always up to date

The law changes, but Nolo is always on top of it! We offer several ways to make sure you and your Nolo products are always up to date:

1 **Nolo's Legal Updater**

We'll send you an email whenever a new edition of your book is published! Sign up at **www.nolo.com/legalupdater**.

2 **Updates @ Nolo.com**

Check **www.nolo.com/update** to find recent changes in the law that affect the current edition of your book.

3 **Nolo Customer Service**

To make sure that this edition of the book is the most recent one, call us at **800-728-3555** and ask one of our friendly customer service representatives. Or find out at **www.nolo.com**.

2nd edition

What Every
Inventor
Needs to Know About
Business & Taxes

by Attorney Stephen Fishman

SECOND EDITION	MAY 2005
Editor	RICHARD STIM
Cover Design	TERRI HEARSH
Book Design	TERRI HEARSH
CD-ROM Preparation	JENYA CHERNOFF ANDRÉ ZIVKOVICH
Illustrations	SASHA STIM-VOGEL
Index	PATRICIA DEMINNA
Proofreading	RUTH FLAXMAN
Printing	DELTA PRINTING SOLUTIONS, INC.

Fishman, Stephen.
What every inventor needs to know about business & taxes / by Stephen Fishman.--
 2nd ed.
 p. cm.
 Rev. ed. of: Inventor's guide to law, business & taxes / Fishman, Stephen. 1st ed. 2003.
Includes index.
 ISBN 1-4133-0193-2 (alk. paper)
 1. Inventions--United States--Popular works. 2. Inventions--United States--Handbooks,
manuals, etc. 3. Inventors--Taxation--Law and legislation--United States--Popular works.
I. Fishman, Stephen. Inventor's guide to law, business and taxes. II. Title.

KF3131.Z9F57 2005
346.7305'26--dc22

2005040533

For information on bulk purchases or corporate premium sales, please contact the Special
Sales Department. For academic sales or textbook adoptions, ask for Academic Sales. Call
800-955-4775 or write to Nolo, 950 Parker Street, Berkeley, CA 94710.

Acknowledgments

Many thanks to:

Richard Stim and Amy Delpo for their outstanding editing

Terri Hearsh for her solid book design and eye-catching cover

Sasha Stim-Vogel for her clever illustrations

Jenya Chernoff and Andre Zivkovich for their skillful handling of the forms

About the Author

Stephen Fishman received his law degree from the University of Southern California in 1979. He is the author of *Copyright Your Software, Web & Software Development: A Legal Guide, Working for Yourself* and *Hiring Independent Contractors: The Employer's Legal Guide*, all published by Nolo. He can be contacted at Steve_Fishman@nolo.com.

Table of Contents

1 Why Inventors Need to Know About Law, Business and Taxes

  A. Business, Tax, or Law? 1/2

  B. What's Not in This Book 1/3

2 Choosing the Legal Form for Your Inventing Business

  A. Your Business Entity Choices 2/2

  B. Expense and Complexity 2/4

  C. Tax Treatment 2/7

  D. Liability Concerns 2/12

  E. Recommended Business Forms 2/18

3 Setting Up Shop

  A. Choosing a Name for Your Business 3/3

  B. Working at Home 3/6

  C. Leasing a Workplace 3/12

  D. Business Licenses and Permits 3/14

  E. Federal Employer Identification Number 3/16

  F. Insurance 3/17

4 Bookkeeping and Accounting

A. Simple Bookkeeping for Inventors 4/2

B. Length of Time for Keeping Records and Logs 4/12

C. Accounting Methods and Tax Years 4/13

D. Creating Financial Statements 4/14

E. Other Inventing Business Records 4/14

5 Tax Basics

A. Inventors Who Earn Profits 5/2

B. Inventors Who Incur Losses 5/6

C. Inventors Who Hire Employees 5/7

D. How To Handle Your Taxes 5/7

E. IRS Audits 5/10

6 How to Prove to the IRS You're in Business

A. Qualifying as a Business 6/2

B. Passing the 3-of-5 Profit Test 6/4

C. Passing the Behavior Test 6/5

7 Inventor Tax Deductions

A. Tax Deductions: The Basics 7/2

B. Tax Deduction Road Map 7/8

C. Inventing Expenses You May Currently Deduct 7/10

D. Inventing Expenses You Must Deduct Over Time 7/27

E. Special Deduction Rules 7/33

8 Taxation of Inventing Income

A. Capital Gains vs. Ordinary Income 8/2

B. Capital Gains Treatment for Patents Under IRC § 1235 .... 8/3

C. Paying Self-Employment Taxes 8/6

D. Paying Estimated Taxes 8/10

9 Your Inventor's Notebook

A. Why Keep an Inventor's Notebook? 9/2

B. How to Keep Your Notebook 9/5

C. Witnessing Your Notebook 9/7

D. Alternatives to the Inventor's Notebook 9/8

10 Hiring Employees and Independent Contractors

Part I: Determining Workers' Legal Status 10/3

A. ICs Are Business Owners, Employees Are Not 10/3

B. Pros and Cons of Hiring Employees or ICs 10/5

Part II. Hiring Employees 10/7

C. Drafting an Employment Agreement 10/9

D. Tax Concerns When Hiring Employees 10/22

Part III. Hiring Independent Contractors 10/26

E. Drafting an Independent Contractor Agreement 10/26

F. Tax Reporting for Independent Contractors 10/37

11 Who Owns Your Invention?

A. Patent Ownership 11/2

B. Are You an Inventor? 11/3

C. Are You a Solo Inventor? 11/4

D. Are You a Joint Inventor? 11/5

E. Are You an Employee/Contractor Inventor? 11/13

F. Have You Transferred Your Ownership? 11/26

G. Trade Secret Ownership 11/29

12 Introduction to Intellectual Property

A. What Is Intellectual Property and Why Is It Important to Inventors? 12/2

B. Doing the Work of Obtaining IP Protection 12/8

13 Ten Things Inventors Should Know About Trade Secrets

1. All Inventions Begin As Trade Secrets 13/2
2. Any Valuable Information Can Be a Trade Secret 13/2
3. Trade Secrets Are the Do-It-Yourself Intellectual Property 13/3
4. You Can Make Money From Trade Secrets 13/3
5. Trade Secret Protection Is Weak 13/4
6. Trade Secret Laws Don't Protect Against Independent
   Discovery or Reverse Engineering 13/5
7. Trade Secret Protection Has No Definite Term 13/6
8. You Must Choose Between Trade Secret and Patent Protection 13/6
9. You Must Keep Your Trade Secrets Secret 13/9
10. When In Doubt, Use a Nondisclosure Agreement 13/11

14 Fifteen Things Inventors Should Know About Patents

1. Patents Are the Most Powerful IP Protection 14/2
2. A Patent—By Itself—Won't Make You Rich 14/2
3. You Can Profit From Your Invention Without a Patent 14/3
4. Patents Don't Work Well for Inventions With Short Commercial Lives 14/4
5. Patents Are Expensive and Difficult to Obtain 14/5
6. Most Inventions Are Not Patentable 14/7
7. Do a Patent Search Before Anything Else 14/9
8. You Must Document Your Inventing Activities 14/10
9. You'll Lose Your Right to Patent If You Violate the One-Year Rule 14/10
10. Filing a Provisional Patent Application Can Save You Money 14/11
11. Patents Last 17–18 Years 14/12
12. Enforcing a Patent Can Be Difficult and Expensive 14/13
13. U.S. Patents Only Work in the United States 14/13
14. Filing for Patents Helps Show You're in Business 14/13
15. Design Patents Can Protect the Way Your Invention Looks 14/14

15 Ten Things Inventors Should Know About Trademarks

1. Trademarks Can Earn Billions 15/2
2. Trademarks Identify Products and Services 15/2

3. You Must Have Trade to Have a Trademark 15/3

4. You Don't Need a Trademark to License Your Invention (But It Can Help) ... 15/3

5. Trademarks Are Not All Created Equal 15/4

6. Registering a Trademark Is Not Mandatory, But Provides
   Important Benefits 15/4

7. Intent to Use Registration Can Protect Your Mark Before
   You Use It in Trade 15/5

8. Do a Trademark Search Before Selecting Your Mark 15/5

9. Trademark Rights Are Limited 15/6

10. Only Federally Registered Marks Can Use the ® Symbol 15/7

16 Ten Things Inventors Should Know About Copyright

1. Copyright Protects Works of Authorship, Not Inventions 16/2

2. Copyright Can Protect Invention Design 16/3

3. You Can Make Money From Copyrights 16/5

4. Copyright Protection Is Limited 16/5

5. You Get A Copyright Whether or Not You Want It 16/6

6. Copyright Protection Lasts a Long Time 16/6

7. Register Valuable Copyrights 16/6

8. Use a Copyright Notice When You Publish Valuable Works 16/7

9. Copyright Isn't the Only Law That Protects Designs 16/8

10. Watch Out If You Hire an Independent Contractor
    to Create a Copyrighted Work 16/8

17 Ten Things Every Inventor Should Know About Licensing

1. No License Is Better Than a Bad License 17/4

2. You're Licensing Your Rights, Not Your Invention 17/4

3. Sublicensing and Assignments Allow Strangers to Sell Your Invention 17/5

4. You Can License Away the World and Get It Back 17/6

5. A Short Term Is Usually Better Than a Longer Term 17/7

6. Royalties Come in All Shapes and Sizes 17/8

7. Sometimes a Lump Sum Payment Is Better Than a Royalty 17/10

8. GMARs Guarantee Annual Payments 17/12

9. Deductions Can Make Your Royalties Disappear 17/13

10. Audit Provisions Permit You to Check the Books 17/15

18 Help Beyond the Book

A. Patent Websites 18/2

B. Finding and Using a Lawyer 18/5

C. Help From Other Experts 18/8

D. Doing Your Own Legal Research 18/9

E. Online Small Business Resources 18/11

F. State Offices Providing Small Business Help 18/13

Appendix

A How to Use the CD-ROM

A. Installing the Form Files Onto Your Computer A/2

B. Using the Word Processing Files to Create Documents A/3

C. Using PDF Forms A/5

D. Files Included on the Forms CD A/7

Index

Chapter 1

Why Inventors Need to Know About Law, Business, and Taxes

A. Business, Tax or Law? 1/2

B. What's Not in This Book 1/3

*G*enius is not always rewarded. Hungry for cash, John "Doc" Pemberton sold the world's most famous trade secret—the formula for Coca-Cola, for less than $900. Charles Goodyear had a brilliant innovation—rubber that could be used year-round. But Goodyear made many bad deals, failed to protect his patent rights and died in 1860 owing over $200,000. Charles Stahlberg woke the world up with his alarm-clock invention but then, because of business debts, was forced to sell all rights cheaply to the Westclox company. George Ferris had two brilliant ideas—the Ferris wheel and the amusement park—but debts forced him to auction his wheel and eventually he was driven to bankruptcy. Adolph Sax patented his saxophone but died penniless after spending all his money on attorneys to fight patent battles.

From Gutenberg (yes, he died penniless as well) to today, developing a great invention has never been a guarantee of financial success. There are many reasons for these financial failures—bad luck, bad timing, the world's indifference to innovation—but one of the most significant causes is the inventor's lack of basic knowledge in three areas:

- **law**—the array of laws, such as patent law, that protect inventions and thereby enable inventors to make money from them
- **business**—the knowledge of how to properly organize and run inventing activities like a real business, and
- **taxes**—the ability to take advantage of the tax laws to help underwrite inventing efforts.

This book is intended to help the independent inventor fill this knowledge gap. Whether you're a full- or part-time inventor, just starting out or highly experienced with many patents to your name, reading this book will enable you to answer such crucial questions as:

- If I invent something on the job, who owns it—my employer or me? (See Chapter 11.)
- Can I deduct my home-workshop expenses from my taxes? (See Chapter 7.)
- Should I incorporate my inventing business? (See Chapter 2.)
- How can I pay the low 20% capital gains tax rate on my inventing income? (See Chapter 8.)

Reading this book won't guarantee you'll get rich from inventing, but at least you'll be able to avoid some of the mistakes other inventors have made.

A. Business, Tax, or Law?

This book is divided into three conceptual parts:

Starting and Running Your Business. Chapters 2 through 4, 9 and 10 cover starting and running your inventing business, including choosing your form of business, record keeping and hiring employees and contractors.

Taxes. Chapters 5 through 8 cover the tax aspects of inventing, including such issues as showing the IRS that your inventing is not a hobby, deducting your inventing expenses and paying taxes on inventing income.

Ownership and Exploitation. Chapters 11 through 17 cover laws regarding ownership and exploitation of your invention. These laws include intellectual property laws for inventors such as patents, trademarks, trade secrets and copyrights, as well the law relating to invention licensing.

Chapter 18, Help Beyond the Book, tells you how to do further research on your own, and, if necessary, hire an attorney. If you need an answer for a specific question, start with the table of contents at the front of the book. If you don't find the topic you're interested in there, check the detailed index at the back of the book.

B. What's Not in This Book

This book does not cover everything inventors need to know. Specifically, it is not about:

- **How to file for a patent.** This book provides an overview of all forms of intellectual property law, including patents, but it does not explain how to file for a patent. This topic is covered in more detail in *Patent It Yourself*, by David Pressman (Nolo).

- **How to file a provisional patent application.** *Patent Pending In 24 Hours*, by Richard Stim & David Pressman (Nolo) explains how to prepare a provisional patent application.

- **How to do a patent search.** *Patent Searching Made Easy*, by David Hitchcock (Nolo), offers guidance on patent searching.

- **How to do a patent drawing.** If you want to create your own patent drawings, check out *How to Make Patent Drawings Yourself*, by Jack Lo & David Pressman (Nolo). ∎

Chapter 2

Choosing the Legal Form for Your Inventing Business

A. Your Business Entity Choices 2/2
   1. Sole Proprietorship 2/2
   2. Partnership 2/3
   3. Corporation 2/3
   4. Limited Liability Company 2/4

B. Expense and Complexity 2/4
   1. Sole Proprietorship 2/4
   2. Partnership 2/4
   3. Corporation 2/5
   4. Limited Liability Company 2/6

C. Tax Treatment 2/7
   1. Sole Proprietorship 2/7
   2. Partnership 2/7
   3. Corporation 2/8
   4. Limited Liability Company 2/11

D. Liability Concerns 2/12
   1. Sole Proprietors 2/12
   2. Partnerships 2/14
   3. Corporations and Limited Liability Companies 2/15

E. Recommended Business Forms 2/18
   1. Obtaining Investors 2/18
   2. Keeping Money in the Business 2/19
   3. Manufacturing or Selling Your Invention Yourself 2/20

One of the most important decisions you make when you're first starting out is how to legally organize your inventing business. There are several alternatives and the one you choose will have a big impact on your finances, how you're taxed and how much time you have to spend on record keeping and accounting. Keep in mind that your initial choice about how to organize your business is not engraved in stone. You can always switch later.

A. Your Business Entity Choices

There are four forms in which to organize your inventing business:

- sole proprietorship
- partnership
- corporation, or
- limited liability company.

If you're inventing alone, you need not be concerned with partnerships; this business form requires two or more owners. If, like most independent inventors, you're working by yourself, your choice is among being a sole proprietor, forming a corporation or forming a limited liability company.

On the other hand, if you're working with one or more co-inventors who will jointly own the invention, you cannot be a sole proprietor. Your choices are limited to a partnership, corporation or limited liability company.

This section provides an overview of the four types of business entities. Then, in the remainder of the chapter, we'll examine in detail how to decide on which form to use by looking at three main factors:

- **Expense and Complexity:** How expensive and difficult is the entity to form and operate?
- **Tax Treatment:** How is the entity taxed?
- **Liability Concerns:** How and to what extent will you be liable for debts and lawsuits?

After examining these factors, in Section E we provide our recommendations on which business form you should use. As a general rule, when you're first starting out, the sole proprietorship is the best entity for the sole inventor, while a partnership is usually best for co-inventors.

1. Sole Proprietorship

A sole proprietorship is a one-owner business. Unlike a corporation or limited liability company, it is not a separate legal entity. The business owner (proprietor) personally owns all the assets of the business and is in sole charge of its operation. Most sole proprietors run small operations, but a sole proprietor can hire employees and contract with non-employees, too. Indeed, some one-owner businesses are large operations with many employees.

The vast majority of all self-employed people, including inventors, are sole proprietors. Many have attained this legal status without even realizing it: Quite simply, if you start running a business by yourself (or are already engaged in the business of inventing) and do not incorporate or form an LLC, you are automatically a sole proprietor.

2. Partnership

If you are working with one or more co-inventors who will work together to create an invention and share in its ownership and any profits it earns, you can't be a sole proprietor. Sole proprietorships are one-owner businesses. Instead, you must choose among three forms of business that allow for joint ownership by two or more people: a partnership, corporation or limited liability company. Our choice for co-inventors starting out is the partnership business form.

A partnership is a form of shared ownership and management of a business. The partners contribute money, property or services to the partnership and in return receive a share of the profits it earns, if any. They jointly manage the partnership business. This form is extremely flexible because the partners may agree to split the profits and manage the business any way they want.

A partnership automatically comes into existence whenever two or more people enter into business together to earn a profit and don't choose to incorporate or form a limited liability company. Unlike a sole proprietorship, a partnership has a legal existence distinct from its owners—the partners. It can hold title to property, sue and be sued, have bank accounts, borrow money, hire employees and do anything else in the business world that an individual can do.

Because a partnership is a separate legal entity, property acquired by a partnership is property of the partnership and not of the partners individually. This differs from a sole proprietorship where the proprietor-owner individually owns all the sole proprietorship property.

EXAMPLE: Rich and Andrea are mechanical engineers who decide to work together to develop a new type of folding bicycle. The fact that they are working together in their inventing business with a view to eventually earning a profit means they are automatically in a partnership with each other. They're amazed when a lawyer friend mentions this to them at a party. After reviewing their options, they decide to keep the partnership form since it's so cheap and easy to run and gives them favorable tax treatment for their anticipated losses while they're developing their invention. However, they decide to write up a partnership agreement outlining their ownership shares in the partnership and their other rights and responsibilities.

3. Corporation

A corporation, like a partnership, has a legal existence distinct from its owners. It can hold title to property, sue and be sued, have bank accounts, borrow money, hire employees and perform other business functions. In theory, every corporation consists of three groups:
- those who direct the overall business, called directors
- those who run the business day to day, called officers, and
- those who just invest in the business, called shareholders.

However, in the case of a small business corporation, these three groups can be and often are the same person—that is, a single person can direct and run the corporation and own all the corporate stock. So, if you incorporate your one-person inventing business, you don't have to go out and recruit and pay a board of directors or officers.

4. Limited Liability Company

The limited liability company, or LLC, is the newest type of business form in the United States. An LLC is like a sole proprietorship or partnership in that its owners (called members) jointly own and manage the business. Like a partnership, an LLC is a separate legal entity. An LLC is taxed like a sole proprietorship or partnership but provides its owners with the same limited liability as a corporation. LLCs have become popular with self-employed people because they are simpler and easier to run than corporations.

George Ferris
Inventor of the Ferris wheel and the amusement park

B. Expense and Complexity

Some business forms are more expensive to set up and more difficult to run than others. If you'd prefer to spend your time inventing rather than dealing with corporate minutes and other formalities, form a sole proprietorship or partnership, and stay away from the corporate form.

1. Sole Proprietorship

The sole proprietorship is by far the cheapest and easiest way for you to legally organize your inventing business. You don't need permission from the government, you don't pay any fees, and there are no complex legal documents to be drafted, meetings to attend or forms to file. The only exception is if you want to use a name other than your own name to identify your business. In this event, you'll have to file a fictitious business name statement. Depending on where you're located, you might also need to obtain a business license. Neither task is very difficult.

After you get started, running a sole proprietorship is a breeze. There are no legal formalities you need worry about. However, you do need to keep good records and it's wise to have a separate bank account for your inventing business (see Chapter 6).

2. Partnership

Partnerships are the cheapest business form for joint owners to start and operate, but, they are more complicated than sole proprietorships. Partnerships may be operated informally—

that is, there is no need to have annual meetings, elect officers or to document all important
decisions with minutes. However, because
there are two or more owners, the partners
have to decide:

• the duties of each partner
• how each partner will share in the
  partnership profits or losses
• how partnership decisions will be made
• what happens if a partner leaves or dies,
  and
• how disputes are resolved.

Although not required by law, you should
have a written partnership agreement answering these and other questions. You can draft
such an agreement yourself. For detailed
guidance on how to draft a partnership agreement, refer to *The Partnership Book: How to
Write a Partnership Agreement*, by Denis
Clifford & Ralph Warner (Nolo).

There are no special legal formalities you
need to follow, forms you need to file or
registration fees to pay to create a partnership. However, as with a sole proprietorship,
you may need to file a fictitious business
name statement and obtain a local business
license.

One area where partnerships are more
complicated and expensive than sole proprietorships is tax filings. Partnerships must
file their own informational tax returns with
the IRS and with each partner. These returns
are complicated—as is the subject of partnership taxation in general. You may need to
hire a tax professional to help you with them.
Partnership accounting is also more complicated than for a sole proprietorship, especially
if the partners decide to allocate profits and

losses differently than the proportions of their
contributions to the partnership.

3. Corporation

Corporations are the most costly and complex
of all the business forms covered in this
chapter.

a. Corporate formalities

The IRS and state corporation laws require
corporations to hold annual shareholder
meetings and document important decisions
such as choosing a federal or state tax election
with corporate minutes, resolutions or written
consents signed by the directors or shareholders.
Small businesses with only one or a few
shareholders and directors usually dispense
with holding real annual meetings. Instead,
the secretary of the corporation prepares
minutes for a meeting which takes place only
on paper.

If you're audited and the IRS discovers that
you have failed to comply with corporate formalities, you may face drastic consequences.
For example, if you fail to document important
tax decisions and tax elections with corporate
minutes or signed consents, you may lose
crucial tax benefits and risk substantial penalties.

b. More complex bookkeeping

It is absolutely necessary that you maintain a
separate corporate bank account if you incorporate. You'll need to keep a more complex
set of books than if you're a sole proprietor.
You'll also need to file a somewhat more

complex tax return, or file two returns if you form a C corporation (see Section C). And, since you'll be an employee of your corporation, you'll need to pay yourself a salary and file employment tax returns. All this costs time and money. You'll probably need to use the services of an accountant or bookkeeper, at least when you first start out.

c. Some increased taxes and fees

Finally, there are some fees and taxes you'll have to pay if you incorporate that are not required if you're a sole proprietor. For example, since you'll be an employee of your corporation, it will have to provide unemployment compensation for you. The cost varies from state to state, but is at least several hundred dollars per year.

You'll also have to pay a fee to your state to form your corporation and may have to pay additional fees throughout its existence. In most states, the fees are about $100 to $300. In one state—California—you must pay a minimum $800 franchise tax to the state every year after the first year you're in business even if your corporation has no profits.

d. Forming a corporation

You create a corporation by filing the necessary forms and paying the required fees with your appropriate state agency—usually the secretary of state or corporations commissioner. Each state specifies the forms to use and the filing cost. You'll also need to choose a name for your corporation, adopt corporate bylaws, issue stock, and set up your corporate records.

For detailed guidance on how to form a corporation in all 50 states, see *Incorporate Your Business: A 50-State Legal Guide to Forming a Corporation,* by Anthony Mancuso (Nolo). In addition, the following books written by Anthony Mancuso and published by Nolo explain how to form a corporation yourself in three of the most populous states:

- *How to Form Your Own California Corporation*
- *How to Form Your Own New York Corporation*, and
- *How to Form Your Own Texas Corporation*.

4. Limited Liability Company

Setting up an LLC takes about the same time and money as a corporation, but thereafter an LLC is simpler and easier to run. With a corporation, you must hold and record regular and special shareholder meetings to transact important corporate business. Even if you're the only corporate owner, you need to document your decisions. This isn't required for an LLC.

To form an LLC, you must file articles of organization with your state government. Your company's name will have to include the words "limited liability company" or "LLC" or a similar phrase as set forth in your state law. You should also create a written operating agreement setting forth the members' ownership interests, rights and responsibilities. This is similar to a partnership agreement.

For a complete discussion of how to form a limited liability company, see *Form Your Own Limited Liability Company*, by Anthony Mancuso (Nolo).

C. Tax Treatment

Probably the most important single factor to think about when deciding on a business form is taxation. If, like most independent inventors, you expect to incur losses for some time, a sole proprietorship or partnership is your best choice.

1. Sole Proprietorship

When you're a sole proprietor, you and your inventing business are one and the same for tax purposes. Sole proprietorships don't pay taxes or file tax returns. Instead, you must report the income you earn or losses you incur on your own personal tax return, IRS Form 1040. If you earn a profit, the money is added to any other income you have and that total is taxed. If you incur a loss, you can generally use it to offset income from other sources— for example, salary from a job, interest or investment income or your spouse's income if you're married and file a joint tax return. From a tax standpoint, this makes sole proprietorships ideal for independent inventors who expect to incur losses for some time.

Although you are taxed on your total income regardless of its source, the IRS does want to know about the profitability of your business. To show whether you have a profit or loss from your sole proprietorship, you must file IRS Schedule C, Profit or Loss From Business, with your tax return. On this form you list all your business income and deductible expenses. (See Chapter 7.)

Sole proprietors are not employees of their business; they are owners. Their businesses don't pay payroll taxes on a sole proprietor's income or withhold income tax from his or her compensation. However, sole proprietors do have to pay self-employment taxes—that is, Social Security and Medicare taxes—on their net self-employment income. These taxes must be paid four times a year along with income taxes in the form of estimated taxes. (See Chapter 8, Section D.) But, sole proprietor inventors need only pay self-employment taxes if they earn a profit from inventing. Inventors who incur losses don't have to worry about these taxes.

> **EXAMPLE:** Lisa is a sole proprietor inventor who also holds a full-time job as an electrical engineer. During her first year of inventing, she incurs $10,000 in expenses and earns nothing, giving her a $10,000 loss from her inventing business. She reports this loss on IRS Schedule C, which she files with her personal income tax return (Form 1040). Since Lisa is a sole proprietor, she can deduct this $10,000 loss from any income she has, including her $100,000 annual salary from her engineering job. This saves her about $4,000 in taxes for the year. Because Lisa earned no money from inventing for the year, she did not have to pay any self-employment taxes.

2. Partnership

Partnerships receive much the same tax treatment as sole proprietorships. Like proprietorships, partnerships do not pay taxes. Instead, partnership income and losses are passed through the partnership directly to the partners and reported on their individual federal tax returns.

Although partnerships pay no taxes, they are required to file an annual tax form (Form 1065, U.S. Return of Partnership Income) with the IRS. Form 1065 is used to report partnership revenues, expenses, gains and losses. The partnership must also provide each partner with an IRS Schedule K-1, listing the partner's share of partnership income and expenses (copies of these schedules are attached to the Form 1065 sent to the IRS). Partners must then file IRS Schedule E with their returns showing their partnership income and deductions.

Like sole proprietors, partners are neither employees nor independent contractors of their partnership; they are self-employed business owners. A partnership does not pay payroll taxes on the partners' income or withhold income tax. Like sole proprietors, partners must pay income taxes and self-employment taxes (see Chapter 8) on their partnership income.

The partnership form is particularly useful for co-inventors who expect to incur losses while developing their invention. As with a sole proprietorship, these losses generally can be deducted from the partners' income— whether from a job, investments or any other source. Moreover, partners have great flexibility in deciding how to allocate profits and losses with each other. Their share of profits and losses doesn't have to be proportionate to their capital contributions (the rule for corporations).

EXAMPLE: Rich and Andrea (see the example above) decide that Rich should be allocated 60% of their partnership's profits and losses because he will spend more time on the invention than Andrea. Because they are in a partnership, they are free to do this even though they both contributed the same amount of money to the partnership. In its first year, the partnership business loses $10,000. $6,000 of this loss passes through to Rich's personal tax return and $4,000 to Andrea's. When they do their income taxes for the year, they can each deduct these losses from their income, such as the salaries they earn from their regular jobs.

3. Corporation

Your tax affairs are much more complicated when you incorporate your business. First of all, you automatically become an employee of your corporation if you continue to work in the business, whether full-time or part-time. This is so even if you're the only shareholder and are not subject to the direction and control of anybody else. In effect, you wear two hats—you're both an owner and an employee of the corporation.

If you wish, you may pay yourself a salary (of course, you probably won't want to do this if your inventing business is making no money). But, if you do, Social Security and Medicare taxes must be withheld from any employee salary your corporation pays you and money must be paid to the IRS just as for any employee. However, your total Social

Security and Medicare taxes are about the same as if you were a sole proprietor.

In addition, you must decide how you want your corporation to be taxed. You ordinarily have the choice of being taxed as a C corporation (sometimes called a regular corporation), or as an S corporation, also called a small business corporation.

 For additional information on corporate taxation, see *Tax Savvy for Small Business*, by Frederick W. Daily (Nolo). You can also obtain the following IRS publications free by calling the IRS (800-TAX-FORM) or by downloading them from the IRS website (www.irs.gov):

- IRS Publication 542, Tax Information on Corporations, and
- IRS Publication 589, Tax Information on S Corporations.

a. Regular C corporations

When you form a corporation, it automatically becomes a C corporation for federal tax purposes. C corporations are treated separately from their owners for tax purposes. C corporations must pay income taxes on their net income and file their own tax returns with the IRS using either Form 1120 or Form 1120-A. They also have their own income tax rates which are lower than individual rates at some income levels. C corporations generally take the same deductions as sole proprietorships or partnerships to determine their net profits, but have some special deductions as well.

In effect, when you form a C corporation you take charge of two separate taxpayers:

your corporation and yourself. You don't pay personal income tax on C corporation income until it is distributed to you in the form of salary, bonuses or dividends.

This separate tax identity is not good for owners of businesses that lose money. Because a C corporation is a separate taxpaying entity, its losses must be subtracted from its income and can't be directly passed on to you—that is, you can't deduct them from your personal income taxes. This makes the C corporation a poor choice for inventors who expect to incur losses from their inventing businesses.

When you're a sole proprietor and you want to take money out of your business for personal use, you can simply write yourself a check. Such a transfer has no tax impact since all your sole proprietorship profits are taxed to you personally. It makes no difference whether you leave the money in the business or put it in your personal bank account. Things are very different when you form a C corporation. Any direct payment of your corporation's profits to you will be considered a dividend by the IRS and taxed twice. First, the corporation will pay corporate income tax on the profit and then you'll pay personal income tax on it. This is called double taxation.

To avoid double taxation, instead of taking dividends, small C corporation owners try to take any profits out of the business in the form of employee salaries, benefits and bonuses. These items are deductible expenses for corporate income tax purposes; thus, income tax will only be paid once on such employee compensation.

b. S corporations

When you incorporate, you have the option of having your corporation taxed as an S corporation for federal income tax purposes. An S corporation is taxed like a sole proprietorship or partnership. Unlike a C corporation, it is not a separate taxpaying entity. Instead, the corporate income and losses are passed through directly to the shareholders—that is, you and anyone else who owns your business along with you. The shareholders must split the S corporation's profit or loss according to their shares of stock ownership and report it on their individual tax returns. This means that if your business has a loss, you can deduct it from income from other sources including your spouse's income if you're married and file a joint return.

At first glance, since S corporations are "pass-through entities," they would seem to be as good taxwise as sole proprietorships and partnerships for inventors who incur losses. However, this is not the case. This is because the amount of losses that can be passed through to an S corporation shareholder are limited to the shareholder's total "basis" in his or her stock. The stock's basis is equal to the amount paid for it (plus or minus adjustments during the S corporation's life) plus amounts loaned personally by the shareholder to the corporation. Amounts borrowed by the corporation, not by shareholders personally, are not added to basis. Losses that exceed these limits cannot be deducted in the current year. Instead, they must be carried forward to be deducted in future years.

EXAMPLE: Mike and Dave form an S corporation in 2003 to market their automatic basket-weaving invention. They each own 100 shares of stock. Mike and Dave each contributed $10,000 in cash to the corporation and loaned it $5,000. They each have a $15,000 basis in their stock. In 2003, the corporation has a loss of $40,000. Mike and Dave are each entitled to deduct half of the total loss—$20,000—from their personal income tax. However, they can currently deduct only $15,000 of this loss, the amount of the loss equal to their basis. The remaining $5,000 in losses must be deducted in future years.

Inventors who establish partnerships or LLCs may be able to personally deduct more business losses in a given year than inventors who form S corporations. This is because partners and LLC members get to count their pro-rata share of all money borrowed by the business, not just loans personally made by a partner or member, in determining their basis.

An S corporation normally pays no taxes, but must file an information return with the IRS on Form 1120S telling the IRS how much the business earned or lost and indicating each shareholder's portion of the corporate income or loss.

There are some IRS rules on who can establish an S corporation and how it's operated. For example:

- An S corporation can only have 75 shareholders.
- None of the shareholders can be nonresident aliens—that is, noncitizens who don't live in the United States.

- An S corporation can have only one class of stock—for example, you can't create preferred stock giving some shareholders special rights.
- The shareholders can only be individuals, estates or certain trusts—for example, a corporation can't be an S corporation shareholder.

To establish an S corporation, you first form a regular corporation under your state law. Then you file Form 2553 with the IRS. If you want your corporation to start off as an S corporation, you must file the form within 75 days of the start of the tax year of your business.

No Favorable Capital Gains Treatment for Patents Sold by Corporations

A special tax law provision called IRC Section 1235 enables inventors to obtain long-term capital gains treatment on the profits they earn when they sell all their patent rights. This can save you substantial taxes because the long-term capital gains tax rate is 15% (5% for lower income taxpayers), which may be much lower than the income tax you must pay on your ordinary income. However, corporations, whether C or S corporations, may not take advantage of Section 1235. (See Chapter 8, Section B.) Capital gains treatment might be available for corporations under the normal capital gains rules applicable to all capital assets, but these can very be difficult for inventors to satisfy. This factor militates against incorporating an inventing business.

4. Limited Liability Company

IRS rules permit LLC owners to decide for themselves how they want their LLC to be taxed. Ordinarily, LLCs are pass-through entities. This means that they pay no taxes themselves. Instead, all profits or losses are passed through the LLC and reported on the LLC members' individual tax returns. This is the same as for a sole proprietorship, an S corporation or a partnership.

If the LLC has only one member, the IRS treats it as a sole proprietorship for tax purposes. The members' profits, losses and deductions are reported on his or her Schedule C, the same as for any sole proprietor.

If the LLC has two or more members, it must prepare and file each year, the same tax form used by a partnership—IRS Form 1065, Partnership Return of Income—showing the

Ashok Gadgil
Inventor of an inexpensive way to purify water using ultraviolet light

allocation of profits, losses, credits and deductions passed through to the members. The LLC must also prepare and distribute to each member a Schedule K-1 form showing the member's allocations.

Although LLCs are ordinarily taxed the same as a sole proprietorship or partnership, they are subject to one important tax limitation. IRS regulations appear to require LLC owners to work at least 500 hours per year in the LLC business in order to deduct LLC losses from their non-LLC income. 500 hours means you must work at least 10 hours per week (with two weeks off for vacation). Any less, and you could lose valuable deductions for your business losses. This requirement makes the LLC a poor choice for part-time inventors.

D. Liability Concerns

One of the biggest concerns for business owners (including inventors) is liability—that is, whether and to what extent they are responsible for paying for their business's debts and business-related lawsuits. Indeed, this issue is seen as so important that the corporation and limited liability company business forms were created specially to limit the liability of their owners.

It's likely that you're as concerned about your liability as anybody else. For this reason, you might think that you should form a corporation or limited liability company. After all, these business forms are supposed to provide protection from debts and lawsuits. Indeed, many people seem to believe that forming a corporation or an LLC is like having a magic shield against liability. However, the sad truth is that there are so many holes in this shield that limited liability is often a myth for small business owners who have formed corporations or an LLCs. For this reason, it's often not worth the time, trouble and cost to form a corporation or an LLC.

1. Sole Proprietors

Since sole proprietors personally own their businesses, they have what is often called "unlimited liability." This means that a sole proprietor is personally liable for all the business's liabilities and debts. At first glance, lack of liability protection would appear to be a terrible shortcoming of the sole proprietorship. However, the other business entity forms available don't do a much better job of protecting you. For this reason, the sole proprietorship remains a good choice for the inventor.

a. Business debts

When you're a sole proprietor, you are personally liable for all the debts of your business. This means that a business creditor—a person or company to whom you owe money for items you use in your inventing business—can go after all your assets, both business and personal. This may include, for example, your personal bank accounts, stocks, your car and even your house. Similarly, a personal creditor—a person or company to whom you owe money for personal items—can go after your business assets, such as business bank accounts and equipment.

Liability Is Never Unlimited

In olden days (the nineteenth century and earlier) business owners' personal liability was truly unlimited. If a business failed, the owners could lose everything they owned and even be thrown in debtors' prison by their creditors. For example, Charles Goodyear, the inventor of vulcanized rubber, was sent to debtors' prison in 1855 when a rubber company he formed went out of business leaving substantial debts.

In our modern society, however, there is no such thing as unlimited liability. First of all, some of your personal property is always safe from a creditor's reach. How much depends on the state in which you live. For example, creditors may not be allowed to take your car, your business tools or your home and furnishings depending on how much these items are worth. (By the way, debtor's prisons were abolished long ago.)

Moreover, bankruptcy is always an option if your debts get out of control. By filing for bankruptcy, you can partly or wholly wipe out your debts and get a fresh financial start. There are two types of bankruptcy for individuals:

- Chapter 7 bankruptcy is the more familiar liquidation bankruptcy, in which many of your debts are wiped out completely without any further repayment. In exchange, you might have to surrender some of your property which can be sold to pay your creditors. Most people who file for Chapter 7 bankruptcy, however, don't have anything to turn over to their creditors. The whole process takes about three to six months and commonly requires only one trip to the courthouse. You can probably do it yourself, without a lawyer.
- Chapter 13 bankruptcy is a reorganization bankruptcy in which you rearrange your financial affairs, repay a portion of your debts and put yourself back on your financial feet. You repay your debts through a Chapter 13 plan. Under a typical plan, you make monthly payments to the bankruptcy court for three to five years. The money is distributed to your creditors. If you finish your repayment plan, any remaining unpaid balance on the unsecured debts is wiped out.

Note, if your debts are extremely large, you may file for a Chapter 11 bankruptcy. This is like Chapter 13, but is specifically for businesses—corporations, LLCs, partnerships and sole proprietorships with substantial debts (over several hundred thousand dollars).

If you're in a partnership, you can choose Chapter 7 or Chapter 11 bankruptcy. Usually, Chapter 11 is chosen. A partnership is a separate entity for bankruptcy purposes, so a partner's personal bankruptcy doesn't bankrupt the partnership, and vice versa.

For a complete discussion of bankruptcy and the types and amounts of property that your creditors can't reach, see:

- *How to File for Chapter 7 Bankruptcy,* by Attorneys Stephen R. Elias, Albin Renauer & Robin Leonard, and
- *Chapter 13 Bankruptcy: Repay Your Debts,* by Robin Leonard. (Both are published by Nolo.)

EXAMPLE: Arnie, a sole proprietor inventor, fails to pay $5,000 to a supplier. The supplier sues him in small claims court and obtains a $5,000 judgment. As a sole proprietor, Arnie is personally liable for this judgment. This means the supplier can not only tap Arnie's business bank account, but his personal savings accounts as well. And the supplier can also go after Arnie's personal assets such as his car and home.

b. Lawsuits

Besides being liable for debts, inventors are also concerned about lawsuits. If you're a sole proprietor, you'll be personally liable for the costs of business-related lawsuits. Such lawsuits could come in many forms:

- premises liability for injuries or damages occurring at your office, workshop, lab or other place of business
- infringement liability when someone claims that you have infringed on their patent
- employer liability for injuries or damages caused by an employee while working for you
- product liability for injuries or damages caused by a product that is manufactured and sold to the public, and
- negligence liability for injuries or damages caused by your failure to use reasonable care.

2. Partnerships

Partners are personally liable for all partnership debts and lawsuits, the same as sole proprietors as discussed in the preceding section. However, partnership creditors are required to proceed first against the partnership property. If there isn't enough to satisfy the debts, they can then go after the partners' personal property.

In addition, each partner is deemed to be the agent of the partnership when conducting partnership business in the usual way. This means you'll be personally liable for partnership debts your partners incur while carrying on partnership business, whether you knew about them or not. Moreover, each partner is personally liable for any wrongful acts committed by a copartner in the ordinary course of partnership business.

Alexander Graham Bell
Invented the telephone

Limited Partnerships

In this chapter, we've been discussing the normal type of partnership—also called a general partnership. There is also a special kind of partnership, a limited partnership, that has one or more general partners who run the business, and one or more partners who are called limited partners because they invest in the partnership but don't help run it. The limited partners are a lot like corporate shareholders in that they aren't personally liable for the partnership's debts. The general partners are treated just like partners in normal partnerships and are liable for all partnership debts and lawsuits. Limited partnerships are most commonly used for real estate and similar investments.

3. Corporations and Limited Liability Companies

In theory, forming a corporation provides its owners (the shareholders) with "limited liability." This means that the shareholders are not personally liable for corporate debts or lawsuits. The main reason most small business people go to the trouble of forming corporations is to obtain such limited liability. However, limited liability is more a myth than a reality for most small business people. Thus, for many inventors, the limited liability afforded by the corporate form does not justify going to the time, trouble and expense of incorporating.

a. Business debts

Corporations and LLCs were created to enable people to invest in a business without risking all their personal assets if the business fails or is unable to pay its debts. That is, they can lose what they invested in the corporation, but corporate creditors can't go after their personal assets such as their personal bank accounts or homes.

This theory holds true where large corporations or LLCs are concerned. If you buy stock in Microsoft, for example, you don't have to worry about Microsoft's creditors suing you. But it usually doesn't work that way for small corporations and LLCs—especially newly established ones without a track record of profits and a good credit history.

Major creditors, such as banks, don't want to be left holding the bag if your business goes under. To help ensure payment, they will want to be able to go after your personal assets as well as your business assets. As a result, if you've formed a corporation or an LLC, these creditors will demand that you personally guarantee business loans, credit cards or other extensions of credit—that is, sign a legally enforceable document pledging your personal assets to pay the debt if your business assets fall short. This means that you will be personally liable for the debt, just as if you were a sole proprietor or partner.

EXAMPLE: Lisa forms a corporation to run her part-time inventing business. She applies for a business credit card from her bank. She carefully reads the application and finds that it contains a clause providing that she will be personally liable for the credit card balance—even though the credit card will be in the corporation's name, not Lisa's own name. Lisa asks the bank to remove the clause. It refuses, stating that its policy is to require personal guarantees from all small incorporated businesses such as hers. She goes ahead and signs the application. Now, if Lisa's corporation fails to pay off the credit card, the bank can sue her personally and collect against her personal assets, such as her personal bank account.

Not only do banks and other lenders universally require personal guarantees, other creditors do as well. For example, you may be required to personally guarantee payment of your office or workshop lease and even leases for expensive equipment. Standard forms used by suppliers often contain personal guarantee provisions making you personally liable when your company buys equipment and similar items.

You can avoid having to pledge a personal guarantee for some business debts. These will most likely be routine and small debts. But, of course, once a creditor gets wise to the fact that your business is not paying its bills, it won't extend you any more credit. If you don't pay your bills and obtain a bad credit rating, no one may be willing to let you buy things for your business on credit.

b. Lawsuits

If forming a corporation or an LLC could shield you from personal liability for business-related lawsuits, doing so would be worthwhile. However, the small business owner obtains little or no protection from most lawsuits by incorporating or forming an LLC. This is an important point, so let's look at why this is, in detail.

Corporation and LLC owners are personally liable for their own negligence. The people who own a corporation (the shareholders) or LLC (members) are *personally liable* for any damages caused by their own personal negligence or intentional wrongdoing in carrying out corporation business. Lawyers are well aware of this rule and will take advantage of it if it's in their client's interest. If you form a corporation or an LLC, and it doesn't have the money or insurance to pay a claim, you can be almost certain that the plaintiff's lawyer will seek a way to sue you personally to collect against your personal assets. You can be personally liable under a negligence theory for all the different types of lawsuits outlined above. Here are some examples of how you could be sued personally even though you've formed a corporation or an LLC:

- A visitor slips and falls at your workshop and breaks his hip. His lawyer sues you personally for negligence, claiming you failed to keep your premises safe.
- An employee accidentally injures someone while running an errand for you. The injured person sues you personally for damages claiming you negligently hired, trained and/or supervised the employee.
- A prototype of your invention blows up during a demonstration, damaging the office of a potential licensee. The licensee

sues you personally for so negligently designing your invention that it was unsafe.

- You get a manufacturer to produce and sell a product based on one of your inventions. The product is sold to the public and injures several users. The injured people sue you personally for negligently designing the invention.

- You perfect a new invention and license it to a manufacturer. A holder of a patent for a similar invention claims your invention infringes on his patent. Even if you've formed a corporation or an LLC, the patent holder can sue you personally for inducing patent infringement. This is so, even though your corporation or LLC owns the patent, not you personally.

In all these cases, forming a corporation or an LLC will prove useless in protecting you from personal liability.

Piercing the corporate veil. Another way you can be personally liable even though you've formed a corporation is through a legal doctrine called "piercing the corporate veil." Under this legal rule, courts disregard the corporate entity and hold its owners personally liable for any harm done by the corporation *and* for corporate debts. Corporate owners are in danger of having their corporation pierced if they treat it as their "alter ego," rather than as a separate legal entity—for example, they fail to contribute money to the corporation or issue stock, they take corporate funds or assets for personal use, they mix corporate and personal funds or they fail to observe corporate formalities such as keeping minutes and holding board meetings.

Inactive Shareholders Are Not Liable for Corporate Debts or Wrongs

As discussed above, shareholders who actively participate in the management of the company can be held personally liable for their own negligence or other wrongs under the corporate piercing doctrine. However, shareholders who are *not* active in the business face no such personal liability unless they provide a personal guarantee. Since they aren't active, they won't be committing any personal wrongs for which they could be sued. Moreover, inactive shareholders can't be held personally liable under the piercing of the corporate veil doctrine. This is why, for example, the ordinary shareholders in the disgraced Enron Corporation are not personally liable for its debts or wrongdoing. But shareholders who were active in the company—for example, its president and chief financial officer—can be held personally (and even criminally) liable for their actions.

c. The role of insurance

If incorporating or forming an LLC won't relieve you of personal liability, what are you supposed to do to protect yourself from business-related lawsuits? There's a very simple answer: get insurance. Your insurer will defend you in such lawsuits and pay any settlements or damage awards up to your policy limits. This is what all wise business owners do, whether they are sole proprietors, partners, LLC members or corporation owners. Liability and many other forms of business insurance are available to protect you from the types of lawsuits described above.

Note carefully, however, that insurance won't protect you from liability for business debts—for example, if you fail to pay back a loan or default on a lease. This is where bankruptcy comes in.

E. Recommended Business Forms

We believe that the sole proprietorship and partnership forms are best for inventors when they are starting out because these are the cheapest and easiest to establish and they offer favorable tax treatment for inventors who expect to incur initial losses.

Generally, forming a corporation is not the best choice for an inventor—at least when first starting out. This is because corporations cost more to form than other types of business entities and are costlier and more complex to run. Moreover, the limited liability they are supposed to provide is more a myth than a reality (see Section D).

However, always be aware that you don't have to stay with your initial choice of business entity. You can switch to another type of entity after you've been in business for a while. Or, you may be able to keep the same entity and switch the way it's taxed by the IRS. Such switching is very common among small business owners.

There may come a time where switching to another legal form makes sense. Three important reasons to make the switch are to obtain equity investors, keep money in the business and avoid personal liability for products liability lawsuits.

1. Obtaining Investors

One way to obtain money for your business is to borrow it. The only problem is that you are obligated to pay it back. Instead of borrowing, you can obtain financing by selling investors a piece of your business. This way, if your business makes money, they make money. But if it doesn't, you don't have to pay them back.

Although not absolutely necessary, forming a corporation can be advantageous if you want to obtain investors. Investors are used to receiving corporate stock and usually prefer it to other forms of co-ownership. One reason investors like corporate stock ownership is that—so long as they aren't actively involved in the business or providing personal guarantees—they are not personally liable for corporate debts or lawsuits. Only their investment is at risk. The same investor limited liability can be obtained by forming a limited partnership or limited liability company (LLC), but investors are more familiar with corporations. They like those stock certificates.

Incorporating has other advantages as well. For example, it may be helpful for marketing and licensing purposes. Having an "Inc." after your business name makes your inventing operation seem more substantial. Incorporating is also necessary if you ever want to attract investors through a public stock offering. Also, issuing corporate stock options is a good way to motivate and keep key employees.

EXAMPLE: Rich and Andrea have formed a partnership to invent a new type of folding bicycle. Having reached the point where they want to create a prototype, they conclude they need to find an investor to provide some development money. Andrea's father Bill agrees to invest $100,000. In return he wants a one-third ownership interest in the business. Rich and Andrea could make Bill another partner in their partnership, but Bill doesn't want this because he doesn't want to be personally liable for the partnership's debts or lawsuits. All Bill wants to risk is his $100,000. So Rich and Andrea form a corporation and give Bill one-third of the corporate stock. Rich and Andrea continue to run the business and Bill is a passive investor.

2. Keeping Money in the Business

When you're a sole proprietor, your business and personal finances are one and the same. Everything you earn from your business is your personal income and must be taxed as such. If you have losses, this pass-through treatment is great. But if you start earning profits, you might prefer to keep some of your money in the business, instead of having all of it go directly to you. You can do this by forming a regular C corporation.

A C corporation is a separate taxpaying entity. Any profits it earns initially belong to it, not to its shareholders personally. Such profits can be distributed to the shareholders in the form of salaries and fringe benefits (for shareholders who work in the business) and dividends. But they don't have to be distributed.

Instead, the C corporation can keep part of its profits in its own bank accounts and use them for future expansion, to buy equipment or to pay employee benefits such as health insurance and pension benefits or for any other legitimate business purpose. This process is called income splitting.

Of course, your corporation must pay income taxes on these retained profits. But this can be advantageous because corporations pay federal income tax at lower rates than individuals at certain income levels—for example, in 2005, an individual had to pay a 27% tax on income from $29,701 to $53,451, while a corporation only had to pay a 15% tax on income up to $50,000.

You can safely keep up to $250,000 of your business earnings in your corporation—that is, let it stay in the corporate bank account. However, if you keep more than $250,000, you'll become subject to an extra 15% tax called the accumulated earnings tax. This tax is intended to prevent you from sheltering too much money in your corporation.

There is yet another substantial tax benefit to income splitting: you don't have to pay Social Security and Medicare taxes, also called employment taxes, on profits you retain in your corporation. This is a 15.3% tax; so, for example, if you retain $10,000 in your corporation, you'll save $1,530 in taxes.

EXAMPLE: Betty has invented a new type of mousetrap. Betty formed a C corporation and transferred her invention to it. Her corporation licensed her design to a large mousetrap manufacturer and earns a hefty annual royalty. In one year, her corporation had a net profit of $50,000 after paying Betty a healthy $100,000 salary. Rather than pay herself the $50,000 in the form of additional salary or bonuses, Betty decides to leave the money in her corporation. She uses the money to finance the development of new inventions. The corporation pays only a 15% tax on these retained earnings. Had Betty taken the $50,000 as salary, she would have had to pay a total federal income tax of $14,000 on them because she is in the 28% income tax bracket. In contrast, her corporation only pays $7,500 under the 15% corporate tax rates.

If you're a partner in a partnership (or member of an LLC) you don't have to go to the trouble of forming a C corporation to obtain the benefits of income splitting. Instead, you can elect to have your partnership (or LLC) taxed the same as a C corporation. This is easily accomplished by filing IRS Form 8832, Entity Classification Election. When you do this, partnership or LLC income will be taxed at the entity level at corporate tax rates and you can engage in income splitting. (Sole proprietors cannot change their tax treatment by filing Form 8832; that's why they must incorporate or form a partnership or an LLC to obtain the benefits of income splitting.)

3. Manufacturing or Selling Your Invention Yourself

If you're one of the relatively few independent inventors who manufactures or sells your invention yourself, it may be advisable to incorporate or form an LLC. This is because of product liability claims—lawsuits that are brought when someone is injured by a defective product. Depending on the nature of your invention, the cost of defending against such lawsuits and paying damages can be astronomical.

Courts often hold manufacturers or sellers to be strictly liable for any injuries caused by their products. "Strict liability" means that the company must pay damages to the injured person even if it was not negligent in designing or manufacturing the product. In other words, the company must pay for any harm the product causes, even if it was not really at fault.

By incorporating or forming an LLC, you can avoid some of the harshness of this strict liability rule. Your company (corporation or LLC) will be strictly liable, but you'll avoid personal strict liability. This way, your personal assets (bank accounts, real estate), will not be subject to strict liability product liability lawsuits, but your business assets remain subject to them.

However, if an injured person proves you acted negligently or recklessly in designing, manufacturing, placing warnings on or warranting your product, you can be held personally liable even if you've formed a corporation or an LLC. ■

Chapter 3

Setting Up Shop

A. Choosing a Name for Your Business 3/3

    1. Choosing a Legal Name 3/3

    2. Choosing a Trade Name 3/4

    3. Fictitious Business Name Registration 3/5

B. Working at Home 3/6

    1. Advantages and Disadvantages of Inventing at Home 3/7

    2. Legal Restrictions on Inventing at Home 3/7

C. Leasing a Workplace 3/12

    1. Rent 3/12

    2. Term 3/12

    3. Security Deposit 3/13

    4. Permitted Uses 3/13

    5. Improvements 3/13

    6. Maintenance 3/13

    7. Insurance 3/13

    8. Negotiating a Termination Clause 3/14

    9. Negotiating a Sublease Clause 3/14

    10. Negotiating Dispute Resolution 3/14

D. Business Licenses and Permits 3/14

    1. Federal Requirements 3/14

    2. State Requirements 3/15

    3. Local Requirements 3/16

E. Federal Employer Identification Number 3/16

F. Insurance 3/17

    1. Business Property Insurance 3/18

    2. General Liability Insurance 3/19

    3. Patent Infringement Insurance 3/20

    4. Environmental Pollution Insurance 3/21

    5. Car Insurance 3/21

    6. Workers' Compensation Insurance 3/21

    7. Choosing the Right Insurance 3/22

    8. Ways to find and save money on insurance 3/24

    9. Deducting Your Business Insurance Costs From Your Taxes 3/26

*I*f you are in the early stages of developing your invention, you probably want to focus all of your energy on seeing your vision come to fruition, not on the mundane tasks required to actually set up a business. However, resist the urge to devote all your time and effort to inventing. Setting up shop takes a little time and effort and may cost some money, but doing it correctly can save you innumerable headaches down the road.

The various tasks you need to establish your inventing business include:

- choosing a business name (see Section A, below)
- finding a place to work (see Sections B and C, below)
- obtaining any necessary licenses and permits (see Section D, below), and
- obtaining insurance (see Section F, below).

A. Choosing a Name for Your Business

One of the first tasks you must accomplish is to choose the name or names you'll use to identify your inventing business. The subject of business names can be confusing because you have the option of using different names in different contexts:

- **Legal Name:** This is the official name of your business. It is the name you must always use when you sign legal documents (for example, contracts), file tax returns, sign leases, apply for bank loans or file lawsuits. If you are a sole proprietor, your legal name is always your personal or "true" name—for example, Jon Wilcox, sole proprietor. If your business is a partnership, LLC or corporation, you must choose a legal name.
- **Trade Name:** Your trade name is the name you use to identify your inventing business to the public—for example, on your business stationery, in advertising, on business cards, in websites, in marketing literature and so forth. Your legal name and your trade name can be the same or you may use a creative trade name—for example John Wilcox might use the trade name, Wilcox Widget Solutions.

In Section A1, below, we discuss legal names. In Section A2, below, we explain how to choose a trade name—including how to decide whether your legal name and trade name should be the same.

Keep in mind that if you are a sole proprietor and your trade name is different than your personal name, you'll probably have to register with your local county clerk under state "fictitious business" regulations. We explain how to register in Section A3.

1. Choosing a Legal Name

Your legal name depends, in part, on what legal form your choose for your business. If, like the vast majority of self-employed inventors, you're a sole proprietor, your personal (or "true") name will always be your legal name. It couldn't be simpler.

EXAMPLE: Joe Dokes runs his invention business as a sole proprietor. Therefore, his business's legal name is Joe Dokes. This is the name he'll use to sign contracts, file tax returns and so on.

If your business is any form other than a sole proprietorship, you must choose a legal name.

Partnerships. In the case of partnerships, you can choose the last names of all the partners as your legal name—for example, Wilcox, Smith and Hutton—or choose a more creative legal name—for example, the Great Widget Partnership. If you use a name other than your last names, you should draft and sign a written partnership agreement and list the name in the agreement. (We discuss partnership agreements in Chapter 2.)

LLCs and Corporations. If you create a corporation or an LLC, you must choose a legal name. Like racehorses, corporations must have unique names. Once you decide upon a name, you must get permission to use it by registering the name with the appropriate agency in your state (usually the secretary of state's office). (See Section A3, below.)

2. Choosing a Trade Name

Your trade name is your public name—the moniker that consumers and other businesses will use when contacting you. Once you have picked a legal name, you must decide whether you also want to use it as your trade name.

For most inventors, the simplest thing to do is to use the same name for legal and trade purposes. This is especially true when you haven't even begun marketing your invention. If, like most independent inventors, you're a sole proprietor, this means you'll use your personal name as your trade name. If you're a partnership, corporation or LLC, you'll use the name you've chosen as your legal name.

If you're more concerned with the marketing and sales of your invention and you think your legal name is too dry, you may want to create a trade name that is more striking or memorable.

EXAMPLE: Ambrose Burnside, a sole proprietor who patented a new type of widget, seeks a manufacturer to license and sell his invention. Rather than simply identify his business as "Ambrose Burnside, Sole Proprietor," he distinguishes his company as Interactive Widgets, believing it more likely to get the attention of prospective licensees.

Your trade name—regardless of whether it is the same as your legal name—should not be substantially similar to that of another company in your field. If it is so similar that it is likely to confuse the public, you could be sued under state and federal trademark and unfair competition laws. If you lose such a lawsuit, you may be required to change your name and even pay financial damages.

It's always a good idea to do a name search for your trade name. If you find a similar name for a company involved in a field that is the same as yours (or related to it), it's usually best to choose a different name. This avoids potential headaches later on. A name similar to one used by a company in an unrelated field probably won't pose a problem unless the name is a famous trademark like McDonald's. For example, even if your name is McDonald, you may run into problems using "McDonald's Innovations." Companies with famous names are often fanatical about protecting them under a trademark principle known as dilution (see Chapter 15).

Here's how to do a free and quick name search:

- Type your proposed name or names in an Internet search engine such as Google (www.google.com) to see if other people or companies are using similar names.
- Find out if there is a similar federally registered trademark by using the U.S. Patent and Trademark Office website (www.uspto.gov). Click "Search Trademarks" on the home page.
- See if there is a similar unregistered trademark at the Thomas Register (www.thomasregister.com), a comprehensive listing of companies, brand names, products and services.
- See if there is a similar Internet domain name by doing a search at any domain name registration website, for example Register.com (www.register.com) or Network Solutions (www.netsol.com).

For more detailed information on name searching, read *Trademark: How to Name a Business and Product*, by Stephen Elias (Nolo).

3. Fictitious Business Name Registration

In most states, a person or business entity transacting business in the state under a name other than their own "true name" must register that business name with the county clerk or secretary of state's office as a fictitious name or "doing business as" (dba) registration. For a sole proprietorship or partnership, a business name is generally considered "fictitious" unless it contains the full name (first and last name) of the owner or all of the general partners, and does not suggest the existence of additional owners. Generally, using a name which includes words like "company," "associates," "brothers," or "sons," will suggest additional owners and will make it necessary for the business to file. Depending on the state in which you live, you may or may not have to register your name if you

Doc Pemberton
Inventor of the Coca-Cola formula

add a word such as "inventions," "innovations," or "technology."

If you fail to register, you'll have all sorts of problems. For example, you may not be able to open a business bank account. You also may be barred from suing on a contract signed with the name. There is usually a time limit on when you must register—often a month or two after you start business.

To register, you usually file a certificate with the county clerk (most likely at your county courthouse) stating that you are the one doing business under that name. In many states, you must publish the statement in a local newspaper. This is intended to help creditors identify the person behind an assumed business name, supposedly to track down those people who are in the habit of changing their business names to confuse and avoid creditors. Some states also require you to pay additional fees, or to file the statement with the state department of revenue or some other state agency.

Contact your county clerk and ask about the registration requirements in your locale. You'll have to fill out a simple form and pay a fee—usually between $15 and $50. The county clerk will normally check to see if any identical or very similar names have already been registered in the county. If so, you'll have to use another name. In most counties, you can check to see if anyone is using a similar name in your county before you attempt to register—either by doing a search of the county clerk's records at its office, calling the clerk, mailing in a request or using the clerk's website.

Your Business Name Is Not a Trademark

As we explain in Chapter 15, state and federal trademark laws protect the right to exclusively use a name, logo or any device that identifies and distinguishes products or services. A good example of a trademark is the Nike name and the distinctive swoosh logo. If a competitor uses this trademark, Nike can obtain a court injunction and monetary damages.

It's important to understand that registering a legal or trade name by filing a fictitious business name or similar document (or registering a corporate or LLC name) does not make your name a trademark. Such registration gives you no ownership rights in the name in the sense of preventing others from using it. If someone else is the first to use your name to identify a product or service to the public, it doesn't make any difference whether you or they have previously registered it as an assumed or corporate or LLC name. They will still have the right to exclusive use of the name in the marketplace. See Chapter 15 for a detailed discussion of trademarks.

B. Working at Home

There are no statistics on the subject, but it's likely that the majority of independent inventors work at home—whether in a spare bedroom, den, garage, basement or other space.

Before you decide to do your inventing from home, you will have to weigh the advantages and disadvantages (see Section B1, below). You will also have to determine if any legal restrictions prohibit you from working at home. We look at both issues in more detail in this section.

1. Advantages and Disadvantages of Inventing at Home

Working at home has many advantages—for example:

- you don't have to pay any rent
- you don't have to commute to your outside workspace
- you can deduct your home workplace expenses from your income taxes—a particularly valuable deduction if you're a renter (see Chapter 7), and
- you have increased flexibility in your daily schedule and can be around to take care of household and childcare issues.

But it also has some disadvantages. For example, inventing at home is not a good idea if you don't have enough space or it will disrupt your lifestyle or your neighborhood. For reasons explained below, a home workplace also may not work well if you need to have several employees working with you.

Other potential drawbacks to working from home include the following:

- **Obtaining services can be difficult.** Businesses that provide services to businesses sometimes charge higher rates to those who work at home. For example, UPS charges more for deliveries to a home

business than to one at an outside business workplace. Many temporary agencies won't even deal with a home-based business because they're afraid they won't get paid.
- **Lack of security.** Your home may not be as secure an environment as an office building or industrial park that is filled with people, has burglar alarms, employs security guards and has hidden security cameras.
- **Local restrictions.** Local laws regarding home-based businesses might make it illegal for you to work at home (see the following section for a detailed discussion).

2. Legal Restrictions on Inventing at Home

If you plan to work at home, you may have potential problems with your local zoning laws or with land use restrictions in your lease or condominium rules. Even if your community is unfriendly to home workplaces, there are many things you can do to avoid difficulties.

a. Zoning laws

Municipalities have the right to make rules about what types of activities can be carried out in different areas. For example, cities and towns often establish commercial zones for stores and offices, industrial zones for factories and residential zones for houses and apartments.

Some communities—Houston, for example—have no zoning restrictions at all. However, most do, and they have laws limiting the kinds of business you can conduct in a residential zone. The purpose of these restrictions is to help maintain the peace and quiet of residential neighborhoods.

Although your inventing may feel like a hobby to you, it's a business when it comes to these zoning laws. Fortunately, the growing trend across the country is to permit home businesses. Many cities—Los Angeles and Phoenix, for example—have updated their zoning laws to permit many home businesses. However, some communities remain hostile to home businesses.

To find out where your community falls on the issue, carefully read your local zoning ordinance. You can obtain a copy from your city or county clerk's office or your public library.

Zoning ordinances are worded in many different ways to limit businesses in residential areas. Some are extremely vague, allowing "customary home-based occupations." Others allow homeowners to use their houses for a broad but, unfortunately, not very specific list of business purposes—for example, "professions and domestic occupations, crafts and services." Still others contain a detailed list of approved occupations, such as "law, dentistry, medicine, music lessons, photography, cabinet-making." Whether inventing falls within one of these categories is often unclear—meaning it may be difficult or impossible to know for sure whether your local zoning ordinance bars home inventing businesses.

Ordinances that permit home-based businesses typically include detailed regulations on how you can carry out your business activities. These regulations vary widely, but the most common types limit car and truck traffic and restrict the number of employees who can work at your house on a regular basis (indeed, some prohibit employees altogether.) Some ordinances also limit the percentage of your home's floor space that can be devoted to your business. Again, study your ordinance carefully to see how these rules apply to you.

Most ordinances prohibit activities that cause excessive noise, pollution, waste, odors and similar conditions not appropriate in a residential neighborhood. For example, the city of Santa Clara, California (located in Silicon Valley, a hotbed of invention), prohibits activities in the home that create "undue noise, vibrations, dust, odors, smoke, television or radio interference, heat, radiation, or other nuisance." Nor does it permit "the storage of hazardous, flammable, or combustible liquids or materials, other than those customarily found in a dwelling."

If you read your ordinance and don't understand it, you may be tempted to discuss the matter with zoning or planning officials. Unless you are certain of the politics in your locality, however, it may be best to do this without identifying and calling attention to yourself, since this may make local officials suspicious about what you're doing at home. If you think it's worth the expense, you could also consult with a land use lawyer.

Fighting for Change Can Pay Off

If your town has an unduly restrictive zoning ordinance, you can try to get it changed. For example, a self-employed person in the town of Melbourne, Florida, was surprised to discover that his local zoning ordinance barred home-based businesses and decided to try to change the law.

He sent letters to his local public officials, but got no response.

He then reviewed the zoning ordinances favoring home offices from nearby communities and drafted an ordinance of his own that he presented to the city council. He enlisted support from a local home-business association and got a major story about his battle printed in the local newspaper.

After several hearings, the city council voted unanimously to amend the zoning ordinance to allow home offices.

Practically speaking, you may be able to invent at home even if your zoning laws prohibit it. In most communities, such laws are rarely enforced unless one of your neighbors complains to local officials. Complaints usually occur because you make lots of noise or have large numbers of employees or delivery people coming and going, causing parking or traffic problems. If you're unobtrusive—for example, you work quietly in your home workplace all day and rarely receive business visitors—it's not likely your neighbors will complain.

Unfortunately, some communities are extremely hostile toward home businesses and actively try to prevent them. This is most likely to be the case if you live in an affluent, purely residential community. Even if you're unobtrusive, these communities may bar you from working at home if they discover your presence. If you live in such a community, you may want to consider moving—or you'll really need to keep your head down to avoid discovery.

To determine your community's enforcement style, try talking with your local chamber of commerce and other self-employed people you know in your town. Friends or neighbors who are actively involved with your local government may also be knowledgeable.

Neighbor relations are the key to avoiding problems with zoning. If your relationship with neighbors is good, tell them about your plans to invent at home so they'll know what to expect and will have the chance to air their concerns. Explain that there are advantages to your working at home—for example, having someone home during the day could improve security for the neighborhood. You might even offer to accept your neighbors' deliveries.

If any of your neighbors are retired, try to be particularly helpful to them. Retired people who stay at home all day are more likely to complain about a home workplace than neighbors who work during the day.

On the other hand, if your relations with your neighbors are already shaky or you happen to be surrounded by unreasonable people, you're probably better off not telling them you work at home. If you're inconspicuous, they may never know what you're doing.

If your neighbors complain about your home workplace, you may have to deal with your local zoning bureaucracy. When local zoning officials decide to close a home business, they'll first send a letter ordering closure. If this and any subsequent letters are ignored, the municipality may file a civil lawsuit seeking an injunction—that is, a court order prohibiting the business from operating.

If you receive a letter from zoning officials, talk with the person at city hall who administers the zoning law—usually someone in the zoning or planning department. Don't ignore the problem; it won't go away. City officials may drop the matter if you'll agree to make your home workplace less obtrusive.

If this doesn't work, you can apply to your planning or zoning board to grant a variance allowing you to violate the zoning ordinance. To obtain such a variance, you'll need to show that your business does no harm to your neighborhood and that relocation would deprive you of your livelihood. Be prepared to answer the objections of unhappy neighbors who may be at the planning commission meeting loudly objecting to the proposed variance.

You can also try to get your city council or zoning board to change the local zoning ordinance. You'll probably have to lobby some city council members or planning commissioners. It will be useful to enlist the support of the local chamber of commerce and other business groups. Try to get your neighbors on your side as well—for example, have them sign a petition favoring the zoning change.

> ### Keeping Your Home Business Unobtrusive
>
> There are many ways to help keep your home inventing business under wraps in the interest of warding off neighbor complaints. For example, if you get a lot of deliveries, arrange for mail and packages to be received by a private mailbox service such as Mail Boxes, Etc. Don't put your home address on your stationery and business cards. Also, try to visit prospective licensees, investors and others in their workplaces instead of having them come to your home workplace.

Finally, you can take the matter to court, claiming that the local zoning ordinance is invalid or that the city has misinterpreted it. You'll probably need the help of a lawyer familiar with zoning matters to do this. (See Chapter 18.)

 For detailed guidance on how to handle neighbor disputes, see *Neighbor Law*, by Cora Jordan (Nolo).

b. Public nuisance laws

Even if your community doesn't have restrictive zoning laws concerning home businesses, it could take legal action against you if you make a nuisance of yourself. It's illegal to create a public nuisance—that is, do something that may harm public heath or safety; for example, creating excessive noise or offensive odors, or storing hazardous chemicals or waste.

b. Deed restrictions

Property deeds often contain restrictions, called restrictive covenants, limiting how you can use your property. Restrictive covenants can bar or limit the use of home workplaces. These may apply both to homeowners and renters.

You can find out if your deed has such restrictions by reading your title insurance policy or checking your deed. If you're a renter, ask your landlord about such restrictions—preferably before you move in.

If your neighbors believe you're violating these restrictions, they can take court action to stop you. Such restrictions are usually enforced by the courts unless they are unreasonable or the character of the neighborhood has changed so much since they were written that it makes no sense to enforce them.

c. Condominium restrictions

One in six Americans lives in a planned community with a homeowners' association. When you buy property in such a development, you automatically become a member of the homeowners' association and agree to follow its rules, which are usually set forth in a lengthy document called Covenants, Conditions and Restrictions, or CC&Rs for short. CC&Rs often regulate in minute detail what you can do on, in and to your property. The homeowners' association is in charge of modifying and enforcing these rules.

The CC&Rs for many developments specifically bar home workplaces. The homeowners' association may be able to impose fines and other penalties against you if your business violates the rules. It could also sue you in court to get money damages or other penalties. Some homeowners' associations are very strict about enforcing their rules against home businesses, others are much less so.

Carefully study the CC&Rs before you buy into a condominium, planned development or cooperative to see if home workplaces are prohibited. If so, you may want to buy somewhere else.

If you're already in a development that bars home workplaces, you may be able to avoid problems if you're unobtrusive and your neighbors are unaware you have a home workplace. However, the best course may be to seek to change the CC&Rs. Most homeowners' associations rule through a board of directors whose members are elected by all the members of the association. Lobby members of the board about changing the rules to permit home workplaces. If that fails, another strategy is for you and like-minded neighbors to try to get seats on the board and gain a voice in policymaking.

d. Lease restrictions

If you are a renter, check your lease before you start your home business. Many standard lease forms prohibit tenants from conducting a business on the premises—or prohibit certain types of business. Theoretically, your landlord could evict you if you violate such a lease provision. However, in practice, few landlords want to evict their tenants. Most don't care what you do on your premises as long as it doesn't disturb your neighbors, create noise, pollution or landlord liability or cause damage. Keep up good neighbor relations to prevent complaints.

However, if you have business visitors, your landlord may require you to obtain liability insurance in case a visitor has an accident such as a trip or fall on the premises.

C. Leasing a Workplace

If you decide against working at home, you'll have to rent an outside workplace (unless you're one of the few independent inventors who purchases a workspace). If you rent a workspace, you'll be renting commercial property, not residential property, and this means that you will be signing a commercial lease. Renting commercial space is not like renting an apartment or house. Commercial leasing is a business transaction—as a business-person, you are presumed to be an adult who can protect yourself. For this reason, few of the consumer protection laws that protect residential tenants—for example, caps on security deposits—apply to commercial leases.

If the landlord is willing, virtually every term in the lease can be negotiated to suit your needs. This section provides an over-view of some key things to think about and possibly negotiate before signing a commercial lease. For a more detailed step-by-step expla-nation of everything you should know, refer to *Leasing Space for Your Small Business*, by attorneys Janet Portman & Fred Steingold (Nolo).

1. Rent

Probably foremost in your mind is the amount you are going to have to pay for your invent-ing space. Depending on the commercial rental market in your area, the rent amount may be highly negotiable. Commercial rent is typically charged by the square foot—for ex-ample, $10 per square foot. When negotiating your rental term, find out how the square footage is determined; for example—does the square footage you're being charged for include common areas such as hallways, elevators and rest rooms? If it is, you'll be paying more rent than if you're charged only for the workspace you use.

In addition to negotiating a rent amount that is fair and that works for your pocketbook, you should understand exactly what you are paying for. Depending on the type of lease you have, the rent may include nothing or lots of things. There are two basic types of commercial leases:

- **Net Lease.** Your rent pays only for your right to occupy the space. As a result, you must make separate payments for maintenance, insurance and property taxes.
- **Gross Lease.** You make a single payment to the landlord that covers everything— rent, maintenance, insurance and taxes.

2. Term

You can usually negotiate the amount of time that the lease will last—for example, anywhere from 30 days to many years. A short-term lease is probably best when you're first starting out—that is, no more than six months to a year. If you think you might want to stay longer, but want to play it safe, you can include in the lease an option to renew.

3. Security Deposit

Just like with an apartment, you have to make a security deposit. You will have to negotiate with the commercial landlord the amount and when it will be returned. Try to negotiate a lease that provides that a portion of the deposit will be returned to you if you pay rent on time for a specified period—for example, for at least one year.

4. Permitted Uses

Commercial leases typically include a clause providing how you may use the property. These use clauses are written in one of two ways:

- The clause may list everything you're forbidden to do—which means you're free to do anything not on the list.
- The clause may list all the ways you are permitted to use the property. In this event you must make sure your intended use is specifically mentioned as permitted in the lease.

If you're going to be storing waste products or if your work may create a good deal of noise, odors, vibrations or other types of environmental pollution, make sure the landlord is aware of this and specifically permits it in the lease.

Melitta Benz
Inventor of a method of making
coffee using a drip filter

5. Improvements

Is the space going to be improved or modified in any way? Will new fixtures be installed? If so, the lease must state who will pay for such changes and who will own these modifications when the lease ends.

6. Maintenance

The lease should specify who will maintain and repair the leased premises. Some leases state that the landlord will provide basic maintenance services. Others make the tenant pay for everything—including cleaning, building security, heating and maintenance of the air-conditioning system.

7. Insurance

If you're signing a net lease (see Section C1), you'll have to contribute to property and liability insurance payments. (In a gross lease, insurance costs are figured into your rent amount.) If there are multiple tenants at the premises, the landlord will usually obtain the insurance and require you to contribute to the cost. Your contribution should be based on how much space you use—for example, if you're renting 10% of the building, you should have to pay only one tenth of the insurance. If you are the only tenant, you may have to get and pay for the insurance yourself.

If the landlord gets the insurance, make sure you are listed on the policies as an additional insured. This will help you deal with the insurance company if you need to make a claim or share in any payout.

 See Section F below for a detailed discussion of insurance for inventors.

8. Negotiating a Termination Clause

Make sure that the lease includes a clause detailing what happens if you end the lease early. In some leases, you have no right to terminate before the lease term ends. In others, you can terminate before the end of the lease, but you have to pay a penalty to the landlord. It's usually in your interest to be able to get out of a lease as easily, quickly and cheaply as possible.

9. Negotiating a Sublease Clause

You may want the right to sublease—that is, to rent out some or all of your leased space to someone else. Most leases allow you to

sublease only if you get the landlord's prior permission. Some leases permit the landlord to withhold permission for any reason. It's preferable to establish a standard of "reasonableness"—that is the landlord can only deny permission if there is a reasonable basis for doing so.

10. Negotiating Dispute Resolution

Finally, what does the lease say about how disputes are to be resolved? Some leases require mediation and/or arbitration; others don't.

D. Business Licenses and Permits

Depending on the type of inventing you do and where you do it, the federal, state or local government (or all three) may require you to have a license or permit or both. It's wise to comply with all applicable licensing requirements—you can incur fines if you don't. Moreover, having such licenses and permits demonstrates you're running a real business, not engaged in inventing as a hobby, something that is important when tax time comes.

1. Federal Requirements

The federal government doesn't require licenses or permits for most small businesses. One important exception, however, is if your inventing activities produce environmental pollution, hazardous materials or waste or toxic chemicals, or if you need to store toxic materials or waste. In this event, you'll likely need a permit from the federal Environmental Protection Agency (EPA). Penalties for failure to comply with these requirements are severe, so make sure you get a permit if you need one.

 To find out more about the EPA permitting process, visit the agency's website at www.epa.gov.

2. State Requirements

Each of the 50 states (and the District of Columbia) has its own licensing requirements. These can differ greatly from state to state. Generally speaking, there are four possible types of licenses that you may need before you start your inventing business:

- general business license (see subsection a, below)
- occupational license (see subsection b, below)
- environmental permit (see subsection c, below)
- sales tax permit (see subsection d, below).

a. General business licenses

A few states, for example, Alaska and Washington, require all businesses to obtain general business licenses. Other states require certain types of business to obtain general business licenses. Every state explains its licensing requirements on a state website. You can find links to most of these state websites at the SBA's site (www.sba.gov).

b. Environmental permits

As with the federal government, you may need to get a state permit if your activities involve environmental pollution, hazardous materials or waste. If you fail to get an environmental permit you may be fined, ordered to stop doing business or criminally prosecuted.

 A great place to find information on these state requirements is the Small Business Environmental Home Page at www.smallbiz-enviroweb.org. There, you can find links to state government websites organized by category.

c. Sales tax permits

All states—except Alaska, Delaware, Montana, New Hampshire and Oregon—have sales taxes. If you sell your invention to the public and your state has sales taxes, you'll need to obtain a state sales tax permit. You must complete and file the application before you make your first taxable sale. Many states impose penalties if you make a sale before you obtain a sales tax permit. Generally, you pay sales taxes four times a year. Be sure to collect the taxes due. If you fail to do so, you can be held personally liable for the full amount of uncollected tax. (By the way, you'll be personally liable even if you've formed a corporation or limited liability company.)

Each state's sales tax requirements are unique. A product taxable in one state may be tax free in another. The only way to find out if your invention is subject to sales tax is to contact your state sales tax department.

You can find links to every state's sales tax department at the Small Business Administration's business law website at www.businesslaw.gov.

3. Local Requirements

At the local level, you need to investigate whether your inventing activities require you to get one or both of the following:

- hazardous waste permit (see subsection a, below), or
- general business license (see subsection b, below).

a. Hazardous waste permit

In addition to federal and state hazardous waste permits, you may need a permit from your city or county government if your activities involve hazardous waste or materials or create environmental pollution.

b. General business licenses

Many cities, counties and municipalities require business licenses or permits for all businesses—even one-person home-based operations. If you're doing business within city limits, contact your city government to find out if you need a local license. If you're in an unincorporated area, contact your county government. If you're doing business in more than one city or county, you may have to get a license in each city or county in which you do business.

To find out what to do, call the appropriate local official in charge of business licensing.

This is often the city or county clerk, planning or zoning department, city tax office, building and safety department or public works department. Your local chamber of commerce may be able to direct you to the agency or person to contact.

To obtain a business license, you'll be required to fill out an application and pay a fee. Fees vary from locality to locality—from as little as $15 to several hundred dollars. Fees are often based on your projected gross revenues—for example, 10 cents per $1,000 of revenue. Periodically, you'll have to renew your license and pay a new fee, usually every year. It's also likely that your locality will require you to post your license at your place of business.

Many self-employed people, particularly those who work at home, never bother to get a local business license. If your local government discovers you're running an unlicensed business, it may fine you and bar you from doing business until you obtain a license.

E. Federal Employer Identification Number

The federal Employer Identification Number (EIN) is a nine-digit number the IRS assigns to businesses for tax filing and reporting purposes. The state tax authority may also require an EIN on state tax forms—if so, this will be the same as your federal EIN.

Whether or not you must have an EIN depends on what business form you have. If your business is a corporation, partnership or limited liability company, you must obtain an EIN. If your business is a sole proprietorship, you must obtain an EIN if you:

- hire employees
- have a retirement plan (for self-employed people, such a retirement plan is often called a Keogh plan) (see Chapter 8, Section D for more about Keoghs)
- buy or inherit an existing business that you operate as a sole proprietorship
- incorporate, form a partnership or form a limited liability company, or
- file for bankruptcy.

Also, some banks require sole proprietors to have an EIN before they'll set up a bank account for your business.

To obtain an EIN you must file IRS Form SS-4, Application for Employer Identification Number. Although completing the form is relatively simple, there are a few trouble spots that you should watch out for:

- Space 1: List your full legal name if you're a sole proprietor. If you've incorporated, list the corporation's name—the name on your articles of incorporation or similar document establishing your corporation.
- Space 7: Leave this space blank if you're a sole proprietor.
- Space 11: For most self-employed people, the closing month of the tax year is December.
- Space 12: If you don't plan to hire any employees, enter "N/A" in this space. Remember, you are not an employee of your inventing business unless you incorporate; so don't include yourself unless you've formed a corporation.

- Space 13: Put "0" if you don't expect to hire employees in the next year.

You can obtain your EIN by mailing the completed SS-4 to the appropriate IRS service center listed in the form's instructions. The IRS will mail the EIN to you in about a month.

If you need an EIN right away, you can get it over the phone by using the IRS's Tele-TIN program. Here's what to do.

- Complete the SS-4 form.
- Call the IRS at 866-816-2065; an IRS representative will take the information off your SS-4 and assign you an EIN that you can start using immediately.
- Write your EIN in the upper right-hand corner of the SS-4 and sign and date the form.
- Mail or fax the signed SS-4 within 24 hours to the Tele-TIN unit at the IRS service center address for your state; the addresses are provided in the SS-4 instructions, or the IRS representative with whom you speak will give you the fax number.

 A copy of IRS Form SS-4, Application for Employer Identification Number, is contained in the CD-ROM forms disk. You can also download a copy from the IRS website at www.irs.gov or obtain one by calling the IRS at 800-TAX-FORM.

F. Insurance

One last item you may need before setting up shop is insurance. It comes in many forms. What type and how much you need depends on the extent of your business property and the nature of your inventing activities. In the Sections F1-F6, we describe the types of insurance you may need and in Section F7, we help you determine which insurance is best for your particular business.

1. Business Property Insurance

Business property insurance compensates you if something happens to your business assets (such as computers, office furniture, equipment and supplies). If, for example, you lose all of your equipment in a fire or burglary, your business property insurance would cover the loss or some portion of it. If you work at home and have a homeowner's or renter's insurance policy, it will provide some limited business property coverage, but it may not be enough to cover all your property.

How much you have to pay for the insurance will depend in part on choices you make when you tailor the policy to your needs. Before you make these choices, be sure you know exactly what you are insuring—and what it is worth.

Note that losses from earthquakes and floods normally aren't covered by business property policies—regardless of whether it is special form or named peril. You can obtain earthquake insurance through a separate policy or as an endorsement—additional coverage added to your policy—to your business property coverage. Similarly, you can obtain flood insurance through a separate policy. Unfortunately, if you live in a part of the country where such hazards are common,

such insurance can be expensive (or may even be unavailable.)

a. Policy limits

All policies have a maximum limit on how much you will be paid, no matter how great your loss. The greater your policy limit, the more expensive the insurance will be.

b. Replacement or cash value coverage

Your policy can either replace your property or reimburse you for the property's actual present cash value. A replacement cost policy will replace your property at current prices regardless of what you paid for it. An actual cash value policy will only pay you what your property was worth when it was lost or destroyed. If the item has depreciated (gone down) in value, you may obtain far less than the amount needed to replace it. We advise obtaining replacement value business property coverage with a policy limit equal to the amount you estimate it would cost to replace all of your business property. If you can't afford that much coverage, consider a policy with a higher deductible. This is usually wiser than obtaining coverage with a lower policy limit. That way, if you insure your property for less than its full value, you won't be covered if you suffer a total loss.

c. Scope of coverage

Business property insurance comes in one of two forms: named peril and special form.

Named peril policies only cover you for perils listed in the policy. For example, the cheapest type of named peril policy only covers losses caused by fire, lightning, explosion, windstorm, hail, smoke, aircraft, vehicles, riot, vandalism, sprinkler leaks, sinkholes and volcanoes. In contrast, a special form policy will cover you for anything except for certain perils that are specifically excluded—for example, earthquakes. Special form policies cost more than named peril policies because their coverage is broader.

d. Deductible

The deductible is the amount you must pay out of your own pocket before your insurance coverage kicks in. The higher the deductible, the smaller the premium, but the greater your out-of-pocket expenses if you suffer a loss.

Cheap Insurance for Your Computer

If the only valuable business equipment you have is a computer, the only business property insurance you may need is computer insurance. A company called Safeware (www.safeware.com) will insure your computer equipment against any type of loss except theft of computer equipment left in an unattended car. The rates are based on the replacement cost of your computers—not their present cash value—and are quite modest.

2. General Liability Insurance

General liability insurance is not expensive; you can usually obtain it for a few hundred dollars per year. How much coverage do you need? There is no simple answer to this question. Some insurance experts suggest you obtain coverage equal to the value of all your business assets. Your business assets are all the equipment and other property you use in your inventing business. Others say you should get coverage equal to the largest damages award you might have to pay—however, it is difficult for inventors to determine this amount. This is something to discuss with your insurance broker.

Traditionally, this form of insurance only covers you for things that you do or do not do while the policy is in effect. This means, for example, that if you make a claim for damages for an accident that occurred before you got the policy, you would not be covered. However, it is possible to get something called "claims made" insurance that covers you no matter when the actual injury took place, so long as you make the claim while you have insurance coverage. Typical general liability insurance provides coverage for the following types of injuries to other people or businesses:

a. Bodily injury

Bodily injury refers to damage to a person's body or physical well-being caused by your actions or failure to act—for example, a prototype maker visiting your office slips on the newly washed floor and shatters her elbow.

It does not cover damages caused by a product you manufacture or sell.

b. Personal injury

You might think personal injury and bodily injury are the same; they aren't. Personal injury occurs when something you say or publish damages a reputation—for example, you bad mouth a competitor's product in a conversation with a prospective licensee at an inventor's trade show.

c. Property damage or loss

Any type injury to real or personal property belonging to other people may fall under this category—for example, your lab explodes and destroys the building next door. It does not include damages caused by a product you manufacture or sell.

d. Advertising injury

This category of injury covers damages caused by your advertisements or product promotions—for example a competitor sues you for false advertising. This also includes intellectual property infringement claims, including trademark, copyright and trade secret infringement claims. It does not include patent infringement; you need a special policy for that. (See Section F3, below.)

e. Products liability

This coverage is intended to protect you if a product that you design, manufacture or sell injures someone—for example, your invention explodes and injures several users or damages their property. Although your general liability insurance may include this type of coverage, you will need to obtain separate coverage if you manufacture an inherently dangerous product—for example, medical equipment.

 If you license your invention to another company to manufacture and sell, your license agreement should include a provision requiring that the company maintain product liability insurance and that it name you as an additional insured on its policy. The company should also agree to pay for your attorney fees and damage awards in the event that someone sues you for product liability. This sort of agreement is called indemnification.

3. Patent Infringement Insurance

If someone claims that you have copied, used or sold their patented invention without their permission they may sue you in federal court for patent infringement. As you might expect, defending such lawsuits can be very expensive. In recent years, some insurers have begun to provide patent infringement insurance to cover patent litigation costs.

There are two types of patent infringement policies: (1) defensive policies that cover you if someone sues *you* for violating a patent; and (2) offensive policies that help pay your attorney fees and other costs if you sue *someone else* for violating a patent.

For the majority of inventors, we recommend neither type of patent insurance. Defensive patent insurance typically costs 2% to 5% of the insured amount—that comes to $20,000 to $50,000 for $1 million in coverage. That's a lot of money you could be spending to develop or market your invention. Moreover, you must make a co-payment ranging from 15% to 25% of any damage award—for example, if you suffer a $1,000,000 patent infringement judgment and have $1,000,000 in defensive coverage, you'd have to pay the first $150,000 to $250,000 yourself. Just as bad as the expense involved is the strict screening process patent insurers will make you go through before issuing a policy. They'll look very carefully at your patent portfolio and check for conflicting patents. They tend to be very conservative and will refuse to issue you a policy if they think there's even a small likelihood you might be sued. The same defects apply to offensive patent insurance.

4. Environmental Pollution Insurance

General liability insurance does not cover lawsuits arising from environmental pollution—meaning fumes, irritants, waste or contaminants that your inventing business produces. You must purchase a separate policy for this coverage, which can be expensive. However, if you think you might have a problem with environmental pollution, this coverage may be worthwhile.

5. Car Insurance

If you use your automobile for business as well as personal use—for example, transporting supplies and equipment in addition to grocery shopping—you need to make certain that your automobile insurance will protect you from accidents that may occur while you are on business. Some do and some don't, so check. You may need to purchase a separate business auto insurance policy or obtain a special endorsement covering your business use. Whatever you do, make sure your insurer knows you use your car for business—and not just personal trips or driving to and from your office. If you do not inform your company about this, it may cancel your coverage if a claim occurs that reflects a business use—for example, you get into an accident on a business trip.

If you keep one or more cars strictly for business use, you will definitely need a separate business automobile policy. You may be able to purchase such a policy from your personal auto insurer.

6. Workers' Compensation Insurance

General liability insurance doesn't provide coverage for work-related injuries to your employees. Homeowner's and renter's insurance also does not provide this coverage. You must obtain a separate workers' compensation insurance policy for this coverage. This insurance pays an injured employee's medical expenses and provides replacement income while the employee is unable to work.

In some states coverage is mandatory. To find out, contact your state worker's compensation insurance agency. Each state agency has a website describing your state's requirements. You can find links to these websites at the North Carolina Industrial Commission website (www.comp.state.nc.us). (Click on "WC Links" on the left side of the page.)

Even if state law does not require you to get this type of coverage, however, we recommend you do so. When you have workers' compensation coverage, an injured employee usually can't sue you claiming his injuries were caused by your negligence.

Most small businesses buy workers' compensation insurance through a state fund or from a private insurance carrier. If private insurance is an option in your state, you may be able to save money on premiums by coordinating workers' compensation coverage with property damage and liability insurance. Talk to your insurance broker.

7. Choosing the Right Insurance

Now that you know the types of insurance that are available, you must decide what and how much you need. This will depend on a variety of factors but the primary issue is whether you are inventing at home or at some other location.

a. If you work at home

If you invent at home, have little business property, don't receive business visitors and are not engaging in activity that could cause injury to your neighbor's property or body, you probably don't need much insurance at all. If all you need is insurance to cover the loss of a small amount of business property, a homeowner's or renter's insurance policy may

be adequate—but you may want to obtain an endorsement to the policy to provide more coverage for business property.

On the other hand, if you have expensive equipment or other costly items, you need business property insurance. You also need liability coverage if you regularly receive business visitors, your activities might cause damage in your neighborhood or you're actually distributing or selling your invention to the public.

As a home-based inventor, you have several options for obtaining business property and liability insurance:

- adding endorsements to your homeowner's insurance
- purchasing a special home business policy (also known as an in-home policy), or
- purchasing a business owner's packaged policy (also known as a BOP policy).

Let's look at each of these in more detail.

Adding endorsements to your homeowner's insurance. If you have homeowner's insurance, take a careful look at your policy. It may provide you with a limited amount of insurance for business property—usually no more than $2,500 for property damaged or lost in your home and $250 away from your home. Computer equipment may not be covered at all. If you have very little business property, this might be enough coverage for you. You can double the amount of business property covered by your homeowner's policy by purchasing an endorsement—for example, increasing your coverage from $2,500 to $5,000. The cost is usually only about $20 per year. These endorsements typically are available only for businesses that generate $5,000 or less in annual income. Although homeowner's polices usually don't provide coverage for liability claims arising from your business activities, you may be able to add an endorsement to your policy covering injuries to business visitors. You would still need to separately purchase other types of liability insurance.

Purchasing an in-home policy. The insurance industry created this type of policy specifically for people who work at home. These in-home business policies insure your business property at a single location for up to $10,000. The cost is usually around $200 per year. For an additional premium, the policy includes liability coverage from $300,000 to $1 million. Liability premium costs are based on how much coverage you buy. There's also coverage available to protect against lost valuable papers, records, accounts receivable, off-site business property and equipment.

Purchasing a BOP policy. This type of policy is for larger business—regardless of whether they are based at home or someplace else. These policies combine property and general liability coverage into a single policy. BOPs are more expensive than in-home policies, but provide the most comprehensive coverage available for small businesses. However, the liability coverage limits are lower than those you could obtain by purchasing a separate general liability insurance policy known as a commercial general liability or CGL policy. BOP coverage is limited to companies with less than $1 million in revenues and to business premises with limited square footage.

b. If you work outside your home

If you rent an outside workspace, your lease is going to require you either to obtain your own property and liability insurance or to help the landlord pay for his own insurance.

If you have a net lease, you'll have to pay directly for this insurance. If you have a gross lease, the landlord's insurance costs are factored into your rent and you don't separately pay for them. (See Section C1, above, for an explanation of the difference between net and gross leases.)

If you're the only tenant on the premises and have a net lease, you'll likely have to purchase your own business property and liability policies and name the landlord as an additional insured. The lease may specify how much insurance you must carry. Your best bet will probably be to get a BOP policy providing both property and liability coverage. If this doesn't provide enough coverage, you can obtain separate business property and liability policies. Your landlord will probably require you to submit proof that you have insurance—typically a written statement from your insurer called a certificate of insurance.

In multi-tenant net lease situations, the landlord will often have both business property and liability insurance and you'll be required to contribute to the cost. Make sure that you are named as an additional insured under the landlord's policy.

It's important to understand that the landlord's property insurance only covers the landlord's property—for example, the landlord's furnishings, fixtures and maintenance equipment. It does not cover your own business property. You must get your own business property policy for this. In fact, your landlord may insist that you obtain such insurance.

In addition, the landlord's liability coverage may not provide you with all the coverage you need. Have your insurance agent review the landlord's insurance policy to see if you'll need to supplement it with your own liability coverage.

If you have a gross lease, you'll also need to obtain your own business property insurance and may need to supplement the landlord's liability insurance with coverage of your own.

8. Ways to find and save money on insurance

There are a number of things you can do to make it easier to find and pay for insurance.

a. Purchase a comprehensive policy

It's usually cheaper to purchase a comprehensive insurance package that contains many types of coverage than it is to buy coverage piecemeal from several companies. You should be aware, however, that the amount of coverage available when you purchase a comprehensive policy is usually lower than that which you can obtain by purchasing separate policies —that is you can often get greater protection by buying separate policies.

b. Seek out group plans

Often, the cheapest and easiest way to obtain insurance is through a professional organization, trade association or similar membership organization. There are hundreds of such organizations. Because these organizations have many members, they can often negotiate cheaper rates with insurers than you can yourself. Your local chamber of commerce may also offer insurance benefits.

If you don't know the name and address of an organization you may be eligible to join, ask other self-employed people or check out the *Encyclopedia of Associations* (Gale Research); it should be available in most public libraries. Also, many of these organizations have websites on the Internet, so you may be able to find the one you want by doing an Internet search.

c. Use an insurance agent

Insurance agents or brokers are people who sell insurance policies to the public. They can be a useful source of information. The terms agent and broker mean different things in different parts of the country. In some states, an agent is a person who represents a specific insurance company and a broker is a person who is free to sell insurance offered by various companies. Elsewhere, the term insurance agent is used more broadly to cover both types of representatives.

If you want to use an agent, find one who is familiar with businesses such as yours and who represents more than one insurer. Always keep in mind that insurance agents are salespeople who earn their livings through commissions paid by insurance companies. The more insurance they sell you, the more money they make. Agents sometimes recommend insurance from companies paying the highest commissions, whether or not it's the cheapest or best policy for you. If you use an agent, try to get quotes from more than one and compare them with the coverage you can obtain through a professional organization or by dealing directly with an insurer (see below).

d. Buy directly from an insurance company

Instead of using an insurance agent, you could try to purchase insurance from one of the growing number of companies selling policies directly to the public. These companies can usually offer you lower rates because they don't have to pay commissions to insurance agents. If you do decide to buy from an individual company, be sure to talk to more than one (see below).

e. Comparison shop

Insurance costs vary widely from company to company. You may be able to save a lot by shopping around. Also, review your coverage and rates periodically. Insurance costs go up and down. If you're shopping for insurance during a time when prices are low, try locking in a low rate by signing up for a contract for three or more years.

f. Use the internet

You can obtain a great deal of information about insurance from the Internet. Insurance companies, agents and organizations all have their own sites. Two good places to start an Internet search about business insurance are the business insurance directory at Google.com and the list of business insurance links at Yahoo.com.

Check on an Insurer's Financial Health

Several insurance companies have gone broke in recent years. If this happens and you have a loss covered by a policy, you may only receive a small part of the coverage you paid for or none at all. The best way to avoid this is to obtain coverage from an insurer that is in good financial health.

The following reference works rate insurance companies for financial solvency:

- Best's *Insurance Reports* (Property-Casualty Insurance Section)
- *Moody's Bank and Financial Manual* (Volume 2)
- Fitch Ratings, and
- Standard & Poor's.

These services rate insurers on a letter grade scale—for example, *Best Insurance Reports* rates insurance companies from A++ to F. Approximately 80% of all insurers have a Best rating A or better, so you should require at least an A rating.

You can obtain insurance company ratings from Standard & Poor's and Fitch Ratings for free at www.insure.com. An insurance agent should also be able to give you the latest rating from these publications and they may be available in your public library.

9. Deducting Your Business Insurance Costs From Your Taxes

You can deduct the premiums for any type of insurance you obtain for your inventing business from your income taxes. This includes business property insurance, liability insurance, insurance for business vehicles and workers' compensation insurance.

Car insurance and homeowner's or renter's insurance premiums are deductible to the extent you use your car or home for business. ■

Chapter 4

Bookkeeping and Accounting

A. Simple Bookkeeping for Inventors 4/2

    1. Business Checking Account 4/3

    2. Income and Expense Records 4/4

    3. Supporting Documents 4/9

    4. Asset Records 4/11

B. Length of Time for Keeping Records and Logs 4/12

C. Accounting Methods and Tax Years 4/13

    1. Accounting Methods 4/13

    2. Tax Years 4/13

D. Creating Financial Statements 4/14

E. Other Inventing Business Records 4/14

*L*et's face it, bookkeeping and accounting lack the excitement of inventing. But no matter how dry the subject matter, you'll need to develop some expertise in this area. Maintaining proper records will enable you to:

- show that inventing is your business (and not just a hobby), something that is important for tax purposes (see Chapter 6 for more on this)
- monitor the health of your business
- prepare financial statements
- keep track of deductible expenses
- prepare your tax returns, and
- win IRS audits.

This chapter shows you how to set up and maintain a simple bookkeeping system and explains some basic accounting concepts. Read Chapter 7 for a detailed discussion of tax deductions for inventors.

![!] This chapter is for inventors who are sole proprietors. If you are in a partnership, corporation or limited liability company, you'll need to keep some records in addition to those described here. However, the basic principles discussed in this chapter apply to all forms of business.

A. Simple Bookkeeping for Inventors

If, like most independent inventors, you are a sole proprietor and don't manufacture and/or sell your invention yourself, you don't need a fancy or complex set of books. You can get along very nicely with just a few simple items. These include:

- a business checking account (see Section A1, below)
- income and expense journals (see Section A2, below)
- files for supporting documents, such as receipts and canceled checks (see Section A3, below), and
- an asset log to support your depreciation deductions (see Section A4, below).

If, on the other hand, you're a sole proprietor who does manufacture and/or sell your own invention, you'll need to do more than the simple bookkeeping that we describe in this chapter, including keeping track of inventory, sales and costs of goods sold. *Small Time Operator* by Bernard B. Kamoroff (Bell Springs Publishing) provides help on how to do this.

Adolph Sax
Inventor of the saxophone

Patenting Your Books

What if, while dutifully working on your books, you come up with a new or better bookkeeping method. Could your method be patented? Until recently, the answer would have been no. For example, in 1908 a federal appeals court ruled that a bookkeeping system designed to prevent fraud by waiters and cashiers in hotels and restaurants was not patentable because it was a method of doing business. (*Hotel Security Checking Co. v. Lorraine Co.*, 160 F. 467 (2d Cir. 1908) .) However, in 1998, the federal courts changed their tune and found that methods of doing business could be patented. The case involved a method of investing in mutual funds, featuring a central asset pool linked by software to a series of funds. (*State Street Bank & Trust Co. v. Signature Financial Group*, 149 F.3d 1368 (Fed. Cir. 1998).) Since 1998, many business methods patents have been issued by the USPTO including patents related to bookkeeping systems—for example Pat. No. 4,642,767 Bookkeeping and accounting system, and Pat. No. 5,390,113, Method and electronic apparatus for performing book-keeping.

1. Business Checking Account

Although it is not required by law, one of the first things you should do when you become self-employed is to set up a separate checking account for your inventing business. Your business checkbook will be the primary place where you record business expenses and income. Make all inventing business-related payments by check from the account and deposit any inventing income you receive—such as checks from people to whom you license your invention—into the account. Don't use your business account for personal expenses. Don't use your personal account for business expenses.

Your business account will separate your personal expenses and business income and expenses, which will help convince the IRS that you are running a business and not just engaged in a hobby. It will also be quite helpful should the IRS decide to audit you.

a. Opening the account

If you use a trade name to identify your sole proprietorship instead of your real (or legal) name—for example, you use Acme Widget instead of John Jones, sole proprietor—your account should be established under the trade name. (See Chapter 3, Section A for a discussion of the difference between trade and legal names.) In this case, you *must* open a business, not a personal account. Also you will likely have to give your bank a copy of your fictitious business name statement. If you are a sole proprietor doing business in your own name, you may be able to save money by opening a personal account rather than a business account.

Separate Credit Cards Could Save You Money

Use a separate credit card for business expenses instead of using one card for both personal and business items. Credit card interest for business purchases is 100% deductible while interest for personal purchases is not deductible at all. In addition, using a separate card will help you keep track of how much interest you've paid for business purchases. The card doesn't have to be in your business name. It can just be one of your personal credit cards.

b. paying yourself from the account

If your inventing business earns a profit, you may pay yourself all or part of that money by writing a business check to yourself and depositing the money in your personal account.

Personal draws are not a deductible business expense because you're just transferring your own money from one account to another. If you are a sole proprietor, you do not have to report your personal draws on your tax returns.

c. Writing checks on the account

If you already keep an accurate, updated personal checkbook, just follow the same procedures in your inventing checkbook. If, however, you tend to be careless in keeping up your personal checkbook, you're going to have to change your habits. Each time you write a check, make sure you record the following:

- the date
- the amount
- the check number
- the name of the person or company to whom the check is written, and
- the business reason for the check—for example, the equipment or service you purchased.

You can use either the paper register that comes with your checkbook or a computerized register.

 Avoid writing checks payable to cash. Writing cash checks might lead to questions from the IRS if you're audited. If you must write a check for cash to pay a business expense, be sure to include the receipt for the cash payment in your records.

d. Making deposits into the account

When you make deposits into your business checking account, record in your check register:

- the date
- the amount, and
- a description of the source of the funds—for example, a licensee's name.

2. Income and Expense Records

In addition to a business checkbook, you should maintain records that list by category all of your expenses and income. These records, which you should update at least monthly, show how much you are making, how much you are spending and what you are spending your money on—a valuable time saver when preparing your taxes.

There are three different ways you can keep income and expense records:

- **By hand:** First, you can do it the old-fashioned way, using paper ledger sheets or accounting record books and a pencil.
- **Using a computer spreadsheet:** Another way to record your expenses and income is to use a computer spreadsheet program, such as *Excel* or *Quattro Pro*.
- **Using a financial program:** Finally, you can use a computer financial program such as *Quicken* or *MS Money*.

In the following two sections, we describe how to use a manual or spreadsheet record keeping system. We do not cover computerized financial programs. You need to carefully read the instructions that come with the program you have. Make sure you know how to use it. If you don't, you'd be better off with paper ledgers or spreadsheets.

a. Keeping an expense journal

Your expense journal will show what you buy for your business. Create it by using ledger sheets you can get from any stationery or office supply store—preferably ledger sheets with at least 12 or 14 columns. Devote a separate column to each major category of expenses you have. Alternatively, you can purchase accounting record books with the expense categories already printed on them.

Using Computer Financial Programs

There are many computer programs designed to help people with their finances. The two most popular are *Quicken* and *MS Money*. These programs work differently than the manual or spreadsheet system described in this section.

Programs like *Quicken* work off of a computerized check register. You enter your deposits (income) and withdrawals (expenses) from your business checking account into the register. You can also record cash and credit card expenses using separate accounts. You note the category of each income or expense item in the register. *Quicken* can then take this information and automatically create income and expense reports—that is, it will show you the amounts you've spent or earned for each category. It can also create profit and loss statements and balance sheets. You can even import these amounts into tax preparation software, such as *TurboTax*, when you do your income taxes.

Quicken or *MS Money* can do the job for most independent inventors. But far more sophisticated accounting programs are available. Programs such as *QuickBooks*, *Mind Your Own Business* and *Peachtree Accounting* can accomplish more complex bookkeeping tasks, such as double entry bookkeeping. You'll need one of these programs if you manufacture and distribute your invention yourself and maintain an inventory.

These cost more, however, and might not offer categories that meet all your needs.

If you're using a computer spreadsheet, you'll need to set it up by creating and labeling columns with expense categories. Some spreadsheets come with pre-packaged templates you can use; you can also get templates off the Internet—for example *Excel* templates are available from the Microsoft website (www.microsoft.com).

To decide what your expense categories should be, sit down with your first month's bills and receipts and divide them into categorized piles. Common expense categories for inventors include:

- business meals and entertainment
- travel
- telephone
- office supplies
- postage and shipping
- rent
- utilities
- professional dues, publications and books
- business insurance
- payments to other self-employed people, and
- equipment.

You should always include a final category called Miscellaneous for various expenses that are not easily pigeon-holed.

You can add or delete expense categories as you go along—for example, if you find your Miscellaneous category contains many items for a particular type of expense, add it as an expense category.

You don't need a category for automobile expenses, since these expenses require a different kind of documentation for tax purposes. (See Section B below.)

In separate columns, list the check number for each payment, date and name of the person or company paid. If you pay by credit card or check, indicate it in the check number column.

At least once a month, go through your check register, credit card slips, receipts and other expense records and record the required information for each transaction. Also, if you're using a manual system, total the amounts for each category when you come to the end of the page and keep a running total of what you've spent for each category for the year to date.

The example below shows a portion of a manual expense journal.

b. Keeping an income journal

If you are earning money from your inventing, you should keep an income journal to reflect how much money you earn and from where. (If you aren't making any money yet, don't bother with the journal.)

At a minimum, your income journal should have columns for the source of the funds, the amount of the funds and the date you received payment. If you have many different sources of income, you can create different categories for each source and devote separate columns to them in your journal.

An example portion of an income journal is shown below.

Expense Journal										
Expense Details			Expense Category							
Date	Pmt. Type	To:	Equip-ment	Postage/ Shipping	Utilities	Services (Contractors)	Rent	Travel	Meals & Entertainment	Misc.
5/1	Check 123	JJ					1,000			
5/1	Check 124	ABC Rents	500							
5/10	Visa	Comp World	1,000							
5/15	Cash	Café Ole							50	
5/16	Check 127	Telephone			35					
5/20	Check 128	Tommy Edison			50					
5/30	Check 129	Nicky Tesla				500				
Total This Page	1,500	0	85	500	1,000	0	50	0		
Total This Year	3,500	250	250	1,000	5,000	300	3,000	600		

Income Journal

Source	Amount	Date Received
Acme Manufacturing Co.	$5,000	1/15/xx
Acme Manufacturing Co.	4,000	4/15/xx
Acme Manufacturing Co.	6,000	7/15/xx
Total	$15,000	

c. Keeping automobile records

If you use a car or other vehicle for business purposes (other than commuting to an outside workplace where you carry on your inventing business), you can deduct gas and other auto expenses from your taxes. This deduction can be either the actual cost or a standard rate deduction, which is based on the number of business miles you drive. You're generally allowed to use whatever method gives you the largest deduction. (See Chapter 7, Section E for a detailed discussion of the automobile expense deduction.)

As far as recordkeeping is concerned, the standard deduction is by far the easiest method to use. All you need to do is to keep track of the total miles you drive and how many are for your inventing business purposes. However, keep track of your business-related parking expenses. These are fully deductible no matter which auto deduction method you use.

If you use the actual cost method, you get to deduct the cost of all your auto-related expenses, including gasoline, oil, tires, repairs and insurance. You also get to deduct an amount for depreciation of your auto (see Chapter 7). Unfortunately, you must keep records of all these expenses, which can be a hassle. The easiest way to do this is to keep all your receipts in a folder or envelope. At tax time, add them up to determine how big a deduction you'll get using the actual expense method. This will be much easier if you use a separate credit card for your gas and other auto expenses (if you pay cash for gas, you'll need to get a receipt or make a note of the amount).

Regardless of which method you choose, you must record the total business miles you drive during the year. If you use your car for both business and personal reasons, you must take care to separate those miles and figure out the percentage of business vs. personal use. You can do this by keeping track of the total miles you drive each year and then keeping a separate tally of your business miles. Make a note of your odometer reading on January 1 of every year—that way, you'll know how many miles you've driven each year.

EXAMPLE: In one recent year, Sally, who is working on an electronic baby bib invention, uses her Volvo sedan to visit prospective licensees, prototype makers and to attend a trade show in Las Vegas. Her odometer reading at the beginning of the year was 59,000. At the end of the year, it was 69,000, so she knows she's driven a total of 10,000 miles. Her records show that she drove the car 1,000 miles for her inventing business during the year. Thus, she had a 10% business use percentage for the car. If she uses the actual expense method, she can deduct only 10% of her expenses.

The way the IRS would like you to keep track of your business mileage is to use a mileage log book or similar record book and note the miles you drive for each business trip along with odometer readings. An example of a page from such a log book is reproduced below. You can obtain such log books from a stationery or office supply store for just a few dollars.

In real life, however, many people find keeping such a log book too much trouble. If you don't want to use a log book, at least keep track of all your business trips in an appointment book or calendar and note your business miles driven. It's not absolutely necessary to provide odometer readings or precise mileage counts—a good estimate will suffice. Then, when you do your taxes, you'll have to add together the mileage for all your business trips to determine your total business miles for the year.

If you hate doing anything by hand and would rather use your computer, you can keep track of your mileage and car expenses with a spreadsheet program or a financial program like *Quicken Home and Business.*

An example of a portion of a mileage logbook is shown below.

3. Supporting Documents

The IRS lives by the maxim, "Figures Lie and Liars Figure." It knows very well that you can claim anything in your books, since you create them yourself. For this reason, the IRS requires that you have documents to support the entries in your books and on your tax returns. You don't have to file any of these documents with your tax returns, but you must have them available to back up your returns if you're audited.

a. Income records

When the IRS audits a small business, it usually asks for both business and personal bank statements. If you don't have them, the IRS may subpoena them from your bank. If your bank deposits are greater than your reported income on your tax return, the IRS auditor will assume you've underreported your income and impose additional tax, interest and penalties.

Car Mileage Logbook

Date	Destination	Purpose	Beginning Odometer Reading	Ending Odometer Reading	Business Miles
5/1	Sunnyvale, CA	Visited Patent Depository Library to do patent search	50,000	50,025	25
5/10	Portland, OR.	Saw Art Andrews—potential investor	50,500	51,000	500
5/25	Las Vegas, NV	Attended inventor trade show	60,000	60,200	200
				Total Business Miles	725

To avoid this, you need to keep documents showing the sources and amounts of all your income, including bank deposit slips. Keep your bank statements as well.

b. Expense records

You also need supporting documents to prove that an expense was related to your business. Sometimes it will be clear from the face of a receipt, sales slip or the vendor's name on your canceled check that the item you purchased was for your business. But if it's not clear, note what the purchase was for on the document.

In the absence of a supporting document, an IRS auditor will likely conclude that an item you claim as a business expense is really a personal expense and refuse to allow the deduction. If you're in the mid-level income, 27% marginal tax bracket, every $100 in disallowed deductions costs you $27, plus interest and penalties.

The best supporting document for an expense is a paid receipt that shows whom you paid, how much, the date and the item or service purchased.

If you don't have a receipt, keep your canceled check. A canceled check isn't as good as a receipt because it doesn't show what you bought. You can prove this, however, by matching the check with a bill or invoice.

If you use a credit card, keep your credit card slips and save your monthly billing statements. The best approach is to set aside a separate credit card just for business expenses. If you pay an expense with an ATM card or

another electronic funds transfer method, keep your receipt and bank statement.

c. Entertainment, meal and travel expense records

Deductions for business-related entertainment, meals and travel are a hot button item for the IRS because taxpayers have historically stretched these deductions beyond logic. You need to have more records for these expenses than for almost any others, and the IRS will closely scrutinize them during an audit.

Whenever you incur an expense for business-related entertainment, meals or travel, you must document:

- the date
- the amount
- the place
- the business purpose, and
- if the deduction is for either entertainment or meals, the business relationship of the people at the event—for example, their names and occupations and any other information needed to establish their business relation to you.

All this record keeping is not as hard as it sounds. Your receipts will ordinarily indicate the date, amount and place in which you incurred the expense. You just need to describe the business purpose and business relationship if entertainment or meals are involved. You can write this directly on your receipt.

EXAMPLE: Mary has lunch with Harold, president of Acme Technologies, Inc., to discuss licensing her new folding bicycle invention. Her restaurant receipt shows the date, the name and location of the restaurant, the number of people served and the amount of the expense. Since Mary paid by credit card, the receipt even shows the amount of the tip. Mary just has to document the business purpose for the lunch. She writes on the receipt: "Lunch with Harold Pinto, President, Acme Technologies, Inc. Discussed signing license to manufacture folding bicycle invention."

You must keep supporting documents for expenses other than lodging that tally more than $75. Keep your receipts or credit card slips for such expenses. Canceled checks alone are not sufficient; you must have the bill for the expense as well. You don't need to keep supporting documents for expenses that tally less than $75. But you still must make a record of how much you spent, what it was for, who you paid it to, the date paid and the type of expense. It's probably easier to just keep your receipts for all these small expenses than to make a separate record.

d. Filing supporting documents

If you don't have a lot of receipts and other documents to save, you can simply keep them all in a single folder, shoebox or other safe place.

If, on the other hand, you have numerous supporting documents or are the type of person who likes to be extremely well organized, separate your documents by category—for

example, income, travel expenses and equipment purchases. You can use a separate file folder for each category or get an accordion file with multiple pockets.

4. Asset Records

When you purchase property such as computers, office furniture, copiers or cellular telephones to use in your business, you must keep records to verify:

- when you bought the item
- the purchase price
- the cost of any improvements to the item—for example, upgrading your computer
- whether you use the asset for business or personal purposes, or both
- when and how you disposed of the asset, and
- if you've sold the asset, the selling price and expenses of the sale.

Be sure to keep copies of all your receipts, purchase and sales contracts, repair invoices and similar items.

If you have assets that can be used for either personal or business purposes, you may have to keep special records for these assets. This type of asset is called listed property, and it includes such things as:

- cars, boats, airplanes and other vehicles
- computers
- cellular phones, and
- any other property generally used for entertainment, recreation or amusement— for example, VCRs, cameras and camcorders.

Unless you use your listed property 100% for your inventing business and keep it at your business location, you must follow the IRS's special rules if you want to depreciate or take a Section 179 deduction for the property (basically, Section 179 allows you to take all your depreciation in one year; see Chapter 7.) (If you work from home, keeping your property at home is the same as keeping your property at your business location.)

These special rules require you to document how you use the property—both for business and personal use. Keep a log book, business diary or calendar showing the dates, times and reasons that you used the property. You can purchase log books for this purpose at stationery or office supply stores. You can also use a computer spreadsheet or an advanced financial program such as *QuickBooks*.

> **EXAMPLE:** Bill purchases a computer he uses for his inventing business and to play video games. He must keep a log showing his business use of the computer. Following is a sample from one week in his log.

Use Log for Personal Computer

Date	Business Use Time	Business Use Reason	Personal Use Time	Personal Use Reason
5/1	4.5 hours	Prepared patent drawings	1.5 hours	
5/2			3 hours	
5/3	8 hours	Prepared patent application		
5/4				

Ordinarily, you're supposed to keep listed property records all year long for every year you have the property and use it in business. (See Section B, below, for information on how long you should keep logs and records.) However, if this is too much trouble, there is an alternative. You may keep the records described above for only part of each year—for example, for the first week of each month or for the first three months of the year. If you do this, be prepared to show the IRS that the sample period is representative of the way you used the property for the entire year. A good way is through your inventor's notebook, showing that you spend roughly the same amount of time inventing each month or each quarter of the year.

B. Length of Time for Keeping Records and Logs

Unless we've stated otherwise in the preceding section, keep all your income and expense supporting documents for at least three years after you file your tax returns. Keep your asset records for three years after the depreciable life of the asset ends. For example, keep records for five-year property such as computers for eight years. (See Chapter 7 for a list of the depreciation period for various types of business property.)

If you hire employees, you must create and keep a number of special records, including payroll tax records, withholding records and employment tax returns. And you must keep these records for four years. (See Chapter 10 for guidance on hiring employees.)

C. Accounting Methods and Tax Years

To put it mildly, accounting methods and tax years are rather dry subjects, but it's worthwhile understanding the basics because it can help you defer your taxes.

1. Accounting Methods

There are two basic accounting methods that you can choose from: cash basis and accrual basis.

Using the cash basis method is like maintaining a checkbook. You record income only when you receive the money, and you record expenses only when you actually pay them.

In accrual basis accounting, you report income when you earn it (not necessarily when you receive the money), and you record expenses when you incur them (and not necessarily when you pay them).

Whether the cash or accrual method is used becomes really important at the end of the year. Under the accrual method, expenses incurred in December, but not paid until the following year, can be deducted for the prior year. Under the cash method, an expense is deductible only for the year it is actually paid. The same rules apply to business income you receive.

> **EXAMPLE:** You hire a freelance illustrator to produce drawings for your patent application. He bills you $1,000 in December 2004, but you don't pay the bill until February 2005. Under the cash method, you record the $1,000 expense and take the tax deduction for your 2005 taxes. Under the accrual method, you record the expense for 2004—the year you incurred the debt.

The cash method is by far the simplest and is used by most self-employed people who do not maintain inventory or offer credit. The accrual method can be difficult to use because there are complex rules to determine when income or expenses are accrued. The accrual method must be used by businesses that provide for credit sales or maintain an inventory. So, if you manufacture and/or sell your invention, you'll have to use the accrual method for purchases and sales.

Since you'll likely be using the cash method, be sure to remember that you must actually pay an expense by December 31 to deduct it from your taxes for the year—it's not enough simply to be billed for it. However, for tax purposes, paying by credit counts as a cash payment, even if you don't completely pay off your balance at the end of the month.

2. Tax Years

All businesses must pay taxes for a 12-month period, also known as the tax year. Sole proprietors, partnerships, limited liability companies and S corporations (see Chapter 2 for more information about these business forms) must use the calendar year as their tax year—that is, January 1 through December 31.

However, there are exceptions that permit some small businesses to use a tax year that does not end in December, also known as a fiscal year. You need to get the IRS's permission to use a fiscal year. The IRS doesn't like businesses to use fiscal years, but it might grant you permission if you can show a good business reason for it. To get permission, you must file IRS Form 8716, Election to Have a Tax Year Other Than a Required Tax Year.

D. Creating Financial Statements

Using the information from the simple bookkeeping described above, you can automatically create financial statements which show the financial condition of your inventing business. These include profit and loss statements and balance sheets.

A profit and loss statement shows how your inventing business is doing over a period of time—a month, a quarter, a year or longer. You create one by totaling your revenues and then subtracting your business expenses from that total for the period of time covered by the statement.

A balance sheet shows the financial condition of your business at a specific moment in time—it's like a photograph of your finances. It lists the total value of your business assets (things you own for your business such as equipment) and your liabilities (everything your business owes, such as loans). It also shows your owner's equity or net worth; this is what's left of your assets after subtracting the value of your liabilities.

You'll need these financial statements not just to know whether your inventing business is doing well or poorly, but also to obtain loans or financing from investors or other sources. Financial accounting programs like *Quicken* and *MS Money* can create these statements for you.

For a good introduction to financial statements and basic accounting concepts, refer to *The Accounting Game,* by Darrell Mullis and Judith Orloff (Sourcebooks, Inc.).

E. Other Inventing Business Records

In addition to financial records, you should keep all records showing your attempts to market, license or sell your invention. These may include, for example, correspondence, emails, business cards, notes of telephone conversations, your daily calendar showing the dates and times of business meetings, licenses and contracts. If you wish, you may paste these and similar items into your inventor's notebook. If you do this, it's a good idea to sign and date them and have them witnessed. However, it will probably be easier for you to keep them in a separate file. (See Chapter 9 for a detailed discussion of how to keep an inventor's notebook.)

Why keep these records? Because they will provide very strong evidence that you want to make a profit from your inventing. This will show the IRS or courts that you are engaged in a business, not a hobby (see Chapter 6). In one case a court held that an inventor who never made any money from his inventions was nevertheless in business because he made numerous marketing efforts—for example, he sent letters to 11 pharmaceutical companies in an attempt to license a new antibiotic he developed.

In addition, keep records of your attendance at any educational seminars and of any consultations with experts or professionals. For example, if you attend a seminar on how to market your invention, keep your billing statement, syllabus or other materials you obtain.

Keep good records if you contact a marketing firm, technical expert or patent attorney. These types of activities and contacts also help show you are running a business. ■

Chapter 5

Tax Basics

A. Inventors Who Earn Profits 5/2

    1. Federal Taxes 5/2

    2. State Taxes 5/4

    3. Local Taxes 5/5

B. Inventors Who Incur Losses 5/6

C. Inventors Who Hire Employees 5/7

    1. Federal Employment Taxes 5/7

    2. State Employment Taxes 5/7

D. How To Handle Your Taxes 5/7

    1. Doing the Work Yourself 5/7

    2. Hiring a Tax Pro 5/9

E. IRS Audits 5/10

    1. Audit Time Limit 5/11

    2. Type of Audit 5/11

    3. What the Auditor Does 5/11

    4. Handling Audits 5/12

*W*illiam Harper took early retirement from Westinghouse in 1989 and began to work on an invention—a way to improve trailerable pontoon boats. The technical challenges were substantial as were the research and development costs. He kept careful track of his expenses and, at his accountant's direction, wrote them off each year. Then, two years into his development work, he got an audit letter from the IRS questioning his inventing deductions for the prior year. Thus began a two-year sojourn in which Harper met with an IRS auditor four times and ended up hiring a lawyer. Finally, after two years, the IRS admitted it could find nothing wrong with his deductions and the case was closed.

The IRS cost Harper a lot of time, aggravation and attorney and accounting fees. But it could have been a lot worse. Because Harper kept proper records, filed an accurate tax return and claimed only those deductions to which he was entitled, he was able to beat the IRS. Other inventors have not been so lucky.

William Harper's experience should serve as an object lesson to every self-employed independent inventor: You may not be interested in the IRS, but the IRS is interested in you. You need to pay careful attention to tax matters.

This chapter provides an overview of the brave new world of taxation you are about to enter as an independent inventor and explains some ways to deal with it efficiently.

A. Inventors Who Earn Profits

If you're one of the fortunate independent inventors who earns a profit from inventing, you'll discover that all levels of government—federal, state and local—will want a piece of it. You need to be familiar with the requirements of each.

1. Federal Taxes

The federal government puts the biggest tax bite on all self-employed people, including inventors. When you're in business for yourself, the federal government imposes a number of taxes on you, the primary ones being:

- income taxes, and
- self-employment taxes.

In addition, as explained below, the federal government requires that you pay your income taxes and self-employment taxes quarterly throughout the year—a procedure known as estimated taxes.

a. Income taxes

Unless you've formed a C corporation, you'll have to pay personal income tax on the profits your inventing business earns. In Chapter 7, we explain how to take advantage of a number of business-related deductions to reduce your taxable income.

By April 15 of each year, you'll have to file an annual income tax return with the IRS showing your income and deductions for your inventing business for the previous year and how much estimated tax you've paid. You must file IRS Form 1040 and include a special tax form in which you list all your business income and deductible expenses. If, like most independent inventors, you're a sole proprietor, you use IRS Schedule C, Profit or Loss From Business.

Tax matters are more complicated if you operate your inventing business with others, or choose to incorporate your one-person invention business or form a one-owner LLC.

- If you operate a partnership, you must file a partnership return (IRS Form 1065 also known as Schedule K-1) which lists the partnership's income and deductions and each partner's share of partnership profits or losses. You use this information to report your partnership income or losses on your personal tax return (IRS Form 1040). (For more information, see Chapter 2, Section C2.)
- If you incorporate your business and choose S corporation tax status, the entity must file an information return with the IRS on Form 1120S. This form is also referred to as a Schedule K-1, but it's different from the K-1 partnership's filing. The shareholders use the information on the S corporation K-1 to report their income or losses on their personal tax returns (IRS Form 1040). (For more information, see Chapter 2, Section C3).
- If you incorporate your business as a C corporation, it will have to file its own tax return and pay taxes on its profits. You'll be an employee of your corporation; you'll have to file a personal tax

return and pay income tax on the salary your corporation paid you. (See Chapter 2, Section C3.)
- If you form an LLC, the rules for filing depend on whether you choose to be taxed as a partnership, C corporation or sole proprietorship (if the LLC has only one owner). For more information, see Chapter 2, Section C4.

b. Self-employment taxes

You'll also have to pay Social Security and Medicare taxes on the money you earn from your inventing business. These taxes are called self-employment taxes, or SE taxes. You must pay SE taxes if your net yearly earnings from your business are $400 or more. When you file your annual tax return, you must include IRS Form SE, showing how much SE tax you were required to pay. (We discuss self-employment taxes in more detail in Chapter 8, Section C.)

c. Paying quarterly estimated taxes

Federal income and self-employment taxes are pay-as-you-go taxes. You must pay these taxes as you earn or receive income during the year. Unlike employees, who usually have their income and Social Security and Medicare tax withheld from their pay by their employers, business owners normally pay their income and Social Security and Medicare taxes directly to the IRS. These tax payments, called estimated taxes, are usually made four times every year on April 15, June 15,

September 15 and January 15. You have to figure out how much to pay; the IRS won't do it for you.

2. State Taxes

Life would be too simple if you were only required to pay federal taxes. States get into the act as well, imposing their own income and sales taxes to fund their governments.

a. State income taxes

Except for Alaska, Florida, Nevada, South Dakota, Texas, Washington and Wyoming, all states impose income taxes on business owners. New Hampshire and Tennessee impose income taxes on dividend and interest income only. Most states charge a percentage of the income shown on your federal income return. Depending on the state in which you live, these percentages range anywhere from 3% to 12%.

In most states, you have to pay your state income taxes during the year in the form of estimated taxes. These are usually paid at the same time you pay your federal estimated taxes.

You'll also have to file an annual state income tax return with your state tax department. In all but six states—Arkansas, Delaware, Hawaii, Iowa, Louisiana and Virginia—the return must be filed by April 15, the same deadline as your federal tax return.

If you're incorporated, your corporation will likely have to pay state income taxes and file its own state income tax return.

Each state has its own income tax forms and procedures. Contact your state tax department to learn about your state's requirements and obtain the forms.

b. State sales taxes

If you sell a product based on your invention, you'll likely have to pay sales taxes. Almost all states and many municipalities impose sales taxes of some kind. The only states without sales tax are Alaska, Delaware, Montana, New

Dean Kamen
Inventor of the portable insulin pump, surgical stent and the Segway human transporter

Hampshire and Oregon. You'll have to fill out an application to obtain a state sales tax number. Many states impose penalties if you make a sale before you obtain a sales tax number. Generally, you pay sales taxes four times a year, but you might have to pay monthly if you make lots of sales.

Miscellaneous State Business Taxes

In addition to income and sales taxes, some states impose other, sometimes obscure business taxes. For example, Nevada imposes a Business Privilege Tax of $100 per year per employee. Hawaii imposes a general excise tax ranging from .5% to 4% of the gross receipts businesses earn. Michigan has a Single Business Tax of 2% on businesses with gross receipts over $250,000. These miscellaneous taxes are sometimes difficult to ferret out. Check with your state government website to learn more about miscellaneous business taxes in your state.

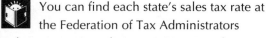 You can find each state's sales tax rate at the Federation of Tax Administrators website (www.taxadmin.org). You can also locate your own state tax rate at your state government website. (Insert the name of your state and the words "sales tax" into your Internet search engine.)

3. Local Taxes

You might have to pay local business taxes in addition to federal and state taxes. For example, many municipalities have their own sales taxes which you may have to pay to a local tax agency.

Some cities and counties also impose property taxes on business equipment or furniture. You may be required to file a list of such property with local tax officials, along with cost and depreciation information. Some cities also have a tax on business inventory. This is why many retail businesses have inventory sales: They want to reduce their stock on hand before the inventory tax date.

A few large cities—for example, New York City—impose their own income taxes. Some also charge annual business registration fees or business taxes.

Your local chamber of commerce should be able to give you good information on your local taxes. You can also contact your local tax department.

Tax Calendar. The following calendar shows you important tax dates during the year. If you're one of the few self-employed people who uses a fiscal year instead of a calendar year as your tax year, these dates will be different. (See Chapter 4, Section C.) If you have employees, you must make additional tax filings during the year. (See Chapter 10.)

The dates listed below represent the last day you have to take the action described. If any of the dates fall on a holiday or weekend, you have until the next business day to take action.

Tax Calendar	
Date	**Action**
January 15	Your last estimated tax payment for the previous year is due.
January 31	If you file your tax return by now, you don't have to make the January 15 estimated tax payment. If you hired independent contractors last year, you must provide them with Form 1099-MISC.
February 28	If you hired independent contractors last year, you must file all your 1099s with the IRS.
March 15	Corporations must file federal income tax returns.
April 15	Your individual tax return must be filed with the IRS and any tax due paid. Or, you can pay the tax due and file for an extension of time to file your return. You must make your first estimated tax payment for the year. Partnerships must file information tax returns. State, individual income tax returns due in all states except Delaware, Hawaii, Iowa, Louisiana and Virginia.
April 20	Individual income tax returns due in Hawaii.
April 30	Individual income tax returns due in Delaware and Iowa.
May 1	Individual income tax returns due in Virginia.
May 15	Individual income tax returns due in Louisiana.
June 15	Make your second estimated tax payment for the year.
September 15	Make your third estimated tax payment for the year.

B. Inventors Who Incur Losses

If you're one of the many inventors who—as of yet—earns no money at all from inventing, you'll have no taxes to pay on your inventing business. Only people who make money need to pay taxes. Likewise, no taxes will be due if your inventing expenses exceed inventing income. However, this doesn't mean you need not be concerned with taxes. On the contrary, inventors who lose money have just as much to fear from the IRS as those who earn substantial profits.

Inventing business losses can be very valuable. You can use them to offset your income from other sources—for example, a job or investment income—and thereby reduce your tax liability for the year. However, the IRS and other tax agencies may closely scrutinize your deductions. To protect yourself in the event of an audit you should:

- be able to show the IRS that your inventing activities are a business, not a hobby (see Chapter 6 for an explanation on how to prove you are operating an inventing business)
- keep accurate records of your expenses (see Chapter 4 for an explanation on bookkeeping and accounting), and
- have a legitimate legal basis for your deductions (see Chapter 7 for an explanation of when and how to deduct inventor expenses).

C. Inventors Who Hire Employees

Whether or not you earn any money from inventing, if you hire employees you'll have to deal with state and federal employment taxes.

1. Federal Employment Taxes

Federal employment taxes consist of half your employees' Social Security and Medicare taxes and all of the federal unemployment tax. You must also withhold half your employees' Social Security and Medicare taxes and all their income tax from their paychecks. You must pay these taxes monthly, by making federal tax deposits at specified banks. You may also deposit them directly with the IRS electronically.

When you have employees, you'll have to keep records and file quarterly and annual employment tax returns with the IRS. (See Chapter 10.)

When you hire other self-employed people, however, you don't have to pay any employment taxes. You need only report payments over $600 for business-related services to the IRS and to your state tax department if your state has income taxes.

2. State Employment Taxes

If you live in a state with income taxes and have employees, you'll likely have to withhold state income taxes from their paychecks and pay the money over to your state tax department. As we explain in Chapter 10, you'll also have to provide your employees with unemployment compensation insurance by paying state unemployment taxes to your state unemployment compensation agency.

D. How To Handle Your Taxes

Many business owners take care of their taxes completely by themselves. Others hire tax professionals to take care of everything for them. Many more are somewhere in between. Your approach will depend on how complex your tax affairs are and whether you have the time, energy and desire to do some or all of the work yourself.

1. Doing the Work Yourself

The more tax work you do yourself, the less money you'll have to pay a tax pro such as a certified public accountant (CPA) to help you through. This will not only save you cash, but also will give you more personal control over your financial life. The subject of taxes might seem daunting, but you don't need to become a CPA to take care of your own tax needs. Nor do you have to do everything yourself— for example, you can hire a tax pro to prepare your annual tax return or to advise you if you encounter a particularly difficult problem. You can do some or all of the following tasks yourself.

a. Bookkeeping

Even if you do hire a tax pro to prepare your tax returns, you'll save money if you keep good records. Tax pros have many horror stories about clients who come in with plastic bags or shoe boxes filled with a jumble of receipts and canceled checks. As you might expect, these people end up paying much more than those who have a complete and accurate set of income and expense records. It is not difficult to set up and maintain a bookkeeping system for your inventing business. You should do so when you first start business. (Chapter 4 describes a simple bookkeeping system adequate for sole proprietor inventors.)

b. Paying estimated taxes

If your inventing business makes money, you'll need to pay estimated taxes during the year. (see Section A1). If you live in one of the 43 states with income taxes—that is, all states but Alaska, Florida, Nevada, South Dakota, Texas, Washington and Wyoming—check with your state tax department to find out whether you must make estimated tax payments.

c. Paying state and local taxes

You may have to pay various state and local taxes, such as a sales tax or personal property tax. (See Section A2.) This is an area where a tax pro can advise you. Otherwise, you'll need to contact your state tax department and local tax office for information. Once you learn about the requirements and obtain the proper forms, it's usually not difficult to compute these taxes on your own.

d. Filing your annual tax returns

The most difficult and time-consuming tax-related task you'll face is filing your annual tax return. If you live in one of the states that has income taxes, you'll have to file a state income tax return as well. Federal and state returns are due by April 15 except in six states that have later dates for state returns. (See the chart in Section A.)

One way to make your life easier is to hire a tax pro to prepare your returns the first year you're in business. You can then use those returns as a guide when you do your own returns in future years.

Taxes at the Touch of a Button

Completing your tax return yourself has been made much easier by the availability of tax preparation computer programs. These programs contain all the forms you need and, not only do all your tax calculations for you, but also contain online tax help and questionnaires you can complete to figure out what forms to use.

Two popular tax preparation programs are *TurboTax* and *Taxcut*. (Specially designed small-business versions of *TurboTax* are recommended.)

e. Paying employment taxes

If you have employees, your tax life will be more complicated than if you work alone or just hire independent contractors. You'll need to file both annual and quarterly employment tax returns. You're also required to withhold part of your employees' pay and send it to the IRS along with a contribution of your own.

This is an area where many business owners seek outside help, since calculating withholding can be complex. Many use an accountant or payroll tax service to perform these tasks. However, if you have a computer, accounting programs such as *QuickBooks* and *PeachTree Accounting* can calculate your employee withholding and prepare employment tax returns.

If you handle your taxes yourself, you'll likely want to obtain a more detailed book specifically on taxation. Many excellent books are available, including *Home Business Tax Deductions: Keep What You Earn,* by Stephen Fishman (Nolo), and *Tax Savvy for Small Business*, by Frederick W. Daily (Nolo).

The IRS also has publications on every conceivable tax topic. These are free, but can be difficult to understand. IRS Publication 910, *Guide to Free Tax Services,* contains a list of these publications and many of the most useful ones are cited in the following chapters. One that you should obtain is Publication 334, *Tax Guide for Small Business.* You can obtain these and all other IRS publications by calling the IRS at 800-TAX-FORM, visiting your local IRS office or downloading them from the IRS Internet site at www.irs.gov.

2. Hiring a Tax Pro

Instead of doing the work yourself, you can hire a tax professional to perform some or all of it for you. A tax pro can also provide guidance to help you make key tax decisions, such as choosing the best setup for your business and helping you deal with the IRS if you get into tax trouble.

a. Types of tax pros

There are several types of tax pros. They differ widely in training, experience and cost.

Tax preparers. As the name implies, tax preparers prepare tax returns. The largest tax preparation firm is H&R Block, but many mom and pop operations open for business in storefront offices during tax time. In most states, anybody can be a tax preparer; no licensing is required. Tax preparers don't have the training to handle taxes for inventing businesses and so are not a wise choice.

Enrolled agents. Enrolled agents or EAs are tax advisors and preparers who are licensed by the IRS. They have to have at least five years of experience and pass a difficult test. Some EAs are very knowledgeable, but most have little or no experience dealing with the special problems of inventors. However, many offer bookkeeping and accounting services that you may find useful.

Certified public accountants. Certified public accountants, or CPAs, are licensed and regulated by each state. They undergo lengthy training and must pass a comprehensive exam. CPAs represent the high end of the tax pro spectrum. In addition to preparing tax returns, they perform sophisticated accounting and tax work. Large businesses routinely hire CPAs for tax help and so should you—they are the most knowledgeable about the technical details of taxation.

Tax attorneys. Tax attorneys are lawyers who specialize in tax matters. The only time you'll ever need a tax attorney is if you get into serious trouble with the IRS or another tax agency and need legal representation before the IRS or in court. Some tax attorneys also give tax advice, but they are usually too expensive for small businesses. You're better off hiring a CPA if you need tax advice.

b. Finding a tax pro

The best way to find a tax pro is to obtain referrals from business associates, friends or professional associations. If none of these sources can give you a suitable lead, local CPA societies can give you referrals to local CPAs. You can also find tax pros in the telephone book under "Accountants, Tax Return."

Your relationship with your tax pro will be one of your most important business relationships. Be picky about the person you choose. Talk with at least three tax pros before hiring one. You want a tax pro who takes the time to listen to you, answers your questions fully and in plain English, seems knowledgeable and makes you feel comfortable. It can also be helpful if the tax pro already has other clients who are inventors or at least are involved in research and development of new products. A tax pro already familiar with

inventors' tax problems can often give you the best advice for the least money.

c. Tax pros' fees

Ask about a tax pro's fees before hiring him or her and, to avoid misunderstandings, obtain a written fee agreement before any work begins. Most tax pros charge by the hour.

E. IRS Audits

In an audit, the IRS examines you, your business, your tax returns and the records used to create the returns. If an IRS auditor determines you didn't pay enough tax, you'll have to pay the amount due plus interest and penalties.

Fortunately, your chances of being audited in any given year are not very high. Indeed, IRS audit rates have declined dramatically in recent years due to reductions in the IRS's staff, a growing number of tax returns being filed and a new IRS emphasis on taxpayer service rather than enforcement.

However, the IRS still needs to be taken seriously. The fact that overall audit rates are low doesn't guarantee you won't get audited. Indeed, if, like many independent inventors, you incur losses each year, you probably have a higher chance of being audited than business owners who report profits. This doesn't mean you shouldn't take all the deductions to which you're legally entitled. But it does mean that you must understand the rules and be able to back up your deductions with proper records.

IRS Audit Rates for Sole Proprietors Filing Schedule C		
	2001	2002
Income under $25,000	2.67%	3.00%
$25,000 to $100,000	1.18%	1.33%
$100,000 and over	1.45%	1.47%

These audit rates, compiled by the IRS itself, are misleading. They don't include the millions of IRS computer-based reviews of taxpayer returns—often called "invisible audits." If the IRS included these in its calculations, the reported audit rates (above) would be three to four times higher.

1. Audit Time Limit

As a general rule, the law allows the IRS to audit a tax return up to 36 months after it's filed. This means you normally don't have to worry about audits for tax returns you filed more than three years ago. The IRS calls the years during which it can audit you "open years."

2. Type of Audit

There are three types of IRS audits:
- correspondence audits
- office audits, and
- field audits.

Correspondence audits: Correspondence audits are handled entirely by postal mail. These are the simplest and shortest type of IRS audit, ordinarily involving a single issue. The IRS sends you written questions about a perceived problem, and may request additional information and/or documentation. If you don't provide satisfactory answers or information, you'll be assessed additional taxes. Correspondence audits are often used, for example, to question a patent owner about unreported income—income the IRS knows the taxpayer received because an IRS Form1099 form listing the payment has been filed by a patent licensee. Correspondence audits are the most common type of IRS audits.

Office audits: Office audits take place face-to-face with an IRS auditor at one of the 33 IRS district offices. These are more complex than correspondence audits, often involving more than one issue or more than one tax year. If you make less than $100,000 per year, this is the type of face-to-face audit you'll likely be subjected to.

Field audits: The field audit is the most comprehensive IRS audit, conducted by an experienced revenue officer. A field audit examines your finances, your business, your tax returns, and the records used to create the returns. As the name implies, a field audit is normally conducted at the taxpayer's place of business—this is so the auditor can learn as much about your business as possible. Field audits are ordinarily reserved for taxpayers who earn a lot of money. It's not likely you'll be subjected to one unless your inventing business earns more than $100,000 per year.

3. What the Auditor Does

IRS auditors look primarily at two issues: whether you've underreported your income and whether you've claimed tax deductions to which you're not entitled—for example, claimed that nondeductible personal expenses were deductible business expenses. Using a separate bank account for your business expenses will help convince the auditor that you're not mixing your personal bills with your business expenses.

The auditor will want to see the business records you used to prepare your tax returns, including your books, check registers, canceled checks and receipts. The auditor will also ask to see your records supporting your business tax deductions.

IRS auditors can also obtain your bank records, either from you or your bank, and check them to see if your deposits match the income you reported on your tax return. If the total of all your deposits is larger than your reported income, the auditor will assume you failed to report all your income, unless you can show that the deposits you didn't include in your tax return weren't income—for example, that they were loans, inheritances, or transfers from other accounts. This is why you need to keep good records of your income.

4. Handling Audits

You have the legal right to take anyone along with you to help during an audit—a bookkeeper, tax pro or even an attorney. If you've hired a tax pro to prepare your returns, it can be helpful for him or her to attend the audit to help explain your business receipts and records and to explain how the returns were prepared. Some tax pros include free audit services as part of a tax preparation package.

However, if you prepared your tax returns yourself, you can probably deal with an office audit yourself. It could cost more to hire a tax pro to represent you in an office audit than the IRS is likely to bill you. If you're worried that some serious irregularity will come to light—for example, you've taken a huge deduction and can't produce a receipt or canceled check to verify it—consult with a tax pro before the audit.

No matter who prepared your tax returns, it usually makes sense to have a tax pro represent you in a field audit, since these can result in very substantial assessments.

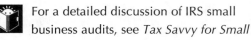 For a detailed discussion of IRS small business audits, see *Tax Savvy for Small Business*, by Frederick W. Daily (Nolo). ■

Chapter 6

How to Prove to the IRS You're in Business

A. Qualifying as a Business 6/2

    1. The Two IRS Tests for a Business 6/2

    2. You Must Have a Profit Motive 6/3

B. Passing the 3-of-5 Profit Test... 6/4

C. Passing the Behavior Test.. 6/6

    1. Act Like a Businessperson 6/7

    2. Have or Get Expertise 6/8

    3. Work Steadily 6/9

*H*obbies are great! They're relaxing, entertaining and can lower your blood pressure. But if the IRS considers inventing to be your hobby—not your business—your blood pressure may rise. That's because a hobbyist can only deduct inventing expenses from inventing income. If there is no income, there's no deduction. And an inventor in this position can't carry over the deductions to use them in future years when income may be generated. The deductions are lost forever. In summary, inventors who are deemed to be hobbyists are in the worst of all possible tax worlds. So, if you're looking for a hobby, try stamp or coin collecting; but make inventing your business.

If you qualify as an inventing business, you'll become one of the pampered pets of the tax code, receiving the best possible tax treatment. You can deduct inventing expenses from other income you earn, such as salary from your job or your spouse's job or interest and investment income. This can be done even though you don't expect to earn any money from inventing for many years. Moreover, the tax law gives inventors who are in business special treatment, making their tax situation even better than that of most businesspeople.

In this chapter we will show the tax rules for qualifying your inventing activities as a business. And if you've already been inventing for a while, it's still not too late to take the few simple steps described below to ensure you can take these deductions.

A. Qualifying as a Business

For IRS purposes, inventing (or any other activity) qualifies as a business if:

- your primary motive for inventing is to earn a profit, and
- you engage in inventing continuously and regularly over a substantial time period.

1. The Two IRS Tests for a Business

The IRS has established two tests to measure these factors. One is a simple mechanical test that asks whether you've earned a profit in three of the last five years. The other is a much more complex test based on whether you behave like a business. We walk you through these tests in Sections B and C. If you can "pass" either test, you can claim the tax benefits discussed in Chapters 7 and 8.

Rear Admiral Dr. Grace Murray Hooper
Pioneer in the development of COBOL
and other computer languages

Note that the IRS only applies these tests if your tax returns are audited. In other words, you may mistakenly presume that inventing is your business only to learn, four or five years later that the IRS has a different opinion. In that case, you would be disallowed any improper deductions made during those years and required to pay any miscalculated taxes and penalties. A disallowance can be quite expensive and for that reason, we strongly recommend that you bolster your position as a business by reviewing this chapter and following the rules set forth in Sections B and C.

2. You Must Have a Profit Motive

Inventing can't qualify as a business unless you do it to earn a profit. Making a profit need not be your sole motive, but it should be your primary one. For example, you may engage in inventing to help mankind, to become famous, to advance technology or just because you enjoy it. This is all fine as long as you also want to make a profit. (In contrast, inventing is a hobby if you engage in it for reasons other than making a profit—for example, to incur deductible expenses or just to have fun.)

If you're like most inventors, you're probably thinking to yourself right now: "Of course, I want to make a profit; why else would I bother working on an invention?" This may well be true, but the IRS can't read your mind to see whether you want to earn a profit. And it certainly isn't going to take your word for it. Instead, it looks to see whether you actually earn a profit, or whether you *behave* as if you want to earn a profit. If you never earn a

profit or behave like you want to, the IRS will determine your inventing activities are a hobby; this is so even though you sincerely believe in your heart that you want to make money.

Moreover, don't think that just because you're working on a serious or important invention that the IRS will conclude you're in business. For example, building a wind-powered ethanol plant sounds like a very serious idea, but a tax court was not impressed enough to permit the business deduction (see below). If you don't earn profits or behave as if you want to, even serious inventing efforts will be deemed a hobby by the IRS.

> **EXAMPLE:** Piszczek, an airline pilot, spent his spare time building a wind-powered ethanol plant in his backyard. Over an 18 year period he never produced any ethanol, never applied for or obtained any patents or consulted with experts in the field. Using commercially available parts, he set out to build a model, rather than to develop the principles on which a new ethanol technology could be based. The court concluded that the ethanol project was "a costly hobby which other taxpayers need not subsidize." (*Piszczek v. United States*, 1995 U.S. App. LEXIS 39490.)

Regardless of whether your invention is characterized as "serious" or "wacky," you are in business for tax purposes if you earn profits or if you act like you really want to. Keep in mind that when it comes to earning money, trivial ideas can be just as lucrative as serious ones (maybe even better)—the Hula Hoop and Frisbee both earned millions in profits.

Why Have a Hobby Loss Rule?

The IRS created the hobby loss rule to prevent taxpayers from entering into ventures primarily to incur expenses they could deduct from their other income. Before the hobby loss rule was enacted in its current form, wealthy people used to do this all the time—for example, they would buy farms or ranches they would run just to incur losses they could deduct from their other income. The hobby loss rule halts this form of tax avoidance by allowing you to take a business expense deduction only if your venture qualifies as a business.

B. Passing the 3-of-5 Profit Test

You usually don't have to worry about the IRS labeling inventing as a hobby if you earn a profit from it in any three of the last five years. If your venture passes this test, the IRS must presume it is a business. This doesn't mean the IRS can't claim your venture is a hobby, but it shifts the burden to the IRS to prove it is a hobby. In practice, the IRS usually doesn't attack ventures that pass the profit test unless it's clear the numbers have been manipulated just to pass it.

You have a profit when the taxable income from an activity is more than the deductions for it. You don't have to earn a big profit to satisfy this test and there is no set amount or percentage of profit you need to earn.

The presumption that you are in business applies to your third profitable year and extends to all later years within the five-year period beginning with your first profitable year.

EXAMPLE: Tom began to work on a new invention in 2001. He earned no income from inventing during 2001–2002 and therefore had no profits from inventing for those years. He obtained a patent in 2003, and licensed it to a manufacturer that same year. Due to his royalty income from the patent, he earned a profit during 2003 through 2005.

Year	Losses	Profits
2001	$10,000	
2002	$5,500	
2003		$9,000
2004		$6,000
2005		$18,000

If the IRS audits Tom's taxes for 2005, the IRS must presume that Tom was in business during that year. Tom earned a profit during three of the five consecutive years ending with 2005, so the presumption that Tom is in business extends to 2008, five years after his first profitable year.

Unfortunately, a great many self-employed inventors can't satisfy the profit test. It may take far more than five years before you see any money at all from an invention, let alone turn a profit (see sidebar, "How Long Does It Take?"). For that reason, the IRS often uses a second test, we've dubbed the "behavior test," to determine whether a venture qualifies as a business.

Postponing an IRS Determination Whether You Are in Business

The IRS doesn't have to wait for five years after you start inventing to decide whether it is a business or hobby—it can audit you and classify your venture as a business or hobby at any time. However, you can give yourself some breathing room by filing IRS Form 5213, which requires the IRS to postpone its determination until you've been in business for at least five years.

Although this may sound like a good idea, filing the election only alerts the IRS to the fact that you might be a good candidate to audit on the hobby loss issue after five years. It also adds two years to the statute of limitations—the period in which the IRS can audit you and assess a tax deficiency. For this reason, almost no one ever files Form 5213. Also, you can't wait five years and then file the election once you know that you will pass the profit test. You must make the election within three years after the due date for

the tax return for the first year you were in business—that is, within three years after the first April 15 following your first business year. So if you started your inventing business in 2005, you would have to make the election by April 15, 2009 (three years after the April 15, 2006 due date for your 2005 tax return).

There is one situation in which it might make sense to file Form 5213. If the IRS has already told you that you will be audited, you may want to file the election to postpone the audit for two years. However, you can do this only if the IRS audit notice is sent to you within three years after the due date for your first business tax return. If you're notified after this time, it's too late to file the election. In addition, you must file your election within 60 days after you receive an IRS audit notice, whenever it is given, or you'll lose the right to make the election.

King Camp Gillette
Inventor of the safety razor

How Long Does It Take?

Being an inventor is usually not a road to quick riches. It may take years for you to perfect your invention, and years more before you obtain a patent. Once you get a patent, it may take even more time before you can commercialize your invention. Here are examples of how long it took several well-known inventions to make money:

- Although invented in 1914, the zip fastener (or zipper as it was later known) was not widely used in clothing until 10 years later.
- Disc brakes were not widely used on cars until 50 years after they were patented.
- Power steering was patented in 1927, but was not introduced in passenger cars until 1951.
- Stereophonic sound was invented in 1933 but was not popularized in consumer recordings until the 1960s.
- The microwave oven was patented in 1945 but consumer models were not available until 1967.
- Though patented in 1938, the first commercial electric photocopiers were not sold until 1958.
- Though bar code technology was patented in 1949, it was not used for supermarket checkouts until 1974.

Form 5213: An Invitation to Audit

The IRS has a form called Form 5213, *Election to Postpone Determination as to Whether the Presumption Applies that an Activity is Engaged In for Profit*. If you file this form, the IRS must wait an extra year before it can determine whether you've shown a profit under the profit test. This may sound like a good deal but filing this form only alerts the IRS that you should be audited on the hobby loss issue. For this reason, almost no one ever files a 5213.

C. Passing the Behavior Test

If, like so many inventors, you keep incurring losses and can't satisfy the profit test, don't worry; you can still show you're running a business by passing the behavior test. Indeed, this is how most inventors show the IRS they are in business. Under this test, the IRS looks at the following "objective" factors to determine whether you are behaving like a real business.

- **Whether You Act Like a Business.** Among other things, acting like a business means you keep good books and other records and otherwise carry on your inventing activities in a businesslike manner.
- **Your expertise.** People who are in business usually have some knowledge and skill relevant to the business. Thus, adequate expertise in the field of invention you're interested in shows you're in

business. If you lack the necessary expertise, you should acquire it through study or by consulting with experts in the field.

- **The time and effort you spend on inventing.** The more time and effort you put into inventing, the more likely it will appear a business.

- **Your track record.** Having a track record of success in other businesses in the past—whether or not related to inventing—helps show your present inventing activities are a business.

- **Your history of profit and losses.** Even if you can't satisfy the profit test, earning at least occasional profits helps show you're in business. However, the IRS is aware that inventors often earn no profits for many years in expectation of a big payoff if and when their invention is perfected and commercialized.

- **The amount of any profits you earn.** Earning only small or occasional yearly profits while you have large losses and/or a large investment in an activity, tends to show a lack of a profit motive. On the other hand, earning a substantial profit one year after years of losses helps show you are in a business. After all, inventing is a highly speculative venture and inventors often earn little or nothing for many years in the hope of a big payday down the road.

- **Are you rich?** The IRS figures you likely have a profit motive and are running a real business if you don't have a substantial income from sources other than inventing. After all, you'll need to earn

money from your inventions to survive. On the other hand, substantial income from sources other than inventing tends to show a lack of a profit motive (particularly if your losses from inventing generate substantial tax deductions). But this factor is not determinative by itself.

- **Are you having too much fun?** Finally, activities that are inherently fun or recreational are less likely to be engaged in for profit than those that are not fun. Although inventing may be pleasurable, it's not so enjoyable that this factor should pose a problem for most inventors.

The first three factors listed above—acting like a business, expertise and time and effort expended—are by far the most important. Studies have shown that no taxpayer who has satisfied these factors has ever been found not to be in business.

Any inventor can satisfy these factors and pass the behavior test. This is so even though you don't expect to earn any money from inventing for many years.

1. Act Like a Businessperson

First and foremost, you must show that you carry on inventing in a businesslike manner. Doing the things outlined below will not only help you with the IRS, they will greatly aid you in actually earning a profit one day or determining that your invention will not be profitable.

- **Keep Good Business Records.** Keeping good records of your expenses and income from inventing is the single most important thing you can do to show you're in business. Without good records, you'll never have an accurate idea of how you stand financially. Lack of records shows you don't really care if you make money or not. You don't need an elaborate set of books. A simple record of your expenses and income will suffice. See Chapter 4 for a detailed discussion of recordkeeping for inventors.

- **Keep Invention Records.** Every inventor should document his or her efforts in writing. Such documentation is vital for obtaining and enforcing a patent. But it also helps to show you have a profit motive and are working regularly at inventing. Laying a documentary foundation for a patent shows you want to make money from your invention. (See Chapter 9 for information about creating an Inventor's Notebook.)

- **Legally Protect Your Inventions.** Seek to legally protect your inventions by using trade secrecy and/or applying for patents. More than one court has observed that only inventors who want to make money bother to obtain patents.

- **Keep a Separate Checking Account.** Open up a separate checking account for your business. This will help you keep your personal and business expenses separate —another factor that shows you're running a business.

- **Get Business Stationery and Cards.** It may seem like a minor matter, but obtaining business stationery and business cards shows you think you are in business. Hobbyists ordinarily don't have such things. You can inexpensively create your own stationery and cards using special software.

- **Obtain All Necessary Business Licenses and Permits.** Obtain any required licenses and permits for your invention activities. (See Chapter 3). For example, an inventor attempting to create a wind-powered ethanol generator was found to be a hobbyist partly because he failed to get a permit to produce alcohol from the Bureau of Alcohol, Tobacco and Firearms.

- **Obtain a Separate Phone Line for Your Home Office.** If, like many inventors, you work at home, obtain a separate phone line for your business. Like an EIN, this helps separate the personal from the professional and reinforces the idea that you're in business.

- **Join Professional Organizations and Associations.** Join and participate in professional organizations and associations. For example, if you're an engineer, join engineering organizations. There are also many associations for inventors you can join. You can find a list in the Appendix.

- **Create a Business Plan.** It is also helpful to draw up a business plan with forecasts of revenue and expenses. This will be a big help if you try to borrow money for your inventing business. For detailed guidance on how to create a business plan, see *How to Write a Business Plan*, by Mike McKeever (Nolo).

2. Have or Get Expertise

If you're already an expert in your field, you're a step ahead of the game. But if you lack all the expertise you need, develop it by attending educational seminars and similar activities and/or consulting with other experts. Keep records to show your attempts to gain expertise—for example, notes documenting your attendance at a seminar.

3. Work Steadily

You don't have to work full-time on inventing to show you're in business. It's fine if you hold a full-time job and only invent part of the time. However, it's best if you work regularly and continuously on inventing instead of only sporadically. For example, it's fine to work ten hours every week on your invention. It's less fine if you only work ten hours every six months. Keep a log showing the time you spend inventing—this doesn't have to be fancy, you can just mark down the time you spend on your calendar or in your inventor's notebook.

> **EXAMPLE:** Levinson owned and operated an electronics store. Over a 40-year period, he worked in his spare time on inventions ranging from microwave power sources to methods for preparing beverages. In 1981, he obtained a patent for a microwave cookware container and later filed suit against a company that infringed on the patent, winning a $210,000 settlement. Even so, the tax court held that Levinson's inventing was not a business because he only worked sporadically at it. He would work at inventing only when an idea came to him, and years could pass between ideas. (*Levinson v. Comm'r.*, T.C. Memo 1999-212.)

If you're like Levinson and only work at inventing when inspiration strikes, you'll have a hard time convincing the IRS or courts that inventing is a business. You don't have to be like Thomas Edison and work 18 hours a day seven days a week, but if you want to avoid the hobby loss rule, you must work steadily at inventing.

The following chart compares the amount of time spent by inventors who were found by the courts to be in business versus those found not to be in business (note that the nonbusiness inventors couldn't even specify exactly how much time they spent inventing).

Inventors Found To Be in Business	Inventors Found Not To Be in Business
20 to 30 hours per week (*Maximoff v. Comm'r.*, T.C. Memo 1987-155.)	No set number of hours each week (*Schell v. Comm'r.* T.C. Memo 1994-164.)
25 hours per week for three years, then 5-10 hours per week for 2 years (*Luow v. Comm'r.*, T.C. Memo 1971-326.)	Inventor couldn't establish how much time, if any, spent on inventing. (*Everson v. Comm'r*, 2001 TNT 115-8.)
72% of working time (*Kilroy v. Comm'r.*, T.C. Memo 1980-489.)	Most of time after work for 6-8 months, then little or no time (*Cherry v. Comm'r.*, T.C. Memo 1967-123.)

The Behavior Test: Pass or Fail

You'll never officially know if you passed or failed the behavior test until you are audited by the IRS. However, if you've done even part of what is suggested above, you have a very good chance of winning. Below are some examples of inventors who passed or failed the test. Besides demonstrating the behavior test at work, these cases also teach another lesson: You don't have to accept a determination by the IRS that you're not in business. The inventors in the examples below refused to accept the results of an IRS audit and appealed to the Tax Court.

Passed: Kilroy, a self-employed person, spent about 70% of his time inventing. He worked on several projects, including an interlocked pallet and container system, a hydraulic mining system, an antibiotic and an anti-allergy substance. He obtained four U.S. and three foreign patents for his mining system. As of the time the IRS determined that he was not engaged in business, he had earned almost nothing from any of these ventures. The tax court reversed the IRS's decision. The court noted that Kilroy made numerous efforts to market his inventions—for example, he tried to license his interlocking pallet and container system to six different packing companies, and wrote 11 letters to pharmaceutical companies to market his antibiotic substance. At various times he employed a microbiologist, patent attorneys and a consulting economist to help him. He also consulted with various experts on how to market his inventions. However, the court was particularly impressed by the

fact that Kilroy had obtained several patents. The court noted that if Kilroy was not interested in making a profit, "there would have been no need for him to patent his inventions or attempt to market them." (*Kilroy v. Commissioner*, T.C. Memo 1980-489.)

Passed: Maximoff, an engineer with a full-time job, spent 20 to 30 hours every week developing a miles-per-gallon indicator for cars and trucks. He produced a test setup combined with a miles-per-gallon indicator for development purposes. After one year, he gave up on the project when he realized that, because of the required complexity of the design and vehicle installation costs, there would be a limited market for the device. Furthermore, when he contacted General Motors regarding his invention, he was told that the company had started the development of the same device with a team of engineers. He decided he couldn't compete with GM. He never finished the indicator, never patented it, never attempted to market it and never made any money from it. Nevertheless, he deducted over $6,000 in expenses incurred working on the invention from his income taxes. The IRS disallowed these expenses, claiming inventing was just a hobby for Maximoff. Maximoff appealed to the U.S. Tax Court and won. The court concluded that Maximoff's inventing was a business. The court was particularly swayed by the fact that he worked steadily on the invention for over a year and had obtained patents for other inventions in the past. Moreover, the court found that his

The Behavior Test: Pass or Fail (continued)

decision to drop the project after he learned about GM's efforts showed he had a profit motive—he dropped the project after he realized he couldn't earn a profit competing against GM. (*Maximoff v. IRS*, TC Memo 1987-155 (1987).)

Failed. Flanagin, a mainframe computer consultant, spent part of his spare time in the late 1980s and early 1990s creating software for the Zenith Z-100 computer. This computer was fast becoming obsolete and had only a few thousand users. Flanagin created a floppy disk device driver for the Z-100 and managed to sell about 300 copies at $39 a piece through a mail-order distributor. Unfortunately, Flanagin's expenses far exceeded his earnings from this activity. Indeed, he incurred losses for 10 straight years, totaling almost $100,000. The tax court agreed with the IRS

that developing software for the Z-100 was a hobby for Flanagin. It concluded that Flanagin flunked the first two factors of the behavior test listed above (see Sections C1 and C2): He did not run his software development activity like a business and he lacked expertise. Most damning of all was the fact that he did not keep adequate records. As a result, the court said "he conducted his activity unaware of the amount of revenue he could expect and had no concept of what his ultimate costs might be or how he might achieve any degree of cost efficiency." In addition, although Flanagin knew how to write software, he was not knowledgeable about the economics of software development. Even so, he never sought professional advice on the economics of this activity. (*Flanagin v. Commissioner*, T.C. Memo 1999-116.)

Tax Purgatory: When Inventing Is Classified as an "Income-Producing Activity"

For some, inventing is not really a hobby, but not really a business either. This could occur where the primary motive for inventing is to earn a profit, but the inventor doesn't engage in inventing sufficiently regularly or continuously for it to be a business. In these cases, inventing could be classified as a for-profit income-producing activity under IRS § 212. An income-producing activity is one you engage in primarily to earn a profit but that does not qualify as a business. A typical income-producing activity would be managing investments. But, although there is little case law on the subject, inventing activities could qualify in this category.

The tax consequences of having an income-producing activity are not as favorable as being in business, but they are still better than engaging in a hobby. Subject to two important exceptions, you're entitled to the same tax deductions as a businessperson. The two exceptions are the research and experimentation deduction and the first-year start-up deductions both discussed in Chapter 7. (You may, however, have to deduct your inventing expenses a little at a time over your invention's useful life, instead of all in the year in which they are incurred—a process called depreciation.) This is a complex area of the tax law. If you believe your inventing activities qualify as an income-producing activity instead of a business or hobby, consult with an experienced tax pro.

■

Inventor Tax Deductions

A. Tax Deductions: The Basics 7/2

    1. You Must Be in Business To Have Business Deductions 7/2

    2. You Must Keep Track of Your Expenses 7/3

    3. You Must Have a Legal Basis for Your Deductions 7/3

    4. How to Deduct Inventing Business Expenses On Your Tax Return 7/3

B. Tax Deduction Road Map 7/9

    Step 1. Determine If the Expense Is Currently Deductible 7/10

    Step 2. Determine If the Expense Must Be Deducted Over Time 7/10

    Step 3. Determine If the Expense Is Not Deductible 7/11

C. Inventing Expenses You May Currently Deduct 7/11

    1. Research and Experimentation Expenses (IRC § 174) 7/11

    2. Currently Deducting Long-Term Property (IRC § 179) 7/18

    3. Deducting Inventing Expenses as Ordinary and Necessary

       Business Expenses (IRC § 162) 7/22

D. Inventing Expenses You Must Deduct Over Time 7/29

    1. Depreciation of Tangible Property 7/29

    2. Amortization of Intangible Property 7/33

    3. Start-Up Expenses (IRC § 195) 7/33

E. Special Deduction Rules 7/34

    1. Deducting Your Home Office Expenses 7/34

    2. Cars, Travel, Meals and Entertainment 7/42

This chapter shows you when and how you can deduct your inventing expenses. This is not a step-by-step tax preparation guide. Rather, it explains basic tax concepts with an emphasis on those that are unique to inventors. You can use the information in this chapter for tax planning purposes throughout the year. Then, when it comes time to prepare your tax return, it will help give you the background you need to deal with a tax pro, or prepare your taxes yourself with the aid of a computer tax preparation program or other do-it-yourself tax preparation tools.

 This chapter provides an overview of a great deal of complex tax law. If, after reading it, you're not sure if an expense is deductible or how to deduct it, consult with a tax pro.

A. Tax Deductions: The Basics

A tax deduction is an expense or the value of an item that you can subtract from your income to determine your taxable income. The more deductions you have, the lower your taxable income and the less tax you pay.

Everyone who pays taxes is entitled to at least some tax deductions. For example, you are entitled to deduct a certain amount from your income each year just for being alive—this is called the personal deduction (in 2005 this deduction was $3,200). However, this chapter is about the large array of deductions available only to people who are in business—

specifically the business of inventing. You don't get these deductions just for being alive, and there is no set business deduction amount established by law as with the personal deduction. Instead, you may only deduct the specific costs you incur in running your inventing business. This way, you only have to pay tax on your profit from your business, if any.

To qualify for any business deduction, you must satisfy three basic requirements:
- you must be in business
- you must keep records of your expenses, and
- you must have a legal basis for the deduction.

1. You Must Be in Business To Have Business Deductions

Obviously, you can't deduct business expenses unless you are in business. Inventing qualifies as a business for tax purposes only if (1) you work at it regularly, and (2) your primary motive for doing it is to earn a profit. If the IRS concludes you have some other motive for inventing—for example, to have fun, please your spouse or avoid your spouse—it may deem your inventing a hobby and you'll find yourself in deduction hell.

How do you show the IRS that your motive for inventing is to earn a profit? You must actually earn a profit, or at least act as if you want to earn profits. Review Chapter 6, discussing the hobby-loss rule, before claiming any deductions.

2. You Must Keep Track of Your Expenses

You can only deduct those expenses you actually incur. This means those expenses you actually paid during the year, whether by cash, credit card or other borrowing. You need to keep records of these expenses to (1) know for sure how much you actually spent; and (2) prove to the IRS you really incurred the expenses listed on your tax return in the event you're audited.

You can keep track of your inventing expenses by using the simple manual system described in Chapter 4 or by using a computer spreadsheet or accounting program.

3. You Must Have a Legal Basis for Your Deductions

All tax deductions are a matter of "legislative grace"—meaning you may take a deduction only if it is specifically allowed by one or more provisions of the tax law. Inventors are fortunate in that the tax law gives them more ways to deduct their expenses than most businesspeople. It is usually not necessary to indicate on your tax return which tax law provision you're relying on for a deduction. But, if you're audited by the IRS, you'll have to provide a legal basis for all your deductions. If the IRS concludes you lack such a basis, it will deny the deduction and you'll have to pay back taxes and penalties.

In short, it helps to know the basics about inventing deductions when you file your taxes. This is true even if you hire a tax pro to prepare your return. You must be able to prove to the IRS that the law permits you to make each deduction claimed. Consider the following example, based on a true story.

EXAMPLE: Gregor invents a software program and pays his attorney $5,000 to prepare a patent application. He deducts the entire $5,000 as a business expense when he files his taxes for the year. Two years later an IRS examiner audits Gregor's return and informs him that he cannot deduct the $5,000 attorney fee payment in one year; he must spread it out and deduct $1/_{15}$ of the $5,000 each year over the life of the patent, telling Gregor he owes back taxes and penalties. Gregor researches the tax law and discovers IRC § 174 that permits an inventor to deduct all costs related to research and experimentation involving his invention in one year, not over the life of the patent. The IRS examiner reviews the law and permits the deduction.

All the possible legal bases for inventing deductions are discussed in detail in Sections C, D and E below.

4. How to Deduct Inventing Business Expenses On Your Tax Return

If, like most independent inventors, you're a sole proprietor, your deductions will be listed on IRS Schedule C, Profit or Loss From Business. If you're not familiar with Schedule C, take a look at the sample shown below, now. In Part I of Schedule C you list your income. (We discuss how to deal with inventing income in Chapter 8.) In Part II you list your expenses (deductions).

Schedule C is like a spreadsheet. You enter numbers and make calculations. You don't provide explanations. For example, Line 17 asks for "Legal and Professional Services." If you hire a lawyer to prepare a patent application, you would list the amount of his or her fee here. Expenses that don't fit into one of the expense categories are listed in the "Other Expenses" section of Schedule C.

a. Line 31: Net Loss

After you have listed all your deductions on Schedule C you will subtract your total expenses from your gross income and enter your net profit or net loss on Line 31. If, as is the case with many inventors, your inventing expenses exceed your inventing income, or you have no inventing income at all, you will have a net loss on Line 31 of your Schedule C. Assuming you meet the IRS business standards established in Chapter 6, you can deduct this loss from all the income you earn for the year, whatever the source—for example, from your salary or investment income, thereby reducing your taxable income for the year.

> **EXAMPLE:** In one year, Chuck earned no money from his ultraviolet rifle scope, but incurred $20,000 in annual expenses that could be currently deducted. Chuck has a net loss from inventing of $20,000. He can deduct his $20,000 inventing loss from all his income for the year, which was $100,000 in salary and investment income. So, instead of having to pay income tax on $100,000 in income, he only had to pay it on $80,000 ($100,000 − $20,000). This $20,000 deduction ends up saving Chuck $7,500 in federal and state income tax for the year—$7,500 he would not have had were he not engaged in the business of inventing.

 For more information on net operating losses, refer to IRS Publication 536, *Net Operating Losses (NOLs) for Individuals, Estates, and Trusts*. You can obtain this and all other IRS publications from the IRS Internet site (www.irs. gov), by calling the IRS at 800-TAX-FORM or visiting your local IRS office.

b. Line 31: Net Profit

If your income exceeds your expenses, you have a net profit. You may or may not have to pay taxes on this income, depending on your income and expenses from other businesses, your job or other sources of revenue. (See Chapter 8.)

 The calculations involved in determining how much you can deduct from prior years' income can be complicated. Tax preparation programs like TurboTax aren't designed to handle net operating losses (NOLs), so it's wise to let a tax pro help you determine your NOL.

SCHEDULE C (Form 1040) Department of the Treasury Internal Revenue Service	**Profit or Loss From Business** (Sole Proprietorship) ▶ **Partnerships, joint ventures, etc., must file Form 1065 or 1065-B.** ▶ **Attach to Form 1040 or 1041.** ▶ **See Instructions for Schedule C (Form 1040).**	OMB No. 1545-0074 20**04** Attachment Sequence No. **09**

Name of proprietor | Social security number (SSN)

A Principal business or profession, including product or service (see page C-2 of the instructions) | **B** Enter code from pages C-7, 8, & 9 ▶

C Business name. If no separate business name, leave blank. | **D** Employer ID number (EIN), if any

E Business address (including suite or room no.) ▶ --
City, town or post office, state, and ZIP code

F Accounting method: (1) ☐ Cash (2) ☐ Accrual (3) ☐ Other (specify) ▶ ----------------------------

G Did you "materially participate" in the operation of this business during 2004? If "No," see page C-3 for limit on losses ☐ Yes ☐ No

H If you started or acquired this business during 2004, check here . . . . ▶ ☐

Part I Income

1	Gross receipts or sales. **Caution.** If this income was reported to you on Form W-2 and the "Statutory employee" box on that form was checked, see page C-3 and check here . . . . . ▶ ☐	1
2	Returns and allowances	2
3	Subtract line 2 from line 1	3
4	Cost of goods sold (from line 42 on page 2)	4
5	**Gross profit.** Subtract line 4 from line 3	5
6	Other income, including Federal and state gasoline or fuel tax credit or refund (see page C-3) . . .	6
7	**Gross income.** Add lines 5 and 6 . . . . ▶	7

Part II Expenses. Enter expenses for business use of your home **only** on line 30.

8	Advertising	8	19	Pension and profit-sharing plans	19
9	Car and truck expenses (see page C-3).	9	20	Rent or lease (see page C-5):	
10	Commissions and fees . .	10	a	Vehicles, machinery, and equipment .	20a
11	Contract labor (see page C-4)	11	b	Other business property . . .	20b
12	Depletion	12	21	Repairs and maintenance . .	21
13	Depreciation and section 179 expense deduction (not included in Part III) (see page C-4)	13	22	Supplies (not included in Part III)	22
			23	Taxes and licenses	23
			24	Travel, meals, and entertainment:	
			a	Travel	24a
14	Employee benefit programs (other than on line 19). .	14	b	Meals and entertainment .	
15	Insurance (other than health) .	15	c	Enter nondeduct-ible amount in-cluded on line 24b (see page C-5) .	
16	Interest:				
a	Mortgage (paid to banks, etc.) .	16a	d	Subtract line 24c from line 24b .	24d
b	Other	16b	25	Utilities	25
17	Legal and professional services	17	26	Wages (less employment credits) .	26
			27	Other expenses (from line 48 on page 2)	27
18	Office expense	18			

28	**Total expenses** before expenses for business use of home. Add lines 8 through 27 in columns . . ▶	28
29	Tentative profit (loss). Subtract line 28 from line 7	29
30	Expenses for business use of your home. Attach **Form 8829**	30
31	**Net profit or (loss).** Subtract line 30 from line 29. • If a profit, enter on **Form 1040, line 12,** and **also** on **Schedule SE, line 2** (statutory employees, see page C-6). Estates and trusts, enter on Form 1041, line 3. • If a loss, you **must** go to line 32.	31
32	If you have a loss, check the box that describes your investment in this activity (see page C-6). • If you checked 32a, enter the loss on **Form 1040, line 12,** and **also** on **Schedule SE, line 2** (statutory employees, see page C-6). Estates and trusts, enter on Form 1041, line 3. • If you checked 32b, you **must** attach **Form 6198.**	32a ☐ All investment is at risk. 32b ☐ Some investment is not at risk.

For Paperwork Reduction Act Notice, see Form 1040 instructions.   Cat. No. 11334P   Schedule C (Form 1040) 2004

Schedule C (Form 1040) 2004   Page **2**

| **Part III** | **Cost of Goods Sold** (see page C-6) |

33 Method(s) used to value closing inventory: **a** ☐ Cost   **b** ☐ Lower of cost or market   **c** ☐ Other (attach explanation)

34 Was there any change in determining quantities, costs, or valuations between opening and closing inventory? If "Yes," attach explanation . . . . ☐ Yes   ☐ No

35	Inventory at beginning of year. If different from last year's closing inventory, attach explanation . .	**35**	
36	Purchases less cost of items withdrawn for personal use	**36**	
37	Cost of labor. Do not include any amounts paid to yourself	**37**	
38	Materials and supplies	**38**	
39	Other costs	**39**	
40	Add lines 35 through 39	**40**	
41	Inventory at end of year	**41**	
42	**Cost of goods sold.** Subtract line 41 from line 40. Enter the result here and on page 1, line 4 . .	**42**	

| **Part IV** | **Information on Your Vehicle.** Complete this part **only** if you are claiming car or truck expenses on line 9 and are not required to file Form 4562 for this business. See the instructions for line 13 on page C-4 to find out if you must file Form 4562. |

43 When did you place your vehicle in service for business purposes? (month, day, year) ▶ ..../.........../..........

44 Of the total number of miles you drove your vehicle during 2004, enter the number of miles you used your vehicle for:

a Business _____   **b** Commuting _____   **c** Other _____

45 Do you (or your spouse) have another vehicle available for personal use?. . . . . ☐ Yes   ☐ No

46 Was your vehicle available for personal use during off-duty hours? . . . . ☐ Yes   ☐ No

47a Do you have evidence to support your deduction? . . . . ☐ Yes   ☐ No

  b If "Yes," is the evidence written? . . . . ☐ Yes   ☐ No

| **Part V** | **Other Expenses.** List below business expenses not included on lines 8–26 or line 30. |

48	**Total other expenses.** Enter here and on page 1, line 27	**48**	

Schedule C (Form 1040) 2004

Tax Savings From Deductions

Most taxpayers, even sophisticated business-people, don't fully appreciate just how much money they can save with tax deductions. Only part of any deduction will end up back in your pocket as money saved. Because a deduction represents income on which you don't have to pay tax, the value of any deduction is the amount of tax you would have had to pay on that income had you not deducted it. So a deduction of $1,000 won't save you $1,000 — it will save you whatever you would otherwise have had to pay as tax on that $1,000 of income.

To determine how much income tax a deduction will save you, you must first figure out your income tax bracket. The United States has a progressive income tax system for individual taxpayers with six different tax rates (called tax brackets), ranging from 10% of taxable income to 35% (see the chart below). The higher your income, the higher your tax rate.

You move from one bracket to the next only when your taxable income exceeds the bracket amount. For example, if you are a single taxpayer, you pay 10% income tax on all your taxable income up to $6,000. If your taxable income exceeds $6,000, the next tax rate (15%) applies to all your income over $6,000—but the 10% rate still applies to the first $6,000. If your income exceeds the 15% bracket amount, the next tax rate (25%) applies to the excess amount, and so on until the top bracket of 35% is reached.

The tax bracket in which the last dollar you earn for the year falls is called your "marginal tax bracket." For example, if you have $60,000 in taxable income, your marginal tax bracket is 25%. To determine how much federal income tax a deduction will save you, multiply the amount of the deduction by your marginal tax bracket. For example, if your marginal tax bracket is 25%, you will save 25¢ in federal income taxes for every dollar you are able to claim as a deductible business expense (25% x $1 = 25¢). The following table lists the 2005 federal income tax brackets for single and married individual taxpayers and shows the tax savings for each dollar of deductions.

Income tax brackets are adjusted each year for inflation. For current brackets, see IRS Publication 505, *Tax Withholding and Estimated Tax*. You can obtain this and all other IRS publications by calling the IRS at 800-TAX-FORM, visiting your local IRS office, or downloading the publications from the IRS Internet site at www.irs.gov.

You can also deduct your inventing business expenses from any state income tax you must pay. The average state income tax rate is about 6%, although seven states (Alaska, Florida, Nevada, South Dakota, Texas, Washington, and Wyoming) don't have an income tax.

If you earn income from your inventing business, you can also deduct most of your inventing expenses for self-employment tax pur-

Tax Savings From Deductions (continued)

2005 Federal Personal Income Tax Brackets

Tax Bracket	Income If Single	Income If Married Filing Jointly	Income Tax Saving for Each Dollar in Deductions
10%	Up to $7,300	Up to $14,600	10¢
15%	From $7,301 to $29,700	$14,601 to $53,450	15¢
25%	$29,701 to $71,950	$53,451 to $119,950	25¢
28%	$71,951 to $150,150	$119,951 to $182,800	28¢
33%	$150,151 to $326,450	$182,801 to $326,450	33¢
35%	All over $326,450	All over $326,450	35¢

poses. The self-employment tax rate is 15.3% on net self-employment earnings up to the Social Security tax cap ($90,000 in 2005). Earnings over the cap are only subject to the 2.9% Medicare tax.

When you add up your savings in federal and state income taxes, you can see the true value of a tax deduction. For example, if you're in the 25% federal income tax bracket, a deduction can be worth 25% (in federal income taxes) + 15.3 % (in self-employment taxes) + 6% (in state income taxes). That adds up to a whopping 46.3%

savings. If you buy a $1,000 computer for your inventing business and you deduct the expense, you save about $460 in taxes. In effect, the government is paying for almost one/third of your inventing expenses. This is why it's so important to know all the deductions you are entitled to take—and to take advantage of every one.

You should get into the habit of thinking about your inventing expenses in terms of "after-tax dollars"—what the item really costs you after you deduct the cost from your income taxes.

Net Operating Losses: When Inventing Losses Exceed Total Annual Income

Sometimes losses from an inventing business are so great that they exceed an inventor's total income for the year. For example, assume that Chuck, in the example above, did not have a salary and investment income and only earned $15,000 in total income from a part-time consulting job, while incurring $20,000 in currently deductible inventing expenses for the year. He would have a net loss for the year of $5,000 ($15,000 –$20,000 = –$5,000). Such a loss is called a "net operating loss," NOL for short.

Although it may not be pleasant to lose money over an entire year, having an NOL does result in important tax benefits—indeed, it's a little like having money in the bank because it can result in a quick tax refund. You can deduct the amount of an NOL against your income for previous years and thereby reduce the tax you needed to pay for those years. This is called "carrying a loss back."

Ordinarily, you may elect to carry back the loss for two years before the NOL year (the year you incurred the loss). However, if you have an NOL for 2001 or 2002, you may carry back the loss five years before the NOL year. The loss is used to offset the taxable income for the earliest year first, and then used for the next year(s). If any of the loss is left over, it may be carried forward up to 20 years—that is, used to reduce your taxable income in future years.

To obtain a refund due to an NOL, you must file either IRS Form 1045 or 1045X. You can get your refund faster by using Form 1045—usually you'll get it within 90 days. However, you must file Form 1045 within one year of the end of your NOL year.

Inventors Who are Not Sole Proprietors

Not every inventor is a sole proprietor. Some co-own their inventing businesses with one or more people. Such inventors are involved in partnerships, corporations or LLCs. An inventor who works alone can also incorporate or form an LLC. If you are in a partnership, corporation or LLC, you won't file a Schedule C as outlined above. Partnerships, S corporations and LLCs taxed as partnerships file information returns with the IRS showing the entitys' income and expenses. The partnership, S corporation or LLC must give the IRS and each business owner a copy of IRS Schedule K listing the owner's share of any profit earned or loss incurred by the business. The owners use this information to report their income or loss on their personal tax returns (Form 1040). Business income or loss is reported on IRS Schedule E, capital gains or losses on Schedule D. Things are very different if you form a C corporation. It is a separate taxpaying entity that files its own income tax return.

B. Tax Deduction Road Map

Figuring out when and how you can deduct your inventing expenses can be confusing because there are several different ways such expenses can be deducted, depending on the nature and amount of the expense and when and how it is incurred. This section provides a road map you can follow to determine how to deduct any inventing expense.

Step 1. Determine If the Expense Is Currently Deductible

First, determine if the expense can be currently deducted—that is, whether the entire amount can be deducted on your taxes for the year the expense is incurred. The following categories of expenses can be currently deducted:

Research and experimentation (R&E) expenses: These are expenses you incur in the course of developing a new invention—for example, rent on the office or lab where you do your development work, patent fees and any property that lasts for less than one year. But R&E expenses don't include long-term assets—things you buy or create that last more than one year, such as computers. (See Section D1 for more information.)

Up to $25,000 of Long-Term Tangible Property: Since you can't deduct long-term (over one year of useful life) property as an R&E expense, you must find another way to currently deduct it. Fortunately, each year you may currently deduct up to $105,000 worth of long-term tangible personal property you buy to use in your inventing business, whether to develop an invention or for other business purposes. (See Section C2 for more information.)

Ordinary and necessary business expenses: You may incur some inventing business expenses that are neither R&E expenses nor the cost of buying long-term-property—for example, invention marketing costs such as payments to a marketing consultant, or administrative expenses such as accounting fees or legal fees not related to obtaining a patent. Generally, these expenses can be currently deducted as ordinary and necessary business expenses. (See Section C3 for further information.)

Step 2. Determine If the Expense Must Be Deducted Over Time

If an expense is not currently deductible, the cost can usually be deducted over a number of years—a process called depreciation or amortization. These costs include:

Long-Term Tangible Property: You may be unable or choose not to deduct certain long-term tangible property under the $105,000 deduction provision listed above. Expenses for this property—tangible property with over one year of useful life that wears out—are deducted over the useful life of the asset as determined by the IRS. (See Section D for more information.)

Long-Term Intangible Property: This is the cost of long-term intangible property you buy that has a determinable useful life—for example, the cost of purchasing someone else's patent, trademark or copyright. These costs are deducted over the property's useful life. The costs you incur in creating a patented invention may also be depreciated on this basis if you can't deduct them currently as described above.

Start-Up Expenses: These are costs you incur, other than for long-term property, before you actually begin business. Once your business begins, $5,000 of your start-up expenses may be currently deducted. Amounts over $5,000 must be deducted over the first 15 years you're in business. (See Section D3 for more information.)

Step 3. Determine If the Expense Is Not Deductible

Certain expenses are not deductible at all. For example, land is not deductible because it never wears out. Personal expenses are not deductible. The cost of purchasing someone else's trade secret may not be deductible.

The flowchart shown below summarizes what we've said above.

C. Inventing Expenses You May Currently Deduct

When it comes to tax deductions, most of us are like children in a candy store: We want everything we can get as soon as we can get it. This makes economic as well as emotional sense because of a concept called "the time value of money"—that is, due to inflation and the fact that money earns interest, money is worth more today than tomorrow. Thus, it's usually advantageous to obtain as big a tax deduction as you can immediately, rather than spreading out over several years. This lowers your tax bill as much tax as possible for the current year, leaving you more money in your pocket.

Unfortunately the fact that you've incurred an expense for your inventing business one year doesn't necessarily mean you can deduct the entire cost on that year's taxes. Some expenses can be currently deducted (deducted in one year), but others must be deducted over several years. Fortunately, the tax code bends over backwards to make it possible for inventors to currently deduct many of their expenses. The inventing expenses you can currently deduct fall into three categories:

- research and experimentation expenses
- Section 179 expenses, and
- ordinary and necessary business expenses.

When you want to figure out whether an expense is currently deductible, go through the categories in the order listed above.

1. Research and Experimentation Expenses (IRC § 174)

If you learn only one section of the Internal Revenue Code, the one to learn is IRC § 174 because it is the inventor's best tax friend. Congress enacted IRC § 174 to encourage inventors and companies engaged in research and development of new technologies.

IRC § 174 is deceptively simple. It says that "a taxpayer may treat research or experimental expenses which are paid or incurred by him during the taxable year in connection with his trade or business as expenses which are not chargeable to capital account." The phrase "not chargeable to capital account" is key: It means that the entire amount of these expenses may be currently deducted from an inventor's gross income.

a. What is research and experimentation?

Only expenses for research and experimentation (R&E) are deductible under Section 174. Research and experimentation is all the work you do as part of your inventing business to discover information that helps eliminate scientific or technical uncertainty concerning

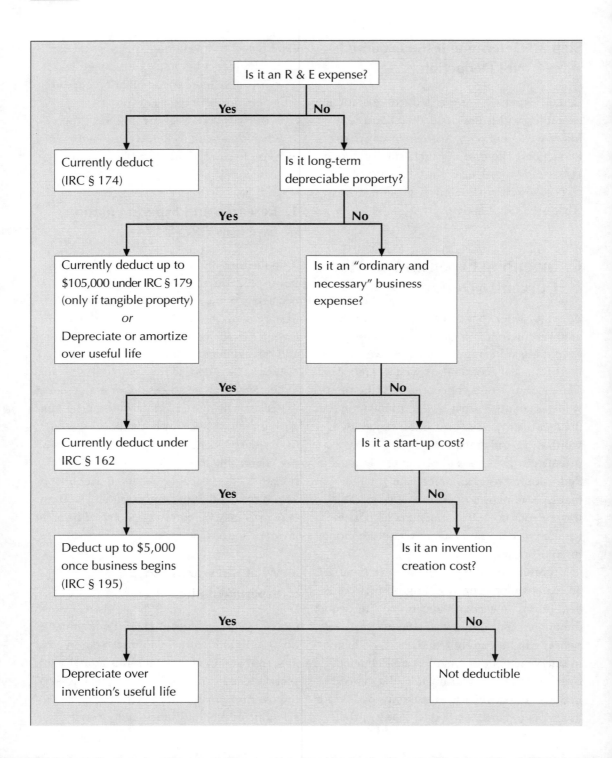

the development or improvement of an invention, patent, process, prototype, formula, technique or similar product.

In other words, you must work to develop or discover something new in the laboratory or experimental sense. You can't, for example, claim a Section 174 deduction to develop an invention that has already been patented or to repeat something that has already been done. Nor can Section 174 be used to claim deductions to discover information that is not scientific or technical in nature—for example, marketing or sales information.

So long as you're doing R&E, it makes no difference if you're attempting to develop a particular invention or are engaged in a general research project. Moreover, your research and experimentation need not be successful—that is, end up as a patented invention or salable product. Indeed, your R&E, may not even have a high probability of being successful.

b. What research and experimentation expenses are deductible?

Subject to one very important exception covered in the following section, any money you spend to perform R&E is currently deductible. Courts have allowed inventors to deduct both direct and indirect R&E expenses.

Direct R&E expenses are the monies you spend for the things you use to actually perform R&E—for example, the laboratory and computer supplies you use for your R&E activities, equipment you rent to conduct R&E, or the money you pay to an employee or independent contractor to assist you in your research.

Indirect R&E expenses are those expenses that help you perform R&E, but are not directly used for that purpose. These primarily consist of the overhead expenses you incur while performing R&E—for example, the rent for your office, lab or workshop, utilities, telephone bills arising from R&E, travel expenses incurred for R&E purposes, and dues and publication expenses incurred for R&E purposes.

Although it may not seem like an R&E expense, the cost of obtaining a patent is also currently deductible under Section 174. This includes both attorney fees and patent filing fees. This is one of the largest expenses many independent inventors have.

c. Cost of long-term property not deductible under section 174

The one thing you buy for R&E that you can't currently deduct under Section 174 is the entire purchase price of long-term property—that is, property that has a useful life of more than one year. This is so even though the property is used for R&E purposes.

> **EXAMPLE:** Mary purchases a $10,000 microscope to aid her in her research to develop a new type of glue. Because a microscope has a useful life of more than one year, the $10,000 expense is not currently deductible under Section 174.

The "useful life" of an asset is not its physical life, but rather the period during which it may reasonably be expected to be useful in your business. Usually it's fairly clear which expenses have a useful life of more than one year—for example, durable lab equipment, vehicles, machinery, buildings, furniture and computer software. (See Section D1 for a more detailed discussion.)

Although Section 174 doesn't apply, you can deduct the cost of long-term property from your taxes, but not necessarily all in one year. Up to $25,000 of tangible personal property you buy for your inventing business can be currently deducted under Section 179 as described in Section C2. If you spend more than $25,000, or the property you buy isn't eligible to be deducted under Section 179, the cost is ordinarily deducted a portion at a time over several years. (See Section D.)

Cost of Constructing Long-Term Property: The prohibition on using Section 174 to currently deduct long-term property applies not just to the cost of buying long-term property from someone else, but to long-term property you build yourself to use in your inventing business—even if the property is used for R&E or is created as a result of your R&E activities. The cost of such long-term property includes the amounts you spend for labor, materials, components, construction and installation.

> **EXAMPLE:** Assume that Mary in the example above decides to construct her own special microscope to use for her glue research. She spends $5,000 for materials and components and pays $5,000 to an optics expert to help her construct and install the microscope. These costs are not currently deductible under Section 174; but she may depreciate them over several years.

Exception—Hiring independent contractors to buy or build long-term property: If you hire an independent contractor to help you conduct R&E, and the contractor buys or builds long-term property to do the work, you may currently deduct the entire cost of the property under Section 174 so long the contractor *retains ownership* of the property.

> **EXAMPLE:** Bill hires the Acme Research Co. to help him develop a new type of explosive. He pays Acme $100,000 for its work. $25,000 of this amount was for new lab equipment Acme needed to buy for the research. Bill agrees that Acme may retain ownership of the equipment. Bill may deduct under Section 174 the entire $100,000 he paid Acme.

However, if you obtain ownership of any long-term property the contractor builds or buys, you may not deduct under Section 174 the cost of parts, labor, materials and installation.

> **EXAMPLE:** Chuck intends to invent a process for infusing soap with caffeine. Chuck hires Ron to construct a machine for isolating caffeine anhydrous, the material to be infused. Chuck will acquire ownership of the completed machine. The cost of building the machine is not currently deductible under Section 174.

Although you cannot deduct labor, materials or installation costs incurred by a contractor, you can deduct the research and experimentation costs incurred when a contractor constructs long-term property you'll own and use in your business.

EXAMPLE: Assume that no one has ever built a machine to isolate caffeine anhydrous before. Ron, from the above example must perform his own extensive research and experimentation to develop and test a design for the device. Once the design is perfected, he buys the materials and parts needed and puts it together. Ron charges Chuck $5,000 for the time he spent researching and $5,000 for the parts and labor involved in building the device. The $5,000 in research costs for the new design are currently deductible under Section 174. The $5,000 for building the machine is not currently deductible under 174.

Because of this rule, whenever you hire independent contractors to perform R&E tasks, make sure that they keep separate track of the expense involved in performing pure research and the expenses of building long-term property you will acquire. Indeed, it's best if you're billed separately for research and labor and materials for constructing property.

Exception—Building prototypes: The cost of building a prototype or working model of your invention is currently deductible under Section 174, including the labor, parts and materials. Building and testing prototypes is part of the development process.

Exception—Leasing instead of buying: There is an easy way around the limits on Section

174 deductions for long-term property: Lease such property to use in your inventing business instead of buying it. The lease payments are entirely deductible in the current year under Section 174. Thus, for example, if Mary in the example above paid a $1,000 annual fee to lease a microscope instead of buying or building it herself, she could deduct the entire amount under Section 174 in the current year.

Deduction of Software Development Costs

The IRS has determined that the costs of developing computer software (whether or not the software is patented) are similar to the type of R&E costs that fall within Section 174. Therefore, R&E expenses incurred to develop software may be currently deducted the same as other 174 expenses. This is so whether the software is developed for an inventor's own use or to sell or license to others. (Rev. Proc. 2000-50.)

Note that this rule doesn't apply to the cost of software you buy from someone else to use in your inventing business, whether to help you with your inventing or for administrative tasks like bookkeeping. Such software must be depreciated over 36 months as described in Section D. Software that comes with a computer you buy is depreciated as part of the computer, unless you're billed separately for the software.

d. Expenses that can't be deducted under section 174

In addition to the money you spend on long-term assets as described above, you can't currently deduct under Section 179 routine expenses to purchase, study, market, sell, test or manufacture an invention or product that already exists. These include, for example:

- quality-control testing
- efficiency surveys
- management studies
- consumer surveys
- advertising or promotions, and
- the cost of buying someone else's patent or trademark.

Indeed, once your invention is perfected, you'll likely have no more R&E expenses deductible under Section 174 (but you may deduct the cost of obtaining a patent as mentioned above).

However, these non-R&E expenses may be currently deductible as ordinary and necessary business expenses (see Section C3).

e. Expenses must be incurred "in connection with a trade or business"

Section 174 requires that R&E expenses be incurred "in connection with a trade or business" to be currently deductible. This requirement is easy to satisfy. An inventor need not be engaged in a long-established, up-and-running business. All that is required is that there be a "realistic prospect" that the inventor's efforts will result in a trade or business at some time. (*Harris v. Commissioner*, (5th Cir. 1994) 16 F.3d 75.)

In practical terms, this means you can just be starting out in inventing and still currently deduct your R&E expenses using Section 174. You're entitled to a deduction even if the only "business" you're conducting is the research itself. You need not have patented any inventions or earned any money from inventing.

All that is required is that there be a realistic prospect that you *could* have an active business some time in the future using the fruits of your research, assuming it proves successful. The future business can involve the licensing or sale of an invention derived from the research, manufacturing and selling products or services derived from the research, or both.

> **EXAMPLE:** Scoggins and Christensen formed a partnership to develop a new type of epitaxial reactor—a machine used in the high-technology industry to apply layers of silicon on substrate silicon wafers. They spent $486,000 on research in 1985-86. At the end of this time, they still had not completed the reactor research. As a result, they made no efforts to market their reactor and had yet to earn any money from their research effort. Nevertheless, they were entitled to currently deduct their R&E expenses under Section 174. This was because, if the research ultimately proved successful and the reactor was completed, they had a realistic prospect of entering a fully-fledged, ongoing business—that is, the business of licensing and/or manufacturing and selling epitaxial reactors. (*Scoggins v. Commissioner*, 46 F.3d 950 (9th Cir. 1995).)

Amortizing Section 174 Expenses Instead of Currently Deducting Them

Most inventors use IRC § 174(a) to deduct the entire amount of their R&E expenses in the current year, rather than deducting them a portion at a time over several years. However, Section 174(b) gives you the option of amortizing your R&E expenses, instead of deducting them all at once. "Amortize" means you deduct an equal portion of the expense each year until the entire amount of the expense is deducted.

The minimum period for such amortization is 60 months. However, if the R&E expenses involved ultimately lead to issuance of a patent, they must then be depreciated over the useful economic life of the patented invention—as long as 17 to 18 years.

If you elect to amortize, you aren't allowed to begin deducting your R&E expenses until the month you first realize benefits from the expenses. This is usually defined to mean the month you put the property to an income producing use. It can be difficult to know exactly when to begin taking your deduction.

If you want to amortize your R&E Expenses, you must include a statement to that effect with your tax return. You may amortize all your R&E expenses or only those for certain projects. Additionally, you are required to make an "accounting segregation" in your books of the R&E costs involved.

Amortization of R&E expenses is not an option most independent inventors choose. However, it can be advantageous if you expect to be in a much higher tax bracket in later years or want to avoid incurring a NOL for the year because, for various reasons, you don't want to have a business that is losing money. If you think you may want to amortize, consult with a knowledgeable tax pro, because of the complexities involved.

f. Section 174 expenses must be reasonable

There is no dollar limit on the amount of Section 174 deductions you can take each year, but your deductions must be reasonable in amount. "Reasonable" means that the amount you spend for R&E must be about what would ordinarily be paid for similar expenses by similar types of businesses.

g. When to claim Section 174 expenses

You must claim your Section 174 deductions in the first year R&E expenses are incurred. If you fail to claim these deductions on your Schedule C for the year in which they were incurred, you must ask the IRS for permission to use Section 174 in subsequent years. You do this by sending a letter to:

The Commissioner of Internal Revenue Washington, DC 20224.

The letter must include:
- your name and address
- the first tax year in which you want to use Section 174
- a description of the project or projects for which you have incurred R&E expenses or will incur such expenses, and
- your signature.

These requests are usually routinely granted by the IRS. However, you must file the request no later than the last day of the tax year you want to use Section 174. If your request is granted, it is not retroactive—that is, you can use Section 174 only for the current and future tax years.

Once you start claiming R&E expenses under Section 174, you are required to stick with this method of deducting such expenses. You need permission from the IRS to switch to a different method of treating R&E expenses. This rule applies on a project-by-project basis.

h. The need to keep good records

If, like most independent inventors, you currently deduct your R&E expenses under Section 174, there is no legal requirement that you record Section 174 expenses as such in your own books or records. (1958-1 C.B. 148.) But, such separate record keeping is required if you amortize R&E expenses under Section 174(b).

However, because of the limitations on Section 174 deductions for depreciable property discussed in Section C1 above, it is essential to keep good records to substantiate your R&E expenses when construction of a

piece of property is the end result (or part) of your research and experimentation. Specifically, you need to be able to show that those expenses you deducted under Section 174 really were for research and experimentation rather than for labor and materials to construct the property.

Keeping a detailed laboratory notebook showing all your research and experimentation efforts will help provide excellent evidence that an expense was for research, rather than construction. Obviously, you should keep all receipts, invoices and other documentation of your research and experimentation expenses as well.

2. Currently Deducting Long-Term Property (IRC § 179)

The previous section explained that the cost of purchasing long-term property (property with a useful life of over one year) is not currently deductible as a research and experimentation expense under Section 174. Fortunately, part of the cost of this property can be currently deducted under another tax law provision—IRC § 179.

Section 179 permits you to deduct up to $105,000 of your long-term property purchases in the year you make them, rather than having to depreciate them over several years as described in Section D below. Tax pros call this "first year expensing" or "Section 179 expensing."

The property you deduct under Section 179 need not be used for research and experimentation purposes, though it can be.

It's deductible so long as you use it for any business purpose.

> **EXAMPLE:** Gary is working to invent a special bed that vibrates to awaken its owner. This year he spends $8,000 for a special sleep monitor he uses to help to test his bed. After perfecting his invention, he buys $10,000 worth of bed-making machinery, and spends $7,000 for a photocopier, fax machine and computer he uses to help market the bed. All $25,000 in expenses are currently deductible under Section 179.

It's up to you to decide whether to use Section 179 to take a current deduction for depreciable assets. You always have the option of depreciating the property instead—this means you deduct a portion of the cost each year over several years. Most taxpayers do take the full amount of the Section 179 deduction because it gives them as large a tax reduction as possible for the current year.

However, in some cases, you may be better off in the long run using depreciation instead of Section 179. This may be so if you expect to earn more in future years than you will in the current year. Remember that the value of a deduction depends on your income tax bracket. If you're in the 15% bracket, a $1,000 deduction is worth only $150. If you're in the 30% bracket, it's worth $300. So spreading out a deduction until you're in a higher tax bracket can make sense.

You may also prefer to use depreciation rather than Section 179 if you want to puff up your business income for the year. This can help you get a bank loan or help your business show a profit instead of incurring a loss—and therefore, avoid running afoul of the hobby loss limitations.

So, think carefully before taking a Section 179 deduction. If you do so, you can't change your mind later and decide to use depreciation instead. Depreciation is discussed in detail in Section D.

a. Property that can be deducted

You can use Section 179 to deduct the cost of any *tangible personal property* you buy for your business that the IRS has determined will last more than one year—for example, computers, business equipment and office furniture. (See Section D.) Special rules apply to cars. (See Section E2.)

You can't use Section 179 for land, buildings or intangible personal property such as patents, copyrights and trademarks. Software you purchase separately is intangible property and thus cannot be expensed under 179. However, the software that comes with a computer you buy and is included in the price, may be expensed along with the computer.

If you use property both for business and personal purposes, you may deduct under Section 179 only if you use it for business purposes *more than half the time.* The amount of your deduction is reduced by the percentage of personal use. You'll need to keep records showing your business use of such property.

> **EXAMPLE:** Lucy buys a computer. She uses it 80% for her inventing business

and 20% to play video games. She can deduct 80% of the cost of the computer under Section 179.

If you use an item for business less than half the time, you can't use Section 179. Instead, you must depreciate the property, deducting the cost over several years. (See Section D.)

b. Deduction limit

There is a limit on the total amount of business property expenses you can deduct each year using Section 179. In 2003, the limit increased from $24,000 to $100,000. For 2005 through 2007 the limit is $105,000 plus an annual adjustment for inflation. Congress enacted these whopping increases on a temporary basis, hoping to jumpstart the faltering U.S. economy. Starting in 2008, the Section 179 limit will shrink to $25,000.

The dollar limit applies to all your businesses together, not to each business you own and run. You do not have to claim the full amount. It's up to you to decide how much of the cost of property you want to deduct. But you don't lose out on the remainder; you can depreciate any cost you do not deduct under Section 179.

If you purchase more than one item of Section 179 property during the year, you can divide the deduction among all the items in any way, as long as the total deduction is not more than the Section 179 limit. It's usually best to apply Section 179 to property that has the longest useful life and therefore the long-

est depreciation period. This reduces the total time you have to wait to get your deductions.

Because Section 179 is intended to help smaller businesses, there is also a limit on the total amount of Section 179 property you can purchase each year. You must reduce your Section 179 deduction by one dollar for every dollar your annual purchases exceed the applicable limit. During 2005–2008, the limit is $420,000 plus an amount to be added to account for inflation. In 2008 and later, the limit is scheduled to go down to $200,000. Thus, for example, if you purchase $450,000 of Section 179 property in 2005, your Section 179 deduction for the year will be limited to $62,000 ($450,000 - $410,000 = $40,000; $102,000 deduction limit - $40,000 = $62,000).

Year	Section 179 Deduction Limit	Property Value Limit
2003	$100,000	$400,000
2004	$102,000	$410,000
2005	$105,000	$420,000
2006	$105,000 + inflation adjustment	$420,000 + inflation adjustment
2007	$105,000 + inflation adjustments	$420,000 + inflation adjustments
2008 and later	$25,000	$200,000

c. Limit on Section 179 deduction

You can't use Section 179 to deduct more in one year than the total of your profit from all of your businesses and your salary, if you have a job in addition to your business. If you're married and file a joint tax return, you can include your spouse's salary and business income in this total as well. You can't count investment income—for example, interest you earn on your savings.

You can't use Section 179 to reduce your taxable income below zero. But you can carry to the next tax year any amount you cannot use as a Section 179 deduction and possibly deduct it then.

> **EXAMPLE:** In 2006, Amelia earned $17,000 ($15,000 profit from her engineering consulting business plus $2,000 from her part-time inventing business). She spent $20,000 for computer and lab equipment. She can use Section 179 to deduct $17,000 of this expense for 2006 and deduct the remaining $3,000 the next year.

d. Minimum period of business use

When you deduct an asset under Section 179, you must continue to use it for business at least 50% of the time for as many years as it would have been depreciated. For example, if you use Section 179 for a computer, you must use it for business at least 50% of the time for five years, because computers have a five-year depreciation period.

If you don't meet these rules, you'll have to report as income part of the deduction you took under Section 179 in the prior year. This is called recapture.

 For more information, see IRS Publication 534, *Depreciation*. You can obtain this

and all other IRS publications by calling the IRS at 800-TAX-FORM, visiting your local IRS office or downloading the publications from the IRS Internet site at www.irs.gov.

e. Special rules for listed property

The IRS imposes special rules on certain items that can easily be used for personal as well as business purposes. These items, called listed property, include:

- cars, boats, airplanes and other vehicles
- computers
- cellular phones, and
- any other property generally used for entertainment, recreation or amusement— for example, VCRs, cameras and camcorders.

The IRS fears that taxpayers might use listed property items for personal reasons but claim business deductions for them. For this reason, you're required to document your business use of listed property. You can satisfy this requirement by keeping a logbook showing when and how the property is used or document your use in your inventor's notebook. (See Chapter 9.)

You normally have to document your use of listed property even if you use it 100% for business. However, there is an exception to this rule: If you use listed property only for business and keep it at your business location, you need not comply with the record-keeping requirement. This includes listed property you keep at your home office if the office qualifies for the home office deduction. (See Section E1.)

EXAMPLE: John, a part-time inventor working on a new digital content management system, works full-time in his home office which he uses exclusively for inventing. The office is clearly his principal place of business and qualifies for the home office deduction. He buys a $4,000 computer for his office and uses it exclusively for his inventing business. He does not have to keep records showing how he uses the computer and he can deduct the computer under Section 179.

f. Claiming the Section 179 deduction

To claim a Section 179 deduction on your income taxes, you complete IRS Form 4562, listing the type and value of all the property you choose to deduct and file it with your tax return for the year. You must claim your Section 179 deduction on your original tax return for the year involved. You can't forget to claim it and then file an amended return in a later year to take the deduction.

3. Deducting Inventing Expenses as Ordinary and Necessary Business Expenses (IRC § 162)

By using the deductions provided by Sections 174 and 179 you've been able to currently deduct all your R&E expenses and up to $105,000 in long-term property. This could well include virtually everything you buy for your inventing business during the year. But what if you have expenses left over? May you currently deduct expenses that don't qualify

under Section 174 or 179? Long-term property you buy that cannot be currently deducted under Section 179 must be depreciated as described in Section D. But your other expenses may be currently deductible under yet another tax law provision—IRC § 162.

IRC § 162 provides that a taxpayer may deduct all the ordinary and necessary expenses paid or incurred during the taxable year in carrying on any trade or business. Section 162 is the true workhorse expense provision of the tax code, allowing business owners to deduct most of their day-to-day business expenses, such as office rent and salaries. Indeed, most business owners other than inventors have to rely solely on Section 162 to currently deduct their expenses (other than those they can deduct under Section 179).

Any expense is deductible under Section 162 as long as it is:

- incurred in carrying out a business
- ordinary and necessary
- directly related to your business, and
- reasonable in amount.

Unfortunately, the first two requirements can be difficult for many independent inventors to satisfy. It is for this reason you should always look first to Section 174 to currently deduct your inventing expenses—it is generally easier and safer for inventors to deduct their expenses under Section 174—which is specifically intended to help inventors—than under Section 162, which applies to all taxpayers.

However, Section 174 can only be used for R&E expenses. If you have non-R&E expenses you want to currently deduct, you must do so under Section 162. These would include expenses for marketing or manufacturing an invention and any other expense not arising directly or indirectly from your invention development efforts. You probably won't incur many non-R&E expenses until you are fairly well along in your development efforts. As you'll see below, the further along you are, the easier it will be to qualify for Section 162 deductions.

If you do qualify to deduct your expenses under Section 162, you'll have a legal basis to currently deduct almost every expense you incur for your inventing business, other than purchases of depreciable property. This may include R&E expenses that are also currently deductible under Sections 174. This means you'll often be able to claim two legal bases for your deductions—both Section 174 and 162. If you're audited by the IRS, it's wise to claim both bases wherever possible.

a. Carrying out a business

You may only currently deduct a business expense under IRC 162 if you are "carrying on any trade or business." This means, of course, that you are not engaged in a hobby. It also means that your business has passed through the start-up stage and has begun to function as a going concern. Only at this point, the day your business actually begins operation, does Section 162 apply. Non-R&E expenses you incur before this point are start-up expenses that must be deducted over 60 months (see Section D3). R&E expenses can be deducted under Section 174 whether or not you've passed through the start-up phase of your business (see Section C1).

This leads to the question of when a business begins for Section 162 purposes. This question is easy to answer for many businesses—for example, a restaurant owner's business begins when the restaurant's doors open and the restaurant is ready to serve food to customers. At this point, the owner can currently deduct all his or her ordinary and necessary business expenses under Section 162.

However, it's not always so clear-cut when an inventor's business passes through the start-up stage and begins operation. If you're a well established independent inventor who has patented several inventions and earned money from selling or licensing them, your business has clearly begun and you're un-doubtedly "carrying on" the business of being an inventor. This means you can take advantage of the Section 162 deduction.

But, what if, like most independent inventors, you haven't reached this point yet—that is, you've been developing an invention but have yet to earn any money from it? What if you haven't even obtained a patent yet? Unfortunately, there is no definitive answer.

The general rule is that a manufacturing or similar business begins when the business begins using its assets *to produce* products for sale—it's not necessary that the products be completed or sales be made. Thus, for example, courts have held that a writer's business begins when he or she starts working on a writing project. The act of production itself is "carrying on" the trade or business of writing. (*Gestrich v. Commissioner*, 681 F.2d 805 (3d Cir. 1982); *Snyder v. U.S.*, 674 F.2d 1359 (10th Cir. 1982).)

Similarly, courts in the examples below have found that inventors who worked on inventions—but never completed or patented them—were carrying on a business.

EXAMPLE: Mr. Lamont, a full-time foreign service officer, started a business with his wife to develop language translation software. The software went through a long development phase, but was never perfected to the Lamonts' satisfaction. They sold only one copy after which they ran out of money to complete testing and were unable to raise any more money. The court held they were carrying on a business under IRC 162. The court reasoned that the Lamonts' business was developing computer software, and they had in fact developed software. Furthermore, "a company need not make a single sale, or earn a single penny of income, in order to be considered an active trade or business." (*Lamont v. Commissioner*, 97-2 USTC P 50,861 (Fed. Cl. 1997).)

EXAMPLE: Maximoff attempted to develop a miles-per-gallon indicator for cars and trucks. However, he gave up on the project after one year when he discovered that, because of the required complexity of the design and vehicle installation costs, there would be a limited market for the device. He never finished the indicator, never patented it, never attempted to market it and never made any money from it. Nevertheless the tax court held that he was "carrying on" a business under IRC

§ 162. (*Maximoff v. IRS*, TC Memo 1987-155 (1987).)

Under the logic of these court decisions, your inventing business begins for tax purposes on the day you actually begin developing an invention. Thinking or dreaming about an invention is not sufficient. You must do real work on it—but it is not necessary for you to finish it, patent it or make money from it. A thorough and complete inventor's notebook documenting your work is the best evidence you can have to prove when you started working on your invention.

These cases are not binding on the IRS and they don't prevent it from claiming that you are not carrying on a business. After all, in all these cases the IRS claimed, albeit unsuccessfully, that the taxpayers involved were not carrying on a business. Nevertheless, if you're audited, they provide valuable ammunition and may help sway an auditor in your favor.

One important factor these cases have in common is that the inventors involved established a clear profit motive and worked diligently and continuously at inventing, even though they never made any money. You need to do the same to pass the "carrying on" test.

Also, keep in mind that, if you're audited, it will likely be some years after you first started inventing. If an auditor sees that you have a record of continuous work on inventions over many years, he or she is more likely to conclude you were carrying on a business during the early years of your inventing activity and allow current deductions for your expenses under IRC §162.

If you're not sure your business has begun for Section 162 purposes, consult with a tax pro.

b. Expense must be ordinary

An expense must be "ordinary" to be currently deductible under Section 162. An expense is ordinary only if it is a current expense—that is, has a useful life of less than one year. This includes anything you buy for your business that gets used up, wears out or becomes obsolete in less than one year.

> **EXAMPLE:** Charles spends $80 each month to rent computer equipment. Obviously, since he gets to use the computer only for a month for each payment, these monthly rental payments do not provide Charles with an asset with a useful life of more than one year. Thus, this is a current business expense that he may deduct all in one year.

Expenses that provide benefits beyond one year are called capital expenses and are not deductible under Section 162. This typically includes, for example, equipment, vehicles, books, furniture, machinery and patents you buy from others.

> **EXAMPLE:** Charles spends $1,000 to buy a computer to use in his inventing business. Since this item can reasonably expected to be useful for several years, it is a capital expense and not deductible under Section 162.

Capital expenses are not limited to the cost of buying or renting an asset such as a computer. The cost of *creating* an asset is also a capital expense if it will provide benefits for more than one year. The cost may not only include materials used to create the asset, but costs that would ordinarily be viewed as normal business expenses such as employee salaries.

> **EXAMPLE:** Charles decides to construct his own highly advanced computer for his inventing business. He hires Tom, a computer expert, to help him design and build it. The cost of computer parts and other materials and Tom's fee amount to $5,000. These costs are capital expenses because they are used to create an asset—a computer—that will benefit Charles's business for more than one year. They are not deductible under Section 162.

The "ordinary" expense requirement usually won't pose a problem for non-R&E expenses—for example, the expenses involved in licensing or marketing your inventions, or other expenses not directly or indirectly related to R&E—for example, administrative expenses, accounting fees and attorney fees other than to patent an invention.

However, R&E expenses do pose a problem. Unfortunately, there never has been a clear answer as to when R&E costs are capital expenses vs. current expenses. As a general rule, R&E expenses would seem to be capital expenses because they are part of the cost of developing or improving an invention, product, formula, process or prototype that would ordinarily provide benefits beyond a single year. On the other hand, R&E costs are arguably current expenses where they are carried on as part of a business's day-to-day operations. In the past, the IRS has permitted some businesses to deduct R&E expenses as current expenses, at least where they were a part of a well-established business's ongoing business operations.

However, treating R&E costs as current expenses has always been potentially subject to attack by the IRS. It was to help inventors avoid this uncertainty that Congress passed Section 174; it permits inventors to currently deduct R&E costs even if they are capital expenses.

c. Expense must be necessary

An expense is necessary if it is common, accepted, helpful and appropriate for your inventing business. An expense doesn't have to be indispensable to be necessary; it need only help your inventing business in some way, even in a minor way. It's usually fairly easy to tell if an expense passes this test.

> **EXAMPLE 1:** Bill, a surgeon who invents in his spare time, hires a technician to help him design a new surgical instrument and pays him $25 per hour. This is clearly a deductible business expense. Hiring assistants is a common and accepted practice among inventors. The assistant's fee is an ordinary and necessary expense for Bill's inventing business.

> **EXAMPLE 2:** Surgeon Bill visits a masseuse every week to work on his bad back. Bill claims the cost as a business expense, reasoning that avoiding back pain helps him concentrate on his inventing. This is clearly not an ordinary or customary expense for an inventor and the IRS would likely not allow it as a business expense.

d. Expense must be related to your business

An expense must be related to your business to be deductible. That is, you must use the item you buy for your business in some way. For example, the cost of a personal computer is a deductible business expense if you use the computer to help create an invention.

You cannot deduct purely personal expenses as business expenses. The cost of a personal computer is not deductible if you use it just to play computer games. If you buy something for both personal and business reasons, you may deduct the business portion of the expense. For example, if you buy a cellular phone and use it half the time for business calls and half the time for personal calls, you can deduct half the cost of the phone as a business expense.

However, the IRS requires you to keep records showing when the item was used for business and when for personal reasons. One acceptable form of record would be a diary or log with the dates, times and reason the item was used. This kind of record keeping can be burdensome and may not be worth the trouble if the item isn't very valuable.

To avoid having to keep such records, try to use items either only for business or only for personal use. For example, if you can afford it, purchase two computers and use one solely for your inventing business and one for personal uses.

e. Deductions must be reasonable

There is usually no limit on how much you can deduct as long as it's not more than you actually spend and the amount is reasonable. Certain areas are hot buttons for the IRS—especially entertainment, travel and meal expenses. The IRS won't allow such expenses to the extent it considers them lavish.

f. Common Section 162 deductions for inventors

Common ordinary and necessary business expenses for independent inventors include:

- accounting fees
- bank fees for your inventing business bank account
- costs of renting or leasing equipment, machinery, and other property used in your inventing business
- education expenses—for example, the cost of attending professional seminars or classes related to your inventing business
- expenses for the business use of your home
- fees you pay to self-employed workers you hire to help your business—for example, the cost of paying a marketing consultant to advise you on how to market your invention

- insurance for your business—for example, liability and business property insurance
- interest on business loans and debts—for example, interest you pay for a bank loan you use to fund your invention
- license fees—for example, fees for a local business license
- office expenses, such as office supplies
- office utilities
- postage
- repairs and maintenance for business equipment such as a photocopier or fax machine
- subscriptions for scientific, technical or business publications
- business-related travel, meals and entertainment, and
- wages and benefits you provide your employees.

George Washington Carver
Inventor of the idea of crop rotation and many products and uses of crops

Inventory Is Not a Business Expense

If you manufacture and sell an invention to the public as a product, you are entitled to deduct on your tax return the cost of those products (called "goods" for tax purposes) actually sold during the year. The cost is what you spent for the goods or their actual market value.

However, money spent for goods to sell is not treated as a business expense. Instead, you deduct the cost of goods you've sold from your business receipts to determine your gross profit from the business. Your business expenses are then deducted from your gross profit to determine your net profit, which is taxed.

Businesses that make, buy or sell goods must determine the value of their inventories at the beginning and the end of each tax year.

For more information on inventories, see the Cost of Goods Sold section in Chapter 7 of IRS Publication 334, *Tax Guide for Small Businesses*; IRS Publication 538, *Accounting Periods and Methods;* and Publication 970, *Application to Use LIFO Inventory Method.*

You can obtain these and all other IRS publications by calling the IRS at 800-TAX-FORM, visiting your local IRS office or downloading the publications from the IRS Internet site at www.irs.gov.

The R&D Tax Credit: IRC § 41

To encourage businesses to engage in research and development, a special tax law provision permits a tax credit for certain research expenses. Unlike a tax deduction, which is an amount you deduct from your gross income (all the money you earn) to determine the amount of your income subject to tax, a tax credit is an amount you may deduct directly from the total tax you owe for the year. Thus, for example, a $1,000 tax credit will reduce the tax you have to pay by $1,000; whereas a $1,000 tax deduction will reduce your taxes by only $280 if your marginal tax rate (top rate) is 28% (28% x $1,000 = $280).

Basically, the credit provision contained in IRC § 41 permits you to claim a credit of up to 20% of the increase in research costs you incur during the current year as compared with a base period—usually the three preceding years. New companies have their base amounts set by a complex formula. The amount of any credit you claim is subtracted from the amount of R&E expenses you may deduct under Section 174.

As this short explanation probably makes clear, this is an exceptionally complex area of taxation. Seek expert help if you're interested in this tax credit. It's worthwhile to look into the credit only if you have substantial R&D expenses.

D. Inventing Expenses You Must Deduct Over Time

After deducting everything you can this year as explained in Section B, do you have any expenses for the year left over? If not, you don't need to read this section and you can skip to Section E. However, it is possible that you have expenses left over that you can't currently deduct. These may include:

- the cost of long-term property you haven't been able to currently deduct under section 179, and
- expenses other than R&E expenses you incur during the start-up phase of your inventing business.

As explained in Sections D1 and D2 below, the cost of long-term property can generally be depreciated or amortized over several years. Start-up expenses can be deducted over 60 months.

1. Depreciation of Tangible Property

Many things you buy for your business lose their value over time because they wear out or become obsolete. This loss of value or usefulness is called depreciation. The tax law permits you to take a deduction for depreciation. This is accomplished by deducting a portion of the cost of the asset over several years—exactly how many depends on the nature of the asset. (IRC § 167(a).)

a. What property can be depreciated

Depreciation is used to deduct the cost of any asset you buy for and use in your business that:

- wears out, decays, gets used up, becomes obsolete or loses value from natural causes, and
- has a determinable useful life of *more than one year;* the IRS, not you, determines an asset's useful life.

Depreciation can be used for tangible business assets—for example, buildings, equipment, machinery and office furniture. The cost of intangible property such as patents and copyrights can also be deducted over time. This is called amortization; see Section D2 for a detailed discussion of amortization of intangible assets. Land cannot be depreciated because it doesn't wear out—you can't depreciate something that could last forever.

You must depreciate the cost of major repairs that increase the value or extend the life of an asset—for example, the cost of a major upgrade to make your computer run faster. However, you may deduct normal repairs or maintenance in the year they're incurred as an ordinary and necessary business expense.

Don't Bother Depreciating Small Items

Technically speaking you're supposed depreciate any item you buy for your business that lasts for more than one year, even if it costs very little. However, the IRS understands that this could create a bookkeeping nightmare. So, as a practical matter you are not required to go to the time and trouble of depreciating inexpensive items. The IRS won't say how much an item must cost for the depreciation requirement to kick in. Most companies set a minimum cost amount for depreciating assets, and currently deduct under IRC § 162, rather than depreciate, items below this amount. For a small business, a reasonable minimum would be anywhere between $100 and $250. Thus, for example, if you buy a metal wastepaper basket for $50, you can currently deduct the entire expense, even though the basket can be expected to last for many years.

b. Mixed use property

If you use property for both business and personal purposes, you can take depreciation only for the business use of the asset.

> EXAMPLE: Carl uses his photocopier 75% of the time for personal reasons and 25% for his inventing business. He can depreciate 25% of the cost of the copier.

Keep a diary or log with the dates, times and reason the property was used to distinguish between the two uses.

c. Depreciation period

Under the regular depreciation rules, depreciation begins during the year you place a depreciable asset in service in an active trade or business. Under these rules, you cannot take any depreciation deductions until your inventing business has passed through the start-up phase and is functioning as a going concern. As discussed in Section C3, it can be difficult to determine when an inventing business begins operation for tax purposes. Fortunately, as far as depreciation goes, this is not an issue most independent inventors need worry much about. A special tax rule just for inventors provides that when depreciable property is purchased for R&E the applicable depreciation deduction may be claimed as an R&E expense under IRC Section 174. (IRC Section 174(c); IRC Reg. 1.174-2(b).) Section 174 deductions may be taken whether your inventing business has begun operation or is still in the start-up stage. (See Section C1.)

You should be able to defeat any IRS claim that you are not entitled to a depreciation deduction because your inventing business has not yet begun operation by claiming the deduction under Section 174, instead of the ordinary depreciation rules (IRC § 167). Note, you don't need to indicate on your tax return that you are claiming depreciation under

Section 174. If the IRS questions such a deduction, it will probably be in your interest to claim that the deduction is allowed under both the normal rules (Section 167 and Section 174).

Keep in mind, however, Section 174 may only be used for depreciable property purchased for R&E. Property purchased for other purposes—for example, marketing an invention—may not be deducted under Section 174.

An asset is "placed in service" when it is ready and available for use in your business, whether or not it's actually used. Ordinarily, this is when you buy it. For purposes of calculating your first year's depreciation, you usually treat an item as being placed in service on July 1. This means you get one-half of the first year's depreciation, regardless of the exact date you placed the property in service. However, the rules differ if you buy over 40% of your depreciable property for the year during the last three months of the year.

The depreciation period lasts for the entire estimated useful life of the asset. The tax code has assigned an estimated useful life for all types of business assets, ranging from 3 to 39 years.

Tangible personal property used in connection with research and experimentation has a five-year recovery period. (IRC §§ 168(e)(3) (B)(v) and (i)(11).) Recovery periods for other types of assets are listed in the table below.

You are free to continue using property after its estimated useful life expires, but you can't deduct any more depreciation.

Asset Depreciation Periods	
Type of Property	**Recovery Period**
Computer software (Software that comes with your computer is not separately depreciable unless you're separately billed for it.)	3 years
Office machinery (computers and peripherals, calculators, copiers and typewriters)	5 years
Autos and light trucks	5 years
Construction and research equipment	5 years
Office furniture	7 years
Residential buildings	27.5 years
Nonresidential buildings purchased before 5/12/93	31.5 years
Nonresidential buildings purchased after 5/12/93	39 years

 If you need to know the depreciation period for an asset not included in this table, see IRS Publication 534, *Depreciation*, for a complete listing. You can obtain this and all other IRS publications by calling the IRS at 800-TAX-FORM, visiting your local IRS office or downloading the publications from the IRS Internet site at www.irs.gov.

d. Calculating depreciation

You can use three different methods to calculate the depreciation deduction: straight line or one of two accelerated depreciation methods. Once you choose your method, you're stuck with it for the entire life of the asset.

In addition, you must use the same method for all property of the same kind purchased during the year. For example, if you use the straight line method to depreciate a computer, you must use that method to depreciate all other computers you purchase during the year for your business.

The straight line method requires you to deduct an equal amount each year over the useful life of an asset.

Most small businesses use one of two types of accelerated depreciation: the double declining balance method or the 150% declining balance method. The advantage to these methods is that they provide larger depreciation deductions in the earlier years and smaller ones later on. The double declining balance method starts out by giving you double the deduction you'd get for the first full year with the straight line method. The 150% declining balance method gives you one and one-half times the straight line deduction.

However, using accelerated depreciation is not necessarily a good idea if you expect your income to go up in future years. There are also some restrictions on when you can use accelerated depreciation. For example, you can't use it for cars, computers and certain other property that are used for business less than 50% of the time.

Determining which depreciation method is best for you and calculating how much depreciation you can deduct is a complex task usually best left to an accountant. If you want to do it yourself, seriously consider obtaining a tax preparation computer program that can help you do the calculations. (See Chapter 5 for information on tax programs.)

e. Listed property

Listed property includes:

- cars, boats, airplanes and other vehicles
- computers
- cellular phones, and
- any other property generally used for entertainment, recreation or amusement —for example, VCRs, cameras and camcorders.

Special record-keeping rules are required for listed property; these are covered in Section C2 above.

If you use listed property for business more than 50% of the time, you can depreciate it just like any other property. However, if you use it 50% or less of the time for business, you must use the straight line depreciation method and an especially long recovery period. If you start out using accelerated depreciation and your business use drops to 50% or less, you have to switch to the straight line method and pay taxes on the benefits of the prior years of accelerated depreciation.

 For more information, see IRS Publication 534, *Depreciation*. You can obtain this and all other IRS publications by calling the IRS at 800-TAX-FORM, visiting your local IRS office or downloading the publications from the IRS Internet site at www.irs.gov.

2. Amortization of Intangible Property

Tangible things like equipment and computers aren't the only business assets that wear out or get used up. Intangible assets can also get used up. Intangible assets include intellectual property—patents, copyrights, trade secrets and trademarks. (See Chapter 12 for an overview of intellectual property.)

The cost of intangible assets that get used up may be deducted over the useful life of the asset. This process is called amortization, but is the same as straight line depreciation. You deduct an equal amount of the cost of the asset each year over its useful life.

If you buy an intangible asset from someone else, the cost (tax basis in tax parlance) is the amount you paid for it. You deduct this amount over the asset's useful life. Amortization is also used to deduct those costs of creating an intangible asset that haven't been currently deducted under Section 174, 179 or 162.

Except for trademarks which are amortized over 15 years, the IRS has not established any set time periods for the useful lives of intangible assets. It's up to the taxpayer to determine the useful life; but this determination is subject to review by the IRS. The useful life of an invention for tax purposes can be complex to determine: It could be the legal duration of a patented invention (up to 20 years) or a shorter time if it can be shown the invention will become valueless or obsolete in less than 20 years.

Inventions which are not patented, but protected as trade secrets, may not have a fixable useful life for tax purposes, since trade secrets have no fixed term of existence. In this event, no deduction for the cost of purchasing the invention would be permitted. Instead, the amount of the creation costs would be added to the invention's tax basis (cost for tax purposes). If the trade secret is sold, the tax basis is subtracted from the sale price to determine the taxable profit. You are also entitled to a deduction if the trade secret becomes worthless.

This same rule would apply to any costs of creating a trade secret yourself that you can't deduct currently or over time. However, one way or another, virtually all the costs of creating a trade secret are ordinarily deductible, so this rule usually doesn't come into play.

This is a complex area of taxation. Consult with a knowledgeable tax pro if you need to amortize an intangible asset.

3. Start-Up Expenses (IRC § 195)

Start-up expenses are expenses you incur before you actually begin your business. Unlike operating expenses, start-up expenses cannot all be deducted in a single year. This is because the money you spend to start an inventing (or any other) business is a capital expense—a cost that will benefit you for more than one year. Normally, you can't deduct these types of capital expenses until you sell or otherwise dispose of the business. However, a special tax rule allows you to deduct up to $5,000 in start-up expenses the first year you are in business, and then deduct the remainder, if any, in equal amounts over the next 15 years. (IRC Sec. 195.)

Start-up expenses include any costs you could deduct under Section 162 once your business begins—for example, license fees, fictitious business name registration fees, advertising costs, attorney and accounting fees, travel expenses, market research and office supply expenses. They do not include research and experimentation expenses currently deductible under IRC § 174. The cost of long-term business assets is also not a start-up cost—these costs are either expensed under Section 179 or depreciated once the business begins.

You can't elect (claim) a deduction for start-up expenses until the month your inventing business begins operation. There is no IRS form for this election. You elect such expenses by attaching a statement to your tax return listing what they are, the dates incurred, the date your inventing business began.

See Section C3, above for a detailed discussion of when an inventing business begins for tax purposes.

 For more information on business start-up costs, see IRS Publication 535, *Business Expenses*. You can obtain a copy by calling the IRS at 800-TAX-FORM or by calling or visiting your local IRS office. You can also download a copy from the IRS Internet site at www.irs.gov.

E. Special Deduction Rules

Special rules govern certain types of tax deductions, including those of particular importance to independent inventors, such as the home office deduction.

1. Deducting Your Home Office Expenses

If, like many independent inventors, you elect to work from home, the federal government is prepared to help you out by allowing you to deduct your home office expenses from your taxes. This is so whether you are a full-time or part-time inventor, and whether you own your home or apartment or are a renter. Although this tax deduction is commonly called the home office deduction, it is not limited to home offices. You can also take it if, for example, you have a workshop or lab at home. (IRC § 280A.)

Unfortunately, there is a major limitation on the home office deduction that has special application to many independent inventors: The amount you may deduct each year is limited to your profit from your home business. The many independent inventors who earn no profits from inventing will not be entitled to a current deduction, but they may carry forward the amount of the unused deduction to use in a future year. This limitation applies whether you claim the home office deduction as an ordinary and necessary business expense under IRC § 162 or an R&E expense under IRC § 174.

If you intend to take the deduction, you should also make the effort to understand the requirements and set up your home office so as to satisfy them.

Is the Home Office Deduction an Audit Flag?

Because some people claim that the home office deduction is an audit flag for the IRS, many self-employed people who may qualify for it are afraid to take it. Although taking the home office deduction might increase your chance of being audited, the chances are still relatively small. Also, you have nothing to fear from an audit if you're entitled to the deduction.

a. Regular and exclusive business use

You can't take the home office deduction unless you regularly use part of your home exclusively for a trade or business. As mentioned above, developing new inventions can qualify as a business.

Exclusive use means that you use a portion of your home *only* for business. If you use part of your home as your business office and also use that part for personal purposes, you cannot meet the exclusive use test and cannot take the home office deduction.

EXAMPLE: Johnny, an electrical engineer and part-time inventor, has a den at home furnished with a desk, chair, bookshelf, filing cabinet and bed. He uses the desk and chair for both his inventing business and personal reasons. The bookshelf contains both personal and books he uses for his inventing business. And the filing cabinet contains both personal and business files. Johnny can't claim a business deduction for the den since it is not used exclusively for business purposes.

You needn't devote an entire separate room in your home to your business. But some part of the room must be used exclusively for your inventing business.

EXAMPLE: Paul, a software engineer and part-time inventor, keeps his desk, chair, bookshelf and filing cabinet in one part of his den and uses them exclusively for his business of inventing new software. The remainder of the room—one-third of the space—is used to store a bed for house guests. Paul can take a home office deduction for the two-thirds of the room uses exclusively as an office.

As a practical matter, the IRS isn't going to make a surprise inspection of your home to see whether you're complying with these requirements. However, complying with the rules from the beginning avoids having to lie to the IRS if you are audited.

This means, simply, that you'll have to arrange your furniture and belongings so as to devote a portion of your home exclusively to your home office. The more space you use exclusively for business, the more your home office deduction will be worth.

Although not explicitly required by law, it's a good idea to physically separate the space you use for business from the rest of the room. For example, if you use part of your living room as an office, separate it from the rest of the room with room dividers or bookcases.

b. Qualifying for the deduction

Unfortunately, satisfying the requirement of using your home office regularly and exclusively for business is only half the battle.

You must also meet *one* of these three requirements:

- your home office must be your principal place of business
- you must use a separate structure on your property exclusively for business purposes, or
- you must meet clients or customers at home.

Stephanie Kwolek
Inventor of Kevlar

Ways to Solidify Home Office Deduction

Here are some ways to convince the IRS that you qualify for the home office deduction.

- Take a picture of your home office and draw up a diagram showing your home office as a portion of your home.
- Have all your inventing business mail sent to your home office.
- Use your home office address on all your inventing business cards and stationery.
- Obtain a separate phone line for your inventing business and keep that phone in your home office. The tax law helps you do this by allowing you to deduct the monthly fee for a second phone line in your home if you use it for business. You can't deduct the monthly fee for a single phone line, even if you use it partly for business; however, you can deduct the cost of business calls you place from that line. Having a separate business phone will also make it easier for you to keep track of your business phone expenses.
- Keep a log of the time you spend working in your home office. This doesn't have to be fancy; notes on your calendar or lab notebook will do.

Home as principal place of business. The most common way for independent inventors to qualify for the home office deduction is to use your home as your principal place of business. If you do all or most of your inventing work in your home office, your home is clearly your principal place of business, and you'll have no trouble at all qualifying for the home office deduction.

Using a separate structure for business. You can also deduct expenses for a separate free-standing structure, such as a separate workshop, garage or studio, if you use it exclusively and regularly for your inventing business. The structure does not have to be your principal place of business.

As always where the home office deduction is involved, exclusive use means you use the structure only for business—for example, you can't use it to store gardening equipment or as a guest house. Regular use is not precisely defined, but it's probably sufficient for you to use the structure 10 or 15 hours a week.

> **EXAMPLE:** Deborah has her main office in an industrial park where she does most of her work on various bath-related inventions, such as an adjustable height showerhead. But she also works on her inventions every weekend in a small workshop in her back yard. Since she uses the workshop regularly and exclusively for her inventing business, it qualifies for the home office deduction.

Meeting clients or customers at home. Another way to satisfy the exclusive use requirement for the home office deduction is to use part of your home exclusively to meet with clients or customers. It's not likely many independent inventors will qualify under this provision; except perhaps for an independent inventor who is heavily engaged in manufacturing and selling an invention and who meets with customers at home.

Storing Inventory or Product Samples at Home

You can take the home office deduction if you're in the business of selling retail or wholesale products and you store inventory or product samples at home. This would apply to inventors who sell products based on their inventions.

To qualify, you can't have an office or other business location outside your home. And you must store your inventory at a particular place in your home—for example, a garage, closet or bedroom. You can't move your inventory from one room to the other. You don't have to use the storage space exclusively to store your inventory to take the deduction. It's sufficient that you regularly use it for that purpose.

> **EXAMPLE:** Janet has invented and patented a new potato peeler she sells door to door. She rents a home and regularly uses half of her attached garage to store her peeler inventory and also uses it to park her Harley Davidson motorcycle. Janet can deduct the expenses for the storage space even though she does not use her garage exclusively to store inventory. Her garage accounts for 20% of the total floor space of her house. Since she uses only half of the garage for storing inventory, she may deduct one half of this, or 10%, of her rent and certain other expenses.

c. Amount of deduction

To figure out the amount of the home office deduction, you need to determine what percentage of your home is used for business. To do this, divide the square footage of your home office by the total square footage of your home. For example, if your home is 1,600 square feet and you use 400 square feet for your home office, 25% of the total area is used for business (400/1600=25%).

Or if all the rooms in your home are about the same size, figure the business portion by dividing the number of rooms used for business by the number of rooms in the home. For example, if you use one room in a five-room house for business, 20% of the area is used for business. Claiming 20% to 25% of your home as a home office is perfectly acceptable. However, claiming anything over 40% will likely raise questions with the IRS unless you store inventory at home.

The home office deduction is not one deduction, but many. You are entitled to deduct from your gross income your home office use percentage of:

- your rent if you rent your home, or
- depreciation, mortgage interest and property taxes if you own your home.

In addition, owners and renters may deduct this same percentage of other expenses for keeping up and running an entire home. The IRS calls these indirect expenses. They include:

- utility expenses for electricity, gas, heating oil and trash removal
- homeowner's or renter's insurance
- home maintenance expenses that benefit your entire home including your home office, such as roof and furnace repairs and exterior painting
- condominium association fees
- snow removal expenses
- casualty losses if your home is damaged —for example, in a storm, and
- security system costs.

You may also deduct the entire cost of expenses just for your home office. The IRS calls these direct expenses. They include, for example, painting your home office or paying someone to clean it. If you pay a housekeeper to clean your entire house, you may deduct your business use percentage of the expense.

> **EXAMPLE:** Jean rents a 1,600 square foot apartment and uses a 400 square foot bedroom as a home office for her inventing business. Her percentage of business use is 25% (400 divided by 1,600). She pays $12,000 in annual rent and has a $1,200 utility bill for the year. She also spent $200 to paint her home office. She is entitled to deduct 25% of her rent and utilities and the entire painting expense for a total home office deduction of $3,350. [($12,000+$1,200+$200)/.25=$3,350]

Be sure to keep copies of all your bills and receipts for home office expenses—for example, keep:

- IRS Form 1098 sent by whoever holds your mortgage, showing the interest you paid on your mortgage for the year
- property tax bills and your canceled checks

• utility bills, insurance bills and receipts for payments for repairs to your office area, along with your canceled checks paying for these items, and

• a copy of your lease and your canceled rent checks, if you're a renter.

The home office deduction can be very valuable if you're a renter because you get to deduct part of your rent—a substantial expense that is ordinarily not deductible. If you own your home, the home office deduction is worth less because you're already allowed to deduct your mortgage interest and property taxes.

Taking the home office deduction won't increase your income tax deductions for these items, but it will allow you to deduct them from your self-employment taxes. You'll save $153 in self-employment taxes for every $1,000 in mortgage interest and property taxes you deduct. You'll also be able to deduct a portion of repairs, utility bills, cleaning and maintenance costs and depreciation.

Depreciating Office Furniture and Other Personal Property

Whether or not you qualify for or take the home office deduction, you can depreciate or deduct under Section 179 the cost of office furniture, computers, copiers, fax machines and other personal property you use for your business and keep at home. These costs are deducted directly on your Schedule C, Profit or Loss From Business. They don't have to be listed on the special tax form used for the home office deduction.

---

d. Profit limit for deduction

There is an important limitation on the home office deduction: It may not exceed the net profit you earn from your home office. If, like many independent inventors, you earn no money at all from inventing, you won't be able to currently deduct your home office expenses. However, it's still worthwhile to keep a record of such expenses because you can carry forward the amount of the deduction to use in a future year when you do earn a profit from inventing.

If you do earn money from inventing, you'll have to determine your profit, if any, for purposes of the home office deduction. This can be complex.

First, you have to figure out how much money you earn from using your home office. If you do all your inventing work at home, this will be 100% of your inventing income. But if you work in several locations, you must determine the part of your gross income from inventing that came from working in your home office. To do this, consider how much time you spend in your home office and elsewhere and the type of work you do in each location.

Then, subtract from this amount:

• the business percentage of your otherwise deductible mortgage interest and real estate taxes; you'll only have these expenses if you own your home, and

• business expenses that are not attributable to the business use of your home—for example, supplies, depreciation of business equipment, business phone, advertising or salaries.

The remainder is your profit—the most you can deduct for using your home office.

EXAMPLE: Sam has patented several pizza-box inventions and exclusively uses 20% of his home to engage in this part-time business. In one recent year, his gross income from inventing was $6,000. He does all his inventing work at home, so this entire amount is attributable to his home office. He determines how much of his home office expenses he may deduct as follows:

First, he subtracts 20% of his home mortgage interest and property taxes from his $6,000 gross income. This is $3,000, so he has $3,000 left. Next, he subtracts his business expenses other than for the use of his home office. These amount to $2,000, so he is left with $1,000. Sam may only deduct $1,000 of home office expenses. These expenses totaled $2,000 for the year, so Sam has $1,000 left over that he may not deduct for the year. He may deduct this amount next year if he has sufficient income from his business.

You can carry over any excess in home office deductibles and deduct them in the first year in which your business earns a profit. However, whether or not your business incurs a loss, you can still deduct all your home mortgage interest and property taxes as an itemized deduction on IRS Schedule A because you're a homeowner.

e. Special concerns for homeowners

Until recently, homeowners who took the home office deduction were subject to a special tax trap: If they took a home office deduction for more than three of the five years before they sold their house, they had to pay capital gains taxes on the profit from the home office portion of their home. For example, if you made a $50,000 profit on the sale of your house, but your home office took up 20% of the space, you would have had to pay a tax on $10,000 of your profit (20% x $50,000 = $10,000).

Fortunately, IRS rules no longer require this. As long as you live in your home for at least two out of the five years before you sell it, the profit you make on the sale—up to $250,000 for single taxpayers and $500,000 for married taxpayers filing jointly—is not taxable. (See IRS Publication 523, *Selling Your Home.*) If you sold your house after May 6, 1997 and paid capital gains tax on the home office portion, you may be entitled to amend your return for the year you sold the house and receive a tax refund from the IRS.

However, you will have to pay a capital gains tax on the depreciation deductions you took after May 6, 1997 for your home office. This is the deduction you are allowed for the yearly decline in value due to wear and tear of the portion of the building that contains your home office. These "recaptured" deductions are taxed at a 25% rate (unless your income tax bracket is lower than 25%).

EXAMPLE: Sally bought a $200,000 home in the year 2000 and used one of her bedrooms as her office for her inventing business. She sold her home in 2004 for $300,000, realizing a $100,000 gain (profit). Her depreciation deductions for her home office from 2000 through 2004 totaled $2,000. She must pay a tax of 25% of $2,000, or $500.

Having to pay a 25% tax on the depreciation deductions you took in the years before you sold your house is actually not a bad deal. This is probably no more—and is often less—tax than you would have had to pay if you hadn't taken the deductions in the first place and instead paid tax on your additional taxable income at ordinary income tax rates.

f. IRS reporting requirements

All unincorporated taxpayers who take the home office deduction must file IRS Form 8829 with their tax returns. Renters who take the deduction must also file Form 1099-MISC with the IRS.

If you qualify for the home office deduction and are a sole proprietor or partner in a partnership, you must file IRS Form 8829, Expenses for Business Use of Your Home, along with your personal tax return. The form alerts the IRS that you're taking the deduction and shows how you calculated it. Even if your business has no profits and you're not allowed to deduct your home office expenses, you should file this form. By filing, you can apply the deduction to a future year in which you earn a profit.

If you organize your inventing business as an S corporation instead of a sole proprietorship or partnership, you don't have to file Form 8829. This is one of the major advantages of forming an S corporation. Filing Form 8829 calls your home office deduction to the attention of the IRS. If you can avoid filing it, you are less likely to face an audit.

 For additional information, see IRS Publication 587, *Business Use of Your Home*. You can obtain this and all other IRS publications by calling the IRS at 800-TAX-FORM, visiting your local IRS office or downloading the publications from the IRS Internet site at www.irs.gov.

If you're a renter and take the home office deduction, you should file IRS Form 1099-MISC each year reporting the amount of your rental payments attributable to your home office.

EXAMPLE: Bill rents a house and takes the home office deduction. He spends $12,000 per year on rent and uses 25% of his house as a home office. He should file a Form 1099 reporting $3,000 of his rental payments. ($12,000 x .25 = $3,000)

You should file three copies of Form 1099:
- File one copy with the IRS by February 28.
- Give one copy to your landlord by January 31.
- File one copy with your state tax department, if your state has income taxes. (See Chapter 5.)

Your landlord may not appreciate receiving a Form 1099 from you, but it will definitely be helpful if you're audited by the IRS and your home office deduction is questioned. It helps to show that you were really conducting a business out of your home.

Form 1099 is not required if your landlord is a corporation. Form 1099 need not be filed for payments to corporations. A Form 1099 is also not required in the unlikely event that your rental payments for your home office total less than $600 for the year.

2. Cars, Travel, Meals and Entertainment

Special deduction rules apply to expenses for cars, travel, meals and entertainment. These are not very common expenses for inventors, so we won't go into them in great detail here.

For more information about the rules for claiming these expenses, see IRS Publication 463, *Travel, Entertainment, Gift and Car Expenses*. You can obtain this and all other IRS publications by calling the IRS at 800-TAX-FORM, visiting your local IRS office or downloading the publications from the IRS Internet site at www.irs.gov.

a. Car expenses

You are allowed to deduct your driving expenses when you use your vehicle for your inventing business—for example, to pick up or deliver work, to obtain supplies or to attend seminars. These expenses are usually deducted as an ordinary and necessary business expenses under IRC § 162. However, some car expenses can also be deductible as

R&E expenses under IRC § 174—but only when your driving is done in the course of research and experimentation. For example, your could deduct as an R&E expense the cost to drive to a laboratory that is conducting a test on your new invention; but you couldn't similarly deduct the cost to drive to a licensor's office, because licensing an invention does not constitute research and experimentation.

If you claim a mileage expense as an R&E expense, the rules listed below don't apply. All that is required is that your deduction be reasonable. Deductions that come within the normal rules described below would doubtless be viewed as reasonable by the IRS.

There are two ways to calculate the car expense deduction. You can:

- deduct a specific amount—called the standard mileage rate—for every mile you drive, or
- deduct your actual car expenses—gas, oil, repairs and depreciation.

In 2005, the standard mileage rate was 40.5 cents per mile. When you use this method, you need only keep track of how many business miles you drive, not the actual expenses for your car such as gas or repairs. You can use the standard mileage rate only for a car that you own. You must choose to use it in the first year you start using your car for your business. In later years, you can choose to use the standard mileage rate or actual expenses.

If you own a late-model car worth more than $15,000, you'll usually get a larger deduction by using the actual expense method because the standard mileage rate doesn't include enough for depreciation of new cars. On the other hand, the standard mileage rate will be better if you have an inexpensive or old car and put in a lot of business mileage.

Either way, you'll need to keep records showing how many miles you drive your car for business during the year—also called business miles.

b. Travel expenses

You may need to do some traveling for your inventing business, for example, to visit or work with licensees, prototype makers or customers, attend trade shows or attend professional seminars or business conventions.

You may deduct your airfare, hotel bills and other expenses for such traveling. (Meals are deductible, but subject to the 50% limitation described below.) These expenses may be deducted as an ordinary and necessary business expense under IRC § 162. Such expenses can also be deductible as R&E expenses under IRC § 174—but only when your traveling is done in the course of research and experimentation. In this event, the rules listed below don't apply. All that is required is that your deduction be reasonable. However, deductions that come within the rules described below would doubtless be viewed as reasonable by the IRS.

You can deduct a trip within the United States only if:

- it's primarily for business
- you travel outside your city limits, and
- you're away at least overnight or long enough to require a stop for sleep or rest.

If you travel outside the United States for no more than seven days and you spend the majority of your time on business, you can deduct all of your travel costs. More stringent rules apply if your foreign trip lasts more than one week. To get a full deduction for your expenses, you must spend at least 75% of your time away on business. You must keep good records of your expenses.

c. Entertainment and meal expenses

You may find it helpful or even necessary to entertain people who may be helpful in your inventing business—for example, potential licensees, investors, advisors, suppliers or employees. It's often easier to do business in a nonbusiness setting. Entertainment includes, for example, going to restaurants, the theater, concerts, sporting events and nightclubs, throwing parties and boating, hunting or fishing outings.

To deduct an entertainment expense, you must discuss business either before, during or after the entertainment. Moreover, you're allowed to deduct only 50% of your expenses —for example, if you spend $50 for a meal in a restaurant, you can only deduct $25. The 50% limitation applies whether you claim your entertainment expenses as an ordinary and necessary business expense under IRC § 162 or an R&E expense under IRC § 174. (IRC § 274(n).)

You must keep track of all you spend and report the entire amount on your tax return. The IRS closely scrutinizes this deduction because many taxpayers cheat when taking it. You'll have to comply with stringent record-keeping requirements.

Charles the Inventor Does His Taxes

To give you an example of how deductions work for an inventor, consider Charles—a research chemist employed by a large chemical company. Charles works in his spare time developing a new type of plastic he hopes will be used in place of sheet metal, for example, in automobile bodies. Charles has incurred $46,00 in expenses. His expenses are listed below along with his legal bases for deducting them.

Expense Amount	Expense Purpose	Currently Deductible?	If Not Currently Deductible, Deductible Over Time?	Legal Basis for Deduction
$7,000	Attorney and filing fees for patent application	Yes		R&E expense (IRC § 174), or alternatively, if qualified, an ordinary business expense (IRC § 162)
$5,000	Salary for a part-time lab assistant	Yes		R&E expense (IRC § 174), or alternatively, if qualified, an ordinary business expense (IRC § 162)
$6,000	Laboratory rent ($500 a month)	Yes		R&E expense (IRC § 174), or alternatively, if qualified, an ordinary business expense (IRC § 162)
$5,000	Home office to handle administrative tasks	Yes		If qualified, an ordinary business expense (IRC § 162)
$4,000	Laboratory supplies used in one year	Yes		R&E expense (IRC § 174), or alternatively, if qualified, an ordinary business expense (IRC § 162)
$4,000	Consulting fees to marketing expert	Yes		If qualified, an ordinary business expense (IRC § 162)
$400	Photocopying expenses	Yes		If for R&E, under IRC § 174; if not, then, if qualified, an ordinary business expense (IRC § 162)
$200	Telephone Calls	Yes		If for R&E, under IRC § 174; if not, then, if qualified, an ordinary business expense (IRC § 162)

Charles the Inventor Does His Taxes (continued)

Expense Amount	Expense Purpose	Currently Deductible?	If Not Currently Deductible, Deductible Over Time?	Legal Basis for Deduction
$2,000	Buy lab computer	Yes		Deductible in full under IRC § 179
$3,000	Rent lab computer	Yes		If for R&E, under IRC § 174; if not, then, if qualified, an ordinary business expense (IRC § 162)
$1,500	Customized software for developing invention	No	Yes	Depreciable over life of asset (36 months)
$2,000	Payment to prototype maker for invention prototype	Yes		R&E expense (IRC § 174)
$1,000	Registering trademark	No	Yes	Amortize over 15 years
$5,000	Building plastic mold machines to manufacture plastics	No	Yes	Depreciable over life of asset (5 years)

Chapter 8

Taxation of Inventing Income

A. Capital Gains vs. Ordinary Income 8/2

B. Capital Gains Treatment for Patents Under IRC § 1235 .... 8/3

    1. You Must Be a Holder of a U.S. or Foreign Patent 8/4

    2. You Must Transfer All Substantial Rights in Your Patent 8/5

    3. You May Not Transfer Your Rights to a "Related Person" 8/6

C. Paying Self-Employment Taxes 8/6

    1. Who Must Pay? 8/6

    2. SE Tax Rates 8/6

    3. Earnings Subject to Self-Employment Tax 8/7

    4. Computing the SE Tax 8/8

    5. Paying and Reporting SE Taxes 8/9

    6. Paying Self-Employment Taxes When You Have a Job 8/9

D. Paying Estimated Taxes 8/10

    1. Who Must Pay Estimated Taxes? 8/10

    2. How Much You Must Pay 8/12

    3. When to Pay Estimated Tax 8/15

    4. How to Pay 8/16

    5. Paying the Wrong Amount 8/17

*I*n this chapter, we'll discuss the tax rules for inventors whose ledgers have gone from red to black. Earning a profit from your invention triggers new tax obligations including income and self-employment taxes. The amount and timing of your tax payments depend on several factors, the most important of which is how you earned the money.

For example, if you earned money by manufacturing and selling your invention, or by licensing your patent to a manufacturer, your income is taxed at one rate (ordinary income); if you earned the money by selling your patent to a manufacturer and you meet the requirements discussed in Section B, the income is taxed at a different rate (capital gains).

In the following sections, we'll discuss capital gains, ordinary income, and self-employment taxes for inventors and we'll explain how to pay estimated taxes. Every inventor—whether you are earning big bucks or dreaming about it—should understand these basic rules for taxing income because they affect your decisions for marketing and promoting your invention and they will provide the necessary ammunition needed to deal with the taxman in the event you are ever audited.

A. Capital Gains vs. Ordinary Income

As you are probably aware, the IRS taxes your income either as capital gains or ordinary income. Below is a table showing the comparative tax rates for ordinary income and long term capital gains—the gain (profit) on the sale of a capital asset held (owned) for more than one year.

Ordinary Income vs. Capital Gains Rates 2005			
Income (If Single)	Income (If Married Filing Jointly)	Ordinary Income Rate	Long Term Capital Gains Rate
Up to $7,300	Up to $14,600	10%	5%
7,301 to $29,700	$14,601 to $53,450	15%	5%
$29,701 to $71,950	$53,451 to $119,950	25%	15%
$71,951 to $150,150	$119,951 to $182,800	28%	15%
$150,151 to $326,450	$182,801 to $326,450	33%	15%
All over $326,450	All over $326,450	35%	15%

As you can see, as of 2005, the long term capital gains tax rate was 15% for all taxpayers except for those in the lowest 10–15% income tax brackets whose capital gains were taxed at 10%. (Note, capital assets held for less than one year are taxed at ordinary income rates.) It should be clear, then, that inventors with higher incomes can pay substantially less taxes if they can treat the money they receive from the sale of a patent as a long term capital gain rather than ordinary income.

EXAMPLE: Myron sold his invention and earned a $10,000 profit. If Myron's profit is characterized as ordinary income, he must pay $3,000 in federal income tax and $1,530 in self-employment taxes. If the $10,000 profit is treated as a long term capital gain, he pays only $1,500 in federal income taxes.

Capital gains treatment is available only when you sell a capital asset—this commonly includes such things as real estate and stocks and bonds. A patent can also be a capital asset. Unfortunately, there are complex tax rules governing when long term capital gains tax treatment can be obtained. Some inventors can qualify for capital gains treatment under these rules, but many cannot. Fortunately, a special tax law called IRC § 1235 allows inventors who sell their patents to obtain long term capital gains treatment on their profits whether or not such treatment would be available under the rules applicable to other taxpayers. Congress accorded this preferential treatment to inventors because it wants to encourage them to create new inventions.

There's more to capital gains. If you fail to qualify for capital gains treatment under IRC § 1235 as described in Section B below, you might still be able to obtain such treatment under the normal capital gains rules applicable to all capital assets. However, independent inventors who sell or license their inventions as a business generally cannot obtain capital gains treatment under these rules. These rules are contained in IRC §§ 1221, 1231 and 1245. Note also that different capital gains rates apply to collectibles, certain depreciable real estate and property held over five years—but these are usually of little concern to inventors. If you find yourself with capital gains questions, consult with a tax pro for advice.)

 For more information on capital gains, refer to IRS Publication 544, *Sales and Other Dispositions of Assets*. You can obtain a copy by calling the IRS at 800-TAX-FORM, visiting your local IRS office or downloading it from the IRS Internet site at www.irs.gov.

B. Capital Gains Treatment for Patents Under IRC § 1235

IRC § 1235 provides that individual inventors who sell their patents may treat their earnings as a long term capital gain, taxable at the 20% or 10% capital gains rate. Moreover, self-employment tax need not be paid on the earnings (see Section C).

Ordinarily, a capital asset must be held for at least one year to receive long term capital gains treatment. But Section 1235 allows for capital gains treatment no matter how long the inventor holds the patent.

> **EXAMPLE:** Rick develops a new floor wax that can be applied as a spray. He files a patent application for the invention and immediately enters into an agreement transferring all his rights in the invention to the Acme Floor Wax Co. In exchange, he receives $100,000 up front and a 50 cent royalty on each bottle of wax sold. Rick is a high-income taxpayer who would ordinarily pay income tax at the 35% rate on the payments he receives from Acme.

However, because the transaction falls within IRC § 1235, the transaction may be treated as long-term capital gains even though the entire transaction, from the development of the invention, to the sale to Acme, took less than a month. Thus, Rick need only pay the long term capital gains rate of 15% on his income from Acme.

To qualify for capital gains treatment under IRC § 1235, you must satisfy the following requirements.

1. You Must Be a Holder of a U.S. or Foreign Patent

You are the holder of a patent if you are the named inventor of the patented invention. (A person who buys an interest in a patent from the inventor can also qualify as a patent holder, as described below.) If there is more than one inventor, they can each be patent holders and obtain capital gains treatment.

Although you will not become a patent holder until the patent is actually issued by the USPTO or foreign patent agency, you may nonetheless transfer your future patent rights before a patent issues. This can be done after you've filed a patent application, or, even before, if the invention has been reduced to practice by the creation of a written description that enables a person of ordinary skill to construct an actual model of the invention.

Section 1235 treatment is available no matter how an inventor's activities are characterized for tax purposes—that is, it makes no difference if the inventor is running a business, is engaged in a hobby or an income-producing activity. (See Chapter 6 for information about the hobby loss rule.)

However, only an individual can be a patent holder. Corporations do not qualify. Thus, for example, a corporation whose employee creates a patented invention may not obtain capital gains treatment under Section 1235. But, joint inventors who are in a partnership can still qualify as patent holders so long as all the partners are human beings, not business entities such as corporations.

A person who buys an interest in a patent from the inventor can also qualify as a patent holder, but only if: (1) the purchase is made before the invention was tested and operated successfully (also called "reduction to practice"), and (2) the purchaser is neither related to, nor the employer of, the inventor.

EXAMPLE: Harry, a wealthy investor in the top 35% income tax bracket, has a friend named Dick who is a part-time inventor. Dick tells Harry about his idea for a toothbrush that cleans teeth using a low frequency sound wave. Harry, wowed by the idea, agrees to give Dick $10,000 to develop the toothbrush in exchange for 50% of all the patent rights in the invention. Within six months, Dick creates a prototype and he and Harry sell all their patent rights to the Acme Toothbrush Co. for $1,000,000. Because the transaction qualifies for capital gains treatment under IRC § 1235, Harry only has to pay the 20% capital gains tax on his $500,000 share of the proceeds, instead of the 35% tax rate on ordinary income.

2. You Must Transfer All Substantial Rights in Your Patent

The key to obtaining capital gains treatment under Section 1235 is that you must transfer "all substantial rights" in your patent. A U.S. patent gives you the exclusive right to make, use, sell or import an invention based on your patent for up to 20 years from the date of filing. You must give up all these rights forever. (If a foreign patent is involved, you must give up all the same or similar rights as for a U.S. patent.)

Thus, for example, the agreement you have with the purchaser of your patent cannot be limited as to:

- geography—the transfer must cover the entire country that issued the patent—for example, a transfer of a U.S. patent must cover the entire U.S.
- time—your rights must be transferred for the entire remaining life of the patent
- field of use—the transfer cannot be limited to a particular field of use (whether a product, industry or area of use) provided the patent has substantial value in more than one field of use.
- claims—you must transfer the rights to all the claims contained in your patent.

It makes no difference what the agreement with the person or company that obtains your patent rights is called—whether an assignment, license or transfer agreement. What matters is that the agreement does in fact transfer all your substantial rights for the life of the patent.

However, you are allowed to retain certain rights and still qualify under Section 1235. Most important, the agreement can provide that it will terminate and your patent rights revert to you if the buyer doesn't perform as promised—for example, if the purchaser fails to pay minimum royalties required by the agreement or otherwise fails to make payments. Also, you are allowed to retain a security interest (such as a lien) in your patent. Under IRS § 1235, the agreement may also terminate on the occurrence of certain specified conditions beyond the patent owner's control—for example, the purchaser's bankruptcy or insolvency. (Note, however, even if your agreement permits this, termination provisions based on bankruptcy are generally unenforceable under bankruptcy law.)

Finally, the purchaser of your patent need not pay you the entire purchase price in a lump sum. All or part of your payment can take the form of royalties payable periodically —for example, every quarter or year. And the royalties don't have to be a guaranteed amount; they can be based on a percentage of net or gross sales, productivity gains attributable to the patented invention, profits the purchaser earns from re-selling the patent or some other measure. Moreover, your payment doesn't even have to take the form of money—for example, you could be paid in property or services (this type of remuneration for a patent is called "moneysworth").

 For a detailed discussion of patent licensing issues, refer to *License Your Invention*, by Richard Stim (Nolo).

Transferring All Your Patent Rights May Not Always Be Wise

To obtain capital gains treatment under IRC § 1235, you must put all your eggs in one basket by selling all your patent rights to one purchaser. In many cases you can make substantially more money by licensing your invention to many different people or companies especially if the technology you have patented has different uses in multiple industries.

3. You May Not Transfer Your Rights to a "Related Person"

IRC § 1235 does not apply if you transfer your patent rights to a person who is related to you. This includes your spouse and all your ancestors and lineal descendants (children, grandchildren, etc.). But it does not include your brothers, sisters, half-brothers or half-sisters. A corporation in which you own more than 25% of the stock is also a related person.

C. Paying Self-Employment Taxes

If you have a profit from your inventing business you'll have to pay Social Security and Medicare taxes (referred to as self-employment or "SE" taxes). You must pay SE taxes unless your losses from other business ventures offset the profit or unless your net inventing income is less than $400 during the tax year. When employees have these taxes directly deducted from their paychecks by their employers (who must make matching contributions), such taxes are referred to as FICA taxes. But, when you're a self-employed inventor, you must pay these taxes to the IRS yourself. You pay self-employment taxes only on your net self-employment income, not your entire income. This section shows you how to determine how much SE tax you must pay.

For additional information on self-employment taxes, see IRS Publication 533, *Self-Employment Tax*. You can obtain this and all other IRS publications by calling the IRS at 800-TAX-FORM, visiting your local IRS office or downloading them from the IRS Internet site at www.irs.gov.

1. Who Must Pay?

Sole proprietors, partners in partnerships and members of limited liability companies must all pay SE taxes if their net earnings from self-employment for the year are $400 or more.

Corporations do not pay SE taxes. However, if you're incorporated and work in your inventing business, you are an employee of your corporation and will ordinarily be paid a salary. Instead of paying SE taxes, you must pay FICA taxes on your salary just like any other employee. Half of your Social Security and Medicare taxes must be withheld from your salary and half paid by your corporation. (See Chapter 10.)

2. SE Tax Rates

The self-employment tax consists of a 12.4% Social Security tax and a 2.9% Medicare tax for a total tax of 15.3%. But in practice, the bite it takes is smaller because of certain deductions. (See Section C4.)

The SE tax is a flat tax—that is, the tax rate is the same no matter what your income level. However, there is an income ceiling on the Social Security portion of the tax. You need not pay the 12.4% Social Security tax on your net self-employment earnings that exceed the ceiling amount. The Social Security tax ceiling is adjusted annually for inflation. In 2005, the ceiling was $90,000.

However, there is no similar limit for Medicare: you must pay the 2.9% Medicare tax on your entire net self-employment income, no matter how large. Congress enacted this rule a few years ago to save Medicare from bankruptcy.

> **EXAMPLE:** Manny earned $150,000 in net self-employment income from his inventing business in 2005. He must pay both Social Security and Medicare taxes on the first $90,000 of his income—a 15.3% tax. He only pays the 2.9% Medicare tax on his remaining $60,000 in income.

3. Earnings Subject to Self-Employment Tax

To determine your net self-employment income, you first figure the net income you've earned from your inventing business. Your net business income includes all your income from your business, minus all business deductions allowed for income tax purposes. However, you can't deduct retirement contri-

butions you make for yourself to a Keogh or SEP plan or the self-employed health insurance deduction. If, like most independent inventors, you're a sole proprietor, use IRS Schedule C, Profit or Loss From Business, to determine your net business income.

Capital gains are not included in self-employment income. Thus, if the income you receive from the sale of a patent qualifies for capital gains treatment under IRC § 1235, you need not pay self-employment taxes on it. (IRC § 1402(a)(3)(A); Rev. Rul. 68-129.) Also, capital gains income is not included in Schedule C. You list it instead in IRS Schedule D, Capital Gains and Losses and then transfer the amount directly to the "Other Income" line of your Form 1040.

If you have more than one business—for example, you have both an inventing business and a business as a consultant—combine the net income or loss from them all. If you have a job in addition to your business, your employee income is not included in your self-employment income. Nor do you include investment income, such as interest you earn on your savings.

You then get one more valuable deduction before finally determining your net self-employment income. You're allowed to deduct 7.65% from your total net business income. This is intended to help ease the SE tax burden on the self-employed. To do this, multiply your net business income by 92.35% or .9235%.

> **EXAMPLE:** In 2005, Billie earned $70,000 in ordinary income from licensing her invention—a sundial that can be attached

to a gravestone. She had $20,000 in business expenses, leaving a net business income of $50,000. She multiplies this amount by .9235 to determine her net self-employment income, which is $46,175. This is the amount on which Billie must pay SE tax.

Because of this extra deduction, the "real" self-employment tax rate is about 12% rather than the official rate of 15.3%.

4. Computing the SE Tax

It's easy to compute the amount of your SE tax. First, determine your net self-employment income as described above. If your net self-employment income is below the Social Security tax ceiling—$90,000 in 2005—multiply it by 15.3% or .153.

> **EXAMPLE:** Mark had $50,000 in net self-employment income from his inventing business in 2005. He must multiply this by .153 to determine his SE tax, which is $7,650.

If your net self-employment income is more than the Social Security tax ceiling, multiply your income up to the ceiling by 12.4% and all of your income by the 2.9% Medicare tax; then add both amounts together to determine your total SE tax.

> **EXAMPLE:** Martha had $100,000 in net self-employment income from her inventing business in 2005. She multiplies the first $90,000 of this amount by .153 resulting in a tax of $13,770. She then multiplies the amount over $90,000 ($10,000) by the 2.9% (.029) for Medicare tax, resulting in a $290 tax. She adds these amounts together to determine her total SE tax, which is $14,060.

In another effort to make the SE tax burden a little lighter for the self-employed, the IRS allows you to deduct half of the amount of your SE taxes from your business income for income tax purposes. For example, if you pay $10,000 in SE taxes, you can deduct $5,000 from your gross income when you determine your taxable income.

Frank Zamboni
Invented the self-propelled
single-operator ice resurfacer.

5. Paying and Reporting SE Taxes

You pay SE taxes directly to the IRS during the year as part of your estimated taxes. You have the option of either:

- paying the same amount in tax as you paid the previous year, or
- estimating what your income will be this year and basing your estimated tax payments on that.

When you file your annual tax return, you must include IRS Form SE, Self-Employment Tax, along with your income tax return. This form shows the IRS how much SE tax you were required to pay for the year. You file only one Form SE no matter how many unincorporated businesses you own. Add the SE tax to your income taxes on your income tax return, Form 1040, to determine your total tax.

Even if you do not owe any income tax, you must still complete Form 1040 and Schedule SE if you owe $400 or more in SE taxes.

6. Paying Self-Employment Taxes When You Have a Job

A great many independent inventors have full- or part-time jobs. If you have a job in which you're classified as an employee and have Social Security and Medicare taxes withheld from your wages, you must pay the Social Security tax on your wages first. If your wages are at least equal to the Social Security tax ceiling ($90,000), you won't have to pay the 12.4% Social Security tax on your SE income. But no matter how much you earn from your job, you'll have to pay the 2.9% Medicare tax on all your SE income.

EXAMPLE: Anne earned $100,000 in employee wages and $10,000 in self-employment income from her inventing business in 2005. She did not have to pay Social Security taxes on her earnings above the $90,000 Social Security tax ceiling for the year. Her employer withheld 7.65% in Social Security taxes up to $90,000 of her wages and 1.45% (the Medicare portion of an employee's FICA taxes) on her earnings between $90,000 and $100,000. Anne also had to pay the 2.9% Medicare portion of the SE tax—but not the 12.4% Social Security tax—on her $10,000 in self-employment earnings.

However, if your employee wages are lower than the Social Security tax ceiling, you'll have to pay Social Security taxes on your SE income until your wages and SE income combined exceed the ceiling amount.

EXAMPLE: Bill earned $20,000 in employee wages and $80,000 in self-employment income from his inventing business in 2005. His wages were lower than the $90,000 Social Security tax ceiling for the year. His employer withheld a 7.65% FICA tax on his wages and he had to pay a 12.4% Social Security tax on $70,000 of his SE income. He stopped paying the Social Security tax after his wages and income combined equaled $90,000. This meant he didn't have to pay the Social Security tax on $10,000 of the $80,000 he earned from his inventing business. However, he had to pay the 2.9% Medicare tax on all his SE income.

D. Paying Estimated Taxes

Estimated taxes are taxes you pay directly to the IRS during the year for income that is not subject to withholding. This includes income from self-employment, interest, dividends, alimony, rent, gains from the sale of assets (including patents), prizes and awards. Estimated tax is used to pay both income tax and self-employment tax. You need to figure out the amount you must pay yourself and send it to the IRS four times each year.

You don't have to worry about this when you're an employee because your income and Social Security and Medicare taxes are withheld from your paychecks by your employer and sent to the IRS. However, no taxes are withheld from the money you earn as an independent inventor. This is so whether the money you earn from an invention is ordinary income or qualifies as a capital gain under IRC § 1235 (see Section A).

Most States Have Estimated Taxes, Too

If your state has income taxes, it probably requires the self-employed to pay estimated taxes or increase their employee withholding. The due dates are generally the same as for federal estimated tax. State income tax rates are lower than federal income taxes. The exact rate depends on the state in which you live. Contact your state tax office for information and the required forms.

---

1. Who Must Pay Estimated Taxes?

You must pay estimated taxes if you're a sole proprietor and expect to owe at least $1,000 in federal tax for the year on your inventing business income. This includes the net business income shown on your Schedule C for your inventing business and any capital gain income from selling your patents or any other business property.

> **EXAMPLE:** Joe expects to earn a profit of $10,000 from his inventing business this year. He is in the 28% tax bracket, so he will owe $2,800 in taxes. Thus, he has to pay estimated taxes during the year.

There is one exception to this rule: If you paid no taxes last year, you don't have to pay any estimated tax this year no matter how much tax you expect to owe. But this is true only if you were a U.S. citizen or resident for the year and your tax return for the previous year covered the whole 12 months.

Moreover, if, in addition to being an independent inventor, you hold a job and have taxes withheld from your paycheck by your employer, you need not pay estimated tax if the amount withheld is at least equal to the lesser of:

- 90% of your total tax due for the current year, or
- 100% of the tax you paid the previous year (110% if you earned over $150,000).

Partnerships, LLCs and Corporations

Most independent inventors are sole proprietors —they solely own their inventing business. However, some are owners of partnerships, limited liability companies (LLCs) or corporations. Partners or LLC members must pay individual estimated tax on their shares of partnership or LLC income. This is so whether it's actually paid to them or not. The partnership or LLC itself pays no tax. The only exception is if the owners of an LLC elect to be taxed as a C corporation, which is unusual.

If you form a regular C corporation, you will ordinarily be its employee and receive a salary from which income and employment taxes must be withheld just as for any employee. You won't need to pay any estimated tax on your salary. But if you receive dividends or distributions from your corporation, you'll need to pay tax on them during the year—unless the total tax due on the amounts you received is less than $500. You can cover the taxes due either by paying estimated tax or by increasing the tax withheld from your salary; it doesn't make much practical difference which you choose.

If you've formed a C corporation, it must pay quarterly estimated taxes if it will owe $500 or more in corporate tax on its profits for the year. These taxes are deposited with a bank, not paid directly to the IRS. However, most small C corporations don't have to pay any income taxes or estimated taxes because all the profits are taken out of the corporation by the owners in the form of salaries, bonuses and benefits. (See Chapter 2.)

S corporations ordinarily don't have to pay estimated taxes because all profits are passed through to the shareholders, as in a partnership. (See Chapter 2, Section C3.)

For detailed guidance on C corporation estimated taxes, see IRS Publication 542, *Tax Information for Corporations*. You can obtain this and all other IRS publications by calling the IRS at 800-TAX-FORM, visiting your local IRS office or downloading them from the IRS Internet site at www.irs.gov.

EXAMPLE: Assume that Joe in the example above has a full-time engineering job with an annual $120,000 salary. Given the relatively small amount of inventing income he expects to earn, he is confident that the amount his employer will withhold from his substantial salary will easily equal 90% of his total tax due for the year, so he need not pay estimated taxes.

If the amount you currently have withheld from your paychecks does not meet the above test, you may be able to avoid having to make estimated tax payments by asking your employer to take more tax out of your earnings. To do this, file a new Form W-4 with your employer. However, you'll have more control over your cash flow if you don't have more withheld each month and make your own quarterly estimated tax payments instead.

2. How Much You Must Pay

You should determine how much estimated tax to pay after completing your tax return for the previous year. Most people want to pay as little estimated tax as possible during the year so they can earn interest on their money instead of handing it over to the IRS. However, the IRS imposes penalties if you don't pay enough estimated tax. (See Section C5.) There's no need to get excessively concerned about these penalties. They aren't terribly large in the first place and it's easy to avoid having to pay them. All you have to do is pay at least the lesser of:

- 90% of your total tax due for the current year, or

- 100% of the tax you paid the previous year —or more if you're a high-income taxpayer (see below).

You normally make four estimated tax payments each year. There are three different ways you can calculate your payments. You can use any one of the three methods without paying a penalty as long as you pay the minimum total the IRS requires, as explained above. One of the methods—basing your payments on last year's tax—is extremely easy to use. The other two are more complex to figure out, but might permit you to make smaller payments.

a. Payments based on last year's tax

The easiest and safest way to calculate your estimated taxes is to simply pay 100% of the total federal taxes you paid last year, or more if you're a high-income taxpayer as described below. You can base your estimated tax on the amount you paid the prior year even if you weren't in business that year, but your return for the year must have been for a full 12-month period.

You should determine how much estimated tax to pay for the current year at the same time that you file your tax return for the previous year—no later than April 15. Take the total amount of tax you had to pay for the year and divide by four. If this comes out to an odd number, round up to get an even number. These are the amounts you'll have to pay in estimated tax. You'll make four equal payments throughout the year and the following year. (See the chart in Section C3 to learn when you must make your payments).

TAXATION OF INVENTING INCOME

EXAMPLE: Gary earned $50,000 from his inventing business last year. He figures his taxes for the prior year on April 1 of this year and determines he owed $9,989.32 for the year. To determine his estimated tax for the current year he divides this amount by four: $9,989.32 divided by four equals $2497.33. He rounds this up to $2,500. He'll make four $2,500 estimated tax payments to the IRS. As long as he pays this much, Gary won't have to pay a penalty even if he ends up owing more than $10,000 in tax to the IRS for the year because his inventing income goes up, his inventing business deductions go down or both.

High-income taxpayers must pay more. High-income taxpayers—those with adjusted gross incomes of more than $150,000 or $75,000 for married couples filing separate returns—must pay more than 100% of their prior year's tax.

Your adjusted gross income (or AGI) is your total income minus deductions for:

- IRA, Keogh and SEP-IRA contributions
- health insurance
- one-half of your self-employment tax, and
- alimony, deductible moving expenses and penalties you pay for early withdrawals from a savings account before maturity or early redemption of certificates of deposit.

(To find out your AGI, look at line 33 on your last year's tax return, Form 1040.)

The estimated tax amount you must pay is 110% for returns filed in 2003 and after.

EXAMPLE: Mary earned $250,000 in gross income from her inventing business in 2005. Her adjusted gross income was $200,000 after subtracting the value of her Keogh Plan contributions, health insurance deduction and half her self-employment taxes. Mary paid $50,000 in income and self-employment taxes in 2005. In 2006, Mary must pay 110% of the tax she paid in 2005—$5,550 in estimated tax. As long as she pays this amount she won't have to pay a penalty to the IRS even if she earns more than she did in 2005.

Mid-course correction. Your third estimated tax payment is due on September 15. By this time you should have a pretty good idea of what your income for the year will be. If you're reasonably sure that your income for the year will be at least 25% less than what you earned last year, you can forgo the last estimated tax payment due on January 15 of next year. You have already paid enough estimated tax for the year.

If it looks as if your income will be greater than last year, you don't have to pay more estimated tax. The IRS cannot penalize you so long as you pay 100% of what you paid last year—or more if you're a high-income taxpayer.

You may owe tax on April 15. Basing your estimated tax on last year's income is generally the best method to use if you expect your income to be higher this year than last year. You'll be paying the minimum possible without incurring a penalty. However, if you do end up earning more than last year, using this method will cause you to underpay your taxes. You won't have to pay a penalty, but you'll have to make up the underpayment when you file your tax return for the year. This could present you with a big tax bill if your income rose substantially from last year. To make sure you have enough money for this, it's a good idea to sock away a portion of your income in a separate bank account just for taxes.

b. Payments based on estimated taxable income

If you're absolutely certain your net income will be less this year than last year, you'll pay less estimated tax if you base your tax on your taxable income for the current year instead of basing it on last year's tax. This is not worth the time and trouble, however, unless you'll earn at least 30% less this year than last.

The problem with using this method is that you must estimate your total income and deductions for the year to figure out how much to pay. Obviously, this can be difficult or impossible to compute accurately. And there are no magic formulas to look to for guidance. The best way to proceed is to sit down with your tax return for the previous year.

Take comfort in knowing that you need not make an exact estimate of your taxable income. You won't have to pay a penalty if you pay at least 90% of your tax due for the year.

IRS Form 1040-ES contains a worksheet to use to calculate your estimated tax. You can obtain the form by calling the IRS at 800-TAX-FORM, visiting your local IRS office or downloading it from the IRS Internet site at www.irs.gov.

c. Payments based on quarterly Income

A much more complicated way to calculate your estimated taxes is to use the annualized

Thomas Edison
Invented the lightbulb and
the phonograph.

income installment method. It requires that you separately calculate your tax liability at four points during the year—March 31, May 31, August 31 and December 31—prorating your deductions and personal exemptions. You base your estimated tax payments on your actual tax liability for each quarter.

This method is often the best choice for people who receive income very unevenly throughout the year. If you use this method, you must file IRS Form 2210 with your tax return; this form shows your calculations. You really need a good grasp of tax law and mathematics to use the annualized income installment method. The IRS worksheet used to calculate your payments using this method contains 43 separate steps. If you want to use this method, give yourself a break and hire an accountant or at least use a tax preparation computer program to help with the calculations.

See IRS Publication 505, *Tax Withholding and Estimated Tax*, for a detailed explanation of the annualized income method. You can obtain the form by calling the IRS at 800-TAX-FORM, visiting your local IRS office or downloading it from the IRS Internet site at www.irs.gov.

3. When to Pay Estimated Tax

Estimated tax must ordinarily be paid in four installments, with the first one due on April 15. However, you don't have to start making payments until you actually earn income from your inventing business. If you don't receive

any income by March 31, you can skip the April 15 payment. In this event, you'd ordinarily make three payments for the year, starting on June 15. If you don't receive any income by May 31, you can skip the June 15 payment as well and so on.

The following chart shows the due dates and the period each installment covers.

Estimated Tax Due	
Income received for the period	**Estimated tax due**
January 1 through March 31	April 15
April 1 through May 31	June 15
June 1 through August 31	September 15
September 1 through December 31	January 15 of next year

Also, you can skip the January 15 payment if you file your tax return and pay all taxes due for the previous year by January 31 of the current year. This is a little reward the IRS gives you for filing your tax return early.

However, it's rarely advantageous to file early because you'll have to pay any tax due on January 15 instead of waiting until April 15—meaning you'll lose three months of interest on your hard-earned money.

Your estimated tax payment must be postmarked by the dates noted above, but the IRS need not actually receive them then. If any of these days falls on a weekend or legal holiday, the due date is the next business day.

The Year May Not Begin in January

Don't get confused by the fact that the January 15 payment is the fourth estimated tax payment for the previous year, not the first payment for the current year. The April 15 payment is the first payment for the current year.

4. How to Pay

The IRS wants to make it easy for you to send in your money, so the mechanics of paying estimated taxes are very simple. You file federal estimated taxes using IRS Form 1040-ES. This form contains instructions and four numbered payment vouchers for you to send in with your payments. You must provide your name, address, Social Security number (or EIN if you have one) and amount of the payment on each voucher. You file only one payment voucher with each payment, no matter how many unincorporated businesses you have.

If you're married and file a joint return, the names on your estimated tax vouchers should be exactly the same as those on your income tax return. Even if your spouse isn't self-employed, he or she should be listed on the vouchers so that the money gets credited to the right account.

If you made estimated tax payments last year, you should receive a copy of the current year's Form 1040-ES in the mail. It will have payment vouchers preprinted with your name, address and Social Security number. If you did not pay estimated taxes last year, get a copy of Form 1040-ES from the IRS.

You may pay all or part of your estimated taxes by credit card (Visa, MasterCard, Discover Card or American Express Card). You must do this through one of two private companies providing this service. You'll have to pay the company a fee based on the amount of your payment (the fee does not go to the IRS). You can arrange to make your payment by phone or through the Internet through LINK2GOV Corporation (www.PAY1040 .com), or Official Payments Corporation (www.officialpayments.com).

Keep Your Canceled Checks

It's not unheard of for the IRS to make a bookkeeping error and then claim that you paid less estimated tax than you did or to apply your payment to the wrong year. If this happens, provide the IRS with a copy of the front and back of your canceled estimated tax checks. The agency encodes a series of tracking numbers on the endorsement side of any check that enables it to locate where payments were applied in its system. This points up the importance of keeping your canceled estimated tax checks.

Don't use money market checks to pay estimated taxes or checks from an account in which the bank doesn't return the original checks to you. Even if your bank promises to give you free copies of your checks, the copies may be so poor the IRS can't read them.

Tell the IRS If You Move

You're supposed to notify the IRS if you are making estimated tax payments and you change your address during the year. You can use IRS Form 8822, Change of Address, for this purpose. It's a simple change of address form. Or you may send a signed letter to the IRS Center where you filed your last return stating:

- your full name and your spouse's full name
- your old address and spouse's old address (if different)
- your new address, and
- Social Security numbers for you and your spouse.

5. Paying the Wrong Amount

If you pay too little estimated tax, the IRS will make you pay a penalty. The percentage is set by the IRS each year and has ranged between 6% and 8% in recent years. Many self-employed people decide to pay the penalty at the end of the tax year rather than take money out of their businesses during the year to pay estimated taxes. If you do this, though, make sure you pay all the taxes you owe for the year by April 15 of the following year. If you don't, the IRS will tack on additional interest and penalties. The IRS usually adds a penalty of 1/2% to 1% per month to a tax bill that's not paid when due.

If you pay too much, you can get the money refunded or apply it to your current year's estimated taxes. Unfortunately, you can't get back the interest your overpayment earned while sitting in the IRS coffers; that belongs to the government. ■

Chapter 9

Your Inventor's Notebook

A. Why Keep an Inventor's Notebook? 9/2

    1. Showing You're in Business 9/3

    2. Protecting Your Patent Rights 9/3

    3. Establishing Patent Ownership 9/4

B. How to Keep Your Notebook 9/5

C. Witnessing Your Notebook 9/7

D. Alternatives to the Inventor's Notebook 9/8

    1. Disclosure Document Program 9/8

    2. Provisional Patent Application 9/9

*A*t about one o'clock in the morning of November 9, 1957, Gordon Gould, a Columbia University physics doctoral student, sat up in bed. One of the most important scientific insights of the 20th century had just come to him in a flash. He got up, opened a lined laboratory notebook and started to write: "Some rough calculations on the feasibility of a LASER: Light Amplification by Stimulated Emission of Radiation." He continued writing through the night and much of the next three days. When he was done, he had nine notebook pages describing a way of amplifying light and using the resulting beam to cut and heat substances and measure distance. He had the notebook witnessed and dated. However, Gould didn't file for a patent until 1959, after other laser researchers had already filed. This resulted in a 20-year legal battle, which

Gordon Gould
Inventor of laser and optical devices

Gould finally won in 1977, when the first of his laser patents was issued. Today, Gould earns many millions of dollars per year in patent royalties from his laser invention.

The main reason Gould was ultimately recognized as the true inventor of the laser was because his inventor's notebook proved that he had been the first to conceive of it. Your inventor's notebook might not turn out to be as valuable as Gordon Gould's, but it will still be the most important inventing record you can have.

A. Why Keep an Inventor's Notebook?

An inventor's notebook is a journal that shows when and how you conceived of your invention and the procedures, dates, actions, failures, successes, contacts and other events that occur while building and testing the invention. It is, in effect, the daily diary of your inventing life. Keeping an inventor's notebook will benefit you in numerous ways, both legal and practical.

On the legal side, your notebook will help:

- show that you are engaged in a business and not merely a hobby (see Section A1, below). (See Chapter 6 for information on why the hobby/business distinction is important.)
- protect your patent rights (see Section A2, below), and
- establish your patent ownership (see Section A3, below).

On the practical side, your notebook will help you monitor your invention's progress and determine what remains to be done. For example, by going carefully through his notebook, Alexander Graham Bell found a positive result he had obtained earlier, and wondered why he had not followed up on it. This led to a key discovery that helped him obtain his second telephone patent. (Copies of Bell's notebook pages can be seen online at the Library of Congress website. Visit www.loc.gov, click "American Memory Project," then click "Alexander Graham Bell.")

1. Showing You're in Business

An inventor's notebook is an essential tool to show that you are in business and not simply engaging in a hobby. This is vital if you want to deduct your inventing expenses from all income you might have, such as salary from a job. Your notebook, paired with your financial records discussed in Chapter 4, will provide solid evidence that you are serious about making a profit from your inventing activities. Moreover, your notebook will enable you to tie specific expenses to your inventing work—for example, if you buy an expensive piece of equipment, you'll have a record showing how and when you actually used it to help develop your invention.

> **EXAMPLE:** Alec is attempting to create a synthetic fiber that will repel dirt. He buys a $5,000 microscope to create fiber magnifications and includes these images in his notebook. In this way, the notebook entries demonstrate that Alec actually used the microscope as part of his inventing business.

As discussed in Chapter 4, you should keep all receipts, credit card bills and other documents showing the money you spend on your inventing work. If you wish, you can paste these directly into your inventor's notebook and have these pages dated and witnessed. Note, this is not required; you may prefer to file receipts in a folder.

2. Protecting Your Patent Rights

The United States has a "first-to-invent" patent system—the first person to come up with an invention has the right to patent it. The earliest possible date you can invent something is the date you conceived the invention (the "date of conception")—that is, the date you completely imagined the thing to be patented or discovered the solution to a problem. However, conceiving an invention is not enough to establish the date of conception as the date of your invention. You must be reasonably diligent about completing the invention; this is called "reduction to practice" in patent parlance. You can reduce an invention to practice in one of three ways:

- build and test a prototype and confirm that it will work
- file a regular patent application, or
- file a provisional patent application and file a regular application within one year.

You can't wait forever to do any of these things. You must proceed with reasonable diligence—that is, you must work relatively steadily on the invention. However, gaps in your progress may be excused if you have a good reason—for example, illness, poverty, you had to work a full-time job or needed a vacation.

The main purposes of an inventor's notebook are to establish the date you conceived your invention and to show that you were diligent about reducing it to practice. You do this by writing in your notebook all the pertinent facts about your work on your invention—including:

- a functional description of the invention—that is, an explanation of what it does and how it works
- a structural description of the invention—that is, a static description of how the invention is constructed
- descriptions of all experiments (these should be detailed enough to allow someone else to replicate the experiment—for example, list the equipment you used and the methods and conditions of the experiment)
- calculations
- test results—both successes and failures
- sketches of the invention (these don't have to be artistic renderings and don't need to conform to special patent application rules)
- how your invention differs from previous similar inventions, and
- if other people are working on the invention with you, their identities and roles in the invention process.

Each page of the notebook should be signed, dated and witnessed as described below. This signed and dated notebook is admissible in court as evidence of the dates

of your conception and reduction to practice of your invention. It will provide extremely strong evidence if, like laser inventor Gordon Gould, you get into a dispute with another inventor about who first conceived the invention.

Some inventors believe that you can document the date of conception of an invention by mailing a description of the invention to yourself by certified or registered mail and keeping the sealed envelope. This is not true. The U.S. Patent Office says that post office patents have little legal value.

3. Establishing Patent Ownership

An inventor's notebook can help you establish your patent ownership in two ways:

- If you are an employee, you can use your notebook to show that your invention was not developed during your hours of employment and that you did not use employer resources or knowledge. This evidence could affect whether you or your employer own the patent rights to your invention. (See Chapter 14 for more about patent rights.)
- Also, if you work with others on your invention, the notebook can help document each person's contributions. This evidence may help defeat claims by others that they are co-inventors who should share ownership of your invention. (See Chapter 11 for more about invention ownership.)

B. How to Keep Your Notebook

Keeping an inventor's notebook is not difficult. You can copy the format in the sample page at the end of this chapter.

 The Inventor's Notebook by Fred Grissom & David Pressman (Nolo) provides organized guidance for properly documenting your invention. You can also purchase lab notebooks through Eureka Lab Book, Inc. (www.eurekalabbook.com) or Scientific Notebook Company (www.snco.com/index.htm).

Your inventor's notebook should provide clear and convincing proof of the date you conceived your invention and of your diligent work toward making your invention a reality. To be proof that would convince a judge and jury in the event of a patent or tax dispute, the notebook must not look like it has been tampered with or otherwise altered after the fact to strengthen your case. To avoid these problems, follow these simple rules:

- Use a bound notebook (either softcover or hardcover) so that pages can't easily be removed or inserted.
- List your name and address on the front of the notebook.
- Make all entries in nonerasable ink; use the same pen for a whole page.
- Leave the first few pages of the notebook blank so you can use them later as a table of contents.
- Date the first entry in the upper right-hand corner and fully describe the idea for your invention. If you've already spent time working on your invention, summa-rize the work you've done. Also, record the date you conceived the invention, the names of people with whom you've discussed your idea and any tests or experiments you've performed.
- Write legibly.
- Make regular entries in chronological order—preferably every day you work on your invention.
- Date and sign every page. Never back-date a page.
- Use the past tense ("I did") when you're writing about work that has actually been performed; use the future tense ("I will do") to describe work not yet done.
- Describe your work clearly and concisely; don't use jargon.
- Never erase or "white out" mistakes. To correct an entry, draw a line though it and then make a new entry. Be sure to initial the changes.
- Don't leave any blank pages or large blank spaces in the notebook. Write from one edge of the page to the other and fill each page from top to bottom. Fill in blank areas with one or two diagonal lines.
- If you use a computer to take notes, make drawings or store data, print them out and have them dated, signed and witnessed. Then paste them into your notebook. The pasted material should be referred to by handwritten entries in the notebook—this helps show the material wasn't added after the fact.
- Paste photographs, drawings and other material that can't be directly signed and witnessed into your notebook. Write a

Record of Conception of Invention

Title of invention:

"Orange Peeling Knife" or "knife that can score oranges through skin without cutting pulp."

Circumstances of conception:

On March 2 or 3 of this year, when visiting my sister Shirley Goldberger in Lancaster, PA, I decided to eat an orange just before we all went shopping. When I tried to score through the orange's skin to peel it, I cut too deeply, and the juice dripped onto my lap. It stained my new pants and embarrassed me in front of Shirley, my wife and my mother. I had to change my pants, delaying everyone in the process.

   After we eventually got in the car, I remarked that there must be a better way to score and peel oranges. The problem preoccupied me so much that I didn't go shopping; instead, I came up with a solution while waiting in my car for my family. I remember telling them, on the way back, "Why not make a knife with an adjustable blade stop so that the depth of the cut could be controlled? That way you wouldn't cut into the orange's pulp, it would be easier to peel and it wouldn't drip."

   I didn't make any record of the invention at that time since I didn't know I should until I read this book yesterday.

Purpose or problem solved:

To peel oranges (or grapefruits or pomelos), it is desirable to score them first, preferably with two encircling cuts that cross at the blossom and stem ends so that the skin can be neatly peeled off in quarters. However, this is difficult with an ordinary knife because one inevitably cuts past the skin into the pulp, making the orange drip and the peel difficult to remove without removing some of the pulp with it. The problem is compounded because the thickness of orange peels varies among varieties. A tool that could neatly score oranges with peels of various thicknesses without cutting into the pulp would solve the problem.

Invented by: _Edward R. Furman_____ Date: _July 23, 200–_

Invented by: _____ Date: _____

The above confidential information is witnessed and understood by:

_Ruben Santiago_____ Date: _July 23, 200–_

_____ Date: _____

caption for the material that briefly describes it (for example, "photo of mousetrap operating to exterminate a mouse") and draw a line from the caption to the pasted material.

- Make at least one entry every month to avoid the appearance that you've abandoned your invention.
- Each page should be signed and dated by at least one, preferably two, witnesses (see below).
- Keep your notebook in a safe place. You don't need to put it in a bank safe-deposit box, but at least lock it in a desk drawer.

C. Witnessing Your Notebook

Each entry in your inventor's notebook should be witnessed. This means you must ask someone to read the page, sign it and date it. If you ever need to use your notebook as evidence in court, this same person can testify that the entry in your notebook was made on the date stated and has not subsequently been altered or forged.

You can use one witness, but it's best to have two. This way you have a better chance of having a witness available—perhaps years later—to testify in court. Moreover, two witnesses who say the same thing are more believable than just one.

Not just anybody can serve as your witnesses. First, the people you pick must be disinterested—that is, they won't benefit financially or any other way from your invention. This means you can't use your spouse or other

family members, investors or co-inventors as witnesses. A knowledgeable friend or colleague might make a good candidate. In addition, your witnesses must actually be able to read and understand the entries. If your invention is quite simple, any intelligent, disinterested person can serve as a witness. But if the invention is complex, you must use witnesses who have the scientific and/or technical background necessary to understand what you're doing.

The following phrase (or one similar to it) should be used before the witnesses' signatures: "The above confidential information was read and understood by me on (date)". Neither the witnesses' signatures nor your signature need to be notarized.

If getting every page of your notebook witnessed is too difficult, at least be sure to have witnessed those pages showing your conception of the invention and any building

Louis Pasteur
Invented the process of pasteurization

and testing of it that you do. These are the key entries in the notebook for patent purposes.

Thomas Edison's Notebooks

Thomas Edison, who obtained more than a thousand patents—more than any other individual inventor—was an avid notebook keeper. In his early days, he would keep notes on any scrap of paper at hand and just throw them in a drawer. However, after he established his research laboratory at Menlo Park, New Jersey, he systematized his record keeping. He placed hardcover notebooks all over his lab and ordered assistants to draw out and sign every experiment they performed. The notebook entries were frequently dated, signed and witnessed. Since he worked on many projects at once, Edison assigned separate notebooks to each project. The Edison National Historic Site archives in Orange, New Jersey, has more than 3,000 of Edison's inventor notebooks, each containing approximately 280 pages.

D. Alternatives to the Inventor's Notebook

If keeping an inventor's notebook or obtaining witnesses is too difficult for you, there are alternatives for documenting disclosure and reduction to practice—the Disclosure Document Program and the Provisional Patent Application Program. For purposes of obtaining a patent, both alternatives are accepted by the U.S. Patent Office. However, these alternatives are less valuable than an inventor's notebook for tax purposes because they don't document your day-to-day inventing activities—that is, they don't clearly demonstrate that you're a businessperson, rather than a hobbyist.

1. Disclosure Document Program

Instead of relying on an inventor's notebook to establish the date you conceived your invention, you may file a signed disclosure document with the U.S. Patent Office under its Disclosure Document Program (DDP). The disclosure document must contain a clear and complete explanation of how to make and use the invention. This must be detailed enough to enable someone who has ordinary knowledge in the field of the invention to make and use the invention. If appropriate, a drawing or sketch should be included. The invention's purpose and use must also be described.

You must sign the disclosure document, but you don't have to find people to witness it. Provided it adequately discloses your invention (that is, explains what it is and how it works), the date you file the disclosure document will serve as the date you conceived your invention for patent ownership purposes.

Filing a disclosure document with the Patent Office is not a substitute for diligently filing a regular complete patent application or building and testing your invention. Moreover, if you build and test your invention, you should still keep records of your work, preferably in a witnessed inventor's notebook to show you were diligent.

Filing a disclosure document does not increase the time you have to file your patent application. You must file your patent application within two years after filing your disclosure document, or the Patent Office will destroy it. This means the disclosure document won't be able to establish the date you conceived your invention.

The disclosure document (including drawings or sketches) must be on white letter-size (8½- by 11-inch) or A4 (21.0- by 29.7-cm) paper, written on one side only, with each page numbered. Text and drawings must be sufficiently dark to permit reproduction with commonly used office copying machines. Oversized papers, even if foldable to the required dimensions, will not be accepted. In addition, the Patent Office will not accept attachments such as videotapes and working models.

Sign and date this document and photocopy it. Send the photocopy to the Patent Office and keep the signed original. You don't have to have your document witnessed.

When you file your disclosure document with the patent office, you must include a cover letter (or form) and a fee. The cover letter should state that you are the inventor and that the documents are for the Disclosure Document Program. If you want, you can use the following language: "The undersigned, being the inventor of the disclosed invention, requests that the enclosed papers be accepted under the Disclosure Document Program, and that they be preserved for a period of two years."

If you don't want to write a cover letter, you can use a pre-printed Patent Office form called a Disclosure Document Deposit Request Form (PTO/SB/95). You can find a copy of the form on the forms disk at the end of this book. You can also obtain this form from the Patent Office website (www.uspto.gov) or by calling the General Information Services Division (800-786-9199).

The current fee for filing a disclosure document is $10. Make your check or money order payable to "Commissioner for Patents."

The Patent Office prefers that applicants send two copies of the cover letter or Disclosure Document Deposit Request form and one copy of the disclosure document, along with a self-addressed stamped envelope. The Patent Office will date stamp the second copy of the cover letter or form and return it to you. Be sure to save this notice, because it will show the date that the Patent Office received your document.

Mail the disclosure document with payment to Mail Stop DD, Commissioner for Patents, P.O. Box 1450, Alexandria, VA 22213-1450.

2. Provisional Patent Application

You can use the disclosure document procedure discussed in the previous section to establish the date you conceived your invention, but it will not show that you diligently worked to reduce it to practice. This is normally accomplished by using an inventor's notebook or filing a full patent application. However, you have the option of documenting your reduction to practice by filing a provisional patent application with the patent office. This is a document that fully explains how to make and use your invention.

If you file your regular patent application within one year after filing your provisional application, then the date of your provisional application is the official date that you reduced your invention to practice—an important date for establishing that you, and not someone else, should hold the patent to your invention. If you fail to meet this one-year deadline, the provisional application will be worthless and won't help you prove anything relating to dates and your invention.

Filing a provisional patent application is much simpler than applying for a patent. The filing fee is only $100 and you do not have to include claims or formal patent drawings with the provisional application as you would with the patent application. You don't have to get it witnessed, nor do you have to actually build and test your invention to prove you reduced it to practice.

By filing a provisional application, you obtain an additional year to assess whether your invention has potential and whether it's worth the expense, time and trouble of filing a regular patent application. During this time you may publish, sell or show the invention to others without losing any of your patent rights. You may also use the phrase "patent pending" on your invention. See Chapter 14 for more information on the benefits of filing a PPA.

For a good step-by-step explanation of how to complete and file a provisional patent application yourself, refer to *Patent Pending In 24 Hours*, by Richard Stim & David Pressman (Nolo). ■

Chapter 10

Hiring Employees and Independent Contractors

Part I: Determining Workers' Legal Status 10/3

A. ICs Are Business Owners, Employees Are Not 10/3

1. Right of Control Test 10/4

2. Eight Tips for Dealing With ICs 10/5

B. Pros and Cons of Hiring Employees or ICs 10/5

Part II. Hiring Employees 10/7

C. Drafting an Employment Agreement 10/9

1. Employer's Confidential Information 10/10

2. Nondisclosure of Trade Secrets 10/10

3. Confidential Information of Others 10/12

4. No Conflicting Obligations 10/12

5. Return of Materials 10/12

6. Confidentiality Obligation Survives Employment 10/12

7. Disclosure of Developments 10/12

8. Assignment of Developments 10/12

9. Post-Employment Assignment 10/14

10. Notice Pursuant to State Law 10/14

11. Signing Documents 10/16

12. Prior Developments 10/16

13. Enforcement 10/16

14. Mediation and Arbitration 10/16

15. General Provisions 10/18

16. Signatures 10/20

17. Exhibit A 10/22

D. Tax Concerns When Hiring Employees 10/22

1. Federal Taxes 10/22

2. State Payroll Taxes 10/24

Part III. Hiring Independent Contractors 10/26

E. Drafting an Independent Contractor Agreement 10/26

1. Services Performed by Contractor 10/27

2. Contractor's Payment 10/27

3. Expenses 10/27

4. Materials 10/27

5. Record Keeping 10/30

6. Invoices 10/30

7. Worker an Independent Contractor 10/30

8. Disclosure and Ownership of Developments 10/30

9. Confidential Information 10/30

10. Termination of Agreement 10/30

11. Return of Materials 10/32

12. Warranties and Representations 10/32

13. Indemnification 10/32

14. Mediation and Arbitration 10/32

15. Attorney Fees 10/32

16. Entire Agreement; Modifications 10/35

17. Applicable Law 10/35

18. Notices 10/35

19. No Partnership 10/35

20. Assignment and Delegation 10/37

21. Signatures 10/37

F. Tax Reporting for Independent Contractors 10/37

1. $600 Threshold for IC Income Reporting 10/39

2. Obtaining Taxpayer Identification Numbers 10/39

3. Filling Out Your Form 1099 .... 10/40

*S*ooner or later, most independent inventors need to hire people to help them—for example, to build prototypes, conduct research, provide technical and marketing assistance or just to generally help out. This chapter explains the legal and tax aspects of dealing with your helpers. It is divided into three parts:

- Part I shows you how to determine whether a worker is an employee or independent contractor.
- Part II provides a sample employment agreement and explains the tax details you need to know when hiring an employee.
- Part III provides a sample independent contractor agreement and discusses tax reporting requirements when you hire contractors.

Part I: Determining Workers' Legal Status

Whenever you hire people to help you in your inventing business and pay them (either money or something else), they automatically fall into one of two legal categories—they can be:

- employees, or
- independent contractors (ICs).

How a worker is categorized has important consequences for tax purposes, copyright ownership of the worker's work product and application of the myriad federal and state laws designed to protect employees.

Initially, it's up to you to determine whether a person you hire is an employee or an IC. If you decide that a worker is an

employee, you should have the worker sign an employment agreement and you must comply with the federal and state tax requirements discussed in Section D. If you decide the worker is an IC, you should have him or her sign an independent contractor agreement and comply with the income reporting and tax identification number requirements for ICs covered in Section F.

However, your decision about how to classify a worker is subject to review by various government agencies, including:

- the IRS
- your state's tax department
- your state's unemployment compensation insurance agency, and
- your state's workers' compensation insurance agency.

All these government agencies prefer that workers be classified as employees, rather than ICs. That way, taxes are withheld from their pay and various laws designed to protect employees apply. Any agency that determines that you misclassified an employee as an IC may impose back taxes, fines and penalties.

On the other hand, you can save substantial time and money by treating workers as ICs. For this reason, it's important to have a basic understanding of how to determine if a worker is an employee or IC.

A. ICs Are Business Owners, Employees Are Not

ICs are called by a variety of names, including freelancers, self-employed workers or consultants. But whatever they're called they have one thing in common—they are in business for themselves. Anyone with an independent business qualifies. In contrast, employees are not in business for themselves. They work for other peoples' businesses.

People who have their own businesses usually have certain working characteristics in common. They typically:

- offer their services to the general public, not just one person or company
- have their own business offices
- invest in tools, equipment and facilities
- take care of their own taxes, and
- make a profit if the business goes well, but if it goes badly they risk going broke.

Good examples of ICs are professionals with their own practices such as doctors, lawyers, dentists and accountants. However, a worker doesn't have to be a highfalutin' doctor or lawyer to be an IC. A person you hire to paint your office or fix your computer can also be in business for himself or herself and qualify as an IC.

1. Right of Control Test

Very often, it will be perfectly obvious whether someone you hire is running his or her own business or is an employee.

EXAMPLE 1: Bill completes the conception of his mousetrap invention and hires Tom to build a prototype. Tom runs his own company with two employees, and its own workshop and equipment. Tom offers his prototyping services to the

general public and typically performs services for numerous customers at the same time. Tom pays his own taxes and earns a profit if business is good, but may incur a loss if it is bad. Tom is obviously an independent businessperson.

EXAMPLE 2: Andrea hires Sammy as a lab assistant to help her develop a synthetic fuel invention. Sammy works full-time for Andrea at her lab. Andrea provides Sammy with all the equipment he uses and carefully supervises his work. Sammy is paid a guaranteed weekly salary that he will earn regardless of whether Andrea's invention is successful or not. Sammy is clearly not in business for himself. He is an employee.

In some cases, however, it can be difficult to say for certain whether a worker is or is not in business. This can be especially hard where workers perform specialized services by themselves—that is, without the help of assistants.

EXAMPLE: Ken hires Mike, a computer consultant, to create custom software to test his invention. Mike has no employees, and performs all the work for Ken personally. He ends up spending several months working full-time on the project. It's difficult to say for sure that Mike was in business for himself while he worked for Ken.

To decide whether a worker is an independent contractor or an employee, the IRS and courts assess the degree of control the hiring party has over the worker. An independent contractor maintains personal control over the way he or she does the work contracted for, including the details of when, where and how the work is done. The hiring party's control is limited to accepting or rejecting the final result of the independent contractor's work. An independent contractor is just that—independent.

To help determine whether a worker is an employee or independent contractor, the IRS has developed a set of factors it uses to measure how much control the hiring firm has over the worker. These factors are an attempt by the IRS to synthesize the results of court decisions on who is and is not an independent contractor. They are intended to serve as flexible guidelines for IRS auditors, not as a strict series of tests. Not all the factors may apply to a given worker, and some may be more important than others. The factors are summarized in the chart shown below.

2. Eight Tips for Dealing With ICs

Here are eight things you can do to ensure that workers you treat as ICs really qualify as such:

- **Sign a written contract before the work begins.** The contract should specify the work to be performed and make it clear that the worker is an independent contractor.
- **Don't provide ongoing instructions or training.** If the IC needs special training, he or she should procure and pay for it.

- **Don't supervise the IC or establish working hours.** It's up to the IC to control when and how to accomplish the job.
- **Don't require formal written reports.** An occasional phone call inquiring into the work's progress is acceptable, but requiring regular written status reports indicates the worker is an employee. However, contracts for specific projects can (and should) have performance benchmarks.
- **Don't ever fire an IC.** Instead, terminate the contract if he or she fails to meet the specifications or standards set forth in it.
- **Don't ever refer to an IC as an "employee" (either verbally or in writing).**
- **Set up a separate vendor file for each IC you hire.** Keep in this file the IC's contract, invoices, copies of 1099 forms and any other information that shows the worker is operating an independent business. This may include the IC's business card and stationery, and evidence that the IC has workers' compensation insurance coverage for employees.
- **Don't pay ICs like you pay employees.** Rather, require all ICs to submit invoices, which are paid at the same time you pay other outside vendors, such as your office supply company.

B. Pros and Cons of Hiring Employees or ICs

Hiring an IC instead of an employee can save you money because you need not provide ICs with office space, equipment, workers'

IRS Control Factors		
	A worker will more likely be considered an IC if you:	**A worker will more likely be considered an employee if you:**
Behavioral Control Factors that show whether a hiring firm has the right to control how a worker performs the specific tasks he or she has been hired to do	• do not give him or her instructions how to work • do not provide training, and • do not evaluate how the worker performs	• provide instructions that the worker must follow about how to work • give the worker detailed training, and • evaluate how the worker does the job (as opposed to evaluating the results of his or her work)
Financial Control Factors showing whether a hiring firm has a right to control a worker's financial life	• has a significant investment in equipment and facilities • pays business or travel expenses himself or herself • markets his or her services to the public • is paid by the job, and • has opportunity for profit or loss	• you provide equipment and facilities free of charge • you reimburse the worker's business or traveling expenses • the worker makes no effort to market his or her services to the public • you pay the worker by the hour or other unit of time, and • the worker has no opportunity for profit or loss—for example, because you pay by the hour and reimburse all expenses
Relationship of the Worker and Hiring Firm Factors showing whether you and the worker believe he or she is an IC or employee	• you don't provide employee benefits such as health insurance • you sign an IC agreement with the worker, and • the worker performs services that are not a part of your regular business activities	• you provide employee benefits • you have no written IC agreement, and • the worker performs services that are part of your core business

compensation insurance or any fringe benefits such as health insurance or vacation. Nor need you withhold any taxes from an IC's pay or pay half of his or her Social Security tax as you do with an employee.

On the other hand, you can't closely supervise an IC or provide him or her with extensive training. Nor can an IC work for you on a permanent ongoing basis like an employee can. Also, you don't have an unrestricted right to fire an IC as you normally do with an employee.

As a general rule, hiring an IC works particularly well where you need specialized expertise for a limited period of time—for example, where you need an expert model maker to prepare a prototype of your invention. You don't want or need to train, supervise or otherwise control such a specialist. On the other hand, if you need long-term help and want to closely supervise what the worker does, hiring an employee is appropriate.

The chart below summarizes the pros and cons of hiring employees and ICs.

Part II. Hiring Employees

Whenever you hire an employee, you should have him or her sign an employment agreement as described below. You will also need to take steps to comply with federal and state employment tax laws.

Thomas A. Watson— The Man Bell Wanted

Thomas A. Watson is undoubtedly the most famous employee who ever worked for an inventor. Leaving school at the age of 14, Watson began work in an electrical shop in Boston, where he met Alexander Graham Bell. He served as Bell's assistant when he invented the telephone in 1877. In one of the most famous stories in inventing history, Bell discovered his telephone invention worked when he spilled some acid on his pants and called out "Come here Watson, I want you." Watson, listening in the next room on Bell's prototype telephone receiver, heard Bell's call and the telephone was born. When the Bell Telephone Company was formed, Watson received a share in the business and became its head of research and technical development. Watson later left Bell and went on to have careers as an actor, lecturer and successful shipbuilder. He died in 1934.

Thomas A. Watson
Alexander Graham Bell's assistant

Pros and Cons of Hiring Employees and ICs

There are advantages and disadvantages to hiring employees and ICs.

Hiring Employees

Pros	Cons
You can closely supervise employees.	You must pay federal and state payroll taxes for them.
You can give employees extensive training.	You must usually provide them with workers' compensation coverage.
You automatically own any intellectual property employees create on the job.	You must provide them with office space and equipment.
You don't need to worry about government auditors claiming you misclassified employees.	You ordinarily provide them with employee benefits such as vacations and sick leave.
Employees can't sue you for damages if they are injured on the job, provided you have workers' compensation insurance.	You're liable for their actions.
Employees can generally be fired at any time.	You can be sued for labor law violations.

Hiring ICs

Pros	Cons
You don't have to pay federal and state payroll taxes for ICs.	You risk exposure to audits by the IRS and other agencies.
You don't have to provide workers' compensation insurance for ICs.	You can't closely supervise or train them.
You don't have to provide office space or equipment for ICs.	ICs usually can't be terminated unless they violate their contract.
You don't have to provide employee benefits to ICs.	ICs can sue you for damages if they are injured on the job.
You're generally not liable for ICs' actions.	You may lose copyright ownership if you don't obtain an assignment of rights.
You face reduced exposure to lawsuits for labor law violations.	ICs may usually work for your competitors as well as you.

C. Drafting an Employment Agreement

It is essential that you enter into written agreements with any employees you hire to help in your invention business. Using employment agreements helps accomplish the following:

- to make clear to employees that they are in a confidential relationship with you and have a duty not to disclose confidential information to outsiders without your permission
- to identify as specifically as possible what information you regard as confidential
- to assign to you, in advance, all proprietary rights (patent, trade secret and copyright) the employee may have in his or her work product.

Be sure to give a new employee the agreement before he or she starts work—preferably, at the same time a job offer is made. This way, the hiree can take the agreement home and study it and even have his or her lawyer look at it. Don't wait until the employee has actually started work; the employee may feel he or she has no choice but to sign the agreement as written. If you later need to enforce the agreement, a court may conclude that it was not a freely bargained contract and refuse to enforce it.

That said, if you've already hired an employee and now want him or her to sign an employment agreement, it's not too late to do so. To ensure that the agreement will be legally enforceable, give the employee something of value in return for agreeing to abide by the agreement—perhaps a bonus, some time off or some other consideration. The fact that you pay the employee a salary and benefits may not, by itself, be sufficient, because the employee was receiving these before you asked him or her to sign the agreement. (See below.)

You can use the following employment agreement with any employee you hire. The agreement can be simplified if you hire nontechnical employees who will not help you develop your invention.

 The full text of the following agreement is on the CD-ROM forms disk at the back of this book.

In the introductory paragraph, select Alternative 1 if a new employee will be signing the agreement, and fill in your name.

Select Alternative 2 if the agreement is with a current employee. Fill in your name. To ensure that the agreement will be a legally binding contract, give the employee a small cash bonus, a pay raise that he wouldn't have gotten anyway, stock options, vacation time or some other remuneration. This costs you something, but it ensures that the agreement will be enforceable. (It will also encourage the employee to sign the agreement.) The value of what you give a continuing employee for signing an employment agreement doesn't have to be enormous. But the greater the amount, the clearer it will be that there was a benefit to the employee and a binding contract was thereby created. Specify here the compensation to be provided.

1. Employer's Confidential Information

As discussed in Chapter 10, an employee who learns your confidential information (also called trade secrets) as a result of a confidential relationship with his or her employer has a legal duty not to disclose this information to others without the employer's permission. This clause defines your confidential information; the next clause addresses the employee's nondisclosure obligations.

Like all provisions in an employment agreement (or any other contract), this clause must be reasonable. It should not cover everything in the employee's brain. A clause that attempts to do so will likely be unenforceable in court, because it is unreasonable. You don't need to add anything to this clause; it sets out the types of information and material that should be considered to be confidential information.

2. Nondisclosure of Trade Secrets

This clause bars the employee from making unauthorized disclosures of your confidential information. There are several good reasons for an employer to include a nondisclosure clause in employment agreements. As discussed in Chapter 13, information qualifies as a trade secret only if reasonable precautions are taken to keep it confidential. The use of nondisclosure clauses (or separate nondisclosure agreements) is perhaps the single most important reasonable precaution. Confidential information may not be deemed to be a trade secret where an employer does not use such agreements.

Including a nondisclosure clause in an employment agreement makes clear to the employee that he has a duty to protect the employer's trade secrets. It also shows that you are serious about keeping trade secrets secret.

This clause clearly defines employee obligations regarding trade secrets, which will also make it easier to obtain relief in court if an employee or ex-employee makes unauthorized disclosures.

However, as explained in this clause, the employee's nondisclosure obligation should not extend to information the employee knew before coming to work for the you, information he learns from sources outside your employ and information that is not

Employment Agreement

Alternative 1 (for use with new employee):
In consideration of the commencement of my employment with [*your name*] (the "Employer") and the compensation hereafter paid to me, I agree as follows:

Alternative 2 (for use with continuing employee):
In consideration of my continued employment with [*your name*] (the "Employer") and also in consideration of [*choose one*: the amount of $[*amount*] or [*list other form of consideration*], the receipt and sufficiency of which I hereby acknowledge, I agree as follows:

1. Employer's Confidential Information

I understand that in performance of my job duties with Employer I will be exposed to Employer's confidential information. "Confidential information" means information or material that is commercially valuable to Employer and not generally known in the industry, including:

(a) information concerning Employer's inventions, patents, processes, research projects, product development, test results and know-how;

(b) information concerning Employer's business, including business and marketing plans, business strategies and financial information; and

(c) any other information not generally known to the public which, if misused or disclosed, could reasonably be expected to adversely affect Employer's business.

2. Nondisclosure of Trade Secrets

I will keep Employer's confidential information, whether or not prepared or developed by me, in the strictest confidence. I will not use or disclose such secrets to others without Employer's written consent, except when necessary to perform my job. However, I shall have no obligation to treat as confidential any information which:

(a) was in my possession or known to me, without an obligation to keep it confidential, before such information was disclosed to me by Employer;

(b) is or becomes public knowledge through a source other than me and through no fault of mine; or

confidential because it is public knowledge (so long as the employee didn't make it public).

3. Confidential Information of Others

It's a good idea to remind new employees that they have a duty not to disclose to the employer trade secrets learned from prior employers or others. Employers who take advantage of such information can easily end up being sued.

4. No Conflicting Obligations

Many technical employees have previously signed employment agreements or consulting agreements that may conflict with their ability to work for you—for example, because they contain noncompetition restrictions or restrictions on disclosure of trade secrets that may touch upon the work the employee will perform for you. To make sure this isn't a problem, the agreement asks the employee to list any such prior agreements. If there are any, obtain copies and review them to make sure the employee isn't in any way barred from working for you.

5. Return of Materials

It's important that employees understand their obligation to return all materials containing trade secrets when they leave the company. They should be reminded of this obligation in their employment agreement and before they leave.

6. Confidentiality Obligation Survives Employment

It's important to make clear that the employee's duty not to disclose her employer's confidential information does not end when she leaves the company, but continues for as long as the material remains a trade secret.

7. Disclosure of Developments

The employee must be required to disclose promptly to the employer any and all work-related inventions and other developments she creates. This clause complies with state restrictions on invention assignments discussed in the "Assignment of Developments" clause, below.

In the state of Washington you must include the paragraph on disk that states that Employer will maintain a written record of all such disclosures for at least five years.

8. Assignment of Developments

This is the most important part of the employment agreement. It requires the employee to assign (transfer) any rights he or she might have in the work performed on your behalf. Without such an assignment, you might not end up owning what you pay the employee to create. Or, at the very least, you may be subject to a costly and bitter legal fight over ownership rights. (See Chapter 11.)

If an assignment is executed long after an employee is hired, the employer should give the continuing employee a raise or other

(c) is or becomes lawfully available to me from a source other than Employer.

3. Confidential Information of Others

I will not disclose to Employer, use in Employer's business, or cause Employer to use, any information or material that is a trade secret or confidential information of others. My performance of this Agreement will not breach any agreement to keep in confidence proprietary information acquired by me prior to my employment by Employer.

4. No Conflicting Obligations

I have no other current or prior agreements, relationships or commitments that conflict with this Agreement or with my relationship other than the following: [*Specify; if none, so state*]

5. Return of Materials

When my employment with Employer ends, for whatever reason, I will promptly deliver to Employer all originals and copies of all documents, records, media and other materials containing any of Employer's confidential information. I will also return to Employer all equipment, files, software programs and other personal property belonging to Employer.

6. Confidentiality Obligation Survives Employment

I understand that my obligation to maintain the confidentiality and security of Employer's confidential information remains with me even after my employment with Employer ends and continues for so long as such confidential information remains a trade secret.

7. Disclosure of Developments

While I am employed by Employer, I will promptly inform Employer of the full details of all my inventions, discoveries, improvements, innovations and ideas (collectively called "Developments")—whether or not patentable, copyrightable or otherwise protectible—that I conceive, complete or reduce to practice (whether jointly or with others) and which:

compensation to ensure that the assignment is enforceable.

9. Post-Employment Assignment

This provision is optional. Many high-tech employers require inventive employees to agree to assign patentable works they create for some time after the employment relationship ends. This is to prevent employees from developing inventions and then quitting and patenting them themselves without telling their former employers about it.

Such post-employment assignments are enforceable in most states if they are reasonable. To be reasonable, a post-employment assignment must:

- be for a limited time—probably no more than six months to one year after employment ends, and
- apply only to inventions conceived as a result of work done for the former employer.

If you're concerned about an employee hiding an invention from you, include this provision. However, provisions such as these are not looked on favorably by prospective employees.

10. Notice Pursuant to State Law

To protect employees, several states impose restrictions on the permissible scope of assignments of employee-created inventions. These restrictions apply only to "inventions" an employee creates—that is, creations for which a patent is sought. The restrictions

apply only to employees, not to independent contractors.

The California restrictions are typical. Under California law, an employee cannot be required to assign any of his or her rights in an invention he or she develops "entirely on his or her own time without using the employer's equipment, supplies, facilities, or trade secret information" unless:

- when the invention was conceived or "reduced to practice" (actually created or a patent application filed) it related to the employer's business or actual or "demonstrably anticipated" research or development, or
- the invention resulted from any work performed by the employee for the employer (California Labor Code, § 2870).

The following states impose similar restrictions:

- Delaware (Delaware Code Annotated, Title 19, § 805)
- Illinois (Illinois Compiled Statutes, Chapter 765, § 1060/2)
- Kansas (Kansas Statutes Annotated, Chapter 44, § 130)
- Minnesota (Minnesota Statutes Annotated, Section 181.78)
- North Carolina (North Carolina General Statutes, §§ 66-57.1, 66-57.2)
- Utah (Utah Code Annotated, §§ 34-39-2, 34-39-3), and
- Washington (Washington Revised Code Annotated, §§ 49.44.140, 49.44.150).

If the employee will work in California, Illinois, Kansas, Minnesota or Washington State, state law requires that the employee be

(a) relate to Employer's present or prospective business, or actual or demonstrably anticipated research and development; or

(b) result from any work I do using any equipment, facilities, materials, trade secrets or personnel of Employer; or

(c) result from or are suggested by any work that I may do for Employer.

In Washington state, add the following:
"Employer will maintain a written record of all such disclosures for at least five years."

8. Assignment of Developments

I hereby assign to Employer or Employer's designee, my entire right, title and interest in all of the following, that I conceive or make (whether alone or with others) while employed by Employer:

(a) all Developments;

(b) all patent applications filed and patents granted on any Developments, including those in foreign countries; and

(c) all copyright, trade secret and trademark rights in Developments.

9. Post-Employment Assignment

I will disclose to Employer any and all computer programs, discoveries actually made, or copyright registration or patent applications filed, within [*number of months; six to 12 is recommended*] months after my employment with Employer ends. I hereby assign to Employer my entire right, title and interest in such programs, inventions, improvements and discoveries, whether made individually or jointly, which relate to the subject matter of my employment with Employer during the [*number of months; six to 12 is recommended*] month period immediately preceding the termination of my employment.

10. Notice Pursuant to State Law

Alternative 1 (California employees):
I understand that this Agreement does not apply to any invention that qualifies fully under the provisions of California Labor Code § 2870, the text of which is attached as

given written notice of state law restrictions on an employer's right to obtain an assignment of employee inventions. If this is not done, the assignment might be unenforceable. If the employee will work in any other state, delete this entire clause. Otherwise, include the appropriate state notice on the disk that states that an Exhibit A is attached, which provides written notice of state assignment restrictions. The applicable Exhibit A, setting forth the text of the state law, must also be attached to the Agreement. (This is covered below.)

11. Signing Documents

This clause simply requires the employee to execute any documents necessary to effect the assignment of intellectual property rights. If the employee is unable to do so because of sickness or for any reason, the employer is appointed the employee's attorney-in-fact and may execute such documents on the employee's behalf.

12. Prior Developments

In addition to an assignment provision, many employment agreements contain a provision requiring the employee to list all inventions he or she conceived or patented before starting work. The employee is then required to waive any right to claim that any other invention was created before his or her employment. This eliminates one important defense an employee may have against a pre-invention assignment: that the invention was conceived before he or she began working for the

company and is therefore not covered by the assignment agreement. It's very much in your interest, as the employer, to include this provision in your Agreement.

13. Enforcement

If the employee breaches, or threatens to breach the Agreement, this clause gives the employer the automatic right to an injunction to prevent such a breach. This clause does not preclude the employer's right to seek additional remedies.

14. Mediation and Arbitration

This provision is optional. As you doubtless know, court litigation can be very expensive. To avoid these costs, alternative forms of dispute resolution have been developed that don't involve going to court. These include mediation and arbitration.

Under this clause, you and the employee first try to resolve your dispute through mediation. Mediation, an increasingly popular alternative to full-blown litigation, works like this: You and the employee agree on a neutral third person to try to help you settle your dispute. The mediator has no power to impose a decision, only to try to help you arrive at one. In other words, unless both parties agree with the resolution, there is no resolution.

Insert the place where the mediation meeting will occur. You'll usually want it in the city or county where your office is located. You don't want to have to travel a long distance to attend a mediation.

Exhibit A. This section shall serve as written notice to me as required by California Labor Code § 2872.

Alternative 2 (Illinois employees):
I understand that this Agreement does not apply to any invention that qualifies fully under the provisions of Illinois Revised Statutes, Chapter 140, § 302(1) and (2), the text of which is attached as Exhibit A. This section shall serve as written notice to me as required by Illinois Revised Statutes, Chapter 140, § 302(3).

Alternative 3 (Kansas employees):
I understand that this Agreement does not apply to any invention that qualifies fully under the provisions of Kansas Statutes Annotated §§ 44-130(a) and (b), the text of which is attached as Exhibit A. This section shall serve as written notice to me as required by Kansas Statutes Annotated § 44-130(c).

Alternative 4 (Minnesota employees):
I understand that this Agreement does not apply to any invention that qualifies fully under the provisions of Minnesota Statutes Annotated §§ 181.78(1) and (2), the text of which is attached as Exhibit A. This section shall serve as written notice to me as required by Minnesota Statutes Annotated § 181.78(3).

Alternative 5 (Washington state employees):
I understand that this Agreement does not apply to any invention that qualifies fully under the provisions of Washington Revised Code Annotated § 49.44.140(1), the text of which is attached as Exhibit A. This section shall serve as written notice to me as required by Washington Revised Code Annotated § 49.44.140(3).

11. Signing Documents

Both while employed by Employer and afterwards, I agree to execute and aid in the preparation of any papers that Employer may consider necessary or helpful to obtain or maintain any patents, copyrights, trademarks or other proprietary rights at no charge to Employer, but at its expense.

12. Prior Developments

As a matter of record, I have listed below all prior developments [*if many, add*: "relevant to the subject matter of my employment by Employer"] ("Prior Developments")

If mediation doesn't work, you must submit the dispute to binding arbitration. Arbitration is usually like an informal court trial without a jury, but involves arbitrators instead of judges.

You and the employee can agree on anyone to serve as the arbitrator. Arbitrators are often retired judges, lawyers or persons with special expertise in the field involved. Businesses often use private dispute resolution services that maintain a roster of arbitrators. The best known of these is the American Arbitration Association, which has offices in most major cities.

You may be represented by a lawyer in the arbitration, but it's not required. The arbitrator's decision is final and binding—that is, you can't go to court and try the dispute again if you don't like the arbitrator's decision, except in unusual cases where the arbitrator was guilty of fraud, misconduct or bias.

By using this provision, then, you're giving up your right to go to court. The advantage is that arbitration is usually much cheaper and faster than court litigation.

This provision states that the arbitrator's award can be converted into a court judgment. This means that if the losing side doesn't pay the money required by the award, the other party can easily obtain a judgment and enforce it like any other court judgment—for example, have the losing side's bank accounts and property seized to pay the amount due.

The provision leaves it up to the arbitrator to decide who should pay the costs and fees associated with the arbitration.

You must insert the place where the arbitration hearing will occur. You'll usually want it in the city or county where your office is located. You don't want to have to travel a long distance to attend an arbitration.

For a detailed discussion of mediation and arbitration, refer to *Mediate Your Dispute*, by Peter Lovenheim (Nolo Press).

15. General Provisions

These provisions are customarily lumped together at the end of an agreement. This does not mean they are unimportant.

(a) This clause provides that the Employee's rights and duties under the Agreement continue even after the employee no longer works for you and also apply to the employee's heirs. This means, for example, that the employee's confidentiality obligation continues after he or she leaves your employer. Likewise, the Agreement will bind your successors and assigns—for example, someone who purchases or inherits your business.

(b) This clause specifies which state law governs the contract. This should be the state in which you do business.

(c) This clause helps ensure that the Agreement remains in effect, even if part of it is found invalid by a court.

(d) This clause helps make it clear to a court or arbitrator that the parties intended the contract to be their final agreement. A clause such as this helps avoid claims that promises not contained in the written contract were made and broken.

that have been conceived or reduced to practice or learned by me, alone or jointly with others, before my employment with Employer, which I desire to remove from the operation of this Agreement. Any inventions or discoveries not so listed shall be deemed made or conceived during my employment. This provision does not apply to inventions I patented before the start of my employment.

The Prior Developments consist of: [*List all prior developments or "None."*]

13. Enforcement

I agree that in the event of a breach or threatened breach of this Agreement, money damages would be an inadequate remedy and extremely difficult to measure. I agree, therefore, that Employer shall be entitled to an injunction to restrain me from such breach or threatened breach. Nothing in this Agreement shall be construed as preventing Employer from pursuing any remedy at law or in equity for any breach or threatened breach.

14. Mediation and Arbitration

If a dispute arises under this Agreement, the parties agree to first try to resolve it with the help of a mutually agreed upon mediator in the following location [*list city or county where mediation will occur*]. Any costs and fees other than attorney fees associated with the mediation shall be shared equally by the parties.

If it proves impossible to arrive at a mutually satisfactory solution through mediation, the parties agree to submit the dispute to binding arbitration at the following location [*list city or county where arbitration will occur*] under the rules of the American Arbitration Association. Judgment upon the award rendered by the arbitrator may be entered in any court with jurisdiction to do so.

15. General Provisions

(a) Successors: The rights and obligations under this Agreement shall survive the termination of Employee's service to Employer in any capacity and shall inure to the benefit of and shall be binding upon: (1) Employee's heirs and personal representatives, and

(2) Employer's successors and assigns.

(e) This clause, which is very important, states that any changes to the Agreement must be in writing and agreed to by both parties to be effective. This provision protects both parties; reducing all modifications to writing lessens the possibility of misunderstandings. In addition, oral modifications are not legally binding.

(f) This clause permits you to assign your rights under the Agreement. An "assignment" is the process by which rights or benefits under a contract are transferred to someone else. For example, you might assign the right to receive the benefit of the employee's services to someone else. This might be useful, for example, if you sell your business. In contrast, the employee is barred from making assignments without your prior written consent.

16. Signatures

The end of the main body of the Agreement should contain spaces for the employee to sign. The employee should sign two copies and be allowed to keep one.

It's not necessary that the employer sign this Agreement, but you can sign as a witness to the employee's signature. For information on who should sign when representing a partnership, LLC or corporation, see sidebar, "Business Signatures," below.

Business Signatures

Partnerships: If a joint owner is a partnership, a general partner should sign on the partnership's behalf. Only one partner needs to sign. The signature block for the partnership should state the partnership's name and the name and title of the person signing on the partnership's behalf—for example:

> The Argus Partnership
> A Michigan Partnership
> By: _Randy Argus_
> Randy Argus, a General Partner

Corporations: If a joint owner is a corporation, the agreement must be signed by someone who has authority to sign contracts on the corporation's behalf. The corporation's president or chief executive officer (CEO) is presumed to have this authority. The signature block for a corporation should state the name of the corporation and indicate by name and title, the person signing on the corporation's behalf—for example:

> Kiddie Krafts, Inc.
> A California Corporation
> By: _Susan Ericson_
> Susan Ericson, President

Limited liability companies: If a joint owner is a limited liability company (LLC), it must be signed by the owner or owners (called "members") or by the manager of the LLC. For example:

> Great Inventions, LLC
> A California Limited Liability Company
> By: _Amy Smart_
> Amy Smart, Member

(b) Governing Law: This Agreement shall be construed and enforced in accordance with the laws of the State of _____.

(c) Severability: If any provision of this Agreement is determined to be invalid or unenforceable, the remainder shall be unaffected and shall be enforceable against Employer and Employee.

(d) Entire Agreement: This Agreement supersedes and replaces all former agreements or understandings, oral or written, between Employer and Employee, except for prior confidentiality agreements Employee has signed relating to information not covered by this Agreement.

(e) Modification: This Agreement may not be modified except by a writing signed both by both Employer and Employee.

(f) Assignment: This Agreement may be assigned by Employer. Employee may not assign any rights or delegate any duties under this Agreement without Employer's prior written approval.

16. Signatures

I have carefully read and considered all provisions of this Agreement and agree that all of the restrictions set forth are fair and reasonably required to protect the Employer's interests. I acknowledge that I have received a copy of this Agreement as signed by me.

_____   _____
Employer's Signature   Employee Signature

_____   _____
Date   Date

17. Exhibit A

To protect employees, several states impose restrictions on the permissible scope of assignments of employee-created inventions. If the employee will work in California, Illinois, Kansas, Minnesota or Washington State, include the appropriate notice of state law provided on the disk. Delete all state law notices that don't apply.

D. Tax Concerns When Hiring Employees

Whenever you hire an employee, you become an unpaid tax collector for the government. You are required to withhold and pay both federal and state taxes for the worker. These taxes are called payroll taxes or employment taxes.

You must also satisfy these requirements if you incorporate your inventing business and continue to actively work in it. In this event, you will be an employee of your corporation.

1. Federal Taxes

The IRS regulates federal payroll taxes, which include:

- Social Security and Medicare taxes—also known as FICA
- unemployment taxes—also known as FUTA, and
- income taxes—also known as FITW.

It's important to withhold and pay these taxes on time and in the proper amount because IRS penalties for failure to do so are substantial.

 IRS Circular E, *Employer's Tax Guide*, provides detailed information on federal payroll taxes. It is an outstanding resource that you should have if you hire employees. You can get a free copy by calling the IRS at 800-TAX-FORM, by calling or visiting your local IRS office or by downloading it from the IRS website at www.irs.gov.

a. FICA

FICA is an acronym for Federal Income Contributions Act, the law requiring employers and employees to pay Social Security and Medicare taxes. The IRS imposes FICA taxes on both employers and employees. If you hire an employee, you must collect and remit his or her part of the taxes by withholding it from paycheck amounts and also pay a matching amount yourself.

Employers and employees are each required to pay a tax equal to 7.65% of the employee's annual wages up to the Social Security tax ceiling, which is adjusted annually for inflation. You can find the Social Security tax ceiling for the current year in IRS Circular E.

There is no Social Security tax on the portion of an employee's annual wages that exceed the ceiling. However, the Medicare tax marches on: Both you and the employee must pay the 1.45% Medicare tax on any wages over the ceiling.

b. FUTA

FUTA is an acronym for the Federal Unemployment Tax Act; the law establishes federal unemployment taxes. Most employers must pay both state and federal unemployment taxes. But even if you're exempt from the state tax, you may still have to pay the federal tax. Employers alone are responsible for FUTA. You may not collect or deduct it from employees' wages.

You must pay FUTA taxes if:

- you pay $1,500 or more to employees during any calendar quarter—that is, any three-month period beginning with January, April, July or October, or
- you had one or more employees for at least some part of a day in any 20 or more different weeks during the year. The weeks don't have to be consecutive, nor does it have to be the same employee each week.

Technically, the FUTA tax rate is 6.2%, but in practice, you rarely pay this much. You are given a credit of 5.4% if you pay the applicable state unemployment tax in full and on time. This means that the actual FUTA tax rate is usually 0.8%. In 2005, the FUTA tax was assessed on the first $7,000 of an employee's annual wages. The FUTA tax, then, usually is $56 per year per employee.

c. FITW

FITW is an acronym for federal income tax withholding. When you hire an employee, you're not only a tax collector for the government, but you are a manager of sorts of your employee's income. The IRS fears that employees will not save enough from their wages for their tax bill on April 15 and wants, of course, to speed up tax collections. So the IRS tells you, the employer, not to pay the employees

their entire wages but to send part of the money to the IRS.

You must calculate and withhold federal income taxes from all your employees' paychecks. You normally deposit the funds in a bank, which transmits the money to the IRS. Employees are solely responsible for paying federal income taxes. Your only responsibility is to withhold the funds and remit them to the government.

You must ask each employee you hire to fill out IRS Form W-4, Employee's Withholding Allowance Certificate. The information on this form is used to help determine how much tax must be withheld from the employee's pay.

By January 31 of each year, you must give each employee you hired the previous year, a copy of IRS Form W-2, Wage and Tax Statement, showing how much he or she was paid and how much tax was withheld for the year. You must also send copies to the Social Security Administration.

You can obtain copies of these forms by calling the IRS at 800-TAX-FORM, by visiting your local IRS office or by downloading them from the IRS Internet site at www.irs.gov.

 For detailed information on FITW, see IRS Publication 505, *Tax Withholding and Estimated Tax*. You can obtain a copy by calling the IRS at 800-TAX-FORM, by visiting your local IRS office or from the IRS Internet site (www.irs.gov).

d. Paying payroll taxes

You pay FICA, FUTA and FITW either electronically or by making federal tax deposits at specified banks. The IRS will tell you how often you must make your payroll tax deposits. The frequency depends on the total taxes you pay. If you pay by mail, you must submit an IRS Federal Tax Deposit coupon (Form 8109-B) with each payroll tax payment. You must also report these payments to the IRS on Form 941, Employer's Quarterly Federal Tax Return, after each calendar quarter that you have employees. Form 941 shows how many employees you had, how much they were paid and the amount of FICA and income tax withheld.

Once each year you must also file IRS Form 940, Employer's Annual Federal Unemployment Tax Return or the simpler Form 940-EZ. This form shows the IRS how much federal unemployment tax you owe.

Figuring out how much to withhold, doing the necessary record keeping and filling out the required forms can be complicated. If you have a computer, accounting programs such as *QuickBooks* can help with all the calculations and print out your employees' checks and IRS forms.

You can also hire a bookkeeper or payroll tax service to do the work. Payroll tax services are usually not expensive, especially if you only have one or two employees.

e. Rules for family members

If you hire your child, spouse or parent as an employee in your inventing business, you may not have to pay FICA and FUTA taxes.

- **Employing your child.** If you're a sole proprietor or in a partnership with your spouse as your only partner, you need not pay FICA taxes for services performed by your child who is under 18 years old. The same rule applies to FUTA taxes so long as your child is under 21.

- **Employing your spouse.** If you employ your spouse, her salary is subject to FICA taxes and federal income tax withholding, but not to FUTA taxes. But this rule does not apply—and FICA, FUTA and FITW must all be paid—if your spouse works for: (1) a corporation, even if you control it, or (2) a partnership, even if your spouse is a partner along with you.

- **Employing a parent.** The wages of a parent you employ are subject to income tax withholding and FICA taxes.

2. State Payroll Taxes

Employers in all states are required to pay and withhold state payroll taxes for employees. These taxes include:

- state unemployment compensation taxes in all states
- state income tax withholding in most states, and
- state disability taxes in a few states.

a. Unemployment compensation

Federal law requires that all states provide most types of employees with unemployment compensation, also called UC, or unemployment insurance.

Employers are required to contribute to a state unemployment insurance fund. Employees make no contributions, except in Alaska, New Jersey, Pennsylvania and Rhode Island where employers must withhold small employee contributions from employees' paychecks. An employee who is laid off or fired for other than serious misconduct is entitled to receive unemployment benefits from the state fund. You need not provide unemployment for ICs.

If your payroll is very small—below $1,500 per calendar quarter—you probably won't have to pay UC taxes. In most states, you must pay state UC taxes for employees if you're paying federal UC taxes, also called FUTA taxes. However, some states have more strict requirements. Contact your state labor department for the exact service and payroll amounts.

b. State income tax withholding

All states except Alaska, Florida, Nevada, South Dakota, Texas, Washington and Wyoming have income taxation. If you're in a state that imposes state income taxes, you must withhold the applicable tax from your employees' paychecks and pay it to the state taxing authority. No state income tax withholding is required for workers who qualify as ICs.

It's easy to determine whether you need to withhold state income taxes for a worker: If you are withholding federal income taxes, then you must withhold state income taxes as well. Each state has its own income tax withholding forms and procedures. Contact your state tax department for information.

c. State disability insurance

In a few states, employers must withhold disability insurance premiums from their

employees' pay and remit them to the state disability insurance agency. The states with disability insurance are: California, Hawaii, New Jersey, New York and Rhode Island. Employers must also make their own disability insurance contributions on their employees' behalf in Hawaii, New Jersey and New York. Contact your state disability insurance agency for more information.

d. Workers' compensation insurance

Subject to some important exceptions, employers in all states must provide their employees with workers' compensation insurance to cover work-related injuries. Workers' com-

Charles Goodyear
Inventor of a process for
vulcanizing rubber

pensation is not a payroll tax. You must purchase a workers' compensation policy from a private insurer or state workers' compensation fund. Contact your state workers' compensation agency for more information.

Virtually all state governments have highly informative websites describing their payroll tax requirements and containing forms you can download. Links to state government websites organized by category can be found at www.businesslaw.gov.

Part III. Hiring Independent Contractors

The government imposes far fewer legal burdens on you when you hire an independent contractor (IC) rather than an employee. However, it's vitally important to have the worker sign an IC agreement. There are also some relatively simple tax requirements you must satisfy.

E.   Drafting an Independent Contractor Agreement

You should use the independent contractor agreement described below whenever you hire an IC who will be (or might be) exposed to any of your trade secrets or develop anything on your behalf that you will want to own. This includes, for example, prototype makers, researchers and technical or marketing consultants. Using such an agreement accomplishes many purposes; among other things, it:

- ensures that you will own the intellectual property rights to anything the contractor creates on your behalf
- helps you safeguard your trade secrets by imposing a duty of confidentiality on the contractor
- avoids disputes about the contractor's performance by providing a written description of the work the contractor will perform, the deadline for performance and the contractor's payment, and
- helps establish that the contractor is an independent contractor, not your employee.

The agreement is self-explanatory, with the following clarifications.

 The full text of the Independent Contractor Agreement is on the CD-ROM forms disk at the back of this book.

When completing the introductory paragraph, avoid referring to an IC as an employee or to yourself as an employer. Initially, it's best to refer to the IC by his or her full name. If an IC is incorporated, use the corporate name, not the IC's own name. For example: "John Smith Incorporated" instead of just "John Smith." If the IC is unincorporated but is doing business under a fictitious business name, use that name.

For the sake of brevity, it is usual to identify yourself and the IC by shorter names in the remainder of the agreement. You can refer to the IC simply as "Contractor" or "Consultant." Refer to yourself initially by your company name and subsequently by a short version of the name or as "Client" or "Firm."

Put the short names in quotes after the full names. Also include the address of the principal place of business of the IC and yourself.

1. Services Performed by Contractor

The agreement should describe, in as much detail as possible, what the contractor is expected to do and when it should be done. Make sure to cover everything the contractor should deliver.

If the project is complex or will take a lot of time to complete, it is often helpful to break down the project into discrete parts or stages—often called phases or "milestones." This makes it easier to monitor the contractor's progress and may aid the contractor in budgeting her time. For example, the contractor's pay could be contingent upon the completion of each milestone. (Payment schedules are covered below, under "Contractor's Payment.")

You can include the description in the main body of the agreement. Or, if it's a lengthy explanation, put it on a separate document labeled "Exhibit A" and attach it to the agreement.

2. Contractor's Payment

There are several ways an IC may be paid; choose the alternative that suits your needs:

Alternative 1: Fixed Fee. The simplest way for an IC to be paid is to pay a fixed fee for the entire project. This way, you know exactly how much the work will cost you and the contractor won't have an incentive to pad the bill by working more hours.

Alternative 2: Installment Payments. Paying an IC a fixed fee for the entire job, rather than an hourly or daily rate, can pose problems for the contractor due to difficulties in accurately estimating how long the job will take. One way to deal with this problem is to break the job down into phases or "milestones" and pay the contractor a fixed fee upon completion of each phase. If you use this approach, you must describe in the agreement what work the contractor must complete to receive each payment.

Alternative 3: Payment by the Hour/Day/ Week/Month. If a fixed fee for the job is impractical, you can pay the IC by the hour, day, week or month. It's generally a good idea to place a cap on the contractor's total compensation. This may be a particularly good idea if you're unsure how reliable or efficient the IC is.

3. Expenses

Select one of the two alternatives. Alternative 1 provides you will not pay any of the contractor's expenses. Alternative 2 provides that you will reimburse only those expenses you agree to in writing in advance.

4. Materials

[Use Alternative 1 if the contractor will furnish all materials to do the work. Use Alternative 2, if you're going to provide the contractor with materials. This may be necessary, for example, if you hire someone to create a prototype of your invention. State as specifically as possible what materials you're going to provide.

Independent Contractor Agreement

This Agreement is between _____ ("Client") with a principal place of business at ___*[address]*_____ and _____ ("Contractor") with a principal place of business at _____.

Alternative 1 (Services described in agreement):

Contractor agrees to perform the following services for Client: [*Describe services consultant will perform, including any agreed-upon work schedule*]. The services shall be completed by the following date: _____.

Alternative 2 (Services described in attachment):

Contractor agrees to perform the services described in Exhibit A, which is attached to and made part of this Agreement. The services shall be completed by the following date: _____.

2. Contractor's Payment

Alternative 1 (Fixed fee):

Contractor shall be paid $[*state amount*] upon completion of the work as detailed in Clause 1.

Alternative 2 (Installment payments):

Client shall pay Contractor a fixed fee of $[*total amount*], in [*number of installments*] installments as follows:

(a) $[*first installment amount*] upon completion of the following services: [*describe*].

(b) $[*second installment amount*] upon completion of the following services: [*describe*].

[*The project can be divided into as many phases as desired; add additional installment schedule clauses as needed.*]

(c) $[*final installment amount*] upon completion of all the work to be performed and the services to be rendered in accordance with the schedule set forth in Clause 1 above, and written acceptance by Client.

Alternative 3 (Payment by the hour/day/week/month):
Contractor shall be compensated at the rate of $[*payment rate*] per [*specify "hour," "day," "week" or "month"*]. [**Optional:** "Unless otherwise agreed upon in writing by Client, Client's maximum liability for all services performed during the term of this Agreement shall not exceed $[*maximum amount*]."]

3. Expenses

Alternative 1 (No expenses):
Contractor shall be responsible for all expenses incurred while performing services under this Agreement.

Alternative 2 (Expenses paid if pre-approved):
Contractor will not be reimbursed for any expenses incurred in connection with the performance of services under this Agreement, unless those expenses are approved in advance in writing by Client.

4. Materials

Alternative 1:
Contractor will furnish all materials, tools and equipment used to provide the services required by this Agreement.

Alternative 2:
Client will furnish Contractor with the following materials: _____.

5. Record Keeping
Contractor shall keep detailed records distinguishing between costs and charges for research and experimentation and the costs of labor, materials and installation of any depreciable property. Such costs shall be separately stated on all invoices submitted to Client.

6. Invoices

Contractor shall submit invoices for all services rendered. Client shall pay Contractor within [*choose one: "30," "45," "60"*] days after receipt of each invoice.

5. Record Keeping

This provision requires the contractor to keep separate track of the costs of performing research and the costs for labor, materials and installation of depreciable property—for example, building a prototype or machine for use in your business. This will help you when it comes time to do your taxes. An inventor's costs for pure research performed by an independent contractor can be currently deducted (deducted in one year) under a special tax law provision (IRC § 174). But costs of hiring an IC to build depreciable property—property that lasts more than one year but wears out over time—are often not so easy to currently deduct. That's why it's helpful to keep these two costs separate. (See Chapter 7, Section C.)

6. Invoices

An independent contractor should never be paid weekly, bi-weekly or monthly the way an employee is. Instead, he or she should submit invoices, which should be paid at the same time and in the same manner as you pay other vendors. You need to decide how long after you receive the invoice you will pay the contractor; 30 days is a common period.

7. Worker an Independent Contractor

This clause helps establish that the contractor is an IC, not your employee. But such a clause is not a "magic bullet." Simply signing a piece of paper will not make a worker an independent contractor. The agreement must reflect reality—that is, you must actually not have the right to control the worker (see Section A).

8. Disclosure and Ownership of Developments

This clause requires the contractor to disclose and assign (transfer) to you ownership of anything he or she creates or conceives as a result of working for you. Without such an assignment, you might not own any patentable inventions or trade secrets the contractor develops (see Chapter 11). And, in the absence of an assignment, you definitely won't own any copyrightable works of authorship the Contractor creates. This clause makes such works of authorship "works made for hire," which means you are considered the author for copyright purposes.

9. Confidential Information

In the course of his or her work, the contractor may be exposed to your most valuable trade secrets. It is reasonable, therefore, for you to seek to include a nondisclosure provision in the agreement. This provision states that the contractor may not disclose your trade secrets to others without the your permission.

10. Termination of Agreement

Many contractors and hiring firms want to have the right to terminate their agreements

7. Worker an Independent Contractor

Contractor is an independent contractor, and neither Contractor nor Contractor's staff is, or shall be deemed, Client's employees. In its capacity as an independent contractor, Contractor agrees and represents, and Client agrees, as follows:

(a) Contractor has the sole right to control and direct the means, manner and method by which the services required by this Agreement will be performed.

(b) Client shall not provide insurance coverage of any kind for Contractor or Contractor's staff.

(c) Client shall not withhold from Contractor's compensation any amount that would normally be withheld from an employee's pay.

8. Disclosure and Ownership of Developments

"Developments" means:

- Any work product created by Contractor for Client under this Agreement; and

- All inventions, discoveries, improvements, innovations and ideas that Contractor conceives, completes or reduces to practice (whether jointly or with others) as a result of performing services under this Agreement, and that directly or indirectly relate to Client's present or future anticipated business.

Contractor agrees to promptly disclose all Developments to Client. Contractor hereby assigns to Client its entire right, title and interest, including all patent, copyright, trade secret, trademark and other proprietary rights, in Developments. Contractor acknowledges that all Developments that constitute works of authorship under the Copyright Act shall be works made for hire.

Contractor shall, at no charge to Client, execute and aid in the preparation of any papers that Client may consider necessary or helpful to obtain or maintain—at Client's expense—any patents, copyrights, trademarks or other proprietary rights. Client shall reimburse Contractor for reasonable out-of-pocket expenses incurred under this provision.

for any reason on two weeks' notice. Unfortunately, the IRS considers such an unfettered termination right to be an indicator of an employment relationship (an employee normally can quit or be fired at any time). This clause attempts to reach a compromise between the parties' desire to be able to get out of the agreement and at the same time satisfy the IRS and others that the worker is an independent contractor. Of particular note are:

(a) This paragraph permits either party to terminate the agreement if the other has breached it and failed to remedy the breach within 30 days.

(b) This paragraph permits the client to terminate the agreement only if in the client's "reasonable judgment," the contractor's performance is inadequate or unnecessary. This stops short of giving the client a completely unfettered right to fire the contractor at will.

11. Return of Materials

This clause requires both you and the contractor to return each others' materials at the end of the agreement.

12. Warranties and Representations

A warranty is a promise or statement regarding the quality, quantity, performance or legal title of something being sold. This clause provides that the contractor has the authority to perform as promised. This means, for example, that the contractor is not prevented from working for you because he or she has previously signed a noncompetition agreement for a previous client. The contractor also promises that his or her work product and materials will not infringe on others' copyrights, patents, trade secrets or other intellectual property rights.

13. Indemnification

Indemnification is a fancy legal word that means a promise to repay someone for their losses or damages if a specified event occurs. This clause requires the contractor to indemnify you or your business if someone sues or threatens to sue because the contractor breached any of the warranties made in the agreement. For example, if you hire an IC to create a computer program and the contractor copies code from a third party, the contractor would be required to pay for your legal defense and any damages a court awards if the third party sues for infringement.

14. Mediation and Arbitration

This provision is optional. It is discussed in detail in Section C14 above.

15. Attorney Fees

If you have to sue the contractor in court or bring an arbitration proceeding to enforce the agreement and win, you normally will not be awarded the amount of your attorney fees unless your agreement requires it. Including such an attorney fees provision in the agreement can be in your interest. It can help make filing a lawsuit economically feasible. It will also give the contractor a strong incentive to negotiate with you if you have a good case.

9. Confidential Information

For purposes of this Agreement, "Confidential Information" includes all information or material that has or could have commercial value or other utility in Client's present or future anticipated business. Confidential Information includes, but is not limited to:

- information concerning Client's inventions, patents, patent applications, invention prototypes, processes, research projects, product development, test results and know-how;

- information concerning Client's business, including business and marketing plans, business strategies and financial information; and

- any other information not generally known to the public which, if misused or disclosed, could reasonably be expected to adversely affect Client's present or anticipated business.

Contractor shall hold and maintain Client's Confidential Information in strictest confidence for Client's sole and exclusive benefit. Contractor shall carefully restrict access to Confidential Information to employees, contractors and third parties as is reasonably required and only to persons subject to nondisclosure restrictions at least as protective as those set forth in this Agreement. Contractor shall not, without Client's prior written approval, use for Contractor's own benefit, publish, copy, or otherwise disclose to others or permit the use by others for their benefit or to the detriment of Client, any Confidential Information. Contractor shall return to Client any and all records, notes and other written, printed or tangible materials in its possession pertaining to Confidential Information immediately if Client requests it in writing.

Contractor's obligations not to disclose Confidential Information do not extend to information that is: (a) publicly known at the time of disclosure under this Agreement or subsequently becomes publicly known through no fault of Contractor; (b) discovered or created by Contractor prior to disclosure by Client; (c) otherwise learned by Contractor through legitimate means other than from Client or Client's representatives; or (d) is disclosed by Contractor with Client's prior written approval.

10. Termination of Agreement

(a) Each party has the right to terminate this Agreement if the other party has materially breached any obligation herein and such breach remains uncured for a period of 30 days after notice thereof is sent to the other party.

(b) If at any time after commencement of the services required by this Agreement, Client shall, in its sole reasonable judgment, determine that such services are inadequate, unsatisfactory, no longer needed or substantially not conforming to the descriptions, warranties or representations contained in this Agreement, Client may terminate this Agreement upon [*state notice period—anything from 5 to 30*] days' written notice to Contractor.

11. Return of Materials

Upon termination of this Agreement, each party shall promptly return to the other all data, materials and other property of the other held by it.

12. Warranties and Representations

Contractor warrants that:

- contractor has the authority to enter into this Agreement and to perform all obligations hereunder, and

- all Developments created by Contractor under this Agreement shall not infringe any intellectual property rights or violate any laws.

13. Indemnification

Contractor agrees to indemnify and hold harmless Client against any claims, actions or demands, including without limitation reasonable attorney and accounting fees, alleging or resulting from the breach of the warranties contained in this Agreement. Client shall provide notice to Contractor promptly of any such claim, suit or proceeding and shall assist Contractor, at Contractor's expense, if defending any such claim, suit or proceeding.

14. Mediation and Arbitration

If a dispute arises under this Agreement, the parties agree to first try to resolve it with the help of a mutually agreed upon mediator in the following location [*list city or county where mediation will occur*]. Any costs and fees other than attorney fees associated with the mediation shall be shared equally by the parties.

On the other hand, an attorney fees provision can also work against you. It may help the contractor find an attorney to sue you and make you more anxious to settle. If you think it's more likely you'll violate the agreement than the contractor will, an attorney fees provision is probably not a good idea.

Under this provision, if either person has to sue the other in court or bring an arbitration proceeding to enforce the agreement and wins—that is, becomes the prevailing party—the loser is required to pay the other person's attorney fees and expenses.

16. Entire Agreement; Modifications

"This provision establishes that the agreement is the final version and that any further modification must be in writing."

17. Applicable Law

A contract is ordinarily interpreted according to the law of the place where it is to be performed, or, if the place of performance is not indicated in the agreement, the law of the place where the contract was made.

If you and the IC have offices in the same state, that state's law will apply. This law will determine, for example, how long you have to file a lawsuit if the IC breaks the agreement. But if your offices are in different states, or if the work is done in a different state, you'll need to decide which state's law should govern the agreement. It's best to decide this ahead of time and set forth what state's law will be controlling in your agreement. Failure to

identify which state's law should govern can result in an expensive choice-of-law battle if a dispute with the IC arises.

There is some advantage to having the law of your own state govern, since your local attorney will likely be more familiar with that law. Insert the state whose law will govern in this provision.

18. Notices

When you want to do something important involving the agreement—terminate it, for example—you need to tell the IC about it. This is called giving notice. The following provision gives you several options for providing the IC with notice—by personal delivery, by mail, or by fax or telex followed by a confirming letter.

If you give notice by mail, it is not effective until three days after it's deposited in the mail. For example, if you want to end the agreement on 30 days' notice and mail your notice of termination to the IC, the agreement will not end until 33 days after you mailed the notice.

19. No Partnership

In the course of performing the services, the IC may have to order materials, hire assistants and incur many other expenses. If the IC doesn't pay his or her bills, his or her creditors may want to come after you for payment. If the IC's creditors convince a court that you and the IC are partners, you'll be liable for his or her debts. No writing is required to become a partner in a partnership. All that is

If it proves impossible to arrive at a mutually satisfactory solution through mediation, the parties agree to submit the dispute to binding arbitration at the following location [*list city or county where arbitration will occur*] under the rules of the American Arbitration Association. Judgment upon the award rendered by the arbitrator may be entered in any court with jurisdiction to do so.

15. Attorney Fees

If any legal action is necessary to enforce this Agreement, the prevailing party shall be entitled to reasonable attorney fees, costs and expenses.

16. Entire Agreement; Modifications

This is the entire Agreement between Contractor and Client. It may be modified only by a writing signed by both parties.

17. Applicable Law

This Agreement will be governed by the laws of the State of [*list applicable state*].

18. Notices

Notices: All notices and other communications given in connection with this Agreement shall be in writing and shall be deemed given as follows:

- when delivered personally to the recipient's address as appearing in the introductory paragraph to this Agreement

- three days after being deposited in the United States mail, postage prepaid to the recipient's address as appearing in the introductory paragraph to this Agreement, or

- when sent by fax or electronic mail. Notice is effective upon receipt provided that a duplicate copy of the notice is promptly given by first-class or certified mail, or the recipient delivers a written confirmation of receipt.

Any party may change its address appearing in the introductory paragraph to this Agreement by giving notice of the change in accordance with this paragraph.

required is that two or more people voluntarily intend to carry on a business for profit as co-owners.

This clause makes clear that you *don't* intend to carry on a business with the IC. This ensures that you and the IC will be viewed as separate legal entities, not partners or co-venturers. You need add no information here.

20. Assignment and Delegation

An "assignment" is the process by which rights or benefits under a contract are transferred to someone else. For example, you might assign the right to receive the benefit of the IC's services to someone else. Such a person is called an "assignee." When this occurs, the assignee steps into the your shoes. The IC must now work for the assignee, not for you.

"Delegation" is the flipside of assignment. Instead of transferring benefits under a contract, you transfer the duties. For example, you could transfer the duty to pay the IC to someone else. However, the person delegating duties under a contract usually remains responsible if the person to whom the delegation was made fails to perform.

Unless a contract provides otherwise, you can ordinarily freely assign and delegate it subject to some important legal limitations. One important limitation is that the IC can't delegate his or her duties without your consent if it would decrease the benefits you would receive. Moreover, if the work the IC has agreed to do involves "personal services," the IC cannot delegate it to someone else without your consent. Personal services would include

such things as performance of artistic or creative work, or other work requiring the unique skills of the IC. Personal services also include those of professionals such as lawyers, physicians or architects.

There may be some situations in which you really don't want an IC to delegate his or her contractual duties without your consent. If you have hired a particular IC because of his or her special expertise, creativity, reputation for performance or financial stability, you may not want someone else performing the services, even if the person is technically qualified to do the work. In this event, include the optional provision above to prevent assignment or delegation by the IC under any circumstances without your written approval in advance. Unfortunately, requiring such approval tends to indicate an employment relationship, so don't include it your agreement unless absolutely necessary.

21. Signatures

It is not necessary for the parties to sign the agreement in the same room or on the same day. At least two copies should be signed, with each party retaining one.

F. Tax Reporting for Independent Contractors

When you hire an IC, you don't have to worry about withholding and paying state or federal payroll taxes or filling out lots of government forms. However, if you pay an

19. No Partnership

This Agreement does not create a partnership relationship. Contractor does not have authority to enter into contracts on Client's behalf.

20. Assignment and Delegation

[*Optional:*] Contractor may not assign its rights or delegate its obligations under this Agreement without Client's prior written consent. Client may freely assign its rights and delegate its obligations under this Agreement.

21. Signatures

_____
Contractor's Signature

_____
Client's Signature

_____
Date

_____
Date

unincorporated IC $600 or more during the year for business-related services, you must:

- file IRS Form 1099-MISC telling the IRS how much you paid the worker, and
- obtain the IC's taxpayer identification number.

The filing and ID requirements apply to all ICs you hire who are sole proprietors or partners in partnerships, which is the vast majority of ICs. However, they don't apply to corporations (with the exception of legal or medical corporations). This means that if you hire an incorporated IC, you don't have to file anything with the IRS.

However, it's wise to make sure you have the corporation's full legal name and obtain its federal employer identification number. Without this information, you may not be able to prove to the IRS that the payee was incorporated. An easy way to do this is to have the IC fill out IRS Form W-9, Request for Taxpayer Identification Number, and keep it in your files. This simple form merely requires the corporation to provide its name, address and EIN. (A copy of this form is included on the disk at the back of this book.)

1. $600 Threshold for IC Income Reporting

You need to obtain an unincorporated IC's taxpayer ID number and file a 1099 form with the IRS only if you pay the IC $600 or more during a year for business-related services. It makes no difference whether the sum was one payment for a single job or the total of many small payments for multiple jobs.

EXAMPLE: Andre hires Thomas, a self-employed programmer, to help create a computer program. Andre classifies Thomas as an IC and pays him $2,000 during the year. Thomas is a sole proprietor. Since Andre paid Thomas more than $599 for business-related services, Andre must file Form 1099 with the IRS reporting the payment and obtain Thomas's taxpayer ID number.

In calculating whether the payments made to an IC total $600 or more during a year, you must include payments for parts or materials the IC used in performing the services. For example, if you hire a prototyper, the cost of the prototyper's materials would be included in the tally. However, not all payments you make to ICs are counted towards the $600 threshold.

2. Obtaining Taxpayer Identification Numbers

Some ICs work in the underground economy —that is, they're paid in cash and never pay any taxes or file tax returns. The IRS may not even know they exist. The IRS wants you to help it find these people by supplying the taxpayer ID numbers from all ICs who meet the requirements explained above.

If an IC won't give you his or her number or the IRS informs you that the number the IC gave you is incorrect, the IRS assumes the person isn't going to voluntarily pay taxes. So it requires you to withhold taxes from the compensation you pay the IC and remit them to the IRS. This is called backup withholding. If you fail to backup withhold, the IRS will impose an assessment against you equal to 30% of what you paid the IC.

Backup withholding can be a bookkeeping burden for you. Fortunately, it's very easy to avoid it. Have the IC fill out and sign IRS Form W-9, Request for Taxpayer Identification Number, and retain it in your files. (A copy of this form is included on the disk at the back of this book.) You don't have to file the W-9 with the IRS. This simple form merely requires the IC to list his or her name and address and taxpayer ID number. Partnerships and sole proprietors with employees must have a federal employer identification number (EIN), which they obtain from the IRS. In the case of sole proprietors without employees, the taxpayer ID number is the IC's Social Security number.

3. Filling Out Your Form 1099

One 1099-MISC form must be filed for each IC to whom you paid $600 or more during the year. You can obtain original 1099 forms from the IRS or from office supply stores. You cannot photocopy this form because it contains several pressure-sensitive copies. Each sheet of 1099 forms contains three parts and can be used for three different workers. All your 1099 forms must be submitted together along with one copy of Form 1096, which is a transmittal form—the IRS equivalent of a cover letter. You must obtain an original Form 1096 from the IRS; you cannot submit a photocopy. Obtain these forms by calling the IRS at 800-TAX-FORM or by contacting your local IRS office.

Filling out Form 1099-MISC is easy. Follow this step-by-step approach.

- List your name, address and telephone number in the first box titled Payer's name.
- Enter your taxpayer identification number in the box entitled Payer's Federal identification number.
- The IC you have paid is called the "Recipient" on this form, meaning the person who received the money. You must provide the IC's taxpayer identification number, name and address in the boxes indicated. For sole proprietors, you must list the individual's name first, and then may list a different business name, though this is not required. You may not enter only a business name for a sole proprietor.
- Enter the amount of your payments to the IC in Box 7, entitled "Nonemployee compensation." Be sure to fill in the right box or the Form 1099-MISC will be deemed invalid by the IRS.
- Finally, if you've done backup withholding for an IC who has not provided you with a taxpayer ID number, enter the amount withheld in Box 4.

The 1099-MISC form contains five copies. These must be filed as follows:

- Copy A, the top copy, must be filed with the IRS no later than February 28 of the year after payment was made to the IC. If you don't use the remaining two forms for other ICs, leave them blank. Don't cut the page.
- Copy 1 must be filed with your state taxing authority if your state has a state

income tax. The filing deadline is probably February 28, but check with your state tax department to make sure. Your state may also have a specific transmittal form or cover letter you must obtain.

- Copy B and Copy 2 must be given to the worker no later than January 31 of the year after payment was made.
- Copy C is for you to retain for your files.

All the IRS copies of each 1099 form are filed together with Form 1096, the simple transmittal form. You must add up all the payments reported on all the 1099 forms and list the total in the box indicated on Form 1096. File the forms with the IRS Service Center listed on the reverse of Form 1096.

New Hire Reporting Requirements for Independent Contractors

Several states require that businesses that hire independent contractors file a report with a state agency providing the contractor's contact information and how much the worker is paid. The purpose of these requirements is to aid in the enforcement of child support orders issued against independent contractors. The following states impose reporting requirements for independent contractors:

State	Contact Information
California	(916) 657-0529 (phone); (916) 255-0951 (fax); www.edd.ca.gov/taxrep/txner.htm
Connecticut	(860) 263-6310 (phone); (800) 816-1108 (fax); www.ctnewhires.com Email: ctnewhires@po.state.ct.us
Iowa	(515) 281-5331 (phone); (800) 759-5881 (fax); https://secure.dhs.state.ia.us/epics/
Massachusetts	(617) 626-4154 (phone); (617) 887-5049 (fax); www.cse.state.ma.us/programs/newhire/nh_temp.htm Email: PDUmail@shore.net
New Jersey	(888) 624-6339 (phone); (800) 304-4901 (fax); www.nj-newhire.com E-mail: newjersey@nj-newhire.com
Ohio	(888) 872-1490 (phone); (888) 872-1611 (fax); www.oh-newhire.com E-mail: oh-newhire@policy-studies.com

Chapter 11

Who Owns Your Invention?

A. Patent Ownership 11/2

B. Are You an Inventor? 11/3
   1. Conception 11/3
   2. Reduction to Practice 11/3
   3. Inventor Is Original Owner 11/4

C. Are You a Solo Inventor? 11/4

D. Are You a Joint Inventor? 11/5
   1. Voluntary Joint Inventorship and Ownership 11/6
   2. Involuntary Joint Inventorship and Ownership 11/7
   3. Joint Ownership Agreement 11/10

E. Are You an Employee/Contractor Inventor? 11/13
   1. Pre-Invention Assignment Agreements 11/13
   2. Default Ownership Rules Where There Is No Assignment or State Law 11/19
   3. Special Employment Situations 11/21
   4. Strategies for Dealing with Your Employer 11/24

F. Have You Transferred Your Ownership? 11/26
   1. Licenses Are Not Patent Assignments 11/28
   2. Assigning Patent Ownership to Your Business 11/29
   3. Recording an Assignment 11/29

G. Trade Secret Ownership 11/29
   1. Have You Developed a Trade Secret? 11/30
   2. Are You an Employee/Contractor? 11/30
   3. Have You Transferred Ownership? 11/30

*T*he fact that you've invented something doesn't necessarily mean that you own it. This chapter covers invention ownership rules under the patent and trade secret laws—the primary laws used to protect inventions. Although patents and trade secrets are very different, their ownership rules are essentially the same. Ownership of copyrights, which can be used to protect nonfunctional design elements of inventions, is discussed separately in Chapter 16.

For an overview of the various forms of intellectual property and how to use them to protect your invention, see Chapter 12.

A. Patent Ownership

When a patent is issued by the U.S. Patent and Trademark Office (USPTO), the patent owner obtains the exclusive right to make, use, offer to sell or sell the invention covered by the patent, or to import the invention into the U.S.

Patent ownership rights don't begin until the patent is issued by the USPTO. It usually takes the USPTO one and one/half to three years after the application is filed to issue a patent, sometimes longer. But ownership issues must be sorted out by the time the application is filed—that is, long before a patent issues and any patent rights actually exist.

This is because all people who will own the invention, if and when a patent issues, must join in the patent application. At this point—before a patent issues—these people

own potential, rather than actual, patent rights. Although these are only potential rights, they are subject to the same patent ownership rules that are applied to inventions that have received a patent. Moreover, they can be transferred (sold or licensed) the same as the rights in a patented invention.

As explained below, the inventor is always the initial owner of the potential patent rights in an invention, but this ownership is often transferred to, or shared with, others. To determine who owns a patent, you need to answer the following questions.

- **Are you the inventor?** If you qualify as the inventor, you will be the original owner of an invention. (See Section B.)
- **Are you a solo or joint inventor?** If you are a solo inventor, you will be the only original owner of your invention. If you're a joint inventor, you'll have to share original ownership with your fellow inventor(s). Solo inventorship is covered in Section C. Joint inventorship is discussed in Section D.
- **Are you an employee/contractor inventor?** If you're an employed or independent contractor inventor, you may have a legal obligation to assign your ownership rights to your employer or client, or at least give it the right to use and sell your invention for free. (See Section E.) This is so whether you are a solo or joint inventor.
- **Have you transferred your ownership?** If you're a solo inventor, you may permanently transfer all or part of your ownership through an assignment. (See Section

F.) If you're a joint inventor, you'll need to get the approval of the other joint owners. (See Section D.)

B. Are You an Inventor?

For purposes of obtaining a patent, the inventor is the original owner of an invention. Being an "inventor" for patent purposes is a two-step process:

- first, the inventor must conceive the invention, and
- then the inventor must reduce it to practice.

1. Conception

Conception of an invention occurs when the inventor imagines it so completely that all that is left to do is build and test it. In the words of one court: "Conception is complete only when the idea is so clearly defined in the inventor's mind that only ordinary skill would be necessary to reduce the invention to practice, without extensive research or experimentation." (*Burroughs Wellcome Co. v. Barr Laboratories, Inc.*, 40 F.3d 1223 (Fed. Cir. 1994).)

Giving someone suggestions, advice, or ideas is not enough to be an inventor. Nor does building and testing an invention conceived by another, or filing for a patent, make you an inventor. Conceiving all or part of the invention is what matters.

EXAMPLE: On November 10, 1877, after thinking about the problem of recording speech for several months, Thomas Edison sketched a drawing of a lathe-like device with a hand crank that turned a large, grooved cylinder wrapped in tinfoil mounted on a long shaft. At this moment, Edison's conception of the phonograph was complete. He completely imagined it, so that all that was left to do was to reduce it to practice (see below).

2. Reduction to Practice

Conceiving an invention is a necessary first step in obtaining original patent ownership, but it is not sufficient by itself. In addition to conceiving the invention, the inventor must reduce it to practice. "Reduction to practice" occurs when the inventor:

- builds and tests the invention, or
- files a regular or provisional patent application (see Chapter 14).

You can't conceive an invention and just keep the idea in your head. To obtain patent ownership, you must actually make the invention or file a regular or provisional patent application.

EXAMPLE: Edison gave his drawing of the first phonograph to a machinist to build and the machinist constructed the device from the drawing. Edison and his assistants then tested it for the first time: To everyone's amazement, it worked. The age of sound recording was born. Moreover, by building and testing his invention, Edison had reduced it to practice—this, combined with his conception, made Edison the inventor of the phonograph and entitled him to ownership rights to any patent that resulted from his invention.

Although you must conceive the invention yourself, you need not reduce it to practice yourself. You can hire others to build and test it or file a patent application on your behalf; or, if there is more than one inventor, a co-inventor can do it for you.

What If You're Not an Inventor?

If you don't qualify as an inventor, you can't be the original owner of an invention. But you can obtain ownership from the inventor if:

- you acquire ownership though an assignment (see Section F), or
- someone who works for you as an employee or independent contractor creates an invention (see Section E), or
- you are part owner of a business entity that owns an invention (see Section F2).

3. Inventor Is Original Owner

Inventorship and ownership of an invention are not the same thing. The inventor is the original owner of an invention. The inventor must be listed as such on any patent applica-

tion filed with the USPTO. This is so even though the inventor no longer owns the patent rights in the invention—which is usually the case with employee-inventors.

As the original owner, the inventor has the right to use, make and sell the invention. But the vast majority of inventors are unable to retain these rights because employers and others acquire ownership from them. The people or companies who acquire ownership are not inventors; but, as invention owners, they—not the inventor—have the legal right to make, use or sell the invention.

If you qualify as an inventor, whether you'll be able to keep ownership or have to share it with others or assign it away all depends on how you answer the remaining questions in this chapter.

C. Are You a Solo Inventor?

You're a solo inventor if you conceive your invention completely by yourself, are not anyone's employee and do not perform work for others as an independent contractor (non-employee). If you qualify, you will be the unquestionable sole inventor and original owner of your invention.

EXAMPLE: Kilroy, a retired engineer, spent much of his "golden years" working on inventions. Among them was an interlocked pallet and container system designed to prevent spillage from crates on top of pallets. Kilroy worked for himself and conceived his invention himself.

He obtained two patents for the system. Kilroy was a true independent inventor and was the sole inventor and owner of his invention. (*Kilroy v. Commissioner*, T.C. Memo 1980-489.)

⚠️ **Beware of holdover clauses.** If you've worked in the past as an employee or independent contractor, be sure to read any employment or contractor agreement you signed. Such agreements typically contain provisions requiring you to assign your patent rights to the employer. Moreover, they often include "holdover clauses" providing that you must assign your inventions for some time after your employment ends. So, even if you're self-employed now, an agreement you've signed in the past could come back to haunt you.

D. Are You a Joint Inventor?

Inventions are often jointly invented by two or more people. Joint inventors are also joint owners of their invention. Joint owners (sometimes called co-owners) share in the ownership rights to an invention. If you're a joint owner, your life is more complicated than that of a sole owner. The most important consequences of joint ownership are that:

- Absent an agreement to the contrary, joint owners each own a pro-rata undivided interest in the entire invention— for example, if there are three joint inventors, they each own a one-third interest in the whole invention. Every joint owner must be involved in any action before the USPTO, such as filing a patent application, and they must all join in any patent infringement suit. A patent on a joint invention issued to only one inventor is invalid.

- All joint owners of a patented invention must consent to an assignment of all rights to the invention. That is, none of the owners can give up *all* rights to the invention without obtaining agreement from the other owners. (35 U.S.C. § 262.) Generally, the joint owners decide amongst themselves how to split the revenue from sales and licensing (for example a 50-50% split). If the joint owners cannot decide and a dispute results, a court will make the final determination.

- Most important of all, unless they agree to the contrary, *any* joint owner of a patented invention can make, sell or use the invention without the other owners' consent and without compensating them. For example, one owner can enter into a nonexclusive license with someone to manufacture and sell the patented invention and keep all the revenue. The easiest way for the joint owners of a patented invention to protect their interest is to enter into a Joint Ownership Agreement, as provided below. (Note: this rule only applies to joint owners of patented inventions. It does not apply to trade secret ownership or to inventions that are licensed before a patent is obtained.)

1. Voluntary Joint Inventorship and Ownership

Voluntary joint ownership comes about whenever two or more people deliberately jointly invent something. (Joint invention can also come about without your intending it to happen; see Section D2.)

To be a joint inventor and therefore joint owner of the patent rights in an entire invention, a person must make a contribution to at least one novel and nonobvious concept that makes the invention patentable. In patent-drafting terms, the joint inventor must contribute something substantial to one of the major or minor patent claims. That's all that's required—a substantial contribution to the conception of one claim; this is so even though the invention contains many patent claims.

It is not necessary that joint inventors work in the same place or at the same time. Nor is it necessary that the idea for the entire invention occur to each. One joint inventor may take a step at one time, the other an approach at different times. One may do more of the experimental work while the other makes suggestions from time to time. The fact that joint inventors play different roles and that the contribution of one may not be as great as that of another is unimportant so long as each makes an original contribution to the final solution of the problem solved by the invention.

EXAMPLE: Steve and Rich invented a new type of folding bicycle. Steve conceived the basic idea for the invention and solved the problem of how to easily fold the both the bike frame and handlebars into a 14" by 27" package. Rich conceived a new type of folding pedal. They then promptly filed a patent application and obtained a patent two years later. Steve and Rich are now joint inventors and joint owners of the entire patented invention, even though Steve contributed more than Rich. Since they are joint owners, unless they sign an agreement to the contrary, both can license the invention without sharing the license royalties with the other. This means that, if he's a good salesman, Rich could earn more money than Steve, even though Steve contributed more to the invention.

2. Involuntary Joint Inventorship and Ownership

Joint inventorship, and therefore joint ownership, can come about even though you don't want it. This often leads to expensive and time-consuming patent litigation. Consider the following true example:

EXAMPLE: Dr. Yoon, a surgeon, conceived of a vastly improved trocar, an instrument used for tiny-incision abdominal surgery. In the course of development, Dr. Yoon enlisted the help of an electronics technician named Choi, who worked as an unpaid assistant and was neither Yoon's employee nor an independent contractor. In the course of this work, Choi contributed a novel, though small, element to the invention. Dr. Yoon put the whole invention together and patented it, naming himself as the sole inventor and owner. The trocar became a big hit among surgeons and was worth a lot. Dr. Yoon licensed the trocar to Ethicon, Inc. In the meantime, Choi decided he had ownership rights, too, because he was a joint inventor along with Dr. Yoon. Choi licensed the trocar to the United States Surgical Corporation. Ethicon and Surgical both filed patent lawsuits. After extensive litigation, Surgical and Choi won. The court found that Choi had contributed to two of the 55 claims in Dr. Yoon's patent and was therefore entitled to be a joint owner of the entire patent. As such, Choi had the legal right to license the invention to Surgical. To add insult to injury, since Choi and Dr. Yoon had never made any agreement regarding joint ownership rights, Choi did not have to give Yoon any part of the royalties he received from Surgical. (*Ethicon, Inc. v. United States Surgical Corporation*, 135 F.3d 1456 (Fed. Cir. 1998).)

As the *Ethicon* case shows, employees, independent contractors or even friends or colleagues may have a legitimate claim to joint ownership of your invention if they contribute in any way to its conception and therefore qualify as joint inventors. However, not every contribution leads to joint inventorship and ownership.

a. Ideas and suggestions from others

Remember, a person must contribute to the conception of at least one important or necessary element of the invention to be a joint inventor and owner—for example, contribute to the conception of the physical structure of the invention or its operative steps. Following directions or providing ideas and suggestions is not enough to be a joint inventor unless they amount to the conception of at least part of the claimed invention. For example, suggesting a problem to be solved is not enough to be a joint inventor; a joint inventor must help provide the solution to the problem.

EXAMPLE: Famed inventor Edwin Land went to the beach with his family in 1943. He took a picture of his three-year-

Edwin Land
Inventor of the Polaroid camera

old daughter with a standard camera for the era—one that required that the film be sent to a photo lab for developing. His daughter asked him why she had to wait to see the finished photo. Land's daughter posed a problem—why can't pictures be developed right away? In 1947, Land patented the first instant camera. He eventually obtained many patents for instant photography and marketed his cameras and film through a company he previously founded: the Polaroid Corporation. Land's daughter was not a co-inventor of instant photography. All she did was pose a problem—why can't you see a photograph right away? It was Land who found the solution.

b. Reduction to practice

Reducing an invention to practice—that is, building and testing a prototype or applying for a patent—does not by itself make a person a joint inventor.

> **EXAMPLE:** Thomas Edison didn't build his phonograph invention himself. Instead, he gave a drawing he created of the first phonograph to a machinist in his employ named John Kruesi to build. Kruesi followed the drawing and constructed the phonograph. This did not make him a joint inventor of the phonograph with Edison.

On the other hand, if a prototype builder comes up with valuable contributions and at least one of these contributions finds its way into a patent claim, both people would be joint inventors and should be named as such on the patent application. For this reason, it's wise to keep as much control as you can over the building and testing of your invention.

c. Team efforts

Special difficulties can arise where creating an invention is a team effort, where each member of the team has contributed something. To determine ownership, it is necessary to separate those team members who actually contributed to the conception of the invention from those members who merely acted under the direction and supervision of the conceivers. Only the former are joint inventors and owners.

EXAMPLE: Again, Thomas Edison provides a good example. Most of his greatest inventions were team efforts. For example, many people helped Edison design, build and test the light bulb. One of these helpers was chemist Otto Moses who, at Edison's request, performed a systematic study of the scientific literature on carbon substances. This research helped Edison find the best filament for his light bulb, which turned out to be bamboo. Nevertheless, Moses was not a joint inventor of the light bulb because he did not contribute to the invention's conception.

d. Avoiding involuntary joint inventorship/ownership

Fortunately, it's relatively easy to avoid the whole problem of claims of joint ownership by contractors, assistants and others who perform tasks for you. Have those who help you sign an agreement assigning any rights they may have in the invention to you. Had Dr. Yoon (in the example at the beginning of this section) done this with Choi, Choi's claim that he was a joint owner would not have been successful.

You need to obtain an assignment *before* you get another person to help you with your invention. You especially need to use such assignments with any employees and independent contractors you hire. But you should also obtain assignments from others who provide guidance, ideas, suggestions and other help; this includes colleagues, friends and experts you consult with. You should develop assignment agreements (which should also contain confidentiality provisions) ahead of time to use with such people. You can find sample agreements to use with employees and independent contractors in Chapter 10. Agreements to use with others can be found on the disk at the back of this book.

If you are unable or unwilling to obtain an assignment, all is not lost. If someone falsely claims to be a joint inventor, you'll be able to disprove these claims by keeping good records —principally an inventor's notebook (see Chapter 9). Also, document your third-party contacts—for example, keep copies of correspondence and email. If you have an invention conversation with someone, write a memo summarizing what was said and paste it into your inventor's notebook (or keep it in a separate file). If your invention is successful, you may be surprised at how many people, including friends and colleagues, claim they contributed.

What if someone conceives part of your invention and you don't have an assignment agreement? In this event, you have three options:

- share ownership with the other person, in which case you should sign a joint ownership agreement (see Section D3),
- acquire the other person's ownership interest through an assignment (see Section F), or
- if possible, don't claim those elements of the invention contributed by others—this way, you'll be sole owner of the patent. Seek help from a patent attorney if you're considering this option.

3. Joint Ownership Agreement

Ordinarily, joint owners agree to share any money their invention earns. When they do this, they automatically enter into a partnership with each other—whether they know it or not. A partnership comes into existence whenever two or more people voluntarily enter into a venture together to earn a profit.

Joint Owners, But Not Partners

In some instances (for example, cases of involuntary joint ownership) joint owners may not wish to share the proceeds from their invention. The patent law permits any joint owner to manufacture, sell or license a jointly owned invention without having to share the revenue with the other owners. In this event, the joint owners would not be in a partnership because they don't intend to engage in business together; instead, the joint owners are working for themselves. This is apparently what happened in the case involving the surgical instrument discussed in Section D2, above. A doctor and a technician became involuntary joint owners and each one licensed the invention to different, competing companies. It seems clear that neither shared the royalties he received with the other.

It is not necessary to have a written agreement to have a partnership, but it is advisable to have something in writing establishing the partners' rights and responsibilities. If you don't create a written agreement, your state's partnership law will govern your partnership. Among other things, these laws provide that partners share profits and losses equally after repayment of contributions to the partnership. You may not care for this or other provisions of your state partnership law. The only way to avoid them is to draft a partnership agreement. For detailed guidance on how to draft one, refer to *The Partnership Book: How to Write a Partnership Agreement*, by Denis Clifford & Ralph Warner (Nolo).

In lieu of a full-blown partnership agreement, you can use the simpler Joint Ownership Agreement described below. (A complete version of the agreement is included on the disk at the back of this book). This agreement deals with the most crucial joint ownership issues—although it doesn't cover all the bases of a regular partnership agreement. (You can always create a definitive partnership agreement later on—for example, when it becomes clear the invention is valuable.) All joint owners should sign a Joint Ownership Agreement before a patent is obtained or the invention is licensed or otherwise exploited.

The full text of a Joint Ownership Agreement is on the CD-ROM forms disk at the back of the book.

The following discussion explains the provisions of the agreement and shows you how to fill it out. However, this agreement is not engraved in stone. You may alter it and we suggest some alterations you might want to make.

a. Identifying the parties

The first paragraph of the agreement identifies the joint owners; insert their names. If there are more than two joint owners, add the additional owners' names. If any of the owners are corporations, partnerships or limited liability companies (LLCs), indicate the correct business form (for example, The Techno Consortium, a New Jersey general partnership).

b. Purpose of agreement

Insert a description of your invention in this clause. Choose the correct option, patent, patent application or no patent. If you have two patents or a patent and a patent application, create separate agreements for each invention.

c. Ownership percentage interests

This clause provides the percentage interest and proportionate share of revenues each owner is to receive and, likewise, the proportionate share of expenses and liabilities. The owners must agree on what percentage each of them will receive (for example, each partner receives one-half of the revenue). Insert the percentage interests. The total of all of the owner percentages must equal 100%.

d. Decision making

The parties to a joint ownership agreement can decide which issues require unanimous (all parties must agree) or majority approval (or 2/3 approval if you wish). However, entering into an assignment of all rights to the invention should be with the consent of all parties. In the sample, all other decisions are listed for majority vote. These decisions include:
- entering into agreements with other parties to make, license, use, distribute or sell the invention,
- permitting any party to make, use, distribute or sell the invention,
- filing foreign patent applications,
- filing a lawsuit to stop infringement of the invention, or
- hiring someone to help prepare and file the patent application or help file an infringement lawsuit.

If you want any decisions to be made by unanimous vote (for example, entering into an exclusive license), you may list them as requiring a unanimous vote section.

The owners can establish any decision-making process that suits them and if necessary they also may establish a method of breaking a tie. The sample agreement provides for the use of mediation and arbitration to break ties.

e. Rights to manufacture and sell

This provision permits any joint owner to sell the invention (provided the owner sells it on the same terms as nonowner licensees). If you want, you can alter this clause to provide that only certain joint owners can sell the invention. The clause may also be changed to authorize a joint owner to negotiate deals; or it could permit an individual owner to make, use or sell the invention.

f. Improvements, revisions

This provision permits all co-owners to share in improvements of the invention, provided that the owners have made themselves available to assist in such improvements. If, for example, the relationship between the owners becomes hostile and they can no longer work together to improve the invention, then the income from improvements will be divided according to their ownership percentage interests.

This is not the only way the agreement can deal with income from improvements and revisions. For example, some agreements give more money to the joint owner or owners who made the improvement. Some joint owners use a sliding scale—for example, splitting one quarter of the income from the first improvement among those who contributed to it, and dividing the rest according to the original ownership percentages. The percentages can change as more improvements are made.

g. Disputes

The sample agreement, below provides for discussion, mediation and then, arbitration. (See Chapter 10, Section C.)

h. Effective date

The agreement takes effect when it's signed by all the joint owners. They don't have to sign at the same time.

i. Attorney fees

This clause provides that the prevailing party (winner) in any dispute under the agreement is entitled to an award of attorney fees and other costs. This means the losing side has to pay them. Without such a clause, you normally cannot obtain such fees if you successfully sue a joint owner.

j. General provisions

If you want an explanation of the provisions in this section, refer to Chapter 10, Section C. In the blank space, insert the name of your state of residence or the state agreed upon by the joint owners.

k. Signatures

Most joint owners are individuals acting as sole proprietors and can simply sign the agreement. However, if any joint owner is signing as a general partner representing a partnership or on behalf of a corporation, that person must have the authority to sign the agreement. If you have any doubt about any joint owner's authority to sign the agreement review the section on "signatures" in Chapter 10, Section C.

E. Are You an Employee/ Contractor Inventor?

Many independent inventors work full- or part-time, whether as employees or independent contractors—and invent during their spare time. If you work for somebody else, that person or company could end up owning your invention or at least have a right to use and sell it for free. If the hiring firm obtains ownership of your invention, it could pay you a portion of the money it earns from it, or it could give you nothing beyond the salary you already earn. This is something for you and the hiring firm to negotiate, preferably before you start work.

Note that being an employee or independent contractor is not the same. An independent contractor is a person who performs services for a company or person without having the status of an employee. Independent contractors are often called consultants, freelancers, dailies or self-employed. (For more information on the employee/independent contractor distinction, see Chapter 10.) However, for patent ownership purposes, employees and independent contractors are treated the same, subject to one exception noted below, so both are covered in this section. When we use the word "employee" here, we also include independent contractors, while "employer" includes firms that hire independent contractors.

It's vitally important that you understand what your employer does and does not have the right to own, so you can focus your inventing time on inventions to which your employer has no ownership claim.

1. Pre-Invention Assignment Agreements

Today, it's a nearly universal practice for employers to require employees involved in research and development (R & D) or other technical work to sign agreements assigning in advance to the employer their ownership interest in any inventions they create while employed. Such pre-invention assignment agreements are perfectly legal in all states. However, eight states, including California, impose restrictions on them (see subsection 4b).

If you disregard an agreement and attempt to license your invention, the employer will be able to sue you for breach of the employment agreement. If your employment agreement is found valid and your employer wins the lawsuit, you may have to pay monetary damages.

Before you begin work on any invention on your own, read your employment agreement (and any other agreements you have with your employer or former employers) to determine if they contain any pre-invention assignment provisions. These provisions might also be located in your employee manual or in other employee guidelines—which may or may not be considered legally binding terms of your employment agreement.

 If you've already developed an invention and are not sure whether it falls within your pre-invention assignment agreement, consult with an intellectual property attorney.

a. What they contain

There are no standard forms for pre-invention assignments. They can vary widely. That's why it's so important to read yours carefully. If you don't understand it, ask your employer for an explanation or take it to an intellectual property attorney.

A pre-invention assignment typically includes at least three parts: an assignment provision, a disclosure provision and a power of attorney. Many agreements contain additional clauses as well.

1. Assignment provision

The assignment provision requires the employee to assign his or her inventions to the employer. This is the most important (and the only necessary) requirement for the employer's total ownership of the patent. Be sure to read this provision very carefully, because they are not all the same. Some only cover employee inventions, others cover virtually anything the employee creates, including ideas.

Sample Assignment Clause

Assignment of Developments. I agree that all inventions that (a) are developed using equipment, supplies, facilities or trade secrets of the Company; or (b) result from work performed by me for the company; or (c) relate to the Company's current or anticipated research and development will be the Company's sole and exclusive property and are hereby assigned by me to the Company.

2. Disclosure provision

The employer won't know it owns an employee's invention unless the employee informs the employer of its existence. This clause requires you to do that. These clauses can also differ from agreement to agreement. Many are limited like the following sample. Others purport to cover anything the employee creates while employed.

Sample Disclosure Clause

Disclosure. While I am employed by the Company, I will promptly inform the Company of the full details of all inventions, discoveries, improvements and innovations, whether or not patentable, copyrightable or otherwise protectible, that I conceive, complete or reduce to practice (whether jointly or with others) and which (a) relate to the Company's present or prospective business, or actual or demonstrably anticipated research and development; or (b) result from any work I do using any equipment, facilities, materials, trade secrets or personnel of the Company; or (c) result from or are suggested by any work that I may do for the Company.

3. Power of attorney provision

This clause guarantees that the employer can register and administer the ownership rights without the employee, even if he or she is willing and able to assist. For example, the employer can apply for a patent without the employee's help. This provision is fairly standard in all agreements, and shouldn't be a cause of controversy.

Sample Power of Attorney

Power of Attorney. If the Company is unable to secure my signature on any document necessary to obtain or maintain any patent, copyright, trademark or other proprietary rights, whether due to my mental or physical capacity or any other cause, I hereby irrevocably designate and appoint the Company and its duly authorized officers and agents as my agents and attorneys-in-fact to execute and file such documents and do all other lawfully permitted acts to further the prosecution, issuance and enforcement of patents, copyrights and other proprietary rights with the same force and effect as if executed by me.

4. Holdover clause

In addition to the three clauses listed above, many pre-invention assignment agreements require employees to assign ownership of their inventions for some time after their employment ends. Of all the provisions in pre-invention assignments, "holdover clauses" are the most legally suspect. The reason employers use such clauses is obvious: They're afraid you'll walk out the door without telling them about an invention you created while employed and later develop and patent it yourself. However, courts don't like such post-employment assignment provisions (also called "holdover clauses") because they can make it impossible for an employee to get a new job. After all, a prospective new employer doesn't want to be subject to lawsuits by a former employer claiming that it owns an invention developed by its ex-employee. To protect employees, courts will enforce holdover clauses only if they are reasonable. To be reasonable, a holdover clause must (1) be for a limited time—probably no more than six months to one year after employment ends, and (2) apply only to inventions conceived as a result of work done for the former employer. Some courts are even more restrictive and will enforce such clauses only for inventions made using the ex-employer's trade secrets.

Sample Holdover Clause

Holdover Clause: I will disclose to the Company any and all inventions, improvements or discoveries actually made or copyright registration or patent applications filed, within six months after my employment with the Company ends. I hereby assign to the Company my entire right, title and interest in such inventions, improvements and discoveries, whether made individually or jointly, which relate to the subject matter of my employment with the Company during the six month period immediately preceding the termination of my employment.

Patenting Immediately After Quitting Creates Suspicion

Don't assume you can get out of a pre-invention assignment by quitting your job and immediately patenting the invention listing yourself as owner. For example, a chemist employed by an optics company signed a pre-invention agreement without a holdover clause. He quit his job and four days later prepared a patent disclosure describing his discovery of four chemical compounds useful to the manufacture of contact lenses. The company filed suit, claiming that the chemist must have developed the compounds while employed with the company. The court agreed that it was highly implausible that the chemist could have conceived the compounds—which related directly to his work for the company—so soon after quitting. Therefore, the pre-invention assignment applied and the chemist had to assign ownership to the company. (*Syntex Ophthalmics, Inc. v. Tsuetaki,* 701 F.2d 677 (7th Cir. 1983).)

4. Waiver Provision

Finally, in addition to the assignment provision discussed above, many agreements contain a provision requiring the employee to list all inventions he or she conceived or patented before starting work with the company. Then, the employee is required to waive any right to claim that any other invention was created before his or her employment. This eliminates one important defense an employee may have against a pre-invention assignment: that the invention was conceived before he or she began working for the company and is therefore not covered by the assignment agreement. If your agreement contains such a clause, be sure to list *all* your inventions you haven't patented. You could lose your ownership rights in those you fail to list. (The waiver can't apply to patents you already hold, since the existence of the patent would prove you created the invention before your employment began.)

Sample Waiver Provision

Waiver: I have listed on the back of this agreement all inventions and discoveries that, before the start of my employment, I made or conceived and owned or had an interest in. Any inventions or discoveries not so listed shall be deemed made or conceived during my employment. This provision does not apply to inventions I patented before the start of my employment.

Garrett Morgan
Inventor of a device to control traffic—
a folding traffic signal

b. State limitations on pre-invention assignments

A prospective or continuing employee and his or her employer are usually in an unequal bargaining position—the employer generally has the upper hand. Some employers have attempted to take advantage of their leverage by requiring their employees to agree to very broadly worded assignments that purport to transfer to the employer, in advance, owner-ship of everything the employee creates, whether related to the job or not. In the words of one court, these employers try to obtain "a mortgage on a man's brain" (*Aspinwall Mfg. Co. v. Gill*, 32 F. 697 (3d Cir. 1887)).

To protect employees, eight states, including California, impose restrictions on the permissible scope of assignments of employee-created inventions. These restrictions apply only to "inventions" an employee creates—that is, items for which a patent is sought.

The California restrictions are typical. Under California law, an employee cannot be required to assign any of his or her rights in an inven-tion he or she develops "entirely on his or her own time without using the employer's equipment, supplies, facilities, or trade secret information" unless:

- when the invention was conceived or "reduced to practice" (actually created or a patent application filed) it related to the employer's business or actual or "demonstrably anticipated" research or development, or
- the invention resulted from any work performed by the employee for the em-ployer (California Labor Code, § 2870).

As you can see, these limitations on employee invention assignments are not very generous to employees. The only inventions an employee can't be required to assign to the employer are true independent inventions —those that are developed completely with-out company resources and that don't relate to the employee's work or the employer's current business or anticipated future business.

The following states impose restrictions similar to California's:

- Delaware (Delaware Code Annotated, Title 19, § 805)
- Illinois (Illinois Revised Statutes, Chapter 140, §§ 301-303)
- Kansas (Kansas Statutes Annotated, §§ 44-130)
- Minnesota (Minnesota Statutes Annotated, § 181.78)
- North Carolina (North Carolina General Statutes, §§ 66-57.1, 66-57.2)
- Utah (Utah Code Annotated, §§ 34-39-2, 34-39-3), and
- Washington (Washington Revised Code Annotated, §§ 49.44.140, 49.44.150).

If you work in California, Illinois, Kansas, Minnesota or Washington State, state law requires that you be given written notice of your state's restrictions on an employer's right to obtain an assignment of employee inventions. If this is not done, the assignment could be unenforceable.

What if you live in one of the 42 states that do not have laws restricting invention assign-ments? Even in most of these states, pre-invention assignments can't be grossly unfair. Because they want their pre-invention assign-ment agreements to be legally enforceable, employers in these states sometimes track the rules used in the other eight states when drafting assignments.

c. Is your agreement enforceable?

Courts sometimes find pre-invention assignments to be legally invalid. If a court finds your assignment to be invalid, it won't enforce it and you'll retain ownership of your invention. A pre-invention assignment you signed might be unenforceable if:

- **The assignment is unconscionable:** Courts generally will refuse to enforce assignments that are grossly unfair to the employee. The courts call such agreements unconscionable—that is, so unfair that enforcing them goes against public policy. For example, an assignment that said your employer owned any inventions you created while employed, even if they don't relate to the employer's present or anticipated business and were created by you on your own time without the employer's resources, would likely be found unconscionable by your state courts.

- **The assignment was procured by fraud:** An assignment may be unenforceable if it was procured by fraud—for example, your employer lied or tricked you into signing it.

- **You signed the assignment after you were hired:** All legal agreements, including invention assignments, must be supported by something lawyers call "consideration" —that is, each party must receive something of value for signing the agreement. If consideration is lacking, the agreement won't be legally binding. If you sign a pre-invention assignment before you start work, there is no problem with consideration: The salary you will be paid is deemed to be consideration for signing the agreement. However, some employers forget to get employees to sign an assignment when they are first hired. Often, such employers will later realize their mistake and require the employee to sign an assignment long after being hired. Courts in some states have held that if the employer doesn't give the continuing employee something of value in exchange for signing such an "afterthought" assignment—for example, a raise, stock option, extra vacation—the assignment lacks consideration and is therefore unenforceable.

- **The employer waited too long to enforce the assignment:** A court may decide not to enforce the agreement if your employer waited so long that it would be unfair to enforce it against you. This is most likely to occur where the delay made you think your employer had no ownership claims and you acted accordingly. For example, a court may decide not to enforce an assignment against an employee who left the company five years previously and patented and licensed the invention, thinking that he owned it.

If you think any of these grounds might apply in your case, you should consult with an intellectual property attorney. Ideally, you would do this before you conceive an invention; but this is often not possible. After all, one never knows when inspiration or "the flash of genius" will strike.

2. Default Ownership Rules Where There Is No Assignment or State Law

Over the last 100 years or so, the courts have developed rules governing patent ownership by employees. These rules apply only if you did not sign a pre-invention assignment giving ownership of your inventions to your employer, or if the assignment you did sign is found by a court to be invalid. In effect, they apply only by default. They usually don't come into play because most companies prefer to have their employees sign pre-invention assignments,

rather than rely on these rather ambiguous rules.

Under these default rules, depending on his or her employment status and the circumstances, an employee may be deemed to have created an implied contract to assign the invention to the employer. This means that the employee has a legal duty to assign ownership to the employer; the same practical result as if the employee had actually signed a pre-invention assignment. In other cases, however, the employee may not have a duty to assign the invention, or may only have to give the employer a shop right, a type of nonexclusive license.

To determine how these rules apply to you, you must know your employment status. Employees are classified under these rules as either employed to invent or noninventive.

a. Employed to invent

Employers obtain ownership of the patent and trade secret rights in any inventions created by employees employed to invent. Employees are employed to invent if, at the time the invention was conceived, their primary job responsibility was:

- to solve a problem or develop or invent a specific product, device or procedure, or
- to be generally inventive—that is, do general research and development (R & D) for the employer in a particular area.

In these situations, employees are deemed to have agreed to assign (transfer) to the employer whatever rights they may have had in any invention or trade secret they create at the employer's request and expense. This assignment is made in return for their salary or other compensation.

> **EXAMPLE:** Teets, an engineer, never signed an assignment agreement giving rights to his inventions to his employer, Chromalloy Gas Turbine Corp. He was assigned as the chief engineer on a project to devise a method of welding a "leading edge" for turbine engines. Teets spent at least 70% of his time on the project. He developed a hot forming process (HFP) for welding a leading edge and built the invention on Chromalloy's time and using its employees, tools and materials. Teets claimed that he was the sole owner of patent rights. A court held that Chromalloy owned the patent rights because it expressly directed Teets to create the HFP process. Therefore, even without a written employment agreement, Chromalloy acquired ownership. (*Teets v. Chromalloy Gas Turbine Corp.*, 83 F.3d 403 (Fed. Cir. 1996).)

However, a person employed to invent may be able to keep ownership of an independent invention. The clearest example of an independent invention is one that is:

- conceived outside the scope of employment
- unrelated to the employer's business, and
- developed without any employer assistance.

> **EXAMPLE:** Assume that Teets in the example above, invented a new type of musical instrument and built and tested it on his own time at home using only his own resources. Such an invention would meet all the requirements for an independent invention—Teets was not hired to create a musical instrument and musical instruments don't relate to Chromalloy's present or future anticipated business; and he created the instrument without any assistance from Chromalloy. Teets would likely be deemed be the owner of his invention.

If your invention was outside the scope of employment and unrelated to your employer's business, but you did use employer resources (for example, developed it on company time or using company equipment), you might still be able to retain ownership. But your employer would likely have a shop right as described in the following section.

b. Non-inventive employees

An employee who has not signed a pre-invention assignment or is not hired to invent or develop new products or technology usually owns the rights to any patentable inventions or trade secrets created by the employee. However, the employer may be entitled make, use and sell the invention without the employee's permission and without paying the employee for the use if:

- the employee used the employer's resources in conceiving the invention or reducing it to practice (building and testing it or filing a patent application)—for example, the employee did a substantial amount of the work during business hours or used the employer's equipment, or

- the invention was closely related to the employee's job duties, or
- the employee allowed the employer to promote the invention with a reasonable expectation of royalty-free use by the employer.

This type of license is called a "shop right." It is nonexclusive (it does not prevent an employee-inventor from transferring patent rights to others) and nontransferable by the employer.

EXAMPLE: Hewett worked as foreman in the Samsonite Corporation's model shop where he helped build prototypes of new products. Hewett wasn't hired to invent anything, so he was not asked to sign a pre-invention assignment. While working in the shop, on his own initiative Hewett invented or helped invent three products that Samsonite later patented, including a soft-sided luggage case. After being laid off by Samsonite, Hewett filed suit claiming he was the owner of these patents. Since there was no enforceable assignment agreement, the default ownership rules applied. The court held that, because Hewett was not hired or paid to invent, he was entitled to ownership of the patents. However, Samsonite was entitled to a shop right because Hewett did his

inventing on company time using company resources. This meant that Samsonite could go on manufacturing and selling products containing Hewett's invention without paying him. However, Hewett could now attempt to license his inventions to others. (*Hewett v. Samsonite Corporation*, 32 Colo. App. 150 (Colo. 1973).)

You need only be concerned about shop rights if the invention was created on the employer's time or using the employer's resources (materials, supplies or trade secrets). If it wasn't, the shop right rule is irrelevant.

3. Special Employment Situations

Special ownership rules apply to government employees and many employees of universities.

a. Government employees

Federal law provides that all rights to inventions created by federal employees (whether civilian or military) belong to the government if the invention was:

- made during working hours, or
- made with the government's resources, including money, facilities, equipment, materials, information, or the help of other government employees on official duty, or
- directly related to the inventor's official duties or made because of those duties. (37 C.F.R. § 501.6.)

If you're a federal employee, you can forget about owning any invention that falls within these rules. But there is one exception: If the government does not plan to file a patent application for the invention or promote its commercialization, it must allow the employee-inventor to retain ownership.

If you are able to keep ownership (either because the three criteria listed above don't apply or the government lacks interest in the invention) the government is entitled to a nonexclusive, irrevocable, royalty-free license in the invention with power to grant licenses for all governmental purposes.

If the government obtains ownership of your invention, you have some solace. Federal law provides that, if the government licenses the invention and earns money from it, it must give 15% of the money to the inventor. This is more generous than most private companies are with their employee-inventors.

None of these rules apply to the Department of Energy, Tennessee Valley Authority or U.S. Postal Service.

Many states have laws similar to the federal government's. For example, Connecticut law provides that the state obtains ownership of any state employee invention (1) conceived during the employee's job duties; or (2) that emerges from any state research or development, or other program; or (3) that was conceived or developed wholly or partly at state expense or with its equipment, facilities or personnel. If you're a state employee, you need to examine your state law to determine its patent ownership policies.

Government Contractors

If you are an independent contractor who contracts with the federal government, your ownership situation is brighter than that of government employees. Federal agencies may waive or omit patent rights when awarding government contracts (although there are some exceptions for space research, nuclear energy or defense). If you are contracting directly with the federal government (that is, you are not working for the federal government through a private company), then you should ask about patent ownership at the time of contracting. You may be able to retain patent rights to a government-sponsored invention. If you are working for an employer who has contracted with the federal government and you want to assert patent rights, (1) your employer would have to retain patent rights from the federal government, and (2) you would have to have some basis to assert your claim to patent rights, as discussed in the previous sections.

b. University employees

Today, many universities own large patent portfolios and earn substantial royalties from them. In 2000, for example, the University of California earned $261 million from its patents, more than any other school. These patent portfolios and royalties are derived from the research conducted by faculty members and others associated with the university.

To keep those royalties flowing, most universities seek to obtain ownership of inventions created by their employees. Moreover, if the research leading to the invention was federally funded, they are required by law to obtain ownership (see the sidebar below).

Universities usually require that faculty and others who might create inventions sign separate formal pre-invention assignment agreements granting the university rights to all discoveries made by the employee. If you have such an agreement, read it carefully. It must comply with the same rules as any other pre-invention assignment. If it does, you must live with its provisions. If it doesn't, it could be invalid.

However, other universities don't use formal assignments. Instead, they rely on invention ownership policies set forth in bylaws,

Federally Funded Inventions and the Bayh-Dole Act

A substantial portion of all university research in the United States is funded by the federal government. How much varies from university to university, but federal funding reaches 90% or more at some schools. If a university accepts federal funding, a law called the Bayh-Dole Act (35 USC §§ 200-212) applies.

The Bayh-Dole Act works like this:

- First, a government agency decides to sponsor (pay for) research by a university's faculty, with the university acting as the contractor.
- The university must have written agreements with its faculty and technical staff requiring disclosure and assignment of inventions.
- If faculty develop an invention arising from the research, they must disclose it to the university and the university must disclose it to the federal government within two months.

- The university then has two years to decide whether to retain title to the invention; if it keeps ownership, the federal government gets a shop right in the invention.
- If the university keeps title to the invention, it must patent it.
- The university may then license the invention, giving preference to companies with 500 or fewer employees (however, if a larger company helped fund the invention, it may receive a license).
- The faculty members who developed the invention must receive a percentage of the royalties the university earns.

If the university doesn't want to keep ownership of the invention, the federal government may elect to take it (something it does relatively rarely). If the government doesn't want it, you can petition the federal agency involved to let you have ownership. These requests are usually granted.

manuals, employment letters or similar documents. An assignment contained in such a document might not be legally enforceable. This is something to discuss with an intellectual property attorney.

If you never assigned your rights to the university or the purported assignment is found invalid, the default ownership rules discussed in Section E2 above would apply. Under these rules, the university would own the invention if you were directed to (1) invent the specific item, or (2) perform inventive work in a particular field and the invention came from that work.

Normally, when an invention or discovery is successful and results in a licensing deal, the school pays some portion of the revenues to the inventor. Some schools are quite generous. At one major university, for example, inventors get 50% of the first $100,000 of net revenue, 40% of the second $100,000 and 30% of any sums after that. However, other schools are far stingier.

4. Strategies for Dealing with Your Employer

Here are some basic strategies for dealing with your employer, whether or not you've signed a pre-invention assignment agreement.

a. Keep good records

If you've signed a pre-invention assignment or are an inventive employee who hasn't signed one, you'll likely be able to retain your invention if:

- it was created on your own time and without your employer's resources, and
- it does not relate to your employer's present or anticipated business or your work with the company.

If you're a noninventive employee who hasn't signed an assignment agreement, you'll have to give your employer a shop right unless you can show you created the invention on your own time with your own resources.

It should be clear, then, that it's very important for you to be able to prove you created the invention without your employer's help. If an ownership dispute ends up in litigation, you'll have the burden of proof on these issues—this means you must convince the judge or arbitrator. The best way to prove these things is to keep a witnessed inventor's notebook showing how, when and where you developed the invention. (See Chapter 9 for detailed guidance on using inventors' notebooks.)

Keep any other documentary evidence that might also help, such as correspondence, copies of email and receipts for equipment you purchased or leased. You can paste these into your inventor's notebook or keep them in a separate file.

b. To disclose or not to disclose

If you've signed a pre-invention assignment agreement, it will contain a provision requiring you to disclose any inventions you create to your employer. The purpose of the provision is to allow the employer to evaluate your inventions and determine if the company has any rights (either by assignment or under the default ownership rules).

Read the disclosure clause in your agreement carefully. Such clauses often provide that you need not disclose an invention if you created it with your own resources and it is outside the scope of the employer's present or future anticipated business. If your invention is covered by your disclosure clause, then be sure to tell your employer about it. If you're unsure whether or not it is covered, consult with a patent attorney before making the disclosure.

But, what should you do if your invention is clearly not covered by a disclosure clause you've agreed to? Or what if you've never agreed to such a clause? There are two schools of thought:

- **Disclose everything:** Some people believe it's best to disclose all your inventions and discoveries to your employer. This is so even though you haven't signed a pre-invention assignment agreement or the invention doesn't fall within the assignment agreement you did sign. Here's why: If you don't disclose the invention and later patent it and license or manufacture it, and your employer finds out about it, it could claim ownership. It's best to have such disputes dealt with before you go to the time, expense and trouble of patenting and exploiting an invention. You don't want the ownership issue hanging over your head like Damocles' sword.
- **Disclose only when necessary:** Some people take the opposite view and say

you should disclose your inventions to your employer only when absolutely necessary. They fear that an employer might claim it owns an invention you've disclosed even when it really doesn't, and either sue you or make it impossible for you to continue working for the company without assigning the invention to it, or both. They think it's better not to disclose an invention when you don't have to. If it later is patented and becomes successful, you'll have more financial resources to fight any unfounded ownership claims by the employer.

If you're unsure about whether you should disclose an invention, discovery, innovation or idea to your employer, consult with a patent attorney before making the disclosure. Some things to think about when deciding whether to disclose or not include:

- the potential value of your invention
- whether the invention is closely related to your work for your employer
- how good your relations are with your employer, and
- your employer's record in handling employee inventions in the past.

Whatever you do about post-employment inventions, before you start work, it's wise to provide your employer with a list of all the inventions or discoveries you've already created. Some employers require this but you should do it whether it's required or not. Such a list can help you prove that your employer has no rights in an invention because you created it before you worked for the company.

c. Deal with ownership disputes

What do you do if you and your employer dispute ownership? Your employment agreement, if there is one, may control how the dispute is resolved. For example, the agreement may call for mediation or arbitration of disputes over the agreement's provisions. If not, you can always invite the employer to submit to arbitration or mediation in an effort to avoid a costly courtroom battle. And if all else fails, you could end up in court.

In any ownership dispute, you should seek the advice of an intellectual property attorney before proceeding. The attorney can assess your position in relation to the state law and explain your options, and will work with you to clear ownership so that you can license the invention freely. If the employer claims a shop right, your attorney may be able to reach an agreement as to the extent of this right.

If your employer owns rights to your invention and is willing to transfer those rights to you, then an agreement should be signed confirming the arrangement. Likewise, if it's unclear whether the employer has ownership rights, the company might be willing to waive any rights it might have. This might happen, for example, if the company is in financial difficulty, is attempting to settle some other dispute with you or believes the invention has no commercial potential. The last reason might be your best bet—every year, employers automatically acquire through pre-invention assignments ownership of thousands of inventions created by their employees that they view as having no potential and never patent or attempt to commercially exploit.

The letter agreement shown below enables an employee to retain control over a specific invention.

The full text of the Letter Confirming Employee's Invention Ownership is on the CD-ROM forms disk. If the invention already has been patented by the company, *do not use this form*. Instead, have the company sign an assignment agreement where a patent has been issued. This form is on the CD-ROM forms disk. The assignment should also be recorded with the USPTO.

F. Have You Transferred Your Ownership?

A patent is actually a bundle of legal rights, including the exclusive right to make, use, sell, offer to sell or import into the U.S. the invention covered by the patent. An owner of actual or potential patent rights may transfer ownership of those rights to one or more people. When you transfer all of these rights, or a percentage of them, the transfer is called an assignment. An assignment, like the sale of a house, is a permanent transfer of ownership rights. The seller of the invention is the assignor and the buyer the assignee.

An assignment must be in writing to be legally valid. Patent rights may be assigned before a patent is issued by the USPTO—for example, the pre-invention assignment agreements. Of course, rights may also be assigned after the patent is issued. In this event, the assignment must be recorded with the USPTO.

Letter Confirming Employee's Ownership of Invention

Dear Employer:

This confirms the agreement between [*name of company*] and me that I shall own exclusive rights to the invention known as [*name of invention*] which is more specifically described below.

[*name of company*] hereby assigns to me [*your name*] any and all rights it may have in [*name of invention*], including all patent, trade secret, copyright and trademark rights. This assignment applies to both the original invention and any derivative versions under copyright law or improvements under patent law.

You represent and warrant that you have the power to grant these rights on behalf of [*name of company*] and that if required, a representative of [*name of company*] will furnish any other necessary documents that are required to demonstrate my ownership.

Description of Invention

[*name of invention*] comprises [*Describe invention in detail. If there is a patent application, use the claims section to describe it.*]

If this letter accurately reflects our agreement, please sign and return one copy to me.

Yours truly,

_____   _____
Inventor   Date

Acknowledged and agreed to:

_____   _____
Name of Company   Date

_____   _____
Signature   Position

In addition to assignments by inventor-employees, inventors may need to assign ownership of their inventions to their businesses. An invention may also be assigned to a manufacturer or other person or company in return for a lump sum payment or periodic royalty payments. You could also assign your invention to an investor, relative, friend, charity or anyone else you want; whether for payment or for free.

When you assign patent rights, you can sell the entire patent or just a percentage of it and share ownership—that is, you can assign 100% or a lesser percentage of your entire bundle of patent rights. When you assign less than 100% of your rights, you and the assignee will be co-owners of the invention. You have the same rights and duties as co-inventors.

> **EXAMPLE:** Susan invents and patents an electronic baby bib. She owns 100% of the patent rights in the invention. To obtain financing, she assigns a 50% ownership interest in the invention to Mark, in return for $100,000. Susan and Mark are now joint owners of the invention—that is, they each own 50% of the entire bundle of patent rights.

 Three sample assignments are provided on the CD-ROM forms disk:

- ASSIGN1 is for the assignment of an invention for which a patent has been issued
- ASSIGN2 should be used if a patent application has been filed, and
- ASSIGN3 can be used if no patent application has been filed.

1. Licenses Are Not Patent Assignments

Although the terms assignment and license are sometimes used interchangeably, a patent license is not the same as an assignment. A license is simply an agreement in which you let someone else commercially use or develop your invention for a period of time. In return, you receive money—either a one-time payment or continuing payments called royalties. The patent owner is called the licensor and the person receiving the license for an invention is called the licensee.

Unlike an assignment, a license for an invention is not considered a transfer of patent ownership. Instead, it is similar to a lease for a house or apartment. You're giving someone permission to exercise your patent rights, just as the owner of a house gives a renter permission to live in the house. A person you license your invention to is not considered a co-owner of the invention, and need not be listed as such on a patent application.

Licenses are very flexible, and the same invention can be licensed in many different ways. Your bundle of patent rights can be carved up and licensed by time, geographic area, market segment or in almost any other way imaginable—for example, you could license the right to manufacture and sell your invention in the U.S. to one manufacturer and in Canada to another manufacturer.

Unlike the case with assignments, there is ordinarily no legal requirement that licenses be in writing, but it is highly advisable to write them down. It is not necessary to record patent licenses with the USPTO.

For detailed guidance on patent licenses, refer to *License Your Invention*, by Richard Stim (Nolo).

2. Assigning Patent Ownership to Your Business

If you are the sole inventor and owner of your invention and you operate as a sole proprietor, your personal and business affairs are essentially one and the same. There is no need to transfer ownership to your business. You will personally own your invention and any money you make from it.

However, if you've formed a corporation, partnership (general or limited), or limited liability company (LLC) to develop and/or exploit the invention, you'll ordinarily transfer ownership of your invention to the business entity you've formed. If you're the only owner of this entity—that is, you've formed a one-person corporation or LLC—such a transfer is little more than a legal formality, since you own the entire corporation or LLC. However, if you're in a partnership or share ownership of a corporation or LLC with one or more people, you'll be effectively giving part ownership of your invention to your fellow business owners—that is, they will be co-owners of an entity that owns your invention.

Note that if you've formed a corporation and are its employee, the employee ownership rules discussed in Section E above will apply. Moreover, if you're an officer or director of a corporation, you may have a fiduciary duty to assign your invention to the corporation. This may be so even if you have no duty to assign your invention to the corporation under patent ownership rules.

3. Recording an Assignment

If the invention is patented, any assignment must be recorded with the USPTO. To record it, you must send the USPTO a copy of the signed, notarized assignment with a completed USPTO cover sheet and fee. As of 2005, the fee was $40 per recorded patent assignment. Be sure to check the USPTO website (www.uspto.gov) for the current fee.

Send the cover sheet and assignment to:

    Mail Stop Assignment Recordation Services
    Director U.S. Patent and Trademark Office
    P.O. Box 1450
    Alexandria, VA 22213-1450

If you assign invention rights before filing a patent, you can record the assignment by sending it in with your patent application.

 A copy of the USPTO Recordation Form Cover Sheet, can be found on the CD-ROM forms disk at the back of this book. The form can also be downloaded directly from the USPTO website (www.uspto.gov). The form number is PTO-1595.

G. Trade Secret Ownership

Trade secrets and patents differ greatly, but the ownership rules for them are basically the same. Therefore, as noted below, most of the discussion above applies to trade secrets as well as patents.

For detailed coverage of trade secret law and how to implement a trade secret protection plan, see Chapter 13.

To determine whether you own a trade secret, answer the following questions:

1. Have You Developed a Trade Secret?

By its very nature, the person who conceives or develops a trade secret will be its original owner. This is because this person will be the only one who initially knows about it. However, as is the case with patents, the original owner may be legally obligated to transfer ownership to an employer or client.

Unlike the case with patents, you need not be an inventor—that is, conceiver of an invention that is ultimately reduced to practice —to own a trade secret. This is because trade secret law may be used to protect a much wider array of things than patent law. Trade secret law can be used to protect inventions, whether or not they are patentable; but it can be used to protect such things as formulae, designs and specifications, methods and processes and know-how. Indeed, trade secrecy can protect any information that is generally unknown in the industry involved that provides a competitive advantage.

Moreover, unlike the case with patent ownership, it's not necessary to reduce a trade secret to practice to own it. That is, you need not write it down or create and test it or file a patent application for it. Indeed, you'll usually end up losing your trade secret rights if you file a patent application (see Chapter 14). However, although a trade secret need not be tangible, it must be more than a vague, abstract concept. It must be something concrete that can be used by a business to obtain a competitive advantage.

2. Are You an Employee/Contractor?

If you are an employee or independent contractor, your employer or client may acquire ownership of trade secrets you develop through an assignment or through the same default ownership rules that apply to patents. (See Section E2, above.)

3. Have You Transferred Ownership?

Just like patents, trade secret ownership may be transferred to others by assignment or by will. (See Section F2.) ∎

Chapter 12

Introduction to Intellectual Property

A. What Is Intellectual Property and Why Is It Important to Inventors? 12/2

    1. A Tale of Two Inventors 12/2

    2. IP Is More Than Just Patents 12/3

    3. Putting It All Together 12/5

B. Doing the Work of Obtaining IP Protection 12/8

    1. Copyright Protection 12/8

    2. Trade Secret Protection 12/8

    3. Trademark Protection 12/8

    4. Design Patent Protection 12/9

    5. Utility Patent Protection 12/9

*S*uccessful inventors—that is, those who make money—not only devise good inventions, they also take advantage of the laws used to protect them. Willis Carrier, the inventor of the air conditioner, amassed over 80 air-conditioning-related patents in his lifetime. Thomas Edison obtained more patents than any individual inventor in U.S. history (over 1000).

It is not necessary that you become an intellectual property lawyer to profit from your invention, but you do need to have at least a working knowledge of intellectual property law in order to best protect your invention.

In this chapter and Chapters 12 through 16, we provide you with a basic background in intellectual property and refer to places where you can obtain more information. This chapter begins the process by providing an overview of the four main IP laws and explaining how they can fit together to protect an invention.

A. What Is Intellectual Property and Why Is It Important to Inventors?

When you're an inventor, you'll often hear the term "intellectual property" ("IP" for short) bandied about. Intellectual property is the legal name for things that people create with their minds that are protected by law. It includes inventions, valuable information or know-how that is kept secret, works of authorship such as writings, music and art, and designs and product names.

Intellectual property is "property" because, over the past 200 years or so, a body of laws has been created that gives owners of such works legal rights similar in some ways to those given to owners of real estate or tangible personal property such as automobiles. Intellectual property may be owned and bought and sold the same as other types of property. But in many important respects, owning intellectual property is very different from owning a house or car.

1. A Tale of Two Inventors

The stories of real-life inventors S. Newman Darby and John Coleman can help you understand why IP is so important. Darby invented the sailboard, Coleman a process for using plasma in manufacturing. Darby earned relatively little from his invention—although it was turned into a very popular product that spawned the sport of windsurfing. Coleman has earned millions from his invention, which is used in the manufacture of computer chips and displays. What's the difference between Darby and Coleman? Darby never patented his invention, while Coleman did.

a. No patent, no profit: The saga of S. Newman Darby

In 1964, Darby conceived the idea of connecting a handheld sail rig to a floating platform with a universal joint. He called the device a sailboard. Although he began manufacturing and selling the boards, he never applied for a patent. As a result, his invention entered the public domain—that is, it became ineligible for a patent and could freely be made and used by anyone. A few years later, two inventors created their own sailboard that was very similar to Darby's. They named their board the Windsurfer and licensed manufacturing rights to dozens of manufacturers and ended up dominating the field. Had Darby patented his invention, he would have had the exclusive right to make and sell the sailboard for 17 years. This means that he alone would have had the legal right to manufacture or license the sailboard to the public. With the field entirely to himself, Darby could have reaped millions from his popular invention.

b. The inventor as happy millionaire: John Coleman

John Coleman—an independent inventor who works out of the garage of his home—specializes in plasma science. (Plasma is the fourth state of matter, along with solids, liquids and gas.) In the 1980s he devised a process to use plasma in manufacturing. Unlike S. Newman Darby, Coleman patented his invention—in fact he obtained three separate patents. At first Coleman didn't try to license or otherwise profit from his invention and earned nothing from his patents. But by the mid-1990s he realized that manufacturers of semi-conductor chips and flat-panel displays were using his patented process. These companies were infringing on his patents. Coleman hired a law firm to file patent infringement lawsuits against them. Eventually, they all agreed to settle and pay for licenses from Coleman. Coleman now has licenses for

his patents from three of the four largest semi-conductor chip manufacturers in the world and from most of the big players in the flat-panel display industry. Because he patented his invention, Coleman was able to profit from it.

2. IP Is More Than Just Patents

Many inventors tend to focus solely on patents when they think about how to legally protect their inventions. However, there are four separate bodies of law that protect intellectual property: patents, trade secrets, copyrights and trademarks. Together, all these laws make up "intellectual property law." Each of these laws can protect different elements or aspects of an invention, although there is some overlap. While patent law often provides the most important legal protection for inventions, trade secrecy, copyright and trademark law all may offer valuable legal protection.

a. Patents

Of course, when you talk about legal protection for inventions, patent law must come first. The federal patent law (35 U.S.C. §§ 100 and following) is the law specifically designed to protect inventions. By filing for and obtaining a patent from the U.S. Patent and Trademark Office, an inventor is granted a monopoly on the use and commercial exploitation of an invention, for approximately 17 to 18 years. Anyone who wants to make, use or sell a patented invention during a patent's term must obtain the patent owner's permission or face a patent infringement lawsuit.

The vast majority of patents are utility patents, which can protect the functional features of a machine, process, manufactured item or composition of matter. Design patents can be used to protect the ornamental design of a functional feature (design patents are covered in Chapter 14).

Not all inventions are patentable. An invention qualifies for a utility patent only if it is new, useful and not obvious to someone versed in the relevant technology. To obtain a U.S. patent, an inventor must file an application with the U.S. Patent and Trademark Office in Washington, DC, and pay a fee. The application must describe with specificity those elements of the invention for which the patent is sought. If the Patent Office determines that the invention is sufficiently new, useful and not obvious, it will issue the inventor a patent. The inventor can then stop others from making, selling, using or importing the invention in the U.S. To stop others in foreign countries, the inventor would need to seek patent protection in those countries.

 See Chapter 14 for a discussion of patents.

b. Trade Secrets

Trade secrets come in a close second to patents in the inventor's IP batting order. A trade secret is information that other people do not generally know and that provides its owner with a competitive advantage in the marketplace. The information can be an idea, written words, formula, process or procedure, techni-cal design, customer list, marketing plan or any other secret that gives the owner an economic advantage.

A person who takes reasonable steps to keep the confidential information or know-how secret—for example, does not publish it or otherwise make it freely available to the public—becomes the owner of the trade secret. The laws of most states will protect the owner from unauthorized disclosures of the secret by:

- the owner's employees
- people who agree not to disclose it, such as independent contractors the owner hires
- industrial spies, and
- competitors who wrongfully acquire the information.

Unlike patents, trade secrets are not issued by the government. Instead, they automatically come into existence by virtue of being valuable and secret. It's up to you to ensure that your trade secrets remain secret—a task that will take some effort on your part.

Trade secrecy is almost always used to protect an invention before a patent is obtained. It may also be relied on in lieu of patent protection. Also, since trade secrecy can protect a much wider variety of things than patent law, it can be used to protect elements of an invention or product that are not patentable but are nevertheless valuable and secret.

 See Chapter 13 for a detailed discussion of trade secrets.

c. Copyrights

The federal copyright law (17 U.S.C. §§ 101 and following sections) protects original works of authorship. Authorship includes all kinds of written works, plays, music, artwork, graphics, photos, films and videos, computer software, architectural blueprints and designs, choreography and pantomimes.

The owner of a copyright in a work of authorship has a bundle of rights that enable him or her to control how the work may be used, including the right to copy and distribute the protected work, to create works derived from it and to display and perform it. These rights come into existence automatically the moment a work of authorship is created. The owner need not take any additional steps or file legal documents to secure a copyright.

You may be wondering what good a copyright is to an inventor. After all, the functional or utilitarian aspects of inventions don't qualify as works of authorship and therefore are not protected by copyright. However, many inventions contain nonfunctional design or ornamental features that can be copyrighted. In addition, copyright can be used to protect such things as product manuals, photos, videos and drawings.

 See Chapter 16 for a detailed discussion of copyrights.

d. Trademark Law

Patent, trade secret and copyright laws do not protect names, titles or short phrases. This is where trademark protection comes in. Trademark law protects the right to exclusively use a name, logo or any device that identifies or distinguishes products or services. In many cases, a product name can be worth even more than a patent.

In addition to protecting product names and logos, trademark law also protects trade dress and product configuration. Trade dress is the product's packaging. Product configuration refers to the shape or design of your invention—for example, a distinctive oval-shaped stapler.

Trademark rights are not created until the public has been exposed to a product or service and its trademark, usually by its first use in commerce.

 See Chapter 15 for a detailed discussion of trademarks.

3. Putting It All Together

You might be a bit confused right now. Given all the different types of intellectual property laws and the different things they protect, it might seem bewildering to determine which laws you should use to protect what. In fact, it's not that difficult.

Just remember that various features of the same invention may be protected by different types of intellectual property. In general:

- The *functional* features of your invention (how it works and what it does) may be protected under:
  - utility patent laws, and
  - trade secret laws.

Types of Intellectual Property			
	What is Protected?	**Examples**	**Length of Protection**
Utility Patent	Machines, compositions, plants, processes, articles of manufacture	Digital cameras, the drug known as *Viagra*, the hybrid rose, the process for ordering airline tickets online, the ironing board	20 years from the date of filing for patent applications filed after June 17, 1995
Design Patent	Ornamental designs for useful objects	External design of Adidas shoe	14 years from date of issue
Copyright	Books, photos, music, recordings, fine art, graphics, videos, film, architecture, computer programs	*Lord of the Rings* (book and movie), Marc Chagall prints, Madonna's *Like a Virgin* (music recording, compact disc artwork and video), architectural plans for design of Euro Disney, Adobe *Acrobat* program.	Life of the author plus 70 years for works created by a single author; other works such as works made for hire, 120 years from date of creation or 95 years from first publication
Trade Secret	Formula, method, device, compilation of facts or any information which is confidential and gives a business an advantage	Coca-Cola formula, special method for assembling a patented invention, new invention for which patent application has not been filed	As long as information remains confidential and functions as a trade secret
Trademark	Word, symbol, logo, design, slogan, trade dress or product configuration	Starbucks' name and distinctive green and white logo, General Electric's "We bring good things to life" slogan, Mr. Clean character, Skyy Vodka bottle	As long as business continuously uses trademark in connection with goods; federal registrations must be renewed every 10 years

• The *nonfunctional* features (the decorative appearance or packaging) may be protected under:
  ▪ trademark laws
  ▪ design patent laws, and
  ▪ copyright laws.

How can you tell if a feature is functional or nonfunctional? Ask the question: "Does this feature make the invention work better or is it done primarily for aesthetic reasons?"

For example, a unique V-shape of an electric guitar is not necessary for the guitar to function. It is primarily a decorative or nonfunctional element. On the other hand, a uniquely shaped hook used on a hanger could be primarily functional if it prevented the hanger from snagging on clothing.

Try viewing your invention in terms of its components. Once you've broken down your invention into components, categorize which laws protect which components. For example, is your product shape protectible under copyright or design patent law? Once you've determined which types of intellectual property apply to the various components of your invention, pursue the legal protection for each component.

EXAMPLE: Jan wants to invent a mousetrap that captures mice, but does not kill them. After years of research and experimentation, she finishes her invention, a trap that captures mice in a cylinder. Instead of using messy bait to attract mice into the trap, Jan employs a device of her own design that creates the smell of Swiss cheese by combining certain chemicals. Jan knows that there are lots of mousetraps available in the marketplace, so she decides to make hers as distinctive as possible. She gives the outer case of the trap a unique ovaloid high-tech design, painted to look like a piece of Swiss cheese. She names the trap the "Mousebuster" and hires an artist to design a fanciful mouse logo.

To determine how she may use the IP laws to protect her invention, Jan divides its components into the functional and nonfunctional.

• **Functional Elements:** The functional component of the invention is the mouse trap itself—that part of the product that actually does the work of catching the mouse. These include the cylinder trapping mechanism, the odor-dispersing mechanism and possibly the chemical formula that compromises the cheese odor. While developing her invention, Jan may use trade secrecy to protect these elements. Jan may apply for a patent when the invention is completed. If she does, and the patent issues or is published, those elements disclosed in the patent application will lose their status as trade secrets.

• **Nonfunctional Elements:** The nonfunctional elements of Jan's invention are those that don't actually do any work. Instead, they are used to ornament or identify the mousetrap. These elements include the product name (Mousebuster), logo, and the ovaloid high-tech design. Copyright, trademark and design patent law might all be used to protect the design. Once Jan began selling the device, the logo and name would be protected by trademark law.

B. Doing the Work of Obtaining IP Protection

Obtaining intellectual property protection for an invention takes work and can cost a good deal of money. You can save money by doing all or part of the work yourself instead of hiring others, such as lawyers and patent agents, to do it for you. However, doing it yourself will take some time and effort on your part—how much depends on the type of legal protection you're seeking. Many types of IP protection can be obtained easily. The chart below illustrates the relative difficulty of obtaining various types of IP protection.

1. Copyright Protection

Copyright protection is by far the easiest form of IP protection to obtain. Indeed, whether you want it or not, it begins automatically the moment you create a copyrightable work of authorship. However, there are two simple formalities that can greatly increase the value of a copyright—registering the copyright with the U.S. Copyright Office and using copyright notices. You can easily do both yourself.

2. Trade Secret Protection

Trade secret protection is a little harder to get than copyright. You must take steps to preserve the secrecy of your trade secrets. Principally, this means using nondisclosure agreements with employees, independent contractors, licensees and others to whom you divulge your secrets. A nondisclosure agreement (NDA) must be drafted and signed. It's not hard to do this yourself and we explain how in Chapter 13.

3. Trademark Protection

Trademark protection begins automatically when you are the first to use a protectible mark on a product or service that is sold to the public. However, many important benefits are obtained from registering a trademark with the USPTO. You can easily do this yourself entirely online through the USPTO website (www.uspto.gov). The USPTO has designed an interactive online trademark registration process in which you're asked a series of questions and given clear guidance.

Copyright   Trade Secrets   Trademarks   Design Patents   Utility Patents

Easy   **Difficult**

Difficulty of Obtaining Intellectual Property Protection

Before registering your mark, however, you should do a trademark search to make sure others aren't already using the mark. You can conduct a trademark search for free over the Internet or you can hire someone to do a search for you.

4. Design Patent Protection

Design patents can be used to protect the ornamental design of a functional feature of an invention. You must file an application with the USPTO to obtain a design patent. This type of patent application is fairly simple to prepare. Basically, all you need to do is provide a drawing of your design, a short written "specification" and pay the required fee. You may need help with the drawing, otherwise you can probably handle the application yourself. Unfortunately, however, a design patent application cannot be completed online as can a trademark application. This makes obtaining a design patent a bit more difficult than registering a trademark.

5. Utility Patent Protection

Utility patents, which constitute the vast majority of patents, are issued by the USPTO. This is by far the most difficult and expensive form of IP protection to obtain. You must file an application containing a drawing of the invention along with a detailed, precise explanation of how to make and use the claimed invention. Even if your invention is fairly simple, the drafting process may seem complex. That said, thousands of inventors have patented their inventions themselves.

From Pizza to Patent

John, an expert consultant on the pizza business, got ideas for two types of improved pizza boxes. He formed a small company, along with his brothers, to market the boxes. He decided he should patent his inventions, so he hired a patent attorney to file patent applications. One year and $12,000 later he obtained two patents. So far so good. But the problem was that once John started inventing he couldn't stop. He kept coming up with new ideas for inventions he wanted to patent, but he couldn't afford the attorney fees. So John decided to do the patent applications himself. Using the book *Patent It Yourself,* by David Pressman as his guide, he has filed for a total of 35 patents since 1994 and has had 24 of his patents issued by the USPTO. He has successfully licensed several of these inventions.

Chapter 13

Ten Things Inventors Should Know About Trade Secrets

1. All Inventions Begin As Trade Secrets 13/2

2. Any Valuable Information Can Be a Trade Secret 13/2

3. Trade Secrets Are the Do-It-Yourself Intellectual Property 13/3

4. You Can Make Money From Trade Secrets 13/3

5. Trade Secret Protection Is Weak 13/4

6. Trade Secret Laws Don't Protect Against Independent
   Discovery or Reverse Engineering 13/5

7. Trade Secret Protection Has No Definite Term 13/6

8. You Must Choose Between Trade Secret and Patent Protection 13/6

9. You Must Keep Your Trade Secrets Secret 13/9

10. When In Doubt, Use a Nondisclosure Agreement 13/11

*O*ften, the best way to protect an invention is simply to keep it secret. Business-related secrets are called trade secrets. This chapter provides you with the minimum amount of information you need to know about trade secrets and shows you how to draft your own nondisclosure agreements.

For more detailed guidance on all aspects of trade secrets, refer to *Nondisclosure Agreements: Protect Your Trade Secrets & More*, by Richard Stim & Stephen Fishman (Nolo).

1. All Inventions Begin As Trade Secrets

On December 17, 1903, Orville and Wilbur Wright accomplished the seemingly impossible: powered flight. Their rickety airplane carried Orville aloft for 852 feet along the beach at Kitty Hawk, North Carolina. What did they do next: Announce their feat to the newspapers? Publish their design in a technical journal or otherwise make it available to the public? No. They kept their plane locked in a garage for the next four and one-half years, allowing no one to see it while they awaited the issuance of a patent and closed licensing deals with many of the world's largest governments.

Many people have criticized the Wright brothers for their obsession with secrecy, but in fact, they were following a common practice among inventors—keeping it a secret. After all, people can't steal what they don't know about.

All inventions begin life as secrets. Only the inventor knows what has been created and some inventors, like the Wright brothers, jealously guard this information until they obtain a patent. Others—like the Dutch electronic firm, Philips, that never patented audiocassette technology—make their innovations freely available in order to establish a scientific or manufacturing standard throughout the world. Which strategy to take is up to you. But before you either lock your invention away behind closed doors or call a press conference to announce it to the world, you need to know a little about trade secrets.

2. Any Valuable Information Can Be a Trade Secret

We live in the "information age" and trade secret law is specifically intended to protect information. Virtually any information can be a trade secret so long as it is:

• valuable
• not generally known, and
• kept secret.

Trade secrecy, then, can protect virtually anything of value you know that others don't know. This makes trade secret protection far broader than any other form of intellectual property. It also makes it ideal for inventors, who quite often know something others don't.

Examples of protectible trade secrets include:

• **Physical Devices and Articles:** Physical devices such as the Wright brothers' airplane and other types of machines, devices or objects can be trade secrets.

- **Processes:** Chemical, mechanical and manufacturing processes are commonly protected under nondisclosure agreements (for example, processes for manufacturing chocolate powder, chicken pox vaccine or marble picture frames).
- **Designs, Blueprints and Specifications:** Designs for products, machines and structures, or other manufacturing specifications, can be protected as trade secrets (for example, the design for a photo-processing machine).
- **Formulas:** Formulas are an obvious choice for trade secret protection—the most well-known is the secret combination of flavoring oils and other ingredients that give Coca-Cola its distinctive taste. Other protectible formulas could be pharmaceutical, chemical or cosmetic compounds.
- **Business Information:** All types of business information can qualify as trade secrets, including business strategies and plans, marketing schemes, costs, pricing, new product names, information regarding new business opportunities, sales information and business books and records.

3. Trade Secrets Are the Do-It-Yourself Intellectual Property

Trade secrets are not issued by the government as are patents or automatically protected by law as are copyrights. Instead, you create a trade secret yourself by developing or discovering valuable information that is not generally known and then taking steps to keep it secret. (These steps are described in Section 9 below.) So long as the information remains secret, trade secret law will protect it.

4. You Can Make Money From Trade Secrets

One way to profit from a trade secret is to grant the right to use it to another person or company in return for money or some other remuneration. Such a transaction is called a trade secret license.

> **EXAMPLE:** J. J. Lawrence devised a secret formula for an antiseptic liquid. In 1881, he agreed to license the formula to Jordan Lambert in return for a royalty of $20 for every 12 dozen of the product sold. The product was to be called Listerine. Listerine is still manufactured and sold by Warner-Lambert Pharmaceutical Company, which paid royalties to Lawrence's heirs for decades.

Instead of licensing a trade secret, you can keep it to yourself and use the information to create your own products. For example, this is what the Coca-Cola Company has done. It has kept the formula for Coca-Cola secret since the 1890s, manufacturing the syrup for the drink itself.

5. Trade Secret Protection Is Weak

So long as a trade secret remains secret, this form of IP works beautifully. No one can copy an invention or idea they don't know about. But, what if someone else discovers your secret or discloses it to the public? In this event, the state and federal trade secret laws will give you certain legal rights, but you'll discover that they are quite limited.

Patent owners have the exclusive legal right to make, use or sell a patented invention —in effect, a monopoly. In contrast, trade secret owners have no monopoly over their information. Indeed, they have no exclusive rights at all. Instead, a trade secret owner has the legal right to prevent only two groups of people from using or disclosing a trade secret without permission:

- people who are bound by a duty of confidentiality not to disclose or use the information (see the sidebar below), and
- people who acquire the trade secret through improper means such as theft, industrial espionage or bribery.

If a person who falls into one of these two groups makes an unauthorized use or disclosure, the trade secret owner can seek relief in court. This relief can take the form of money damages and/or an injunction (court order) preventing a competitor from using the trade secret information.

Trade secret owners have no legal rights at all against anyone else—that is, those who are not in a confidential relationship or don't acquire trade secrets through spying or other improper means. This includes most of the people in the world. Such people are free to rediscover anyone's trade secrets though their own independent research and experimentation or by reverse engineering as described below. They may use the information any way they want—for example, they can maintain it as their own trade secret, seek to obtain a patent for an invention based on the secret or publish it or otherwise make it generally known. A trade secret automatically ceases to exist the moment it becomes public knowledge. Any of these things can happen at any time.

Who Has a Confidential Relationship With You?

People who learn about a trade secret through a confidential relationship with its owner may not use or disclose the trade secret without permission. These are the only people you should purposefully disclose a trade secret to. A duty of confidentiality may be deemed by the courts to arise automatically ("implied in law") from many types of relationships, including those between employers and employees who routinely receive trade secrets as part of their jobs. But by far the best way for a trade secret owner to establish a duty of confidentiality is to have each person to whom trade secrets are disclosed, agree in writing to preserve their confidentiality. This type of agreement is called a nondisclosure agreement or confidentiality agreement (see Section 10 below).

6. Trade Secret Laws Don't Protect Against Independent Discovery or Reverse Engineering

The trade secret laws do not protect against "reverse engineering." This is the process of taking a product or device apart and reducing it to its constituent parts or concepts to see how it works and to learn any trade secrets it contains. Any information learned through reverse engineering is considered to be in the public domain and no longer protectible as a trade secret. Reverse engineering is an accepted business practice and is perfectly legal so long as it does not violate anybody's copyright or patent rights.

Ole Evinrude
Inventor of the first successful outboard motor

EXAMPLE: In 1839, after years of experimentation and struggle, Charles Goodyear discovered how to vulcanize rubber —that is, how to chemically treat natural rubber to make it impervious to heat and cold. Confident that his secret process could not be reverse engineered, Goodyear permitted samples of his rubber to be taken to Great Britain. They found their way to Thomas Hancock, the leading British manufacturer and rubber expert. To Goodyear's amazement and eternal chagrin, Hancock reverse engineered Goodyear's process after many months of hard work. It was he, not Goodyear, who named the process vulcanization. To make matters even worse for Goodyear, Hancock obtained the British patent on the process.

A trade secret owner also has no rights against a person who independently discovers or develops his or her trade secret. Moreover, if such person makes the information generally available to the public, it will lose its trade secret status.

EXAMPLE: Peter has developed a revolutionary new coating that enables shower mirrors to remain fog-free. He maintains the formula as a trade secret and licenses it to a manufacturer who sells the mirrors to the public. Pat knows nothing about Peter's formula, but she is also interested in the problem of bathroom mirror fogging. She independently develops a nonfogging mirror coating that turns out to be identical to Peter's. In addition, she publishes the formula in a technical journal. The mirror coating is no longer a trade secret because it is now generally known in the bathroom mirror industry.

One legal expert has described trade secret protection as a leaky sieve because over time many of the most valuable trade secrets are lost when others independently discover or reverse engineer them. Few people have or develop information that is incapable of being independently discovered or reverse engineered by others.

7. Trade Secret Protection Has No Definite Term

Trade secrets have no definite term; they can last for decades or just a few days. A trade secret continues to receive legal protection as long as the requirements for trade secret protection remain in effect. In other words, as long as secrecy is maintained, the secret does not become generally known in the industry and the secret continues to provide a competitive advantage, it will be protected. Theoretically, a trade secret could last forever—for example, the formula for Coca-Cola has been maintained as a trade secret by the Coca-Cola Company for over 100 years.

On the other hand, if a trade secret is independently discovered or reverse engineered and made publicly known, it will cease to exist. For example, the formula for Listerine ceased to be a trade secret when it was published in a medical journal in 1931. Anyone is free to use that formula to manufacture their own mouthwash.

8. You Must Choose Between Trade Secret and Patent Protection

Everything that qualifies for a patent also can qualify as a trade secret. However, you can't have both patent and trade secret protection simultaneously because at some point the patent process requires public disclosure of the invention. If you have a patentable invention, you must decide whether to seek the powerful protection of a patent or to maintain the invention as a trade secret and rely on the relatively weak protection trade secret laws provide. This is the most important legal decision you'll have to make regarding your invention. The table below summarizes the relative advantages of trade secret and patent protection.

a. Using trade secrecy during development stage

Many inventors protect their patentable inventions as trade secrets during the initial stages of development and then seek patent protection when the invention is perfected. While your invention is being developed, the trade secret laws will give you the right to sue people who steal the invention. They will also protect you against unauthorized disclosures by employees and others in a confidential relationship with you.

A patent application is published verbatim when the patent issues or earlier, as discussed

Trade Secrets vs. Patents	
Trade Secrets	Patents
Length of protection. Trade secret protection lasts for as long as the material remains secret— theoretically, it could last forever.	**Length of protection.** Patent protection lasts for approximately 17-19 years.
Legal rights. A trade secret owner can stop only those who acquire the secret improperly.	**Legal rights.** Patent protection allows you to stop anyone from making, using, or selling the invention, including those who develop it through independent discovery or reverse engineering.
Obtaining protection. Trade secret rights are acquired immediately and inexpensively. No registration is required.	**Obtaining protection.** It often takes several years to acquire a patent from the government. Unless you file the application yourself, patent protection generally entails attorney fees between $5,000 to $10,000.
Breadth. Trade secrets can cover more information than a patent since a trade secret does not have to be novel and nonobvious.	**Breadth.** Patent rights only extend to the novel, nonobvious invention claimed in the patent application.
Value. A trade secret's value may diminish instantly if it is reverse engineered or independently discovered.	**Value.** A patented invention is generally worth more than one protected by trade secrecy and can be easier to license.

below, and at that point all of the trade secrets and know-how become public. This public disclosure doesn't usually hurt the inventor, because the patent can be used to prevent anyone else from commercially exploiting the underlying information.

> EXAMPLE: The Wright brothers kept all information about their airplane proto-type secret. They even painted the plane gray so it couldn't be easily photographed. After the plane first flew in 1903, they kept it locked up until they received a patent. At that point, the design became public knowledge—anyone could get and read a copy of the patent which explained how their invention worked. The airplane was no longer a trade secret. But this didn't hurt the Wright brothers because, now that they had a patent, they could sue anyone who commercially exploited their design without their permission. The Wrights filed many patent infringement suits. Indeed, they were so litigious some believe they held back the development of aviation in the U.S. for many years.

Every pending patent application filed on or after November 29, 2000 is published for the public to view 18 months after its filing date (or earlier if requested by the applicant). The only exception is if the applicant, at the time of filing, informs the USPTO that the application will not be filed abroad. If the patent application is published and later rejected you will be in the unfortunate position of having lost both trade secret and patent rights.

Therefore, if you are unsure of whether you will acquire a patent and do not want to risk losing trade secret rights, you must forego foreign patent rights and state at the time of filing your patent application that the application will not be filed abroad. That way, the information in the patent application will become publicly available only if and when a patent is granted. If unsure how to proceed regarding trade secret and patent rights, consult with a patent attorney.

You may not need to disclose all your trade secret information when you apply for a patent. For example, you could keep confidential the research method by which you arrived at your conclusions or test results. However, as we discuss in Chapter 14, when applying for a patent you cannot conceal any information that is necessary to explain how to make and use and your invention.

b. Relying solely on trade secrecy

You need not patent your invention at all and can instead rely solely on trade secrecy to protect it. This strategy can work well where your invention has a short useful life or doesn't qualify for a patent.

1. Inventions with short commercial lives

It takes at least one to three years to obtain a patent. If your invention is obsolete by the time you get a patent, the patent may prove a waste of time and money. Once you have the patent, you'll have the exclusive right to use, make or sell the invention. But, if it's obsolete, these rights are worthless. This can be a particular problem in areas where innovations occur quickly, such as computer software and high-tech.

In contrast, there's no waiting period to get a trade secret. Trade secret protection begins the moment you discover the secret. You can use trade secrecy to protect against thieves and unauthorized disclosures by employees and others during the development process. This can ensure you'll be the first to market or license your invention. Such a head start is invaluable if you're in a field where new products come and go quickly.

Many successful inventors have used this "get it to market quickly and don't worry about patents" strategy. Among them was aviation pioneer Glenn Curtiss. Unlike the Wright brothers who patented everything, Curtiss patented just a handful of the estimated 500 important aeronautical innovations he developed. Instead, he became successful by producing the best airplanes and didn't worry whether competitors copied his designs.

2. Inventions that don't qualify for patents

You may have no choice but to rely on trade secrecy if your invention cannot satisfy the requirements for patent protection. The most difficult requirements to meet are:

- novelty—that is, the invention must differ in some way from the publicly known or existing knowledge in the field of the invention, and
- nonobviousness—that is, the invention must accomplish something unexpected and surprising (nonobvious) rather than evident or apparent to those in the field.

Neither novelty nor nonobviousness are required for trade secret protection. It does not have to be new to the world, just generally not known within an industry or trade. Moreover, trade secrecy can protect even slight advances over common knowledge—advances that would not satisfy the patent law nonobviousness requirement. There are many inventions that aren't sufficiently novel or nonobvious to be patented, but that nonetheless have economic value and aren't generally known in the relevant industry, thus qualifying for trade secret protection. (Of course, it's hard to know what these inventions are, since they are kept secret.)

9. You Must Keep Your Trade Secrets Secret

Simply saying that information is a trade secret will not make it so. You must behave in a way that shows you want to keep the information secret. You don't have to turn your office, lab or workspace into an armed camp, but you must take reasonable precautions to protect your trade secrets. If you're an independent inventor or working with one or two others, there is no need to implement the kind of elaborate trade secret protection program that a Microsoft or IBM uses. You just need to habitually do a few things:

- identify your trade secrets
- use nondisclosure agreements
- maintain some minimal physical security
- maintain some minimal computer security, and
- label confidential information as such.

a. Identify Your Trade Secrets

First, identify exactly what information and material is a trade secret. As discussed above, a trade secret can be any information used by a person or company that provides an advantage over competitors who do not know or use the information. A trade secret can take almost any form. Unlike a patent, it need not be set forth in a formal drawing or description. It can consist of a roughly drawn sketch in a lab notebook or on the back of an envelope.

Your trade secrets would normally include such things as:

- everything written in your inventor's notebook (see Chapter 9)
- notes, photos, drawings and correspondence relating to the invention that are not included in your inventor's notebook
- pending patent applications
- invention prototypes
- business and marketing plans
- financial and investor information, and
- license agreements and other related agreements.

However, don't make the mistake of assuming that virtually all information concerning your invention is a trade secret that must be protected from disclosure to outsiders. Protecting such a volume of information could prove burdensome or impossible. Use your common sense in deciding whether disclosure of a particular item of information to a competitor would really cause harm.

b. Use nondisclosure agreements

Use nondisclosure agreements before disclosing your trade secrets to anyone (see Section 10 below).

c. Maintain physical security

Take a few minimal steps to ensure the physical security of your trade secrets. For example, keep your office securely locked at the end of the day. If others have access to your office, lab or workspace, implement a "clean desk" and "locked file cabinets and desk drawers" policy. Documents containing trade secrets should not be left on desktops when not in use; rather, they should be locked in desk drawers or filing cabinets.

d. Maintain computer security

Take reasonable measures to prevent unauthorized people from gaining access to your computer system. For example, use secret passwords and access procedures. The passwords should be periodically changed, especially when an employee who knows the current passwords quits or is fired.

Take Care With Email

Make certain that both you and your employees take care not to inadvertently disclose trade secrets in email. Always keep in mind that an email recipient can easily forward copies of a message to any number of other people. Given the enormous volume of email and the fact that it is transmitted over the Internet in small packets rather than all at once, it's unlikely that anyone will intercept a specific email message in transit. Email is most likely to be read by unauthorized people when it is stored on a computer after it's composed and sent. It's wise to encrypt any email that contains any particularly sensitive information. This will make it difficult or impossible for your email to be read without your permission. One well-known encryption program, called PGP, is available for free on the Internet (www.pgpi.org).

---

e. Label trade secrets confidential

Before giving others access to documents (both hard copy and electronic) containing trade secrets, mark them "confidential." This is the best way to alert employees, independent contractors and others that a document contains trade secrets.

Here is some language you can use on any type of trade secret material:

THIS DOCUMENT IS CONFIDENTIAL AND PROPRIETARY TO [*your name*] AND MAY NOT BE REPRODUCED, PUBLISHED OR DISCLOSED TO OTHERS WITHOUT AUTHORIZATION.

You should also obtain a rubber stamp reading CONFIDENTIAL and use it to mark documents when it's inconvenient to use the longer notice above.

⚠️ **Don't mark everything confidential.** Don't go overboard and mark everything in sight confidential. If virtually everything, including public information, is marked "confidential," a court may conclude that nothing was really confidential. It is better not to mark anything than to mark everything.

Try to keep faxing and emailing of trade secrets to a minimum. When it's unavoidable, be sure to include a confidentiality notice such as this one:

THE MESSAGES AND DOCUMENTS TRANSMITTED WITH THIS NOTICE CONTAIN CONFIDENTIAL INFORMATION BELONGING TO THE SENDER.

IF YOU ARE NOT THE INTENDED RECIPIENT OF THIS INFORMATION, YOU ARE HEREBY NOTIFIED THAT ANY DISCLOSURE, COPYING, DISTRIBUTION OR USE OF THE INFORMATION IS STRICTLY PROHIBITED. IF YOU HAVE RECEIVED THIS TRANSMISSION IN ERROR, PLEASE NOTIFY THE SENDER IMMEDIATELY.

Although this notice cannot prevent the public disclosure of material that is faxed or emailed to the wrong location, it demonstrates your diligence in preserving trade secrecy and makes it clear to people receiving the fax or email that it contains trade secrets and should be treated with care. The notice can be placed on a fax cover sheet or at the beginning of an email message.

Advanced Trade Secret Protection Programs

There are other more advanced trade secret protections you may wish to employ as your enterprise grows in size and you have employees, contractors and others working for you. These may include beefing up physical security and controlling business visitors, screening employee publications, restricting photocopying by employees and shredding documents containing trade secrets. For detailed coverage of these techniques, see *Nondisclosure Agreements: Protect Your Trade Secrets & More*, by Richard Stim & Stephen Fishman (Nolo).

10. When In Doubt, Use a Nondisclosure Agreement

A nondisclosure agreement (often called an "NDA" for short) is a document in which a person who is given access to trade secrets promises not to disclose them to others without permission from the trade secret owner.

Before you give any person access to your trade secrets, make sure that he or she has signed a nondisclosure agreement.

All employees who may have access to trade secrets should be required to sign nondisclosure agreements before they begin work, or on their very first day of work. If you have employees who have not signed nondisclosure agreements, you should ask them to do so if they are given access to any trade secrets. A nondisclosure provision may be part of an employment agreement, which covers other aspects of employment, including confidentiality issues. Chapter 10 contains sample employment agreements including nondisclosure provisions.

Never expose a nonemployee consultant to trade secrets without having a signed nondisclosure agreement on file. The nondisclosure agreement may be contained in an independent contractor agreement, which covers all aspects of the work relationship. This is discussed in detail in Chapter 10; sample forms are included.

Nondisclosure agreements should also be used to protect trade secrets from unauthorized disclosure and/or use by prospective licensees, investors, prototype makers, manufacturers and other third parties. However, some prospective licensees refuse to sign nondisclosure agreements. This is usually not because they want to steal your invention, but because they are afraid of getting sued by paranoid inventors. You may have no choice but to disclose your invention without the benefit of a signed nondisclosure agreement or find another licensee.

If you find yourself in this situation, you should weigh the following factors before deciding whether or not to disclose your trade secrets without the benefit of a signed NDA:

- The reputation of the company—that is, is it a well-known concern with a reputation for treating inventors well, or a fly-by-night operation you've never heard of.
- The value of the trade secret—the more valuable the secret, the more you should want to protect it with a signed NDA.
- The potential economic benefit of entering into a license with the company—is it worthwhile risking your trade secrets?
- The amount of trade secret information you will need to disclose—you may be able to protect yourself by just giving the company an overview of your invention, keeping valuable details secret.

We can't decide for you whether to disclose or not. But we can tell you that theft of trade secrets from independent inventors is relatively rare.

a. Why use NDAs?

Using nondisclosure agreements consistently is the single most important element of any trade secret protection program, accomplishing these basic purposes:

- It conclusively establishes that the parties have a confidential relationship. As discussed above, only people who are in a confidential relationship with a trade secret owner have a legal duty not to disclose the owner's trade secrets without permission.

- Signing such an agreement makes clear to a person who receives a trade secret that it is to be kept in confidence. It impresses on him or her that the company is serious about maintaining its trade secrets.
- If it's ever necessary to file a lawsuit, a signed nondisclosure agreement precludes a court from concluding that you didn't bother to use nondisclosure agreements because you really didn't have any trade secrets.

b. Drafting your own nondisclosure agreements

It's not difficult to create your own nondisclosure agreement. The nondisclosure agreement provided below can be used with any outside individual or company to whom you disclose your trade secrets, including contractors, potential licensees or investors.

 The full text of the nondisclosure agreement is on the CD-ROM forms disk.

 For nondisclosure agreements to be used with employees and independent contractors, use the agreements in Chapter 10.

Introductory Paragraph. Fill in your company name (you are the Inventor). Then fill in the name of the outside individual or company being granted access to your trade secrets (the Recipient).

1. Confidential Information

Select either Alternative A, B or C, and delete the others. Here's how to choose:

Alternative A. Use this clause if you're disclosing information about an invention for which no regular or provisional patent application is pending. Give a general description of your invention here.

Alternative B. Use this clause if you've applied for a patent or filed a provisional patent application and list the application number.

Alternative C. Use this clause if you're disclosing information unrelated to an invention. Describe what this information is. This can be a general or specific description. An example of a general description would be: "All information or material that has or could have commercial value or other utility in the business in which Inventor is engaged."

Note: You need not use an NDA when disclosing information about an invention that has been patented (see Section 8).

2. Duty of Confidentiality

This clause makes clear that your trade secrets must be kept in confidence by the Recipient and may not be revealed to others without your prior written consent.

3. Return of Materials

This clause requires the Recipient to return all materials relating to your trade secrets upon your written request.

4. Exclusions

This provision describes all the types of information that are not covered by the agreement.

Nondisclosure Agreement

This nondisclosure agreement (the "Agreement") is entered into by and between [*insert your name, business form and address*] ("Inventor") and [*insert name, business form and address of person or company to whom you are disclosing information*] ("Recipient") to prevent the unauthorized disclosure of confidential information. Accordingly, Inventor and Recipient agree as follows:

1. Confidential Information

The following constitutes confidential proprietary trade secret information ("Confidential Information") belonging to Inventor:

[Alternative A: If there is no provisional patent application or pending patent application]
All information, data and materials relating to the following Invention: [describe]

_____ .

[Alternative B: If there is a pending patent application or provisional patent application]
All information, data and materials relating to the invention as described in the application for United States patent (U.S. Patent Office Application Serial No. _____ or U.S. Patent Office Provisional Patent application No. _____).

[Alternative C: Other information]

_____ .

2. Duty of Confidentiality

Recipient will treat Confidential Information with the same degree of care and safeguards that it takes with its own Confidential Information, but in no event less than a reasonable degree of care. Without Inventor's prior written consent, Recipient will not:

(a) disclose Confidential Information to any third party;

(b) make or permit to be made copies or other reproductions of Confidential Information; or

(c) make any commercial use of Confidential Information.

These exclusions are based on court decisions and state trade secret laws that say these types of information do not qualify for trade secret protection. These legal exceptions exist with or without an agreement, but they are commonly included in a contract to make it clear to everyone that such information is not considered a trade secret.

5. Term

There are two alternate provisions dealing with how long the agreement will stay in effect. Select the clause that best suits your needs and delete the other:

Alternative 1. This provision has no definite time limit—in other words, the recipient must keep mum until the trade secret ceases to be a trade secret. This may occur when the information becomes generally known, you disclose it to the public, or it ceases being a trade secret for some other reason. This gives you the broadest protection possible.

Alternative 2. Some recipients don't want to be subject to open-ended confidentiality obligations. Use this clause if the recipient insists that the agreement contain a definite expiration date. The Agreement should last as long as the information is likely to remain a trade secret. Five years is a common period, but it can be much shorter, even as little as six months. The time period may need to be shorter for Internet and high-tech related inventions because of the fast pace of innovation.

Whichever alternative you choose, you'll need to insert the date the agreement begins. This can be the date it's signed or a date in the future.

6. No Rights Granted

This clause makes clear that you are not granting any ownership rights in the confidential information to the Recipient.

7. Warranty

A warranty is a promise. Here, you promise the Recipient that you have the right to disclose the information. This is intended to assure the Recipient that it won't be sued by some third party claiming that the trade secrets belong to it and that you had no right to reveal them to the Recipient.

8. Disputes

This provision is optional. As you doubtless know, court litigation can be very expensive. To avoid these costs, alternative forms of dispute resolution have been developed that don't involve going to court. These include mediation and arbitration.

Under this clause, you and the recipient first try to resolve your dispute yourselves. If this doesn't work, either party has the option of requiring mediation. Mediation, an increasingly popular alternative to full-blown litigation, works like this: You and the Recipient agree on a neutral third person to try to help you settle your dispute. The mediator has no power to impose a decision, only to try to help you arrive at one. In other words, unless both parties agree with the resolution, there is no resolution.

If mediation doesn't work, you must submit the dispute to binding arbitration. Arbitration is usually like an informal court trial without a jury, but involves arbitrators instead of judges.

3. Return of Materials

Upon Inventor's written request, Recipient shall immediately return to Inventor any and all materials relating to Confidential Information.

4. Exclusions

This agreement does not apply to any information that:

(a) was in Recipient's possession or was known to Recipient, without an obligation to keep it confidential, before such information was disclosed to Recipient by Inventor;

(b) is or becomes public knowledge through a source other than Recipient and through no fault of Recipient;

(c) is or becomes lawfully available to Recipient from a source other than Inventor; or

(d) is disclosed by Recipient with Inventor's prior written approval.

5. Term

Alternative 1:

This Agreement and Recipient's duty to hold Confidential Information in confidence takes effect on [*date*] and shall remain in effect until Confidential Information is no longer a trade secret or until Inventor sends Recipient written notice releasing Recipient from this Agreement, whichever occurs first.

Alternative 2:

This Agreement and Recipient's duty to hold Confidential Information in confidence takes effect on [*date*] and shall remain in effect until [*date*].

6. No Rights Granted

This Agreement does not constitute a grant or an intention or commitment to grant any right, title or interest in Confidential Information to Recipient.

7. Warranty

Inventor warrants that it has the right to make the disclosures under this Agreement.

8. Disputes

Inventor and Recipient agree that every dispute between them arising under this Agreement will be resolved as follows:

First, they will meet and attempt to resolve the dispute in a good faith manner.

If they cannot resolve their dispute after conferring, either Inventor or Recipient may require the other to submit the matter to nonbinding mediation, utilizing the services of an impartial professional mediator approved by both parties.

If Inventor and Recipient cannot come to an agreement following mediation, they agree to submit the matter to binding arbitration at a mutually agreeable location. The arbitration shall be conducted under the Commercial Arbitration Rules of the American Arbitration Association. Absent an agreement to the contrary, any such arbitration shall be conducted by an arbitrator experienced in intellectual property law. An award of arbitration shall be final and binding on the parties and may be confirmed in a court of competent jurisdiction.

9. General Provisions

a. Relationships
Nothing contained in this Agreement shall be deemed to constitute either party a partner, joint venturer or employee of the other party for any purpose.

b. Entire Agreement
This Agreement expresses the complete understanding of the parties with respect to the subject matter and supersedes all prior proposals, agreements, representations and understandings. This Agreement may not be amended except in a writing signed by both parties.

b. Entire Agreement
This Agreement expresses the complete understanding of the parties with respect to the subject matter and supersedes all prior proposals, agreements, representations and understandings. This Agreement may not be amended except in a writing signed by both parties.

c. Waiver
The failure to exercise any right provided in this Agreement shall not be a waiver of prior or subsequent rights.

You may be represented by a lawyer in the arbitration, but it's not required. The arbitrator's decision is final and binding—that is, you can't go to court and try the dispute again if you don't like the arbitrator's decision, except in unusual cases where the arbitrator was guilty of fraud, misconduct or bias.

By using this provision, then, you're giving up your right to go to court. The advantage is that arbitration is usually much cheaper and faster than court litigation.

9. General Provisions

The following provisions are typically included at the end of an agreement. That does not mean they are unimportant.

a. Relationships

This clause is intended to make clear that you and the Recipient are not in business together. This can help avoid disputes later on.

b. Entire Agreement

This clause is intended to maker clear that this NDA is your final agreement with the Recipient about the disclosure of the confidential information. This avoids any later claims that promises not contained in the agreement were made. The clause also requires any changes to the NDA to be set forth in writing. Again, this helps avoid disputes.

c. Waiver

This provision states that even if you don't promptly complain about a violation of the NDA, you still have the right to complain about it later. Without this kind of clause, if you know the other party has breached the agreement but you let it pass, you give up (waive) your right to sue over it.

d. Injunctive Relief

An injunction is a court order directing a person to do (or stop doing) something. If someone violated your NDA, you would want a court order directing that person to stop using your secrets. This clause provides that the Recipient agrees that the harm caused by a breach is irreparable, so you will have less to prove if and when you seek a court order. This makes it easier to obtain an injunction.

e. Attorney Fees

Under this provision, if either party has to sue the other in court or bring an arbitration proceeding to enforce the agreement and wins—that is, becomes the prevailing party—the loser is required to pay the other party's attorney fees and expenses. If you have to sue the Recipient in court or bring an arbitration proceeding to enforce the agreement and win, you normally will not be awarded the amount of your attorney fees unless your agreement requires it. Including such an attorney fees provision in the agreement can help make filing a lawsuit economically feasible.

f. Governing Law

It's best to decide this ahead of time and set forth which state's law will be controlling in your agreement. There is some advantage to having the law of your own state govern, since your local attorney will likely be more familiar with that law. Insert the state whose law will govern in this provision.

d. Injunctive Relief

Recipient agrees that Inventor will suffer serious harm if Recipient does not honor the terms of this Agreement. Therefore, Recipient agrees that, in addition to any other remedies available to Inventor at law or in equity, it will be subject to the issuance of injunctive relief to enforce this Agreement.

e. Attorney Fees

In a dispute arising out of or related to this Agreement, the prevailing party shall have the right to collect from the other party its reasonable attorney fees and costs and necessary expenditures.

f.   Governing Law

This Agreement shall be governed in accordance with the laws of the State of

_____.

g. Successors and Assigns

This Agreement shall bind each party's heirs, successors and assigns.

10. Signatures

_____   _____

Inventor's Signature   Recipient's Signature

_____   _____

Date   Date

g. Successors and Assigns

It's possible that either party may be succeeded by someone else. For example, a sole proprietor's heirs may inherit the business. In that case you would want to be sure that the heirs were bound by the same nondisclosure requirements.

10. Signatures

It is not necessary for the parties to sign the agreement in the same room or on the same day. At least two copies should be signed, with each party retaining one. ∎

Chapter 14

Fifteen Things Inventors Should Know About Patents

1. Patents Are the Most Powerful IP Protection 14/2

2. A Patent—By Itself—Won't Make You Rich 14/2

3. You Can Profit From Your Invention Without a Patent 14/3

4. Patents Don't Work Well for Inventions With Short Commercial Lives 14/4

5. Patents Are Expensive and Difficult to Obtain 14/5

6. Most Inventions Are Not Patentable 14/7

7. Do a Patent Search Before Anything Else 14/9

8. You Must Document Your Inventing Activities 14/10

9. You'll Lose Your Right to Patent If You Violate the One-Year Rule 14/10

10. Filing a Provisional Patent Application Can Save You Money 14/11

11. Patents Last 17–18 Years 14/12

12. Enforcing a Patent Can Be Difficult and Expensive 14/13

13. U.S. Patents Only Work in the United States 14/13

14. Filing for Patents Helps Show You're in Business 14/13

15. Design Patents Can Protect the Way Your Invention Looks 14/14

This chapter provides an overview of patent law. It focuses on utility patents, those patents that protect what we typically think of as inventions: machines, useful articles, mechanical and industrial processes and other things that do useful work. (Design patents, which can protect the ornamental or aesthetic elements of an invention, are covered briefly in Section 15.)

For expert guidance on every aspect of the patent process, refer to *Patent It Yourself,* by David Pressman (Nolo).

1. Patents Are the Most Powerful IP Protection

Once upon a time (back in the 1980s), the Kodak Corporation manufactured instant cameras and film. Today, you might be able to find an old Kodak instant camera for sale on Ebay, but they are no longer manufactured or sold by Kodak. Why? It's not because the cameras weren't successful products—Kodak sold more than 16 million of them. It's because of patent law. The Polaroid Corporation, the instant photography pioneer, sued Kodak, claiming its cameras and film infringed on several Polaroid patents. After 15 years of litigation, Polaroid won. Kodak was barred from manufacturing or selling the cameras and film and had to pay almost $900 million in damages to Polaroid.

The Kodak case, the largest patent suit of all time, illustrates the enormous potential power of a patent. A person or company that has a valid patent and the means to enforce it has the exclusive right to make, use and sell the invention described in the patent. Like Polaroid, it can exclude all others from the field and manufacture and sell the invention itself, or license it to others. In effect, the patent provides a potential monopoly on the invention for the length of the patent. No other form of intellectual property—trade secrets, trademarks or copyrights—provides such an expansive monopoly.

2. A Patent—By Itself—Won't Make You Rich

Before you jump on the patent bandwagon, be aware that obtaining a patent is no guarantee of financial success. Consider what happened to Abraham Lincoln, the only president to patent an invention. In 1849, Lincoln received Patent No. 6469 for a device he invented to lift boats over river shoals. However, although it qualified for a patent, the invention didn't seem to be very practical. It was never actually used on a boat, never manufactured and never earned Lincoln any money. Lincoln's experience is far from unusual. Indeed, it is generally estimated that less than 3% of patented inventions ever earn a dime for their inventors.

If you have an invention that people want, such as instant photography, a patent can be enormously beneficial. But, if your invention is worthless, your patent will be too. Of course, the problem is that it's often impossible to know in advance which inventions will be successful and which will be failures. So,

Abraham Lincoln
Inventor of a method of using air chambers within a steamboat

inventors dutifully prepare and file patent applications as insurance just in case they strike it rich.

3. You Can Profit From Your Invention Without a Patent

Back in 1957, an Australian who was visiting Richard Knerr and Arthur "Spud" Melin in California, mentioned that Australian children twirled bamboo hoops around their waists in gym class. Knerr and Melin happened to be the owners of a fledgling toy company called Wham-O. They decided to manufacture and sell the device. They made it out of brightly colored plastic (then a relatively new material) and named it the Hula Hoop. The Hula Hoop

was introduced in 1958 and over 100 million were sold worldwide that year alone. However, the Hula Hoop could not be patented because it was not novel (see Section 6). It had been around in one form or another for at least 3,000 years. But the lack of a patent didn't hurt sales. Although other companies began to manufacture similar devices, Wham-O continued to dominate the field because of good marketing and because, under the trademark laws, it was the only company that could call the device the Hula Hoop.

So, you can make money from an invention without a patent. On the other hand, if, like most independent inventors, you don't plan on manufacturing and selling your invention yourself, obtaining a patent can make it easier to license your invention to a manufacturer. Many companies prefer to license patented inventions (or at least those for which a patent application has been filed). Compared to trade secrets which can be lost at any time, patents are a viewed as a "solid" investment, easier to enforce and to value.

If you proceed with the patent application process, you can license your invention before the patent is issued. Sometimes a licensee may condition the license upon the granting of the patent. That is, if the patent does not issue, the license is canceled or the royalties are reduced to reflect only the nonpatentable aspects that have been licensed.

 For expert guidance on how to license an invention, refer to *License Your Invention*, by Richard Stim (Nolo).

Patents Can Help You Get Money

Obtaining, or at least filing for, patents can also help you obtain financing. Consider the case of the brothers David and Gregory Chudnovsky, both brilliant mathematicians who emigrated from Russia to the U.S. in 1978. Over a period of two decades, they devised a number of computer-related inventions that could have been quite valuable, including a novel switching network. However, they never attempted to patent any of these inventions. They talked to many potential investors about helping to finance the development of their inventions; but, although the investors liked the brothers' inventions, none were willing to put up any money. They were simply afraid to invest in an unpatented invention. Then, in 1998, the Chudnovskys came up with one of their best ideas yet—a memory-addressing system that could substantially speed up computer performance and become an industry standard. This time, they decided to go for a patent. They lined up a group of investors who put up the money to hire a patent law firm to file a patent application for their complex invention and then help market it. Their patent issued in 2002 and they began to actively seek companies for licensure.

4. Patents Don't Work Well for Inventions With Short Commercial Lives

Patent rights do not actually begin until the patent is issued. Years may pass between the time a patent application is filed and the issuance of the patent. This time period is known as the *pendency* or *patent pending* period. The owner of a patent cannot prevent any infringing activity that occurs during the pendency period.

Once the patent issues, the patent owner may have some rights against people who infringed during the pendency period if:

- the patent owner did not seek non-publication of the application when filing (see Chapter 13, Section 8)
- the patent application was published by the USPTO under the 18-month rule
- the infringers had notice of the publication, and
- the patent was infringed after notice of the publication.

In this event, the patent owner can sue for damages for infringements occurring after the date of notice. No claims can be brought for patent infringements that occurred before the application was published.

> **EXAMPLE:** On February 1, 2004, Sally applied for a patent for a new type of disco ball. Her patent application was published by the USPTO on August 1, 2005. Sally obtained her patent on February 1, 2006. There was a two-year pendency

period before Sally got her patent—February 1, 2004 through February 1, 2006. During this entire time, PartyOn, an entertainment supply company, manufactured an identical disco ball. Sally found out about this and notified PartyOn on August 2, 2005 that her patent application had been published and it should stop selling the ball. PartyOn ignored her. Sally may sue PartyOn for patent infringement and claim its profits on sales that occurred after August 2, 2005. But Sally can collect no patent infringement damages for PartyOn's sales before that date.

The fact that patents take so long to obtain often makes them less than ideal for inventions that have a short commercial life. By the time you get your patent, the invention may be obsolete or superseded by other products. You won't be able to sue for infringements that occurred before you got the patent, and no infringements may occur after your patent issues because the invention is no longer commercially valuable. So, you'll have a patent for an invention no one wants and have no one to sue—in other words, you'll have a "hunting license" without anything to hunt.

EXAMPLE: Bill invents a new type of back-scratching device. He applies for a patent on February 1, 2005. Three months later, BigCo independently develops the same device. BigCo doesn't worry about patents. Instead, it immediately starts to manufacture and sell the back scratcher.

To everyone's surprise, the device becomes a hit during the 2005 Christmas season and sells quite well. However, by 2006, the market for the back scratcher dries up and BigCo stops making and selling them. It has earned a tidy profit from the product without spending the time and money to get a patent. Bill's patent is published in July 2006 and the patent is finally issued in 2008. Unfortunately, no one wants to buy the back scratcher. He can't find a manufacturer to license it. And he can't sue BigCo for violating his patent because it manufactured and sold the back scratcher only before the patent was published. Bill decides to frame his worthless patent and hang it on the wall.

5. Patents Are Expensive and Difficult to Obtain

You get trade secret, trademark and copyright protection automatically simply by creating or using something that is protectible. Patents are different. There is no such thing as an automatic patent. To obtain patent protection an inventor must file an application with, and be issued a patent by, the U.S. Patent and Trademark Office (USPTO) in Arlington, Virginia, a branch of the U.S. Department of Commerce. A U.S. patent application typically consists of:

- an explanation of why the invention is different from all previous and similar developments (the "prior art")

- a detailed description of the structure and operation of the invention (called a patent specification) that teaches how to build and use the invention
- a precise description of the aspects of the invention to be covered by the patent (called the patent claims)
- all drawings that are necessary to fully explain the specification and claims
- a statement under oath that the information in the application is true, and
- the filing fee.

When the USPTO receives an application, a patent examiner is assigned to it. Typically, the application process takes between one and three years.

The examiner is responsible for deciding whether the application meets all technical requirements and whether the invention qualifies for a patent. Typically, there is a back-and-forth exchange between the applicant and the patent examiner regarding the scope of the patent claims. Once the application is approved, the applicant pays a patent issue fee and receives an official copy of the patent, and the USPTO issues a patent deed.

To keep a patent in effect, three additional fees must be paid over the life of the patent. At present, the total patent fee for a small inventor, from application to issue to expiration, is over $4,000. For large corporations, it is twice this amount.

Patent Claims Are Crucial

As mentioned above, a patent grants you the right to stop others from making, selling or using your invention during the term of the patent. The extent of these rights depends largely upon the scope and boundaries of your invention. Patent claims—which essentially define the scope of your invention—are the heart of your invention and what makes it attractive to licensees. These claims are located in your patent application. The claims define the boundaries of the invention in the same way that a deed establishes the boundaries of real property. Drafting patent claims is a specialized skill (as you will no doubt see from the sample claim for a baby bib below).

EXAMPLE: A baby's bib comprising: a body portion of a first plastic material having an opening to receive a baby's neck; and a bead formed of a second plastic material more compressible than that of the first plastic material and moulded around a defining edge of the opening to be integral with the body portion and, in use, to encircle the neck of the baby, the bead being such as to permit compression of the second plastic material in a direction substantially radially of the bead but to prevent extension of the second plastic material in a direction along the length of the bead. (Patent No. 6,481,016.)

You can prepare and file your own patent application or you can hire a patent attorney or patent agent to do it for you. A patent agent is a nonlawyer with some technical training who is licensed by the USPTO to prepare patent applications and deal with the USPTO, a process called "patent prosecution." A patent attorney is a lawyer with a technical background who is specially licensed to practice before the USPTO. A patent lawyer can do everything an agent can do plus represent you in patent litigation. Hiring an attorney or agent will cost several thousand dollars, depending upon the complexity of the invention.

Before you decide to hire a patent professional or do the work yourself, obtain and read *Patent It Yourself,* by David Pressman (Nolo). This book is the patent filing bible and will show you everything that must be done to get a patent through the USPTO. If, after reading *Patent It Yourself,* you decide that filing by yourself is too daunting, you can and hire a patent professional. But, if you think you can do it yourself, go ahead and give it a try. If you run into problems, you can always hire a patent pro later.

6. Most Inventions Are Not Patentable

You can't get a patent for just any invention. Rather, to be patentable an invention must:

- fall within one or more of five statutory classes of inventions (that is, it must be "statutory subject matter")
- have some utility, no matter how trivial
- be novel (this means that it must have one or more new main elements), and

- be nonobvious (a significant development) to somebody positioned to understand the technical field of the invention.

These requirements are so strict that only a minority of all the inventions that are created every day are patentable. Of the patent applications that are filed each year, almost half are rejected by the USPTO.

a. Statutory Subject Matter

First, the invention must fall within one of the classes of inventions that can be patented, called statutory subject matter. This is the easiest requirement to satisfy. Virtually anything we normally think of as an invention—and many we don't—can qualify. A patent can be issued for any new and useful:

- process—a method of accomplishing a result through a series of steps, for example, a process for sterilizing surgical equipment
- machine—a device that accomplishes a result by the interaction of its parts, for example, a gear shift in a rowing machine
- article of manufacture—a single object without movable parts such as a pencil or a garden rake, or an object with movable parts that are incidental such as a folding chair or an ironing board
- composition of matter—any combination of chemical or other materials, for example Teflon or WD-40, or
- improvement on an already-existing invention—for example, an improvement upon a household plunger.

These categories are interpreted very broadly and it is possible that your invention may fall into more than one category. For example, computer software can usually be described both as a process (the steps that it takes to make the computer do something) and as a machine (a device that takes information from an input device and moves it to an output device). Regardless of the number of categories a particular invention falls under, only one patent may be issued on it.

Unpatentable Inventions

Some things do not qualify for a patent, no matter how interesting or important they are. For instance, mathematical formulas, laws of nature, newly discovered substances that occur naturally in the world and purely theoretical phenomena (for instance a scientific principle like superconductivity without regard to its use in the real world) have long been considered unpatentable. But the law in this area can be subtle and tricky. For instance, some computer software heavily based on mathematical formulas may nevertheless qualify for a patent if the patent application limits the software to specific uses on specific machines. This is because the patent laws may not be used to create a monopoly on an idea per se, but can be used to create a monopoly on a specific application of an idea. For example, no patent may issue on the complex mathematical formulae that are used in space navigation, but a patent is certainly appropriate for the software and machines that translate those equations and make the space shuttle go where it's supposed to go.

b. Usefulness

An invention must have a use or purpose and it must work—that is, be capable of performing its intended purpose—at least in theory. For this reason, no patent has ever issued on a perpetual motion machine (a device that does more work than the energy supplied to it). Patents may issue on inventions that have some type of usefulness (utility), even if the use is humorous, such as a musical condom or a motorized spaghetti fork.

c. Novelty

The patent system is designed to encourage new inventions. So, in addition to being useful, at least some element of an invention must be novel (new) to be patented. (In patent lingo, it must differ from the "prior art," as explained in Section 7, below.) Your invention isn't novel if someone previously invented it, wrote about it or if a year has passed since it was publicly disclosed or sold.

d. Nonobviousness

It's not enough that an invention simply be wholly or partly novel to be patentable—that would be too easy. It must also be "nonobvious." The idea here is that an invention that anyone in the field could think of doesn't deserve a patent. The nonobviousness rule eliminates more inventions from the patent race than any other requirement.

Your invention is most likely to meet the nonobviousness test if:

- it produces new and unexpected results
- it has enjoyed commercial success
- there has been a need in the industry for the invention
- others have tried but failed to achieve the same result
- you did what others said could not be done
- others have copied the invention, or
- the invention has been praised by others in the field.

7. Do a Patent Search Before Anything Else

David Lindsay, a part-time inventor and author of the book *The Patent Files* (Lyons Press), came up with an idea for an invention: a method of spelling out words by stringing shoelaces through a grid of eyelets. This seemed like unusual invention that no one had thought of before, so he filed a patent application. However, the patent examiner found that the USPTO had already issued at least six patents for similar inventions. The examiner rejected his application because the invention was neither novel nor nonobvious. Lindsay spent several thousand dollars on filing and attorney fees for nothing.

The way to avoid this result is to conduct a patent search (also called a "prior art search") to make sure your invention really is new. Remember, over six million patents have been issued by the USPTO, so there is a good chance somebody has already patented an invention similar to the one you've conceived. Even if they haven't patented it, they may have thought of it and written about it.

Doing a patent search involves examining what lawyers call "prior art" to determine if anyone has built, patented or documented the same invention before you. Prior art can come from just about anywhere—it includes all previous developments that are available to the public. All of the following are prior art:

- patents for inventions similar to yours
- publications discussing inventions like yours
- foreign patents for inventions similar to yours
- any commercial sale or use of an invention like yours, and
- any public knowledge or use of a similar invention.

It's easiest to do a patent search in two stages. In the first stage, you do a basic patent search yourself in which you look for prior patents, publications or sales of similar inventions. Today, because of the Internet, it's easier and cheaper to do a basic patent search than ever before. Databases containing copies of nearly every patent ever issued have been placed online and can be searched for free. The Internet also contains vast stores of technical and academic publications and information—all of which can be prior art.

If no prior art shows up in your basic patent search, you can feel encouraged and go ahead and perfect your invention and even build a prototype and perhaps file a provisional patent application (see Section 10). Although a vast number of patents can be read online, keep in mind, however, that some databases only permit you to search the text of U.S. patents issued in the last 25–30 years. Therefore, Internet searching is often

incomplete—there may be other, more relevant prior art in existence that your Internet
search doesn't turn up. At some point before
filing a regular patent application or selling
your invention, you should conduct a prior
art search beyond the Internet in which
someone—you or a professional searcher—
reviews files at the USPTO or at engineering
libraries.

For guidance on how to conduct a patent
search, refer to *Patent Searching Made
Easy*, by David Hitchcock (Nolo)

8. You Must Document Your Inventing Activities

The U.S. patent system is unique in that the
"first to invent" an invention is entitled to the
patent. In the rest of the world, the first inventor to file a patent application (or "first to
file") is granted protection, regardless of who
was first to create the invention. This "first to
invent" rule has important ramifications for all
inventors.

To prove that you were the first to invent
your invention, you have to be able to prove
to the USPTO the date you conceived the invention and that you were diligent about reducing it to practice. Conception of an
invention is a mental process—you formulate
and perceive a method of solving a problem
or carrying out a result. Reducing to practice
means that you can demonstrate, either
through your patent application or a prototype, that your invention works for its intended
purpose. In other words, conception is the

mental part of inventing and reducing to
practice is the physical embodiment—a sufficient demonstration that the invention works.
For a more detailed explanation of conception and reduction to practice read Chapter
11, Section B.

> **EXAMPLE:** Joe, a California grape farmer,
> is concerned about U.S. dependence on
> foreign oil and envisions a process to use
> grape juice as automotive fuel. This is the
> conception. Reduction to practice occurs
> when Joe either creates a prototype
> engine or prepares a patent application
> (or provisional patent application) that
> demonstrates that the engine works for
> the purposes intended.

It will take more than just saying so to
prove that you invented something. You need
documentation. The best way to document
your invention is to use an inventor's notebook in which you carefully record all your
work on the invention. The notebook should
be signed by witnesses. So, if you don't have
one already, get an inventor's notebook right
now and start using it. Read Chapter 9 for
detailed guidance about how to prepare and
use your notebook.

9. You'll Lose Your Right to Patent If You Violate the One-Year Rule

In 1964, S. Newman Darby conceived the
idea of connecting a handheld sail rig to a
floating platform with a universal joint. He
called the device a sailboard. He was so proud

of his invention that he wanted the whole world to know about it. He published his designs in an article in the magazine *Popular Science Monthly* in 1965. Exactly one year later, Darby forever lost the right to file for a patent for his invention.

Darby lost his patent rights because of something known as the one-year rule, a rule all inventors should be aware of. Under this rule, y*ou have one year from the first offer for sale or public disclosure of your invention to file either a regular or provisional patent application.* If you miss the deadline, your invention is not considered novel and will therefore be ineligible for a patent. If the USPTO is unaware of the public use or sale and issues a patent, it will be declared invalid if it's later shown that the invention was publicly shown or sold.

The one-year period for filing your patent application begins to run if you:

- make any public use of the invention— for example, demonstrate it in public
- sell the invention
- offer to sell the invention, or
- describe the invention in a document published anywhere in the world (as Darby did).

More inventors lose their patent rights by failing to comply with the one-year rule than any other way. You need to make a note of the date you first do any of the things listed above and then calendar a date no more than 11 months later. By that time you'll have to decide whether to apply for a patent and, if so, begin the application and make sure it's filed by the 12-month deadline.

10. Filing a Provisional Patent Application Can Save You Money

As mentioned above, filing a patent application is a difficult and expensive process, and there's no guarantee your invention will ever make any money. To make life a little easier for inventors, Congress enacted a law in 1995 allowing them to file an abbreviated patent application known as a provisional patent application (PPA).

A PPA does not take the place of filing a regular patent application. Rather, filing a PPA is a way to preserve your place in line while you decide whether it's worth it to spend the time and money to file a full-blown application.

By filing a PPA, you satisfy the one-year rule discussed in the previous section requiring that a PPA or regular patent application be filed within one year after an invention is offered for sale or publicly disclosed. As a result, the PPA filing gives you one year to publish, sell, offer to sell or show the invention to others. You can use this time to assess the commercial potential of your invention before committing to the high cost of filing and prosecuting a nonprovisional application for patent.

Filing a PPA provides other benefits as well—it:

- serves as an alternative to building and testing your invention (see Section 8).
- establishes an official United States patent application filing date for the invention

- permits you to use a "Patent Pending" notice on your invention and to sell your invention with greater security against having the invention stolen, and
- extends the expiration date of your patent by one year, if the USPTO later approves your regular application.

A provisional patent application can be written in plain English—not the arcane language associated with nonprovisional patent applications. In fact, if you've written a technical article that accurately describes how to make and use your invention, you can submit that. You do not need to hire a draftsperson to prepare formal drawings; you can furnish informal drawings provided they demonstrate how your invention works. Once you overnight the description and the drawings to the USPTO along with the $100 fee, you can begin marking your invention *patent pending*.

If you invent something you think might be patentable, but you're not sure there's a good market for it, by all means file a PPA. Then, during the 12 months before you have to file a regular patent application, you can investigate the commercial potential further. You can never predict with 100 percent certainty whether you will make money, but you can make a decent forecast during those 12 months. If things look bleak, don't bother filing the regular patent application.

On the other hand, if you're sure your invention is a winner and want to get your patent as soon as possible, you probably won't need to file a PPA. Instead, file a regular patent application as soon as you can.

If you're interested in filing a provisional patent application read *Patent Pending In 24 Hours,* by Richard Stim & David Pressman (Nolo). This book tells you everything you need to know.

11. Patents Last 17–18 Years

For U.S. patents filed through June 17, 1995, the patent lasts for 17 years from the date the patent is issued, provided that fees necessary to keep the patent in force (maintenance fees) are paid. For patent applications filed after June 17, 1995, the patent last 20 years from the date of filing. Since applications typically take one to three years to process, most patents filed after 1995 have an effective duration of 17–19 years.

Once a patent has expired, the invention described by the patent falls into the public domain: it can be used by anyone without permission from the owner of the expired patent. The basic technologies underlying television and personal computers are good examples of valuable inventions that are no longer covered by in-force patents.

The fact that an invention is in the public domain does not mean that subsequent developments based on the original invention are also in the public domain. Rather, new inventions that improve public domain technology are constantly being conceived and patented. For instance, televisions and personal computers that roll off today's assembly lines employ many recent inventions that are covered by in-force patents.

12. Enforcing a Patent Can Be Difficult and Expensive

Patents are not self-enforcing; neither the USPTO nor any other branch of U.S. government will help you enforce yours. As David Pressman points out in *Patent It Yourself*, patents are like hunting licenses. If someone uses your invention as described in your patent without your permission you have the right to sue them in federal court. Patent suits are among the most expensive of all forms of litigation. However, the potential rewards of patent litigation are sometime massive if a patent suit is successful (judges have the power to triple the amount due to you in the case of willful infringement).

It is very common for a company or person accused of patent infringement to agree to license (pay for the use of) the invention rather than face the uncertainties and expenses of litigation. However, some accused infringers elect to fight and seek to have the patent overturned in court. Inventors who lack financial resources may find themselves unable to enforce their patents against determined and well-heeled infringers.

13. U.S. Patents Only Work in the United States

U.S. patents are legally enforceable only in the United States. If you want to have patent rights in a foreign country, you must patent your invention in that country under its own patent laws.

Obtaining foreign patents can be difficult and expensive. It's only worthwhile if you're certain your invention has strong commercial potential in the foreign country or you've obtained a patent license for that country. You'll probably need to obtain expert help— a foreign patent agent who is familiar with the law of the country involved. The best way to find a foreign patent agent is to obtain a referral from a U.S. patent attorney.

You'll ordinarily need to file your foreign application within one year after a regular or provisional patent application is filed in the U.S.

Also, be aware that in most foreign countries an inventor must file for a patent before the invention is offered for sale, sold, publicly used or published. There is no one-year-grace period as there is in the U.S. (see Section 9). However, when you file for a U.S. patent, most major countries give you one year to file for a foreign patent and your application date relates back to the date of the U.S. filing. Thus, if you think you might want to get a foreign patent, you must be sure to file in the U.S. before selling or publicizing the invention. This way you can publish or sell the invention freely without losing any foreign patent rights provided you file in foreign countries within one year after the U.S. filing date.

14. Filing for Patents Helps Show You're in Business

Unfortunately, inventors can get into trouble with the IRS. This most often occurs where the IRS concludes that an inventor is engaged in a hobby, rather than a business, and therefore can't deduct inventing expenses.

Consider what happened to John Schell, an airline pilot who conceived of a mortar-fired wire device for entrapping helicopters. Although he built and tested a prototype, Schell never applied for a patent for his invention and never made any money from it. The IRS disallowed his deductions for his inventing expenses because it claimed the invention was just a hobby for Schell, not a real business. Schell appealed, and the tax court agreed with the IRS. Why? In large part, because Schell never tried to get a patent. It said this failure was "persuasive evidence" that Schell really wasn't interested in earning any money from the invention and therefore was not in business. (*Schell v. Commissioner*, T.C. Memo 1994-164.)

The IRS tried to do the same thing to Oliver Kilroy who invented an hydraulic mining system that never earned any money. Like Schell, Kilroy appealed. Unlike Schell, he won and was allowed to deduct his inventing expenses from his income taxes. This time the tax court held Schell was running a real business, not just practicing a hobby. Why? Mainly because Schell had obtained four patents on his invention. The court said that if Schell had not been running a business "there would have been no need for him to patent his inventions." (*Kilroy v. Commissioner*, T.C. Memo 1980-489.)

The experiences of Schell and Kilroy show that filing for a patent is strong evidence that you're engaged in a business instead of a hobby. This enables you to fully deduct all of your inventing expenses, which include the cost of filing for a patent. This is perhaps the most underappreciated benefit of filing for a patent.

See Chapter 6 for a discussion of how to show the IRS your inventing activities are a business.

15. Design Patents Can Protect the Way Your Invention Looks

Some inventions not only perform a useful function, they also look good. Utility patents, the type of patents we've been discussing up until now, only protect the way an invention functions. They cannot protect an invention's purely ornamental or aesthetic elements. One way to obtain protection for these things is to obtain a design patent.

A design patent can protect the ornamental features or aesthetic appearance of an invention —for example, the shape of a lamp or a telephone. The owner of a design patent has the right to exclude others from making, selling or using the design for the term of the patent. However, your patent protection is limited to the category of invention in which you have designed. For example, if you obtained a design patent for a fish-shaped hanging lamp, that would not enable you stop someone from making a fish-shaped clock. Design patents automatically expire 14 years after they're issued and cannot be renewed.

Design patents may only be obtained for nonfunctional design elements of useful articles. Paintings, silk screens, sculpture, books, photographs or two-dimensional surface ornamentation that is separable from the object (such as decals) are not considered "useful articles." These things are generally protected by copyright law. Design features of some useful articles can also be protected by copyright. (See Chapter 16 for information about copyright law.)

To qualify for a design patent, the design must be new, original and ornamental. The requirement of ornamentality means that the design is not utilitarian or functional. For example, a personal computer designed to resemble a classic robot of the type seen in old science fiction movies could qualify for a design patent as long as the design character-istics were purely ornamental. But if the robot characteristics were functional in some way— for instance, they provide the computer with mobility—they would not qualify for a design patent.

A design need not be aesthetically pleasing to be ornamental. Generally, if there are several ways to achieve the same function with different designs, the USPTO will find the design to be ornamental. Thus, for ex-ample, design patents have been obtained for such useful articles as a power supply (U.S.

D298,824), an engine (U.S. D416,265) and a computer battery (U.S. D431,808).

You must file your design patent within a year after you first commercialize or publish your design. Compared to a utility patent application, the design patent application is relatively simple. Basically, you just need to provide a drawing of the design, fill out a short application and pay a $165 fee. Unless you pay for expedited (speedy) processing, a design patent takes 12 to 24 months to obtain and you cannot use it to stop others from copying until the patent is granted. (The USPTO has indicated that it will place design patents on a faster track than utility patents which can take two to three years to obtain.)

Design patents aren't the only way you can protect the way an invention looks. Copyright law can also protect an invention's aesthetic or artistic features. See Chapter 16 for a detailed discussion.

 For information on obtaining design patents, refer to *Your Crafts Business: A Legal Guide*, by Richard Stim (Nolo), and the USPTO website (www.uspto.gov). ■

Chapter 15

Ten Things Inventors Should Know About Trademarks

1. Trademarks Can Earn Billions 15/2
2. Trademarks Identify Products and Services 15/2
3. You Must Have Trade to Have a Trademark 15/3
4. You Don't Need a Trademark to License Your Invention (But It Can Help) 15/3
5. Trademarks Are Not All Created Equal 15/4
6. Registering a Trademark Is Not Mandatory, But Provides
   Important Benefits 15/4
7. Intent to Use Registration Can Protect Your Mark
   Before You Use It in Trade 15/5
8. Do a Trademark Search Before Selecting Your Mark 15/5
9. Trademark Rights Are Limited 15/6
10. Only Federally Registered Marks Can Use the ® Symbol 15/7

*T*his chapter provides you with trademark basics. For detailed guidance on selecting and protecting a trademark, refer to *Trademark: How to Name a Business and Product*, by Stephen Elias (Nolo).

1. Trademarks Can Earn Billions

If you go into any drugstore, you're likely to find Listerine on the shelf. This liquid compound has been sold since the 1880s, originally as an antiseptic and later as a mouthwash. Currently, Warner-Lambert Pharmaceutical Company, the manufacturer of Listerine, holds two-thirds of the mouthwash market in the U.S.

How is Warner-Lambert able to so dominate this market? It's not because the formula for Listerine is protected by a patent—it was never patented; and, even if it had been, the patent would have expired long ago. Nor is the formula a trade secret. Originally a secret, the formula was published in a medical journal in 1931 and is now in the public domain— freely available to anyone. Warner-Lambert dominates the mouthwash market because of one thing: the word "Listerine." The brand name Listerine is a legally protected trademark. Anyone can use the formula for Listerine and manufacture their own version of the product, but, because of the trademark law, they can't call it Listerine. And that makes all the difference.

Famous trademarks like Listerine, Coca-Cola, Sony, Nokia and Nabisco are the most valuable intellectual property on earth. The Coca-Cola trademark alone is thought to be worth between $40 and $70 billion dollars.

It's unlikely your trademarks will obtain this type of value. But coming up with a good trademark for a product based on your invention can increase its value and your profits.

2. Trademarks Identify Products and Services

A trademark is any distinctive nonfunctional feature of a product that is used to identify its source and distinguish it from other products. A trademark can be a:

- word (Microsoft)
- phrase or slogan ("Intel inside" and "finger-lickin' good")
- logo (the unique geometric shape used by Mercedes Benz)
- graphic image (the Morton's salt girl with umbrella)
- combination of letters and/or numbers (WD-40, 7-11, MTV)
- product shape (the distinctive shape of the Mrs. Butterworth syrup bottle)
- color (the distinctive green used to designate John Deere equipment)
- sound (the NBC chimes), or
- smell (a floral fragrance applied to yarn).

Trademarks are protected under state and federal laws. Each state has it own laws establishing when and how trademarks can be protected. The federal trademark law (the Lanham Act, 15 U.S.C. §§ 1050 et seq.), applies in all 50 states and is used to protect marks for products that are sold in more than one state or across territorial or national borders. Generally, state trademark laws are relied upon for marks used only within one particular state.

Trade Names Are Not Always Trademarks

Note that your company name is a trade name. It does not qualify as a trademark unless you use the name to identify a product or service sold in commerce. Many companies do use their company name on their products—for example, Intel microchips, or Coca-Cola soft drinks; and these names serve as trademarks as well as company names.

Trademark law, like copyright law, will not protect a product's functional features. That is, trademark law will not protect a feature that helps a product work or be used by the consumer. For example a day-glow yellow color could not be a trademark for tennis balls because the color functions to make the ball visible in twilight hours. A feature can be trademarked only if it does not help the product work. Trademark disputes about this issue can arise in cases involving product shapes or packaging (sometime called trade dress).

3. You Must Have Trade to Have a Trademark

Trademark law is different from copyrights, patents and trade secrets because trademark protection is not based upon creating something. It is based on selling something that features your trademark. In other words, trademark rights do not occur until the public has been exposed to your invention and its trademark. If you never sell or advertise your invention, you will not have any trademark rights. The first day that you use your trademark in commerce is referred to as the "date of first use" and you acquire superior rights over later users. Trademark protection lasts for as long as you continually use the mark in commerce. Many trademarks have survived for over a century (Coca-Cola and Kellogg's, for example).

Have You Invented a Service?

It's possible that your invention is a process or method. In that case you may be selling or offering a service, rather than a product. For example, Amazon's infamous One-Click patent is for a service—the ability to check out quickly online. Technically, when a trademark is used to identify and distinguish services it's known as a service mark. Throughout this chapter, whenever we refer to a trademark, the same rule applies for service marks. The distinction is only relevant when filing a trademark application or when engaged in a trademark battle.

4. You Don't Need a Trademark to License Your Invention (But It Can Help)

If you manufacture and sell your invention yourself, you will have to name your product, and this name will be protected by trademark law if it's sufficiently distinctive (see Section 5). For example, inventor Robert G. Merrick patented a stick-on transparent calendar for watches. He manufactured and sold the product himself and named it CrystalDate. He credits this clear simple name with helping the product's sales take off.

However, if, like most independent inventors, you license your invention instead of sell it yourself, you don't necessarily have to devise the name for the product. Your licensee might prefer to do this. (Note, however, the licensee, not you, may own rights to the trademark.) Even if you create the name for your invention and retain all rights, the name will not become a protected trademark until it's actually used on a product or service sold in commerce (see Section 3). This would normally occur after the licensee manufactures and starts advertising and selling the invention.

That said, an inventor who has a good idea about how to identify the product to be based on the invention has a leg up in the marketplace and can reserve a mark as described in Section 7. Presenting a prospective licensee not only with a good invention, but a good way to identify it, may tip the balance in favor of obtaining a licensing deal. For example, Richard C. Levy invented a new design for a large tricycle, named it Fluorider and convinced Proctor & Gamble to license it. He says that his licensing pitch to Proctor & Gamble wouldn't have had the same impact had he not come up with the Fluorider name.

5. Trademarks Are Not All Created Equal

Trademarks are not all treated equally by the law. The best trademarks are "distinctive," that is, they stand out in a customer's mind because they are inherently memorable. The more distinctive a trademark is, the "stronger" it will be and the more legal protection it will receive. Less distinctive marks are "weak" and may be entitled to little or no legal protection.

When selecting a trademark, it's advisable to choose a strong mark. As a general rule, strong marks are made up of terms that are:

- arbitrary—a word or image whose common meaning does not suggest the product (Apple Computer or Midas Muffler)
- fanciful—that is, coined or made up words (Intel or Kodak), or
- suggestive—that is, a mark that alludes to or hints at (without describing) the product (Accuride tires or Roach Motel insect traps).

Marks based on an inventor's name or that describe the attributes of the invention are considered to be weak—for example, Smith's Cutter or Super Shingle Slicer would be weak marks for a device that cuts roofing shingles. However, a weak mark—for example, Chap Stick, Beef & Brew or Healthy Favorites—can become strong with sufficient sales and advertising.

Some names are so descriptive that they describe an entire group or class of goods, for example, shingle cutter, screwdriver or hammer. these generic terms can never achieve trademark protection.

6. Registering a Trademark Is Not Mandatory, But Provides Important Benefits

Generally, trademark protection begins automatically once you use the mark in commerce (that is, when you begin selling or advertising your invention). You do not have to register your trademark to acquire this trademark protection. However, if you use your mark in federally regulated commerce (for example, across state lines or foreign exports), you should register your mark with the U.S. Patent and Trademark Office (USPTO). Owners of registered marks can use the federal registration symbol—®—and the use of the symbol serves as notice of your claim to rights. Federal registration can also serve as the basis for filing a trademark application in certain foreign countries and it creates a presumption that you have a right to national ownership of the mark.

However, federal registration will not always give you superior rights. In some cases a person who has not registered a mark may have superior rights over a person who later uses a similar mark and registers it. This is because the rights are based on first use, and not registration. The first to use the mark in commerce has superior rights. For example, if you sell an anti-theft device called The Perpetrator through a national home-shopping cable channel and a large national company later registers and sells a similar device with the same name, you would be able to stop the company even though they had a registration and you did not.

The registration process involves filling out a simple application, paying an application fee ($325 if using the electronic filing system, $375 if filing a paper application) and being willing to work with an official of the USPTO to correct any errors that he or she finds in the application. Unlike the case with patents, the USPTO has made it easy for you to regis-

ter your trademark yourself. An interactive trademark registration application system, eTEAS, at the USPTO's website (www.uspto .gov) enables you to register your trademark online by answering a series of questions and paying the registration fee by credit card.

7. Intent to Use Registration Can Protect Your Mark Before You Use It in Trade

As mentioned above, you can't acquire any trademark rights until you advertise or sell your invention in commerce. However, if you have a bona fide intent to use the trademark, you can *reserve* a mark before using it in commerce by filing an intent-to-use registration with the USPTO. If the mark is approved, you have six months to actually use the mark on a product sold to the public and file papers with the USPTO describing the use (with an accompanying $100 fee). If necessary, this period may be increased by five additional six-month periods if you have a good explanation for each extension. You should file an intent to use registration as soon as you have selected a trademark for a forthcoming product; your competitors are also trying to come up with good trademarks, and they may be considering using a mark similar to the one you want.

8. Do a Trademark Search Before Selecting Your Mark

A mark you think will be good for your product or service could already be in use by someone else. If your mark is confusingly similar to one already in use, its owner may be able to sue you for trademark infringement and get you to change yours and even pay damages. Obviously, you do not want to spend time and money marketing and advertising a new mark, only to discover that it infringes on another preexisting mark and must be changed. To avoid this you should do a trademark search or hire someone to do a search for you.

A trademark search is a systematic hunt for any registered or unregistered trademark that is confusingly similar to a mark you want to use. You can hire an attorney or trademark search firm to do a search for you, but the cheapest way is to do it yourself. The USPTO maintains a trademark database of federally registered marks called TESS that you can use for free through the USPTO's website (www. uspto.gov). On the home page, click "Search Trademarks." You can use TESS to compare your proposed mark with registered trademarks and trademarks that are pending registration. There are other websites you can use for a fee to do even more advanced searches than can be done through TESS—one of the best known is Saegis (www.saegis.com).

However, be aware that a trademark search, whether you perform it yourself or hire a service to do it for you, is rarely conclusive. If you turn up trademarks that might conflict with yours, you need to decide if there'd be a likelihood of customer confusion. For additional peace of mind, you may want to review the results of your trademark search with a lawyer who specializes in intellectual property law, a branch of law that includes not only trademarks but also copyrights and patents.

 For detailed guidance on how to conduct a trademark search, refer to *Trademark: How to Name a Business and Product*, by Stephen Elias (Nolo).

9. Trademark Rights Are Limited

Although trademarks can achieve significant value, trademark rights are sometimes the weakest of intellectual property rights. That's because a trademark owner does not have a monopoly over use of the mark. Rather, the owner has the legal right only to prevent others from using the mark on similar goods in such a way as to cause confusion about the products or services the owner provides, or about their origins.

A mark need not be identical to one already in use to infringe upon the owner's rights. For example, Mr. Rust infringed Mr. Clean; Permanize infringed Simoniz; and Promise infringed Pledge. The key to infringement is whether consumers would be confused by the use of the second mark. If the proposed mark is similar enough to the earlier mark, and the goods or services are related, then the trademark owner has a strong case for infringement. If a trademark owner is able to convince a court that infringement has occurred, he or she may be able to get the court to order the infringer to stop using the infringing mark and to pay monetary damages.

In addition, if the trademark is famous enough, the owner may, under a legal principle known as dilution, stop people from using it in a way that blurs or tarnishes the mark's reputation. For example, the National Basketball Association was able to stop a rap music company from using its logo (a silhouette of a basketball player) so that the logo included a gun. Similarly, Toys "R" Us was able to stop a company from tarnishing its mark by selling pornographic material under the name Adults R Us.

In summary, a trademark owner must be assertive in enforcing its exclusive rights. A failure to enforce these rights could weaken the mark's strength and distinctiveness.

10. Only Federally Registered Marks Can Use the ® Symbol

To make it clear to the public (and potential competitors) that a word, logo or other device has been trademarked, trademark owners like to use trademark notices on their products and advertising. Use of a notice is not mandatory. But, if you do use a notice, you may be able to collect triple damages against an infringer—which makes using a notice very worthwhile.

The most commonly used notice for trademarks registered with the USPTO is an "R" in a circle—®—but any statement establishing that the mark is federally registered, for example, "Reg. U.S. Pat. & T.M. Off." may also be used. Only marks that are federally registered can use the "®" symbol. Any business that uses a mark, registered or not, can place the "TM" symbol after it (or "SM" for service marks) to publicly claim ownership of the mark. The "TM" and "SM" indicators have no legal significance. ■

Chapter 16

Ten Things Inventors Should Know About Copyright

1. Copyright Protects Works of Authorship, Not Inventions 16/2
2. Copyright Can Protect Invention Design 16/3
3. You Can Make Money From Copyrights 16/5
4. Copyright Protection Is Limited 16/5
5. You Get A Copyright Whether or Not You Want It 16/6
6. Copyright Protection Lasts a Long Time 16/6
7. Register Valuable Copyrights 16/6
8. Use a Copyright Notice When You Publish Valuable Works 16/7
9. Copyright Isn't the Only Law That Protects Designs 16/8
10. Watch Out If You Hire an Independent Contractor to
    Create a Copyrighted Work 16/8

*V*irtually every inventor owns copyrights. This chapter provides an overview of copyright law and explains how inventors can use it to their benefit.

For a detailed discussion of copyright law, refer to *The Copyright Handbook: How to Protect & Use Written Works, Copyright Your Software,* and *The Public Domain: How to Find and Use Copyright-Free Writings, Music, Art and More,* all written by Stephen Fishman (Nolo).

1. Copyright Protects Works of Authorship, Not Inventions

Copyright law protects all types of works of authorship, including writings of all kinds, music, movies, videos, drawings, paintings, sculptures, computer programs and photographs. The creator of an original work of authorship (known as the author) is granted the exclusive right to:

- make copies of the work
- distribute the work to the public (for example, through publication)
- create "derivative works," that is, new works based upon the work—for example, an audiotape version of a book, and
- display or perform the work in public.

EXAMPLE: Stan writes a book on how to build your own mousetrap. The book is a work of authorship protected by copyright. As the author, Stan has the exclusive right to copy, publish or create new works from his book. Typically, an author like

Stan would get a publisher to publish the book in return for a royalty. If someone copies or otherwise uses the book without Stan's permission—for example, posts a chapter on a website—Stan can sue them for copyright infringement and collect monetary damages.

Patent Drawings and Copyright Law

An inventor who files a patent application with the U.S. Patent and Trademark Office (USPTO) must include detailed drawings showing how the invention works, as well as a written description of the invention. An important issue—particularly for the owners of design patents—is whether the drawings are protected under copyright law?

Patent and copyright experts maintain that patent drawings are protected under copyright law. This principle is supported by caselaw (*In Re Yardley*, 493 F.2d 1389 (CCPA 1974) and federal regulations (37 CFR § 1.84(s) and MPEP §1512, below)

However, the public is also granted an implied license to freely reproduce the contents of a published patent for purposes of making or using the invention. On that basis, you can download and copy issued patents without violating the patent owner's rights in the drawings. However, other uses may violate the law. (Unfortunately, there are no cases under the current copyright act to offer guidance on the specific issue of protecting patent drawings.)

Patent Office regulations (MPEP §1512) permit a design patent applicant to include a copyright notice on design patent drawings provided that the following disclaimer is also included: "A portion of the disclosure of this patent document contains material to which a claim for copyright is made. The copyright owner has no objection to the facsimile reproduction by anyone of the patent document or the patent disclosure, as it appears in the Patent and Trademark Office patent file or records, but reserves all other copyright rights whatsoever." On the basis of this regulation, design patent applicants should include a copyright notice along with the waiver statement.

(Note, a statement at the USPTO's website (www.uspto.gov/main/ccpubguide.htm) indicates, to the contrary, that published patents are not subject to copyright restrictions. The statement is most likely in error.)

However, copyright does not protect anything that does useful work—in other words, it doesn't protect inventions—or at least those aspects of an invention that make it useful. It might seem, then, that copyright law has little application to inventors, since they try to create things that do useful work. But, in fact, inventors create copyrighted works of authorship all the time, including, for example, drawings, written descriptions of experiments and other inventing activities, photographs, product manuals and advertisements for inventions. Although these works are important and helpful to inventors, they are not considered functional, under copyright law. All of these things can receive the same copyright protection as best-selling novels, movies or works of art.

2. Copyright Can Protect Invention Design

Although the jottings you make in your inventor's notebook are protected, you probably won't make money off these copyrights. After all, it's not likely anyone would want to publish your inventor's notebook or make a movie out of it. However, if someone does publish or modify your notebook, or if an angry employee posts your patent drawings on the Web (prior to a patent being issued), you can sue for copyright infringement for these uses.

Inventors ordinarily make money from their inventions. Although copyright can't protect the functional elements of your invention, it can protect its nonfunctional artistic elements. These can include pictorial, graphic or sculptural features. These design elements may have value, whether or not your invention is patentable.

> **EXAMPLE:** Gina designs a music box that contains original sculptural and pictorial features—dancing figures and a painted background that looks like an English landscape. The music box mechanism is not patentable—it's obvious and not novel—but the pictorial and sculptural elements are protected by copyright. Although anyone can make a music box with the same mechanism, they can't copy the copyrighted artistic features of Gina's music box without her permission.

Not all design elements can be protected. Copyright protects only the nonfunctional design elements of a useful article if they can be *separated* from the functional elements. This separation can be actual physical separation or conceptual separation.

a. Physically separable features

Any feature that can be physically separated from a utilitarian object and stand on its own as a work of art, is copyrightable provided that it is minimally creative and original. For example, the dancing figures on Gina's music box in the example above could be removed from the box and stand on their own as sculptures.

b. Conceptually separable features

However, many design features contained in utilitarian objects cannot be physically separated from the object. In this event, the feature is copyrightable only if it can be conceptually separated—that is, the artistic features can be imagined separately and independently from the useful article without destroying the article's functionality. In other words, the artistic features and the useful article could both exist side by side and be perceived as fully realized, separate works—one an artistic work and the other a useful article that does work.

Sometimes it's easy to tell that an artistic feature is conceptually separable from its utilitarian object. For example, a two-dimensional painting, drawing, or other graphic work is clearly conceptually separable when it is printed on or applied to useful articles such as containers, furniture or the like. Thus, the

painting on Gina's music box in the above example could easily be imagined as being separate from the box itself and the music box could go on functioning just fine.

Sometimes, however, it's difficult to conceive of the art separate from the function—that is, the art and function seem to merge so completely that one cannot exist without the other. When that happens, it's hard to get copyright because the design is considered necessary to the function. Judges or Copyright Office examiners often resolve this issue by asking the question, "Can this work be created in many alternate ways and still function?" If there are many alternate designs, then the design is not crucial to the function. Below are real-life cases that grappled with these issues:

Barry Cord (of Kieselstein-Cord)
Designer of the Winchester
and Vaquero belt buckles

EXAMPLE 1: Jewelry designer Barry Cord sued a company that copied his belt-buckle designs. The court held that the artistic features of the belt buckle were conceptually separable from the functional features, and were therefore protected under copyright. The court reasoned that the design of the buckles was not required by their utilitarian function—to hold up pants. Therefore the artistic and aesthetic features could be conceived of as having been added to an otherwise utilitarian article. (*Kieselstein-Cord v. Accessories By Pearl, Inc.*, 632 F.2d 989 (2d Cir. 1980).)

EXAMPLE 2: In contrast, an undulating tubed bicycle rack was found not to be copyrightable because the design could not be conceptually separated from the rack's function. The court found that the undulating design was in fact necessary to the rack's function of securing parked bicycles. (*Brandir Int'l. v. Cascade Pac. Lumber Co.*, 834 F.2d 1142 (2d Cir. 1987).)

3. You Can Make Money From Copyrights

You can earn money from copyrights in two ways. You can:

- sue people who copy your work without permission, or
- earn money by licensing or selling your rights.

If someone uses your copyrighted work without your permission—in legal terms, infringes your copyright—you can go after them, make them stop and perhaps collect a financial payment for the damage they've done. You can take these actions against anyone who, without your permission, copies your work, displays your work, makes photos of it, broadcasts it on television or makes variations or miniatures of it.

You can also make money by giving your rights to someone else, either temporarily (a license) or permanently (an assignment). The money earned from licensing or selling copyrights can be substantial. For example, the artists who created Cabbage Patch Dolls earned millions from licensing their creation. In return for letting a company "use" their copyrighted designs, they earn a healthy royalty on each doll sold.

4. Copyright Protection Is Limited

A copyright is far weaker than a patent. A copyright owner's exclusive right to copy, distribute or otherwise use a work of authorship extends only to the expressive elements of a work. Copyright does not protect ideas, facts, formulas or discoveries.

Thus, for example, copyright cannot protect the *idea* of creating a bicycle rack in a highly stylized sculptural form. It only protects the particular way that idea is expressed—that is, the particular design the creator gives to the bike rack. Anyone else can come along and independently create a stylized bike rack. This differs from patent law, which in effect does protect the ideas and discoveries embodied in inventions.

The key to separating an unprotectible idea from a copyrightable expression is to examine the amount of detail in the work. A soft doll with a big puffy face, for example, is an idea. There are very few unique details. However, the Cabbage Patch dolls with their unique face, name and "adoption papers" contain many specific details and are a copyrightable expression.

Copyright also will not generally protect names, titles, short phrases, blank forms and any works within the public domain. For detailed guidance on what copyright does and does not protect, see *The Public Domain: How to Find and Use Copyright-Free Writings, Music, Art and More*, by Stephen Fishman (Nolo).

5. You Get A Copyright Whether or Not You Want It

One of the nice things about copyright protection is that it begins automatically the moment you create a work of authorship that qualifies for copyright. There is no need to file an extensive application with a government agency and wait years for it to grant you rights, as there is with patents.

Moreover, the requirements for copyright eligibility are very modest—the work need only be:

- fixed in a tangible medium of expression —for example, written down, saved on a computer disk, videotape or film
- original—that is, not copied from somebody else, and
- minimally creative—that is, the product of a very modest "creative spark," almost any work qualifies except the white pages in the phone book and similar databases.

Unlike patent law, it does not matter who is the first to create a work of authorship. All that matters is that the work is original to the author. Nor need it be nonobvious. So long as it's original, it can be very obvious and still be copyrighted.

As mentioned, copyright protection starts automatically and there is no need to pay a fee to a government agency as you must do for a patent. Copyright is essentially free.

6. Copyright Protection Lasts a Long Time

Another nice thing about copyright protection is that it lasts a very long time. For most copyrighted works, protection generally extends for the life of the author plus 70 years. In other words, if you have a copyrighted work, protection continues for 70 years after your death, allowing your family (or other beneficiaries of your will) to reap financial rewards from the work. For works that are created by companies, the term may be 95 years from date of first publication or 120 years from creation, whichever is longer. The length of copyright protection also depends upon when the work was first published. Different rules apply for works published before 1978.

7. Register Valuable Copyrights

As mentioned above, copyrights need not be applied for from a government agency as must patents. However, copyrights can be registered with the U.S. Copyright Office in Washington, D.C. Registration is not mandatory, but results in such important benefits that you should take care to register any copyright you feel is, or may be, valuable.

a. Benefits of Registration

When you timely register a copyright, you get three important benefits:
- the right to receive special statutory damages if you successfully sue someone for copyright infringement
- the right to make the defendant pay all or part of your attorney fees if you successfully sue someone for copyright infringement, and
- the legal presumption that your copyright is valid.

The statutory damages and attorney fees benefits are of particular importance. Without them, it is often not economically feasible to sue for copyright infringement.

b. When to Register

To obtain the benefits outlined above, you must make sure to register your work within three months of publication or at least before the infringement occurs. (See the following section for a discussion of when publication occurs for copyright purposes.)

c. How to Register

Registration is easy and you can do it yourself without an attorney's help. You just have to fill out a short application form and send it to the Copyright Office with a $30 application fee and one or two copies of the work. Detailed information about the registration process,

including copies of the application forms, can be obtained from the Copyright Office website (www.copyright.gov).

8. Use a Copyright Notice When You Publish Valuable Works

Whenever you publish a valuable work protected wholly or partly by copyright you should include a copyright notice on it. Use of copyright notices is not mandatory, but they provide important benefits. For one thing, it makes clear that the work is copyrighted, which may deter a potential infringer. Moreover, when a work has a notice, a person who copies it can't claim he or she didn't know it was copyrighted. This can enable the copyright owner to obtain greater damages.

a. What is publication?

A copyright notice need only be used when a copyrighted work of authorship is published. A work is published for copyright purposes when it is made available without restriction to the general public. This can be done by offering the work for sale to the public, by renting it, loaning it out or even giving it away.

b. Contents of valid copyright notices

All copyright notices must contain:
- the copyright symbol—©—or the word "copyright", and
- the copyright owner's name.

Most copyright notices must also contain the year the work was published—for example,

2003. However, there is a big exception to this rule. A publication date is not required in copyright notices for useful articles that contain copyrighted pictorial or graphic elements. For example, a publication date would not be required on a lamp, toy or belt buckle. But, you can still include the date if you want.

These elements don't have to appear in any particular order (although they are usually in the order listed here.) You can place the notice anywhere on a useful article, so long as it can be seen.

> **EXAMPLE:** Velda Vidmar creates a fruit juicer that is embellished with drawings of various fruits and bucolic backgrounds. The drawings are copyrighted. Before Velda offers the juicer for sale, she places the following copyright notice on the underside: Copyright 2003 by Velda Vidmar.

9. Copyright Isn't the Only Law That Protects Designs

Copyright isn't the only intellectual property law that can protect the nonfunctional design elements of useful articles. Design patents can also be obtained for this purpose. Design patents are covered in Chapter 14. Copyrights have both advantages and disadvantages compared to design patents.

The main advantage of copyright is that protection is obtained automatically by creating a protectible work and registration is inexpensive ($30). Design patent protection requires filing an application with the U.S. Patent and Trademark Office. It takes one or two years to get the patent, and protection does not begin until the patent is issued. Total costs, including the application fee, will come to $165 to $1,500 depending on whether you use an attorney.

The main disadvantage of copyrights is that to stop someone from infringing a copyright you must prove that they had access to your work and that they copied it. In other words, if they independently developed the work without first seeing your work, they would not be infringing your copyright. In contrast, to stop an infringer under design patent law, you need only prove that you have a valid design patent and that the two works are equivalent. You wouldn't have to prove that the competitor saw your work and copied it.

You can have both design patent and copyright protection for the same useful article. You may wish to do this if the work is particularly valuable.

10. Watch Out If You Hire an Independent Contractor to Create a Copyrighted Work

The copyright law contains a big trap for the unwary. If you hire an independent contractor (that is, a nonemployee) to create a copyrighted work for you, you will not obtain copyright ownership of that work unless the contractor assigns his or her rights to you.

> **EXAMPLE:** James hires Tim, a freelance toy designer, to design a toy robot. James and Tim don't discuss copyright ownership. James just assumes he owns what

he pays Tim to create. However, because he never obtained an assignment of independent contractor Tim's copyright rights, Tim owns the copyright in the robot appearance he creates, not James. This means Tim can license or sell the design to someone else without James' permission or sharing the money he earns.

It's easy to prevent this from happening. All you have to do is obtain a written assignment (transfer) of the contractor's rights in the work. This should be done before the work is created. The independent contractor agreement in Chapter 10 contains a clause accomplishing such an assignment.

In contrast to independent contractors, copyrightable works created by employees are automatically owned by their employers so long as they were created within the scope of employment. Such works are "works made for hire," and the employer, not the employee, is deemed to be the author for copyright purposes.

Thus, it's not absolutely necessary to obtain an assignment of an employee's copyright rights, as it is with independent contractors. But, just to be on the safe side, our sample employment agreement in Chapter 10 contains a clause ensuring that the employer obtains any copyright rights the employee may have in works he or she creates for the employer.

For more detailed information on copyright ownership issues, refer to *The Copyright Handbook: How to Protect & Use Written Works*, by Stephen Fishman (Nolo). ■

Chapter 17

Ten Things Every Inventor Should Know About Licensing

1. No License Is Better Than a Bad License 17/4

2. You're Licensing Your Rights, Not Your Invention 17/4

3. Sublicensing and Assignments Allow Strangers to Sell Your Invention 17/5

4. You Can License Away the World and Get It Back 17/6

5. A Short Term Is Usually Better Than a Longer Term 17/7

6. Royalties Come in All Shapes and Sizes 17/8

7. Sometimes a Lump Sum Payment Is Better Than a Royalty 17/10

8. GMARs Guarantee Annual Payments 17/12

9. Deductions Can Make Your Royalties Disappear 17/13

10. Audit Provisions Permit You to Check the Books 17/15

*L*onnie G. Johnson has amassed 71 patents since 1979 including a smoke alarm, a valve for maintaining soil moisture, a fluid-powered thermodynamic heat pump and a wet-diaper detector that plays nursery rhymes. Although Johnson has invented thermodynamics systems for NASA, he may be remembered best for a toy originally known as the Power Drencher—the first water blaster to incorporate air pressure. After it was renamed the Super Soaker in 1992, Johnson's invention went on to generate $200 million in sales.

Like many inventors, Johnson avoided the hassle of manufacturing and selling his invention himself. Instead, his company, Johnson Research & Development (www.johnsonrd.com) licensed the rights to the Larami toy company. While Johnson toiled on new money-making ideas, Larami promoted and protected the Super Soaker, making it one of the biggest hits in toy history.

Many inventors prefer to take the same route as Lonnie G. Johnson and license their inventions. A license is an agreement in which you let someone else commercially use or develop your invention for a period of time. In return, you receive money—either a one-time payment or continuing payments called royalties.

In a sense, a license is like a lease for a house or apartment. A tenant makes periodic payments to a property owner for the right to use it. Similarly, a company (the licensee) periodically pays you (the licensor) royalties (similar to rent) for the right to manufacture, sell or use your invention for a period of time. If the licensee fails to pay you or otherwise breaches your agreement, the agreement may terminate and you can license your invention to someone else (provided the license is drafted properly).

License agreements usually develop in two stages. First, the licensor and the licensee

Lonnie Johnson
Holder of 71 patents including the Super Soaker

negotiate the basic elements of the agreement (sometimes referred to as the "business terms"). These elements, discussed in more detail throughout this chapter, are the foundation of the license and they include:

- a description of the invention
- a description of the licensee's products containing the invention
- the rights granted by the license
- how long the license will last
- whether or not it will be exclusive
- what territory it will cover, and
- how much and at what intervals you will get paid.

After agreeing on these basic elements, the parties incorporate this information into a more detailed written agreement. A licensee may refer to this second stage as "turning it over to the lawyers," because the licensee's lawyer becomes involved in revising or drafting the agreement. Don't assume that the deal is done just because you have agreed upon the essential business terms. During this second stage, the parties may negotiate over a wide range of contract provisions such as post-termination rights, warranties or indemnity. Although the basic elements establish the heart of the agreement, both stages of contract negotiation are important.

Even if you hire an attorney to assist in your preparation or negotiation of a license agreement, you should still review the material in this chapter as it will assist you when making licensing decisions and save money on attorney fees.

In order to assist you in your negotiation, we have prepared a worksheet located at the end of this chapter that includes each of the essential elements of your license agreement. This worksheet can be converted into an exhibit (a separate document attached to the agreement).

 All of the information in this chapter is adopted from *License Your Invention* by Richard Stim (Nolo). Review that book for more detailed information on licensing, including a sample license agreement with a clause-by-clause explanation.

Alternatives to Licensing

Before considering licensing, it's important for an inventor to consider the two other basic options to licensing—assigning your rights or manufacturing and selling the invention by yourself. Although a license allows you to retain ownership of the invention, some inventors prefer to assign all rights in return for a large one-time payment (or in some cases, a one-time payment and continuing royalties). Manufacturing and selling the invention yourself (referred to as a venture), requires money, knowledge about the industry, connections with distributors and a lot of hard, hard work. Substantial tax implications distinguish assignments, licenses and ventures. For more on these implications review Chapter 8 which discusses taxation of income.

Licensor—Licensee

You, as owner of the invention, will always be the licensor. The company receiving the license, that is the company that exploits your invention, is the licensee.

1. No License Is Better Than a Bad License

Author Sholom Aleichem wrote, "It's not the signature that counts, it's the man that signs." This rule holds true for licensing agreements.

A license agreement—no matter how well drafted—cannot shield you from the aggravation and expense of dealing with the wrong company. Some inventors assume that any license is better than no license at all. This is not true. The goal is not simply to get licensed, but to find the right partner for the license. Generally, this proves to be a much harder proposition than inventing or patenting your invention. You will need to research, as thoroughly as possible, any potential licensee. This type of research involves reviewing the industry, its trade magazines and newsletters and performing online research at financial and business sites.

If you have created an invention that is applicable to the trade in which you work, you have an advantage because you probably already have contacts, understand the economics of the industry, know the trade magazines and trade shows and are aware of the major players. You are also familiar with the technology available in the trade and may be able to find new uses for old inventions.

Get It "Write" the First Time

Often, parties to a licensing agreement are eager to get started and sign a short agreement summarizing the terms. The parties may say "we'll flesh it out later" or "we can always amend the agreement." That may be true but we urge you to work towards creating a final licensing agreement. It's not always easy to agree on modifications, amendments or alterations once the product is licensed and sales have begun. In addition, amendments and modifications are time-consuming. Concentrate on getting the agreement right before you sign it and use amendments only if necessary.

2. You're Licensing Your Rights, Not Your Invention

You do not license your invention, per se. Rather, you license your legal rights to the invention. This distinction causes confusion for some inventors. Legal rights—patent, copyright, trademark, or trade secret rights—are what give you title or ownership of the invention, much like a deed to a house gives you title to the property. When you license your invention, what you are really transferring to the licensee are your legal rights, such as your rights to manufacture, sell and use the invention. The heart of the license agreement—known as the grant—sets out these rights, usually in two parts, as described below:

- **Grant of (Intellectual Property) Rights.** The grant describes the intellectual property rights transferred to the licensee in the license, for example, the right to manufacture the patented invention. The grant also establishes whether the license is exclusive or nonexclusive. If it is exclusive, then only the licensee can have the rights conveyed in the grant provision. Usually the licensee wants every right you possess. For that reason, the licensee (or licensee's attorney) may propose a long list of rights, such as the right to sell, distribute, manufacture, modify, recast and revise, etc. You should only be concerned if this list of rights also conveys ownership. At that point, you may be moving away from a license (which allows you to retain ownership) and towards an assignment (which is an outright sale of all your rights). For example, giving a licensee the right to improve or revise the licensed products does not necessarily mean that the licensee will own the rights to the improvement. Ownership rights of improvements to your invention, particularly if the licensee makes the improvements, can be a tricky issue.

- **Reservation of Rights.** There is a legal presumption that if you have not expressly transferred a right, you have retained (or reserved) it. For example, if you do not convey the right to sell the licensed products in Thailand, then you have reserved that right for yourself—or for anyone to whom you wish to license it. So, technically, you don't have to make an express statement that you reserve a certain right. Unfortunately, disputes can arise about this issue, so we recommend that you specifically reserve whatever rights you don't wish to transfer. The easiest method of reserving rights is to add a sentence in the grant that states: "Licensor expressly reserves all rights other than those being granted in this agreement."

3. Sublicensing and Assignments Allow Strangers to Sell Your Invention

In two situations—a sublicense or an assignment—the licensee can transfer its rights under the agreement to a third party and, depending on how the license is drafted, you may not have any say in the matter. Because these provisions allow a stranger to sell your invention, it's a good idea to become knowledgeable about sublicensing and assignments before entering into your license.

Sublicensing. Under a sublicense, the licensee transfers some of its rights to another company that can make or sell your invention. For example, perhaps the licensee does not have a strong sales force in France, so it sublicenses the right to sell in France to a French company (assuming the French rights were included in the original license). The French company then pays money to the licensee who then pays you a portion of the sublicensing revenue, often 50%. You may not like the idea of sublicensing because a different company—perhaps a company with a philosophy or sales practices you don't agree with—is selling your invention. You can attempt to prohibit sublicensing altogether, but a better solution would be to require the licensee to seek out your prior approval before granting a sublicense. Keep in mind that licensees like to have the freedom to sublicense.

Assignments. If a licensee sublicenses its rights to manufacture or distribute the invention, the licensee is still responsible for overseeing production and sales and for paying you. However, if the licensee assigns its rights, it has permanently removed itself from its obligations and the new company (the assignee) has stepped into the licensee's shoes. This new company will market the invention and pay you royalties.

If possible, you would want your license to be made nonassignable because you do not want to have another company replace the licensee. However, there are two occasions when an assignment may be necessary:

- the licensee might be purchased by another company and wants to reserve the freedom to transfer its rights to that company, or
- the licensee might create a subsidiary company and wants to be able to assign the agreement to its subsidiary.

To accommodate these possibilities, you can make your license nonassignable with the exception of transfers to a purchasing company or a subsidiary.

Inventions vs. Licensed Products

As you discuss the product or process that is the basis for the licensing agreement, you and the licensor will refer to two versions of your invention. One is the invention as you created or patented it. The other is the invention as the licensee sells it, which is usually referred to as the licensed product. In other words, your invention goes in one door and a licensed product (or products) comes out the other. The licensed product is your invention as packaged or modified by the licensee. Both versions of the invention—as you created it and as it is sold—require separate names (for example, "Property" and "Licensed Products"), because your payments are based upon sales of the licensed product.

Do not underestimate the importance of these definitions; both will have an impact on the license agreement. The definition of your invention explains what the licensee is getting from you. The definition of licensed products describes what the licensee is doing with your invention and affects how you are paid.

4. You Can License Away the World and Get It Back

Every license has geographical limits. Generally, if you are licensing a patent, the choice of territory is limited to the country or countries where patent protection has been obtained. However, if you and the licensee agree to seek patent protection in foreign countries, then the territory can go beyond the boundaries of the initial patent protection. If the license is worldwide, then establishing this is simple—the word "worldwide" is inserted in the grant, for example, "Licensor grants to Licensee an exclusive, worldwide license." If the territory is limited to a country or region, then that information is inserted in the territory section of the agreement, such as, "The rights granted to Licensee are limited to the United States and Canada (the "Territory")."

What's the best approach for you as a prospective licensor? If the licensee has a history of worldwide sales and good sales connections throughout the world, then grant a worldwide license. But if the licensee appears to be familiar only with the U.S. market, it doesn't make sense to license rights to other areas. Doing so would restrict your ability to grant a license to another party for a foreign market.

If you have a difference of opinion with the licensee over the territorial scope of the license, one solution would be to initially grant worldwide rights but also provide that if the licensee has not exploited or sublicensed rights in an area after a certain period of time—say two years—then that area would be excluded from the territory. For example, if after three years the licensee has sold the licensed products everywhere but in France, the licensee would lose rights for France. Usually this type of provision is included in another portion of the license agreement, titled "Right to Terminate a Portion of the Agreement."

Licenses Can Be Written or Oral

Most invention licenses are written. However, a license doesn't have to be written to be valid. An oral license may also be enforceable as long as it qualifies as a contract under general contract law principles. However, there are limits on oral agreements. For example, in most states, an oral agreement is only valid for one year. Because of these limitations and because it is usually more difficult to prove an oral agreement than one set out in writing, we strongly recommend against relying on an oral licensing agreement.

5. A Short Term Is Usually Better Than a Longer Term

The time that the license lasts is referred to as the "term." In general, we recommend a short term (two to five years) because if the licensee is not doing a good job or if the product is a success, you can terminate or renegotiate for a better license. A long term can be beneficial if you are happy with the licensee and want to make sure that you are locked in for a long period.

A licensee will usually want as long a term as possible because a long term guarantees a maximum period for exploitation of the invention. Sometimes, however, a product may have a limited life span and a licensee may not want to be locked into a specific time period. Instead, the licensee wants the term to end whenever the licensee stops selling the product. Sometimes the parties compromise on this issue by establishing renewal periods. For example, if certain conditions are met—sales or royalty payments at a certain level, for instance—the licensee will have the right to renew the agreement for a period of time, say one or two years.

In practical terms, you should be aware that if the invention is not profitable, the term makes little difference. It is difficult to force the licensee to keep selling the product if it is losing money. The licensee will either seek to amend the agreement to permit termination, or the agreement will end up terminating in a lawsuit.

Patents and license length. Note that in the case of a patent license, the term cannot be for longer than the length of the patent.

6. Royalties Come in All Shapes and Sizes

Many inventors focus on the royalty numbers and not enough on the type of royalty payment and the permissible deductions. As you'll see from reviewing this section and Sections 7–9, there are many, many ways to shape royalty payments. Before commencing your negotiation, you need an understanding of royalty definitions. Below we provide explanations for common terminology.

- gross sales—This is the total money received from the licensee's sale of the invention.
- net sales—This includes the gross sales minus deductions such as shipping costs

or returns (products returned by retailers).

EXAMPLE: A licensee receives $1,200,000 from gross sales and has shipping deductions and returns of $200,000. Net sales are $1,000,000.

- royalty—A royalty is a payment for licensing your invention. It is usually calculated as a percentage of the sales and is paid periodically. You may receive royalty checks once a year, twice a year or even four times a year. (A system of continuous royalty payments is sometimes referred to as a "running royalty.")
- net sales royalty—This is the most common form of royalty payment—a percentage of net sales. How do you compute your net sales royalty payment? Multiply the royalty rate against net sales.

EXAMPLE: A royalty rate of 5% times net sales of $1,000,000 equals a net sales royalty of $50,000. (Note: In some cases, royalties can be a percentage of unit sales or production. See below for an explanation.)

- per unit royalty—A per unit royalty is tied to the number of units sold, not the money earned by sales.

EXAMPLE: Under a per unit royalty, a licensor could receive $1 for each product sold.

- per use royalty—A per use royalty is based upon the number of times that the invention is used. This royalty is tied to production, not sales. A per use royalty is commonly chosen when the invention is a process, not a product, such as a method of sealing canned goods. The inventor receives a royalty based upon the amount of production (for example, the number of sealed cans produced).

EXAMPLE: Under a per use royalty, a licensor could receive ten cents for every 100 cans produced using his patented system.

- advance—This is an upfront payment to the licensor, usually made at the time the license is signed. An advance is almost always credited or "recouped" against future royalties unless the agreement provides otherwise. It's as if the licensee is saying, "I expect you will earn $10,000 in royalties so I am going to advance you that sum at the time we sign the agreement." When you do earn royalties, the first $10,000 will be kept by the licensee to repay the advance. If you don't earn the $10,000, then the licensee usually takes a loss and you do not have to return the advance. To assure that you do not have to return the advance, your agreement would state the advance is "nonrefundable" (see the sidebar).
- lump sum payment—Instead of receiving royalties, a licensor may prefer a one-time or lump sum payment.

EXAMPLE: The licensor receives a lump sum payment of $100,000. In return, the licensee has the exclusive right to sell the invention for five years. The licensor gets no other payments or royalties regardless of whether the invention sells millions of units or just one.

- minimum annual royalty payment (sometimes referred to as guaranteed minimum annual royalty or GMAR)—This is a guarantee that you will receive a certain royalty payment each year. Think of a minimum annual payment as an advance that is paid every year of the agreement.

Nonrefundable and Nonrecoupable

The terms "nonrefundable" and "nonrecoupable" are sometimes used in license agreements. Nonrecoupable means that the payment cannot be credited against royalties. It is as if the licensee is saying, "Take this $10,000 payment and I won't deduct it from your future royalties." The term nonrefundable is often used to ensure that a licensor will not have to personally pay back an advance or minimum annual royalty payment. For example, you receive a $10,000 advance but the sales are dismal and the royalties never equal the advance. Although a licensor rarely has to return an advance, the use of the term "nonrefundable" is often added as reinforcement to guarantee that you don't have to write a check to the licensee.

7. Sometimes a Lump Sum Payment Is Better Than a Royalty

Assuming you have a choice, how do you choose between the various payment methods? Your options are explained below.

a. Royalties Based on Net Sales

A royalty payment based on net sales is the most common method of licensing payment. In business terminology, it is a direct cost that can be charged against the cost of goods. In other words, it is a predictable expense that is figured as part of the cost of selling the product. If the invention is not successful, there will be no royalties. Licensors prefer this system because if the invention is successful, the licensor will be richly rewarded over the life of the invention. We generally recommend choosing a royalty payment over a lump sum payment for invention licensing.

b. Per Unit Royalties

In some instances, an inventor may not want to use a royalty system based upon net sales. For example, computer hardware prices often drop radically. More units may be sold but the net sales revenue decreases because the price has dropped. If the wholesale price for your product drops, you may be better served with royalties tied to unit sales. A payment of two dollars per unit may be more profitable than 5% of net sales. Unfortunately, licensees generally don't want to risk committing to unit royalties when the wholesale price can

drop dramatically. If you have the bargaining power, look into a per unit royalty system.

c. Per Use Royalties

It's possible that you may have invented something that is used, rather than sold. For example, if you patented a method of coating glass for neon light, your process may be used in the manufacturing operation. That is, you are licensing a procedure that is used as part of a production process. Since the process may be used in a variety of ways, a royalty system based on net sales is difficult to justify and hard to audit. Under these circumstances, inventors choose a use royalty. This is a royalty applied to the number of units produced, or the number of times the method is used in manufacture.

> **EXAMPLE:** Fred has devised a method of compacting and sealing aluminum cans to produce building blocks. He licenses the method to RecyCo and receives a unit royalty of 15 cents for every cubic foot.

d. Lump Sum Payments

Lump sum payments are a gamble. Should you take one large payment or a royalty? If your invention is wildly successful, you may always regret the lump sum choice. If the invention is not successful, you won't see any royalties. You can attempt, if possible, to estimate potential sales over the period of the license. However, that is a speculative approach and the fact is, there is no proven method for successfully picking the form of payment.

There are two reasons that some licensors prefer a lump sum payment. First, the licensor doesn't have to be concerned with accounting or auditing records. Second, some licensors prefer lump sum payments for foreign licenses because of currency conversion rates. These rates—which measure the foreign currency against U.S. currency—may change dramatically, making your foreign royalty payments less valuable. If you are in doubt whether or not to choose a lump sum, you may wish to consult a patent attorney to evaluate your invention's commercial potential.

Note: A lump sum payment for a license is different from a lump sum payment for an assignment. A license may be limited in time, for example, for two or three years. Under an assignment, however, you lose ownership of your invention (see Chapter 11).

e. Fluctuating Royalty Rates

A fluctuating royalty rate (sometimes referred to as a sliding royalty) is a rate that changes during the licensing period. The rate may change each year or it may change because of other circumstances, such as sales or inflation. For example, the royalty rate may go up if sales exceed a million units in one year. Similarly, a licensee may seek a decreasing royalty in the event that sales fall below a certain mark.

> **EXAMPLE:** Page has licensed a device to patch bicycle tubes. His royalty rate is 5%

for net sales up to and including $100,000 and 6% for net sales above $100,000 in any one year. If net sales are $150,000 in one year, Page receives $8,000 [($100,000 x 5%) + ($50,000 x 6%)].

f. Hybrid License Royalties

If you are licensing a pending or issued patent and a trade secret, your arrangement is referred to as a "hybrid license." A hybrid license requires special attention because of antitrust laws. When you license a patent and some other intellectual property rights for an invention (such as a trademark or trade secret), courts presume that the patent is inherently more valuable than the other form of intellectual property. Therefore, if your pending patent does not issue or if your patent expires, it is unfair to require the licensee to pay the same royalty as if the patent existed.

Therefore we suggest a modification to your license agreement if you meet the following criteria:

- you are licensing a patent or pending patent and some other form of intellectual property (such as a trademark or trade secret), and
- your license agreement is expected to continue longer than the life of the patents.

If your license is longer than the life of the patents, you can continue to collect royalties provided that the royalty percentage decreases to reflect the value of the expired patents. We suggest allocating the royalty between the patent and the nonpatented property. For example, 85% of the royalty can be attributable to the patent and 15% for a trademark. After the patent expires, the royalty rate would diminish by 85%.

You do not need a hybrid royalty provision if the term (that is, the length) of your agreement does not exceed the length of your patent protection. For example, if you license a patented invention and trade secrets and your license provides for termination "with the expiration of the patent," then you would not need to include the hybrid language.

8. GMARs Guarantee Annual Payments

The minimum annual royalty or guaranteed minimum royalty (we'll refer to it as a GMAR) is an annual payment. It's a guarantee that the licensor will receive a certain payment, regardless of how well the product sells in any year. How does a GMAR work? Each year, you receive your GMAR payment. At the end of each year, the earned royalties are totaled. (The earned royalties are the actual royalties that accumulated from net sales that year.) What happens next depends upon the agreement.

a. Credits—When Royalties Exceed the GMAR

The GMAR is a minimum payment to compensate you for royalties that are expected that year. But what happens if the royalties exceed the GMAR payment? In that situation, the licensee has paid fewer royalties to you

through the GMAR than you actually earned. Depending upon how your agreement is negotiated, either 1) you may receive a credit payment at the end of the year, or 2) the licensee may hold onto this money as a carry-forward credit, and then deduct it against your account in the following years if you have a loss.

We would recommend against the carryforward credit because it prevents you from receiving earned royalties for another year. However, licensees prefer it because new product sales may be unpredictable. The first year may be booming, but sales may slow down the second year.

b. Deficiencies—When the GMAR Exceeds the Earned Royalties

What happens if the GMAR payment is more than the royalties that you actually earned in a year? For example, say you were paid a $10,000 GMAR but the royalties only totaled $9,000 that year. The licensee paid more royalties to you than you earned.

Depending upon how your agreement is negotiated, 1) the licensee may have to absorb the deficiency, or 2) the contract may permit the licensee to carry forward or cumulate royalty deficiencies, diminishing next year's GMAR payment accordingly, or 3) if there is a carryforward credit provision (see above), then the deficiency is applied against a previous year's credit.

> **EXAMPLE:** Your license agreement provides for a GMAR of $10,000 to be paid on January 1 of each year. The first year's

total royalty was only $6,000, which is $4,000 less than the GMAR, so there is a deficiency of $4,000. The second year's total royalty was $14,000. That's $4,000 more than the GMAR. So, for the second year, there is a credit of $4,000.

If you had a carryforward provision, you would have received a total of $20,000 for the two years because the first-year deficiency of $4,000 would have canceled out the second-year credit of $4,000. If you had no carryforward provision, you would have received a total of $24,000. You would have received the $4,000 credit from the second year and the $4,000 first-year deficiency would have no effect on your payments.

To sum up, if you are fortunate enough to negotiate a GMAR, your preference should be for a GMAR without a carryforward (sometimes referred to as noncumulating) requirement. You should also be aware that GMARs can be suspended (that is, no payment is required) if certain things occur. Sometimes a contract will provide that no GMAR has to be paid if, through no fault of the licensee, it is impossible to manufacture the product or to obtain the raw materials for the product.

9. Deductions Can Make Your Royalties Disappear

Net sales are the most common measurement for royalty payments. In a net sales license, the royalty rate is multiplied against the net sales. There is no standard definition of net sales and it can change in every license agreement.

During negotiations, a licensee will attempt to define net sales in a very narrow way with many deductions. This way, the licensee can make a lower royalty payment. The licensor, on the other hand, wants a broad definition. The big issue when negotiating net sales is what deductions should be included in the definition of net sales. License agreements often include many deductions. In order for you to sort through these deductions, the common ones are explained below.

a. Quantity Discount Deduction

Sometimes a licensee may seek to increase sales by offering a discount on large quantity orders. The licensee then deducts this discount (also referred to as a volume discount) from net sales. This can be favorable to the licensor because it increases sales. If you choose to include it, you should qualify the discount by describing a quantity discount as "a discount made at the time of shipment" or "a discount actually shown on the invoice," since it is possible that an unscrupulous licensee may attempt to offer a discount after items are shipped, splitting the discount with the purchaser and diminishing your royalty payment.

b. Debts and Uncollectible Account Deductions

Sometimes a licensee may seek to deduct bad debts and uncollectible accounts. For example, say a third party orders products and then fails to pay. The licensee feels no royalty should be paid since no money was earned for these sales. On the other hand, you are not a collection agency and should not have to lose money because of the licensee's bad business dealings. Even though insolvency and uncollected debts are not especially common, it would be better for you to avoid this deduction.

c. Sales Commission Deductions

Sometimes a salesperson is paid a commission for each sale of the licensed product. The licensee may seek to deduct these commissions under the net sales definition. We would discourage the deduction of commissions because they are a cost of the licensee's business.

d. Promotion/Marketing/ Advertising Deduction

As we have stated, net sales are supposed to be total sales, not a collection of business deductions. For that reason we would discourage the use of promotional, marketing or advertising deductions in the definition of net sales. Marketing should be a cost of doing business, not a licensor expense.

e. Fee Deduction

This vague term includes a wide range of costs and business expenses. If the term "fees" can be made more specific, you may be more comfortable with the deduction. Otherwise we discourage the deduction of fees from net sales.

f. Freight/Shipping Deduction

Freight and shipping costs of the product, although a cost of doing business, are traditionally treated as a deduction against net sales. We recommend that you accept this as a deduction from net sales.

g. Credits and Returns Deduction

It is acceptable for a licensee to deduct credits and returns from the total net sales, since returns reflect merchandise which was not purchased or was defective. Some licensors prefer to qualify the definition to state "bona fide returns" or "returns actually made or allowed as supported by credit memoranda" in order to weed out returns which are part of some unscrupulous arrangement between distributors and retailers.

h. Tax Deductions

If a product is taxed locally, it is common to include this as a deduction against net sales.

Summing up, it is generally acceptable for net sales to include deductions for shipping, freight, taxes, credits, returns and discounts made at time of sale. It is less desirable—and we recommend against—deductions for sales commissions, debts, uncollectible accounts, promotions, marketing and advertising.

Putting a Cap on Net Sales Deductions

One way to limit net sales deductions is to place a limit on the amount to be deducted. For example, in your license agreement you could include a statement that reads as follows:

"In no event may the total amount deducted from net sales (for discounts, credits or returns) during any royalty period exceed ten percent of the gross sales of the products during that royalty period."

A provision such as this guarantees that the deductions will never be more than 10% of gross sales. Some license agreements forego a listing of the deductions and simply state that net sales are "gross sales minus ten percent for shipping, freight, taxes, returns and other deductions." This provision may not accurately reflect the actual deductions but it does remove any accounting issues. That is, you no longer have to wonder whether net sales deductions are accurate.

So you've negotiated a good royalty, but how do you know the payments you receive are accurate? Since sales figures and deductions are within the control of the licensee, you will want the right to audit, or review licensee records. This right can be provided in the license agreement and is traditionally referred to as an audit provision.

The audit provision generally provides:
- that the licensor (or the licensor's representative) shall have access to the licensee's books and records,
- that the audit information will remain confidential, and
- a method for resolving any disputes over discrepancies.

10. Audit Provisions Permit You to Check the Books

An audit provision will provide who can audit the books and how often. Normally, a licensee will want to limit the frequency of audits. It is common for a licensee to limit the number of audits to once or twice a year. Also, the licensee will want several days' notice before the audit is to occur. Five days' is common.

The licensee may also seek to limit who can audit the books. For example, a licensee may request that you hire a Certified Public Accountant (CPA) to perform the audit. It will be more expensive for you to hire a CPA, and therefore we would recommend that you avoid this requirement. It would be less expensive if any accountant can serve as your representative for an audit. It also would be helpful to obtain the licensee's cooperation by designating an individual at the licensee's company to be available to assist you or your representatives.

Sometimes a licensee will attempt to prohibit a licensor from using an accounting firm that works on a contingency basis. Working on a contingency basis means that the company will not get paid unless it finds a discrepancy. Licensees are not comfortable with these firms because they believe that contingency accountants "manufacture" discrepancies in order to receive a bigger commission. As a general rule, we would recommend that you retain the right to use whomever you want as your representative for an audit.

Since you may not discover or suspect a discrepancy right away, you should negotiate an audit provision that requires the licensee to keep all books and records available for at least two years after the termination of the license agreement.

Since the licensee's books may contain confidential information about sales and prices, your representative may be required to sign a confidentiality agreement. You may be requested to keep the information confidential. This is reasonable, although this confidentiality provision should not apply in the event of litigation about payments.

Finally, in the case of an underpayment in which you receive less money than you should, the license agreement should provide for a method of settling the dispute. Usually, there are three parts to this dispute resolution.

First, the licensee must promptly pay you the money you should have received. Second, you should seek an interest payment. If you had received the proper payment in the first place, you could have deposited it in a bank and earned interest on it. Third, you may seek to have the licensee pay for the costs of your audit if there is an underpayment. A licensee will not want to pay for the audit for just any discrepancy, only substantial ones. What counts as substantial? Some agreements set a dollar amount, for example; $1,000. Other agreements set a percentage; for example, if any underpayment was more than 2% of the amount paid.

The licensing worksheet below is intended to help you keep track of the essential business facts.

Internet License Exchanges

Several Web-based businesses seek to bring patent owners and potential licensees together. Sites such as Yet2.com (www.yet2.com), the Patent and License Exchange (www.pl-x.com), 2XFR.com (www.2xfr.com) and NewIdeaTrade.com (www.newideatrade.com) offer—for a fee—the ability to post information about patented inventions for would-be licensees. To explore these and other patent exchanges, type "patent exchange" into your Internet search engine and review the resulting sites.

William Lear
Inventor of the car radio, the eight-track player and navigation aids

Contract Worksheet

Licensee

Name of licensee business _____

Licensee address _____

_____

Licensee business form

☐ sole proprietorship   ☐ general partnership   ☐ limited partnership

☐ corporation   ☐ limited liability company

State of incorporation _____

Name, position and phone number of person signing for licensee _____

_____

Property Definition

Patent No. _____

Patent Application Serial No. _____

Copyrightable features _____

_____

Copyright Registration No.(s) _____

Trade secrets _____

_____

Trademarks _____

_____

Trademark Registration No.(s) _____

_____

Licensed Product Definition

Industry (Have you limited the license to a particular industry?) _____

_____

Product (Have you limited the license to a particular product or products?) _____

_____

Territory

☐ worldwide   ☐ countries _____

☐ states _____

Rights Granted (check those rights granted to licensee)

☐ sell	☐ make or manufacture	☐ distribute
☐ use	☐ revise	☐ import
☐ lease	☐ right to improvements	☐ derivatives (copyright)
☐ copy (copyright)	☐ advertise	☐ promote

☐ other rights _____

☐ other rights _____

☐ other rights _____

Rights Reserved

☐ all rights reserved (except those granted in license)

☐ no rights reserved

☐ specific rights reserved _____

Have you signed any other licenses? If so, do you need to reserve specific rights?

_____

_____

Term

Have you agreed upon:

☐ a fixed term (How long? _____)   ☐ a term limited by patent length

☐ unlimited term until one party terminates   ☐ an initial term with renewals (see below)

☐ other _____

Renewals

If you have agreed upon an initial term with renewals:

How many renewal periods? _____   How long is each renewal period? _____

What triggers renewal?

☐ Licensee must notify of intent to renew.

☐ Licensor must notify of intent to renew.

☐ Agreement renews automatically unless Licensee indicates it does not want to renew.

Net Sales Deductions

What is the licensee permitted to deduct when calculating net sales?

☐ quantity discounts   ☐ debts and uncollectibles   ☐ sales commissions

☐ promotion and marketing costs   ☐ fees   ☐ freight and shipping

☐ credits and returns   ☐ other _____

Is there a cap on the total amount of the deductions?   ☐ Yes   ☐ No

If so, how much? _____

Royalty Rates

Licensed products _____%   Combination products _____%

Accessory products _____%

Per use royalty _____% or Usage standard _____

Other products _____%   Other products _____%

Do you have any sliding royalty rates? _____

Advances and Lump Sum Payments

Advance $ _____   Date due _____

Lump sum payment(s) $_____   Date due _____

Guaranteed Minimum Annual Royalty (GMAR)

GMAR $ _____   Date due _____

Does the GMAR carry forward credits?   ☐ Yes   ☐ No

Does the GMAR carry forward deficiencies?   ☐ Yes   ☐ No

Audit Rights

No. of audits permitted per year _____

No. of days notice _____

Chapter 18

Help Beyond the Book

A. Patent Websites 18/2

    1. Inventor Resources 18/2

    2. Patent Law and Intellectual Property Law Websites 18/3

    3. Patent Searching Online 18/3

    4. Assessing Foreign Patent Potential 18/4

B. Finding and Using a Lawyer 18/5

    1. Inventor Attorneys 18/5

    2. Business and Tax Attorneys 18/6

C. Help From Other Experts 18/8

    1. Tax Professionals 18/8

    2. Industry and Trade Associations 18/8

    3. Small Business Administration 18/8

D. Doing Your Own Legal Research 18/9

    1. Researching Federal Tax Law 18/9

    2. Researching Other Areas of Law 18/10

E. Online Small Business Resources 18/11

    1. Internet Resources 18/11

    2. Commercial Online Services 18/12

F. State Offices Providing Small Business Help 18/13

*I*n this chapter we offer a wide range of resources for you to pursue your own small business, tax or intellectual property research. We also provide advice on finding, paying and dealing with legal and tax experts.

A. Patent Websites

Below are four groups of patent links. The first group provides sources of information for inventors, the second group includes resources on patent law and intellectual property law, the third provides patent searching databases and the fourth group will help you to assess your foreign patent potential. As with all Internet links, we cannot guarantee the continued accuracy of any of these sites.

1. Inventor Resources

DaVinci Design Resource (www.uspatentinfo. com) provides information and resources that may be helpful to the inventor in building a prototype of an invention.

Intellectual Property Owners (IPO) (www. ipo.org) sponsors the National Inventor of the Year Award and serves owners of patents, trademarks, copyrights and trade secrets.

Invention Convention (www.invention convention.com) includes links, trade show information and advice for inventors.

InventNet Forum (www.inventnet.com) provides an online forum and mailing list if you wish to contact other inventors.

Inventor's Bookstore (www.inventorhelp. com) offers condensed reports and other guidance for inventors.

Inventor's Digest Online (www.inventors digest.com) publishes online information and a print publication for independent inventors.

Minnesota Inventors Congress (www. invent1.org) is one of the oldest and most respected inventor organizations.

National Technology Transfer Center (NTTC) (www.nttc.edu) helps entrepreneurs and companies looking to access federally funded research and development activity at U.S. universities.

Patent Café (www.patentcafe.com), one of the most popular inventor websites, lists inventor organizations and related links and provides information on starting an inventor organization.

Patent Law Links (www.patentlawlinks.com) provides links to everything "patent" on the Internet.

USPTO Independent Inventor Resources (www.uspto.gov) is a new USPTO-sponsored office aimed at providing services and support to independent inventors. Click "Patents" on the left side and then click "Inventor Assistance Center."

Ronald J. Riley's Inventor Resources (www. inventored.org) offers a set of comprehensive links and advice for inventors.

United Inventors Association (UIA) (www. uiausa.org) is a national inventors' organization.

2. Patent Law and Intellectual Property Law Websites

Copyright Office (www.copyright.gov) has numerous circulars, kits and other publications that can help you, including one on searching copyright records.

European Patent Office (EPO) (www. european-patent-office.org/online) is the agency that implements the European Patent Convention—a simplified method of acquiring a patent among member nations—by granting "regional" European patents that are automatically valid in each European Patent Convention member country.

Fedlaw (http://fedlaw.gsa.gov) is a source of federal law links with a thorough collection of intellectual property statutes, case law and readings.

Government Printing Office (www.access. gpo.gov/#info) is a searchable source for U.S. Code of Federal Regulations, Congressional Record and other Government Printing Office products and information.

Intellectual Property Mall (www.ipmall. fplc.edu) has IP links and information.

Internet Patent News Service (www. bustpatents.com) is a source for patent news, information about searching and patent documents.

Legal Information Institute (http://lii.law. cornell.edu) has intellectual property links and downloadable copies of statutes and cases.

Patent & Trademark Office (USPTO) (www. uspto.gov) offers a number of informational pamphlets, including an introduction to patents (*General Information About Patents*) and an alphabetical and geographical listing of patent attorneys and agents registered to practice before the USPTO (*Directory of Registered Patent Attorneys and Agents Arranged by States and Countries*). Most patent forms can be downloaded from the USPTO website, as can many important publications including the *Manual of Patent Examining Procedures*, *Examination Guidelines for Computer-Related Inventions* and *Disclosure Document Program*.

PCT Applicant's Guide (www.wipo.int) provides PCT information and software for facilitating completion of the PCT forms is available through the PCT's website.

Trade Secrets Home Page (www.execpc. com/~mhallign) has explanations of trade secret law online and current trade secret news.

Trademark Office (www.uspto.gov) provides information about trademarks examination and registration.

U.S. Code (http://uscode.house.gov/usc. htm) is a source for United States Code including copyright, trademark and patent laws.

Yahoo Intellectual Property Directory (www.yahoo.com/Government/Law/ Intellectual_Property) is a thorough listing of intellectual property resources on the Internet.

3. Patent Searching Online

Here are several organizations that offer computer searching of patent records and a description of their services. Several of the "for fee" databases also provide foreign patent information.

U.S. Patent & Trademark Office (www. uspto.gov/patft/index.html) offers free online full-text-searchable database of patents and drawings that covers the period from January 1976 to the most recent weekly issue date (usually each Tuesday). In order to view the drawings, your computer must be able to view TIFF files. The USPTO's site is linked to a source that provides a free downloadable TIFF reader program. For faster searching there is also a Bibliographic Database that contains only the text of each patent without drawings.

Delphion (www.delphion.com) provides a fee-based online searchable database with full-text-searching capability for patents issued from 1974 to the present.

MicroPatent (www.micropatent.com) is a commercial database of U.S. patents searchable from 1836 to the present. Users must first set up an account. Also offers delivery of patent copies dating back to 1790 by U.S. mail, fax, and email.

LexPat (www.lexis-nexis.com) is a commercial database of U.S. patents searchable from 1971 to the present. In addition, the LEXPAT library offers extensive prior-art searching capability of technical journals and magazines.

QPAT (www.qpat.com) and Questel/Orbit (www.questel.orbit.com) are both commercial services that access the QPAT database, which includes U.S. patents searchable from 1974 to the present and full-text European A (1987–present) and B (1991–present) patents.

The European Patent Office's (EPO's) Server (http://ep.espacenet.com) allows you to search for foreign and U.S. patents. Presently this site only offers searches of titles and abstracts of patents.

4. Assessing Foreign Patent Potential

Consult the following resources when deciding whether to pursue foreign patent rights.

EUBusiness (www.eubusiness.com/) is a reliable source of information for facts and statistics on EU economy and specific industries.

European Patent Office (www.european-patent-office.org/online/) provides links to patent-licensing exchanges, mailing lists, patent information providers, registered European patent agents, law offices and patent offices for member states.

National Trade Data Bank (http://iserve.wtca.org/intro_ntdb.html) is a fee-based site (you must pay to use it) that provides detailed statistical information on trade in specific products. Print copies of the National Trade Data Bank are sometimes available in large urban public libraries and university libraries.

The Federation of International Trade Associations (FITA) (www.fita.org) has many international business and trade links, leads, statistics and other helpful information.

The U.S. Commercial Service (www.export.gov) offers free online Country Commercial Guides that analyze categories of industry and trade for each nation. The site also provides Customized Market Analysis Reports—one of the most thorough means of determining the market for your product within a nation. Although expensive (ranging from $2,000 to $4,000 per country), these reports answer a wide range of questions about the likelihood of commercial success. (For a listing of the questions answered by each report and the cost per nation, access the site.)

The U.S. Department of Commerce (DOC) (www.doc.gov) and the U.S. Small Business Administration (SBA) (www.sbaonline.sba.gov) are interested in helping the sales of U.S. goods overseas. If an inventor has a good track record and the possibility of actually placing a product in the market (or already has a product and is seeking to market it overseas), the DOC and SBA offer assistance.

VIBES (Virtual International Business & Economic Sources) (http://libweb.uncc.edu/ref-bus/vibehome.htm) provides over 1,600 links to international business and economic sources including statistical tables and research articles.

Nolo's Legal Encyclopedia

Nolo's website (www.nolo.com) features an extensive Legal Encyclopedia that includes a section on intellectual property. You'll find answers to frequently asked questions about patents, copyrights, trademarks and other related topics, as well as sample chapters of Nolo books and a wide range of articles. Simply click on "Legal Encyclopedia" and then on "Patents, Copyright & Trademark."

B. Finding and Using a Lawyer

An experienced attorney may help answer your invention and business questions and allay your fears about protecting your invention and setting up and running your business. Below we have divided attorneys into two groups: inventor attorneys who can help in the protection and licensing of your invention; and business attorneys who can help in setting up and running your business.

1. Inventor Attorneys

In general, there are two groups of inventor attorneys: those licensed to practice before the USPTO (patent attorneys) and those who are not. You should consult a patent attorney for assistance performing patent searching, drafting a provisional or regular patent application, responding to patent examiners and dealing with the USPTO. An attorney does not have to be licensed to practice before the USPTO in order to enforce your patent in a court case. We recommend that you use a patent attorney to prepare or analyze patent-related agreements on your behalf—for example, to prepare invention assignments, license agreements or co-inventorship agreements. That said, many attorneys who are not licensed to practice before the USPTO can negotiate, prepare and enforce license agreements and ventures.

a. Finding an inventor attorney

The best way to get a referral to a good patent lawyer is to talk to other people who have actually used a particular lawyer's services. The worst is to comb through advertisements or unscreened lists of lawyers provided by a local bar association or the phone company.

If you are having difficulty locating an attorney knowledgeable about inventions and patent law, check out the American Intellectual Property Law Association (AIPLA) (www.aipla. org) or the Intellectual Property Law Association of the American Bar Association (www. abanet.org). The USPTO website (www.uspto. gov) also maintains a list of attorneys and patent agents licensed to practice before the USPTO.

b. Inventor attorney fees

Patent and intellectual property attorneys generally charge $200 to $400 per hour, and a full-blown patent lawsuit can run to hundreds or even thousands of hours' work, before it even goes to trial.

To save yourself a lot of money and grief, review the tips in Section B2.

2. Business and Tax Attorneys

There are many attorneys who specialize in advising small businesses. These lawyers are a bit like general practitioner doctors: they know a little about a lot of different areas of law. A lawyer with plenty of experience working with businesses should be able to answer your basic inventor business questions. Such a lawyer can help you:

- start your business—review incorporation documents, for example

- analyze zoning ordinances, land use regulations and private title documents that may restrict your ability to work at home
- review client agreements
- coach or represent you in lawsuits or arbitrations where the stakes are high or the legal issues complex
- deal with intellectual property issues— copyrights, trademarks, patents, trade secrets and business names, or
- look over a proposed office lease.

a. Finding a business lawyer

The best way to locate a small business lawyer is through referrals from other self-employed people in your community. Industry associations and trade groups are also excellent sources of referrals. If you already have or know a lawyer, he or she might also be able to refer you to an experienced person who has the qualifications you need. Other people, such as your banker, accountant or insurance agent, may know of good business lawyers.

Local bar associations often maintain and advertise lawyer referral services. However, a lawyer can usually get on this list simply by volunteering. Very little (if any) screening is done to find out if the lawyers are any good. Similarly, advertisements in the yellow pages, in newspapers, on television or online say nothing meaningful about a lawyer's skills or manner—just that he could afford to pay for the ad. In many states, lawyers can advertise any specialization they choose—even if they have never handled a case in that area of law.

b. Paying a lawyer

Whenever you hire a lawyer, insist upon a written explanation of how the fees and costs will be calculated and paid.

Most business lawyers charge by the hour. Hourly rates vary, but in most parts of the United States, you can get competent services for your business for $150 to $250 an hour. Comparison shopping among lawyers will help you avoid overpaying. But the cheapest hourly rate isn't necessarily the best. A novice who charges only $80 an hour may take three hours to review a consulting contract. A more experienced lawyer who charges $200 an hour may do the same job in half an hour and make better suggestions. If a lawyer will be delegating some of the work on your case to a less experienced associate, paralegal or secretary, that work should be billed at a lower hourly rate. Be sure to get this information recorded in your initial written fee agreement.

Sometimes, a lawyer may quote you a flat fee for a specific job. For example, a lawyer may offer to incorporate your business for a flat fee of $2,000. You pay the same amount regardless of how much time the lawyer spends. This can be cheaper than paying an hourly fee, but not always.

Alternatively, some self-employed people hire lawyers on retainer—that is, they pay a flat annual fee in return for the lawyer handling all their routine legal business. However, few small businesses can afford to keep a lawyer on retainer.

Here are some tips for keeping fees down:

- **Keep it short.** If you are paying your attorney on an hourly basis, keep your conversations short—the meter is always running. Avoid making several calls a day; instead, consolidate your questions and ask them all in one conversation.
- **Get a fee agreement.** Always get a written fee agreement when dealing with an attorney. Read it and make sure you can understand it. Your fee agreement should give you the right to an itemized billing statement that details the work done and time spent. Some state statutes and bar associations require a written fee agreement—for example, California requires that attorneys provide a written agreement when the fee will exceed $1,000.
- **Review billings carefully.** Your lawyer's bill should be clear. Do not accept summary billings such as the single phrase "litigation work," to explain a block of time for which you are billed a great deal of money.
- **Watch out for hidden expenses.** Find out what expenses you will have to pay. Don't let your attorney bill you for services such as word processing or administrative services. This means you will be paying the secretary's salary. Also beware of fax and copying charges. Some firms charge clients per page for incoming and outgoing faxes.

Remember, you can always fire your lawyer. (You're still obligated to pay outstanding bills, though.) If you don't respect and trust your attorney's professional abilities, you should find a new attorney. But switching attorneys is a nuisance, and you may lose time and money.

Using a Lawyer as a Legal Coach

One way to keep your legal costs down is to do as much work as possible yourself and simply use the lawyer as your coach. For example, you can draft your own agreements, giving your lawyer the relatively quick and inexpensive task of reviewing them.

But get a clear understanding about who's going to do what. You don't want to do the work and get billed for it because the lawyer duplicated your efforts. And you certainly don't want any crucial elements to fall through cracks because you each thought the other person was attending to the work.

C. Help From Other Experts

Lawyers aren't the only people who can help you deal with the legal issues involved in being self-employed. Tax professionals, members of trade groups and the Small Business Administration can also be very helpful.

1. Tax Professionals

Tax professionals include tax attorneys, certified public accountants and enrolled agents. Tax pros can answer your tax questions and help you with tax planning, preparing your tax returns and dealing with IRS audits.

2. Industry and Trade Associations

Business or industry trade associations or similar organizations can be useful sources of information and services. Many such groups track federal and state laws, lobby Congress and state legislatures and even help members deal with the IRS and other federal and state agencies. Many also offer their members insurance and other benefits and have useful publications.

3. Small Business Administration

The U.S. Small Business Administration, or SBA, is an independent federal agency that helps small businesses. The SBA is best known for providing loan guaranties to bolster small businesses that want to start or expand, but it provides several other useful services for small businesses, including:

- SBA Answer Desk. The Answer Desk is a nationwide, toll-free information center that helps callers with questions and problems about starting and running businesses. Service is provided through a computerized telephone message system augmented by staff counselors. It is available 24 hours a day, seven days a week, with counselors available Monday through Friday, 9 am to 5 pm Eastern time. The Answer Desk can be reached at 800-8-ASK-SBA.
- Publications. The SBA also produces and maintains a library of publications, videos and computer programs. These are available by mail to SBA customers for a nominal fee. A complete listing of these products is in the Resource Directory for Small Business Management. SBA field offices also offer free publications that describe SBA programs and services.

- SBA Internet site. You can download SBA publications from the SBA Internet site and obtain information about SBA programs and services, points of contact and calendars of local events. The Internet address is www.sba.gov.
- SCORE program. The Service Corps of Retired Executives, or SCORE, is a group of retired businesspeople who volunteer to help others in business. To find a SCORE chapter in your area, visit the SCORE website at www.score.org, or call the national SCORE office at 800-634-0245.

The SBA has offices in all major cities. Look in the phone book under U.S. Government for the office nearest you.

D. Doing Your Own Legal Research

If you decide to investigate the law on your own, your first step should be to obtain a good guide to help you understand legal citations, use the law library and understand what you find there. There are a number of sources that provide a good introduction to legal research, including *Legal Research: How to Find and Understand the Law*, by Stephen Elias & Susan Levinkind (Nolo). This book simply explains how to use all major legal research tools and helps you frame your research questions

Next, you need to find a law library that's open to the public. Your county should have a public law library, often at the county courthouse. Public law schools often contain especially good collections and generally

permit the public to use them. Some private law schools grant access to their libraries— sometimes for a modest fee. The reference department of a major public or university library may have a fairly decent legal research collection. Finally, don't overlook the law library in your own lawyer's office. Many lawyers will agree to share their books with their clients.

1. Researching Federal Tax Law

Many resources are available to augment and explain the tax information in this book. Some are free and others are reasonably priced. Tax publications for professionals are expensive, but are often available at public libraries or law libraries.

a. IRS website

The IRS has perhaps the most useful and colorful Internet site (www.irs.gov) of any government agency. It contains virtually every IRS publication and tax form, IRS announcement and a copy of the IRS *Audit Manual on Independent Contractors*. It's almost worth getting on the Internet just to use this site.

b. IRS booklets

The IRS also publishes over 350 free booklets explaining the tax code, and many are clearly written and useful. These IRS publications range from several pages to several hundred pages in length. Many of the most useful IRS publications are cited in the tax chapters in this book.

The following IRS publications cover basic tax information that every self-employed person should know about:

- Publication 334, *Tax Guide for Small Businesses*
- Publication 505, *Tax Withholding and Estimated Tax*
- Publication 937, *Employment Taxes and Information Returns*, and
- Publication 15, *Circular E, Employer's Tax Guide*.

IRS publications are available in IRS offices, by calling 800-TAX-FORM or by sending in an order form. They can also be downloaded from the IRS's Internet site at www.irs.gov.

⚠ **Don't rely exclusively on the IRS.** IRS publications are useful to obtain information on IRS procedures and to get the agency's view of the tax law. But keep in mind that these publications only present the IRS's interpretation of the law, which may be very one-sided and even contrary to court rulings. Don't rely exclusively on IRS publications for information.

c. IRS telephone information

The IRS offers a series of prerecorded tapes of information on various tax topics on a toll-free telephone service called TELETAX. Call 800-829-4477. See IRS Publication 910 for a list of topics.

You can talk to an IRS representative at 800-829-1040, but expect difficulty getting though from January through May. Double-check anything an IRS representative tells you over the phone; the IRS is notorious for giving misleading or outright wrong answers to tax-payers' questions. The IRS does not stand behind oral advice that turns out to be incorrect.

d. Tax guides

Dozens of privately published self-help tax guides are available. The most detailed and authoritative are:

- Master Tax Guide (Commerce Clearing House)
- Master Federal Tax Manual (Research Institute of America), and
- Federal Tax Guide (Prentice-Hall).

You can find these in many public libraries.

2. Researching Other Areas of Law

Many fields of law other than federal tax law are involved when you're self-employed. For example, your state laws may control how you form a sole proprietorship or corporation, protect trade names, form contracts and resolve disputes.

If you have questions about your state workers' compensation, tax or employment laws, first contact the appropriate state agency for more information. Many of these agencies publish informative pamphlets.

In-depth research into your state law will require you to review:

- legislation, also called statutes, passed by your state legislature
- administrative rules and regulations issued by state administrative agencies such as your state tax department and unemployment compensation agency, and
- published decisions of your state courts.

Many states, particularly larger ones, have legal encyclopedias or treatises that organize summaries of state case law and some statutes alphabetically by subject. Through citation footnotes, you can locate the full text of the cases and statutes. These works are a good starting point for in-depth state law research.

It's also helpful if you can find a treatise on the subject you're researching. A treatise is a book that covers a specific area of law. The West Publishing Company publishes a series of short paperback treatises called the Nutshell Series. If you are facing a possible contract dispute, you may want to look at *Contracts in a Nutshell*, by Gordon A. Schaber and Claude D. Rohwer, and *Corporations in a Nutshell*, by Robert Hamilton.

A relatively unknown resource for quickly locating state business laws is the *United States Law Digest* volume of the *Martindale-Hubbel Law Directory*. It contains a handy summary of laws for each state. Dozens of business law topics are covered, including corporations, insurance, leases, statute of frauds and trademarks, trade names and service marks. *The Martindale-Hubbel Law Directory* is in most public libraries.

E. Online Small Business Resources

The online world includes the Internet, commercial online services such as America Online and CompuServe and specialized computer databases such as Westlaw and Lexis. All contain useful information for the computer-savvy self-employed.

1. Internet Resources

There are hundreds of Internet sites dealing with small business issues, such as starting a small business, marketing and business opportunities. Be aware, however, that no one checks these sites for accuracy. A good way to find these sites is through an Internet directory such as Yahoo. You can access Yahoo at www.yahoo.com. Click on the Business and Economy category and then on the Small Business Information listing.

A few particularly useful websites for self-employed people include the:

- CCH Business Owner's Toolkit (www.toolkit.cch.com)
- Quicken small business website (www.quicken.com/small_business)

Al Gross
Inventor of the walkie-talkie, the proximity fuse and the world's first pager

- Yahoo Small Business Center (http://smallbusiness.yahoo.com), and
- Small Business Taxes & Management website (www.smbiz.com)

A growing number of court decisions are also available on the Internet for free or at nominal cost. You can find a comprehensive set of links to free case law websites at www.findlaw.com. You can also obtain legal decisions from the subscription websites www.westlaw.com and www.lexis.com.

Nolo Internet Site

Nolo maintains an Internet site that is useful for the self-employed. The site contains helpful articles, information about new legislation, book excerpts and the Nolo catalog. The site also includes a legal encyclopedia with specific information for people who are self-employed, as well as a legal research center you can use to find state and federal statutes. The Internet address is www.nolo.com.

Yet another part of the Internet are Usenet newsgroups. These are collections of electronic-mail messages on specific topics, called postings, that can be read by anybody with access to the Internet. Most newsgroups are completely open—meaning anybody can just jump into the discussion by posting anything they want—although users are usually encouraged to keep to the topic of the newsgroup. Other newsgroups are moderated, meaning that there is a moderator who reviews postings before allowing them to appear in that newsgroup. Moderated newsgroups almost always contain more focused discussion since the moderators want to keep the conversation on the track.

You can use newsgroups to network with other self-employed people, ask specific questions and even find work. Some of the many newsgroups of interest to the self-employed include:

- misc.taxes.moderated
- misc.jobs.contract
- misc.entrepreneurs
- misc.business.consulting
- alt.computer.consultants, and
- alt.computer.consultants.moderated.

If you don't know how to access Internet newsgroups, review the instructions for your Web browser for guidance.

2. Commercial Online Services

Some of the best known parts of the online world are commercial online services such as CompuServe and America Online. To access these systems, a person must become a subscriber and pay a monthly (and sometimes hourly) fee. These systems typically offer online chats with other users logged onto the system, posting of public messages on various topics and vast collections of electronic databases. All of these services have special areas devoted to small business people and consultants. For example, MSN has Bcentral, CompuServe has a Working at Home Forum and America Online has a Small Business area. You can also obtain information on taxes and download copies of IRS tax forms.

Nolo Books on Intellectual Property

Nolo, the publisher of this book, also publishes a number of other titles on intellectual property, including:

- *Copyright Your Software*, by Stephen Fishman
- *How to Make Patent Drawings Yourself*, by Patent Agent Jack Lo & David Pressman
- *License Your Invention*, by Richard Stim
- *Nolo's Patents for Beginners*, by David Pressman & Richard Stim
- *Nondisclosure Agreements: Protect Your Trade Secrets & More*, by Richard Stim & Stephen Fishman
- *Patent Searching Made Easy*, by David Hitchcock
- *Patent, Copyright & Trademark: An Intellectual Property Desk Reference*, by Steve Elias & Richard Stim
- *Web and Software Development, A Legal Guide*, by Stephen Fishman
- *The Copyright Handbook,* by Stephen Fishman
- *The Inventor's Notebook*, by Fred Grissom & David Pressman
- *The Public Domain: How to Find & Use Copyright-Free Writings, Music, Art & More*, by Stephen Fishman
- *Trademark: Legal Care for Your Business & Product Name*, by Stephen Elias, and
- *Patent Pending in 24 Hours* by Richard Stim & David Pressman.

F. State Offices Providing Small Business Help

Below we provide a listing of state offices that can assist small businesses.

Alabama
Economic and Community Affairs
401 Adams Ave
PO Box 5690
Montgomery, AL 36130
800-248-0033 (in-state calling only),
  205-242-0400
www.alalinc.net/partner.cfm?
  Location=secretary

Alaska
Division of Community and Business
  Development
Department of Community & Economic
  Development
PO Box 110809
Juneau, AK 99811-0804
907-465-2017
www.dced.state.ak.us/cbd

Arizona
Department of Commerce
3800 North Central Avenue
Suite 1500
Phoenix, AZ 85012
602-280-1300
www.az.gov/webapp/portal/
  topic.ysp?id=1158

Arkansas

Small Business Information Center
Industrial Development Commission
State Capitol Mall
Room 4C-300
Little Rock, AR 72201
501-682-5275
www.sosweb.state.ar.us

California

Office of Small Business
Department of Commerce
801 K Street, Suite 1700
Sacramento, CA 95814
916-327-4357, 916-445-6545
www.ss.ca.gov/business/business.htm

Colorado

Economic Development Commission
1625 Broadway, Suite 1700
Denver, CO 80202
303-892-3725
www.state.co.us/gov_dir/sos/index.html

Connecticut

Department of Economic and Community
  Development
505 Hudson Street
Hartford, CT 06106
203-258-4200
www.state.ct.us/ecd

Delaware

Development Office
PO Box 1401
99 Kings Highway
Dover, DE 19903
302-739-4271
www.state.de.us/corp/index.htm

District of Columbia

Office of Business and Economic
  Development
Twelfth Floor
717 14th Street NW
Washington, DC 20005
202-727-6600
www.dcra.org

Florida

Bureau of Business Assistance
Department of Commerce
107 West Gaines Street, Room 443
Tallahassee, FL 32399-2000
800-342-0771 (in-state calling only),
  904-488-9357
www.dos.state.fl.us/doc/index.html

Georgia

Department of Community Affairs
100 Peachtree Street, Suite 1200
Atlanta, GA 30303
404-656-6200
www.sos.state.ga.us/corporations

Hawaii

Small Business Information Service
2404 Maile Way
Room A 202
University of Hawaii
Honolulu, HI 96819
808-956-7363
www.hawaii.gov/dbedt/index.html

Idaho

Economic Development Division
Department of Commerce
700 W. State Street

Boise, ID 83720-0093

208-334-2470

www.idsos.state.id.us/corp/corindex.htm

Illinois

Department of Commerce and Community
  Affairs

620 East Adams Street

Springfield, IL 62701

800-252-2923 (in-state calling only),
  217-782-3235

www.commerce.state.il.us/bus/index.html

Indiana

Ombudsman's Office

Community Development Division

Department of Commerce

One North Capitol, Suite 700

Indianapolis, IN 46204-2288

800-824-2476 (in-state calling only),
  317-232-8891

www.state.in.us/sos/bus_service

Iowa

Bureau of Small Business Development

Department of Economic Development

200 East Grand Avenue

Des Moines, IA 50309

800-532-1216 (in-state calling only),
  515-242-4720

www.sos.state.ia.us

Kansas

Division of Existing Industry Development

700 SW Harrison, Suite 1300

Topeka, KN 66603

913-296-2741

www.kssos.org

Kentucky

Division of Small Business

2400 Capitol Plaza Tower

Frankfort, KY 40601

800-626-2250 (in-state calling only),
  502-564-7670

www.sos.state.ky.us

Louisiana

Department of Economic Development

Office of Commerce and Industry

PO Box 94185

Baton Rouge, LA 70804-9185

504-342-5365

www.lded.state.la.us

Maine

Business Development Division

Department of Economic and Community
  Development

State House 59

187 State Street

Augusta, ME 04333

800-872-3838 (in-state calling only),
  207-287-2656

www.state.me.us/sos/cec/cec.htm

Maryland

Division of Business Development

Department of Economic and Employment
  Development

217 East Redwood Street

Baltimore, MD 21202

800-873-7232, 410-767-3316

www.dat.state.md.us

Massachusetts
Office of Business Development
1 Ashburton Place, Room 301
Boston, MA 02202
617-727-8380
www.state.ma.us/sec/cor/coridx.htm

Michigan
Michigan Jobs Commission
Ombudsman's Office
201 N. Washington Square
Lansing, MI 48913
517-373-9808
www.michigan.gov/emi/
   1,1303,7-102-115---,00.html

Minnesota
Small Business Assistance Office
Department of Trade and Economic
   Development
500 Metro Square Building
121 E. 7th Place
St. Paul, MN 55101-2146
800-652-9747, 651-297-9706
www.sos.state.mn.us/business/index.html

Mississippi
Mississippi Development Authority
PO Box 849
Jackson, MS 39205
601-359-3349
www.ms.gov/frameset.jsp?URL=http
   %3A%2F%2fwww.mississippi.org%2F

Missouri
Small Business Development Center
300 University Place
Columbia, MO 65211
573-882-0344
http://mosl.sos.state.mo.us

Montana
Business Assistance Division
Department of Commerce
1218 Sixth St.
Helena, MT 59601
800-221-8015 (in-state calling only),
   406-444-3797
www.state.mt.us/sos/biz.htm

Nebraska
Existing Business Division
Department of Economic Development
PO Box 94666
301 Centennial Mall South
Lincoln, NE 68509-4666
402-471-3747
www.nol.org/home/SOS/htm/services.htm

Nevada
Nevada Commission on Economic
   Development
Capitol Complex
5151 S. Carson St.
Carson City, NV 89710
702-687-4325
http://sos.state.nv.us

New Hampshire
Small Business Development Center
108 McConnell Hall
University of New Hampshire
15 College Road
Durham, NH 03824
603-862-2200
www.state.nh.us/agency/agencies.html

New Jersey

Office of Small Business Assistance

Department of Commerce and Economic
  Growth Commission

20 West State Street, CN 835

Trenton, NJ 08625

609-292-2444

www.state.nj.us/njbgs/services.html

New Mexico

Economic Division

Department of Economic Development

1100 St. Francis Drive

PO Box 20003

Santa Fe, NM 87503

505-827-0300

www.edd.state.nm.us/about.htm

New York

Division for Small Business

Department of Economic Development

1515 Broadway

51st Floor

New York, NY 10036

212-827-6150

www.dos.state.ny.us/corp/corpwww.html

North Carolina

Business and Industry Division

Department of Commerce

Dobbs Building, Room 2019

430 North Salisbury Street

Raleigh, NC 27611

919-733-4151

www.ncgov.com/asp/basic/business.asp

North Dakota

Small Business Coordinator

Economic Development Commission

1833 E. Bismark Expressway

Bismark, ND 58504

701-328-5300

www.state.nd.us/sec

Ohio

Small and Developing Business Division

Department of Development

77 S. High Street

Columbus, OH 43215

800-248-4040 (in-state calling only),
  614-466-4232

www.state.oh.us/sos

Oklahoma

Oklahoma Department of Commerce

PO Box 26980

6601 N. Broadway Extension

Oklahoma City, OK 73126-0980

800-477-6552 (in-state calling only),
  405-843-9770

www.state.ok.us

Oregon

Economic Development Department

775 Summer Street NE

Salem, OR 97310

800-233-3306 (in-state calling only),
  503-986-0110

www.sos.state.or.us/corporation/corphp.htm

Pennsylvania

Bureau of Small Business and
Appalachian Development

Department of Commerce

461 Forum Building

Harrisburg, PA 17120

717-783-5700

www.dos.state.pa.us/corp/corp.htm

Rhode Island
Business Development Division
Department of Economic Development
Seven Jackson Walkway
Providence, RI 02903
401-277-2601
www.sec.state.ri.us/submenus/buslink.htm

South Carolina
Enterprise Development
PO Box 1149
Columbia, SC 29202
803-252-8806
www.callsouthcarolina.com

South Dakota
Governor's Office of Economic Development
Capital Lake Plaza
711 Wells Avenue
Pierre, SD 57501
800-872-6190 (in-state calling only),
  605-773-5032
www.sdgreatprofits.com

Tennessee
Small Business Office
Department of Economic and Community
  Development
320 Sixth Avenue North
Eighth Floor
Rachel Jackson Building
Nashville, TN 37219
800-872-7201 (in-state calling only),
  615-741-1888
www.state.tn.us/sos/service.htm

Texas
Small Business Division
Department of Commerce
Economic Development Commission

PO Box 12728
Capitol Station
410 East Fifth Street
Austin, TX 78711
800-888-0511, 512-936-0100
www.tded.state.tx.us/smallbusiness

Utah
Division of Business and Economic
  Development
324 South State St., 5th Floor
Salt Lake City, UT 84114
801-538-8700
www.utah.org/dbcd/welcome.htm

Vermont
Agency of Development and Community Affairs
The Pavilion
109 State Street
Montpelier, VT 05609
800-622-4553 (in-state calling only),
  802-828-3221
www.sec.state.vt.us/corps/corpindex.htm

Virginia
Small Business and Financial Services
Department of Economic Development
PO Box 798
1021 E. Cary Street, 11th Floor
Richmond, VA 23206-0798
804-371-8106
www.state.va.us/scc/division/clk/index.htm

Washington
Small Business Development Center
Krugel Hall, Room 135
Washington State University
Pullman, WA 99164-4727
509-335-1576
www.secstate.wa.gov/corps/default.htm

West Virginia
Economic Development Authority
1018 Kanawha Blvd. E., Suite 501
Charleston, WV 25301
304-558-3650
www.state.wv.us/sos

Wisconsin
Department of Commerce
201 West Washington Avenue
Madison, WI 53717
608-266-1018
www.commerce.state.wi.us

Wyoming
Economic and Community Development
  Division
Commerce Dept.
6101 Yellowstone Road
Cheyenne, WY 82002
307-777-7284
http://soswy.state.wy.us/corporat/
  corporat.htm

Source: National Association for the Self-Employed, USA TODAY research, updated by Nolo.com.

Appendix

How to Use the CD-ROM

A. Installing the Form Files Onto Your Computer A/2

    1. Windows 9X, 2000, Me and XP Users A/2

    2. Macintosh Users A/3

B. Using the Word Processing Files to Create Documents A/3

    Step 1: Opening a File A/3

    Step 2: Editing Your Document A/4

    Step 3: Printing Out the Document A/4

    Step 4: Saving Your Document A/5

C. Using PDF Forms A/5

    Step 1: Opening PDF Files A/6

    Step 2: Filling in PDF Files A/6

    Step 3: Printing PDF Files A/6

D. Files Included on the Forms CD A/7

he forms discussed in this book are included on a CD-ROM in the back of the book. This CD-ROM, which can be used with Windows computers, installs files that can be opened, printed, and edited using a word processor or other software. It is *not* a stand-alone software program. Please read this appendix and the README.TXT file included on the CD-ROM for instructions on using the Forms CD.

Note to Mac users: This CD-ROM and its files should also work on Macintosh computers. Please note, however, that Nolo cannot provide technical support for non-Windows users.

How to View the README File

If you do not know how to view the file README.TXT, insert the Forms CD-ROM into your computer's CD-ROM drive and follow these instructions:

- Windows 9x, 2000, Me, and XP: (1) On your PC's desktop, double click the My Computer icon; (2) double click the icon for the CD-ROM drive into which the Forms CD-ROM was inserted; (3) double click the file README.TXT.
- Macintosh: (1) On your Mac desktop, double click the icon for the CD-ROM that you inserted; (2) double click on the file README.TXT.

While the README file is open, print it out by using the Print command in the File menu.

Two different kinds of forms are contained on the CD-ROM:

- Word processing (RTF) forms that you can open, complete, print, and save with your word processing program (see Section B, below), and
- Forms from government agencies (PDF) that can be viewed only with Adobe Acrobat Reader 4.0 or higher (see Section C below). Some of these forms have "fill-in" text fields and can be completed using your computer. You will not, however, be able to save the completed forms with the filled-in data. PDF forms without fill-in text fields must be printed out and filled in by hand or with a typewriter.

See Section D, below, for a list of forms, their file names, and file formats.

A. Installing the Form Files Onto Your Computer

Before you can do anything with the files on the CD-ROM, you need to install them onto your hard disk. In accordance with U.S. copyright laws, remember that copies of the CD-ROM and its files are for your personal use only.

Insert the Forms CD and do the following:

1. Windows 9X, 2000, Me, and XP Users

Follow the instructions that appear on the screen. (If nothing happens when you insert the Forms CD-ROM, then (1) double click the My Computer icon; (2) double click the icon for the CD-ROM drive into which the Forms CD-ROM was inserted; and (3) double click the file WELCOME.EXE.)

By default, all the files are installed to the \Inventor's Forms folder in the \Program Files folder of your computer. A folder called "Inventor's Forms" is added to the "Programs" folder of the Start menu.

2. Macintosh Users

Step 1: If the "Inventor's Forms CD" window is not open, open it by double-clicking the "Inventor's Forms CD" icon.

Step 2: Select the "Inventor's Forms" folder icon.

Step 3: Drag and drop the folder icon onto the icon of your hard disk.

B. Using the Word Processing Files to Create Documents

This section concerns the files for forms that can be opened and edited with your word processing program.

All word processing forms come in rich text format. These files have the extension ".RTF." For example, the form for the Employment Agreement discussed in Chapter 10 is on the file Employ Agreement.rtf. All forms, their file names, and file formats are listed in Section D, below.

RTF files can be read by most recent word processing programs including all versions of MS Word for Windows and Macintosh, WordPad for Windows, and recent versions of WordPerfect for Windows and Macintosh.

To use a form from the CD to create your documents you must: (1) open the form in your word processor or text editor; (2) edit the form by filling in the required information; (3) print it out; (4) rename and save your revised file.

The following are general instructions. However, each word processor uses different commands to open, format, save, and print documents. Please read your word processor's manual for specific instructions on performing these tasks.

Do not call Nolo's technical support if you have questions on how to use your word processor.

Step 1: Opening a File

There are three ways to open the word processing files included on the CD-ROM after you have installed them onto your computer.

- Windows users can open a file by selecting its "shortcut" as follows: (1) Click the Windows "Start" button; (2) open the "Programs" folder; (3) open the "Inventor's Forms" subfolder; (4) open the "RTF" subfolder; and (5) click on the shortcut to the form you want to work with.
- Both Windows and Macintosh users can open a file directly by double clicking on it. Use My Computer or Windows Explorer (Windows 9x, 2000, Me, or XP) or the Finder (Macintosh) to go to the folder you installed or copied the CD-ROM's files to. Then, double click on the specific file you want to open.

- You can also open a file from within your word processor. To do this, you must first start your word processor. Then, go to the File menu and choose the Open command. This opens a dialog box where you will tell the program (1) the type of file you want to open (*.RTF); and (2) the location and name of the file (you will need to navigate through the directory tree to get to the folder on your hard disk where the CD's files have been installed). If these directions are unclear you will need to look through the manual for your word processing program—Nolo's technical support department will *not* be able to help you with the use of your word processing program.

ets. Be sure to delete the underlines and instructions from your edited document. You will also want to make sure that any signature lines in your completed documents appear on a page with at least some text from the document itself. If you do not know how to use your word processor to edit a document, you will need to look through the manual for your word processing program—Nolo's technical support department will *not* be able to help you with the use of your word processing program.

Where Are the Files Installed?

Windows Users
RTF files are installed by default to a folder named \Inventor's Forms in the \Program Files folder of your computer.

Macintosh Users
RTF files are located in the "Inventor's Forms" folder.

Step 2: Editing Your Document

Fill in the appropriate information according to the instructions and sample agreements in the book. Underlines are used to indicate where you need to enter your information, frequently followed by instructions in brack-

Editing Forms That Have Optional or Alternative Text

Some of the forms have optional or alternative text:

- With optional text, you choose whether to include or exclude the given text.
- With alternative text, you select one alternative to include and exclude the other alternatives.

When editing these forms, we suggest you do the following:

Optional text
If you **don't want to** include optional text, just delete it from your document.

If you **do want** to include optional text, just leave it in your document.

In either case, delete the italicized instructions.

Alternative text
First delete all the alternatives that you do not want to include, then delete the italicized instructions.

Step 3: Printing Out the Document

Use your word processor's or text editor's "Print" command to print out your document. If you do not know how to use your word processor to print a document, you will need to look through the manual for your word processing program—Nolo's technical support department will *not* be able to help you with the use of your word processing program.

Step 4: Saving Your Document

After filling in the form, use the "Save As" command to save and rename the file. Because all the files are "read-only," and you will not be able to use the "Save" command. This is for your protection. *If you save the file without renaming it, the underlines that indicate where you need to enter your information will be lost, and you will not be able to create a new document with this file without recopying the original file from the CD-ROM.*

If you do not know how to use your word processor to save a document, you will need to look through the manual for your word processing program—Nolo's technical support department will *not* be able to help you with the use of your word processing program.

C. Using PDF Forms

Electronic copies of useful forms from government agencies are included on the CD-ROM in Adobe Acrobat PDF format. You must have the Adobe Acrobat Reader installed on your computer to use these forms. Adobe Reader is available for all types of Windows and Macintosh systems. If you don't already have this software, you can download it for free at www.adobe.com.

All forms, their file names, and file formats are listed in Section D, below. These form files were not created by Nolo.

Some of these forms have fill-in text fields. To create your document using these files, you must: (1) open a file; (2) fill in the text fields using either your mouse or the tab key on your keyboard to navigate from field to field; and (3) print it out.

NOTE: While you can print out your completed form, you will NOT be able to save your completed form to disk.

Forms without fill-in text fields cannot be filled out using your computer. To create your document using these files, you must: (1) open the file; (2) print it out; and (3) complete it by hand or typewriter.

Step 1: Opening PDF Files

PDF files, like the word processing files, can be opened one of three ways.

- Windows users can open a file by selecting its "shortcut" as follows: (1) Click the Windows "Start" button; (2) open the "Programs" folder; (3) open the "Inventor's Forms" subfolder; (4) open the "PDF" folder; and (5) click on the shortcut to the form you want to work with.
- Both Windows and Macintosh users can open a file directly by double-clicking on it. Use My Computer or Windows Explorer (Windows 9x, 2000, Me, or XP)

or the Finder (Macintosh) to go to the folder you created and copied the CD-ROM's files to. Then, double click on the specific file you want to open.

- You can also open a PDF file from within Acrobat Reader. To do this, you must first start Reader. Then, go to the File menu and choose the Open command. This opens a dialog box where you will tell the program the location and name of the file (you will need to navigate through the directory tree to get to the folder on your hard disk where the CD's files have been installed). If these directions are unclear you will need to look through Acrobat Reader's help—Nolo's technical support department will *not* be able to help you with the use of Acrobat Reader.

Step 2: Filling in PDF Files

Use your mouse or the Tab key on your keyboard to navigate from field to field within these forms. Be sure to have on hand all the information you will need to complete a form, because you will not be able to save a copy of the filled-in form to disk. You can, however, print out a completed version.

NOTE: This step is only applicable to forms that have been created with fill-in text fields. Forms without fill-in fields must be completed by hand or typewriter after you have printed them out.

Where Are the PDF Files Installed?

- Windows Users: PDF files are installed by default to a folder named \Inventor's Forms in the \Program Files folder of your computer.
- Macintosh Users: PDF files are located in the the "Inventor's Forms" folder.

Step 3: Printing PDF Files

Choose Print from the Acrobat Reader File menu. This will open the Print dialog box. In the "Print Range" section of the Print dialog box, select the appropriate print range, then click OK.

D. Files Included on the Forms CD

The following files are in rich text format (RTF):

File Name	Form Name
Assignment 1.rtf	Assignment of Rights: Patent Issued
Assignment 2.rtf	Assignment of Rights: Patent Application
Assignment 3.rtf	Assignment of Intellectual Property Rights: No Patent Issued or Application Filed
Contract Worksheet.rtf	Contract Worksheet
Copyright Confirm.rtf	Letter Confirming Employee's Ownership of Copyright
Employ Agreement.rtf	Employment Agreement
IC Agreement.rtf	Independent Contractor Agreement
Joint Ownership.rtf	Joint Ownership Agreement
Nondisclosure.rtf	Inventor Nondisclosure Agreement

The following files are in Adobe Acrobat PDF format (asterisks indicate forms with fill-in text fields):

File Name	Form Name
fss4.pdf	Application for Employer Identification Number*
fw9.pdf	Request for Taxpayer Identification Number and Certification*
pto1595-fill.pdf	Recordation Form Cover Sheet*
sb0095.pdf	Disclosure Document Deposit Request

Index

A

Accelerated depreciation, 7/32
Accounting
  accrual method, 4/13
  in calendar versus fiscal year, 4/13–14
  cash method, 4/13
  See also Bookkeeping system
Accrual basis accounting, 4/13
Accumulated earnings tax, 2/19
Adjusted gross income (AGI), 8/13
Adobe Acrobat Reader installation, Appendix A/5
Advertising insurance coverage, 3/20
AGI (adjusted gross income), 8/13
Amortization, defined, 7/33
Amortized assets
  intangible property as, 7/10, 7/29, 7/33
  research and experimentation as, 7/17
  start-up expenses as, 7/33–34
  See also Depreciated assets
Arbitration
  employment agreement clause on, 10/16, 11/26
  nondisclosure agreement clause on, 13/15,
    13/18
  process of, 10/18
Assets
  depreciation of, calculating, 7/31–32
  depreciation periods of, 7/30–31
  how to record, 4/11
  insurance coverage of, 3/18–19, 3/22–23
  intangible, as amortized expense, 7/10, 7/33–34
  listed, as depreciated expense, 4/12, 7/32
  listed, IRS rules on, 7/21
  long-term, deduction rules on, 7/13–15
  ownership of, by business entities, 2/2–4
  for personal/business purposes, 4/11–12,
    7/19–20
  retention of records on, 4/12–13
  tangible, as current expense, 7/10, 7/19–20
  tangible, as depreciated expense, 7/10
  See also Long-term assets
Assignment of rights
  to business entity, 11/29
  defined, 11/26
  in employment agreements, 10/12, 10/14,
    10/16, 16/9
  in independent contractor agreements, 10/30,
    10/37, 16/8–9
  by licensee, 17/6
  versus licensing, 11/28
  recording of, with USPTO, 11/29
  with shared percentage of rights, 11/28
  to trade secrets, 11/30
  See also Pre-invention assignment agreements
Attorney fees
  of business attorneys, 18/7
  with hidden expenses, 18/7
  independent contractor agreement on, 10/32,
    10/35
  joint ownership agreement on, 11/12

nondisclosure agreement on, 13/18
of patent attorneys, 18/6
written agreement on, 18/7
Attorneys
at arbitration hearings, 10/18
business and tax attorneys, 5/10, 18/6, 18/7
how to find, 18/6
as legal coaches, 18/8
for license agreement negotiations, 17/3
patent attorneys, 14/7, 18/5–6
See also Research resources
Automobile expenses. See Car expenses
Automobile insurance, 3/21

B

Backup withholding of taxes
how to avoid, 10/40
from independent contractor's compensation,
10/39–40
Balance sheets, defined, 4/14
Bankruptcy
and termination of patent transfer, 8/5
types of protection with, 2/13
Bayh-Dole Act, 11/23
Bodily injury coverage, 3/19–20
Bookkeeping system
accounting methods of, 4/13
asset records of, 4/11–12
automobile records of, 4/8–9
balance sheets of, 4/14
benefit of, at tax time, 5/7–8
checking account of, 4/3–4
credit card of, 4/4
entertainment/meals/travel expenses of, 4/10–11
expense records, 4/4–6, 7/3
expense records, sample, 4/7
home office expense records, 7/38–39
income records, 4/4–5, 4/6
income records, sample, 4/7
as IRS behavior test, 6/7–8
marketing/licensing records, 4/14–15

patents of, 4/3
profit and loss statements of, 4/14
simple type, for sole proprietors, 4/2
software versions of, 4/5, 4/6
working hours log of, 6/9
BOP insurance policies, 3/23
Business behavior test of IRS
examples of passed/failed tests, 6/10–11
how to pass, 6/6–9
patent application to pass, 14/14
use of, in audit, 6/3
Business debts
bankruptcy options for, 2/13
liability for, 2/12, 2/13
personal guarantee of liability for, 2/15–16
Business entities
assignment of ownership to, 11/29
attracting investors to, 2/18–19
with Employer Identification Number requirement, 3/16–17
fictitious business name registration of, 3/5–6
four types of, 2/2–4
legal name for, 3/3–4
ownership of assets by, 2/2, 2/3
recommended types of, for inventors, 2/18,
2/20
switching between, 2/18
tax filing deadlines for, 5/5–6
tax year of, 4/13–14
See also Corporations; LLCs; Partnerships; Sole
proprietorships
Business licenses and permits
federal requirements, 3/14–15
as IRS behavior test, 6/8
local requirements, 3/16
state requirements, 3/15–16
Business property insurance
assets covered by, 3/18
of landlord's policy, 3/23–24
for replacement versus cash value, 3/18
two forms of, 3/18–19

Business workplace
commercial lease of, 3/12–14
environmental pollution insurance on, 3/21
general liability insurance on, 3/19–20
landlord's insurance on, 3/23–24
property insurance on, 3/18–19
workers' compensation insurance for, 3/21–22
See also Home workplace

C

California restrictions on pre-invention assignment, 11/17
Capital expenses
defined, 7/25
R&E expenses as, 7/25–26
start-up expenses as, 7/33–34
Capital gains
excluded from self-employment net income, 8/7
on home office depreciation deductions, 7/40–41
IRS form for, 8/7
tax rates on, 8/2–3
treatment of patents as, 2/11, 8/3–6
Car expenses
business mileage log of, 4/8–9
calculating deduction for, 7/42–43
deductible types of, 4/8
as R&E expenses, 7/42
Car insurance, 3/21
Cash basis accounting, 4/13
C corporations (regular corporations)
income tax treatment of, 2/9, 2/19–20, 8/11
IRS filing rules for, 5/3, 7/9
See also Corporations
CC&Rs (Covenants, Conditions and Restrictions), 3/11
CD-ROM forms, Appendix A
Certified public accountants (CPAs), 5/9–10, 17/15
CGL (commercial general liability) insurance policies, 3/23
Chapter 7 bankruptcy, 2/13
Chapter 11 bankruptcy, 2/13

Chapter 13 bankruptcy, 2/13
Checking accounts
for business expenses, 4/3
as IRS behavior test, 6/8
personal draws from, 4/4
"Claims made" insurance, 3/19
Co-inventors
reduction to practice by, 11/4
types of business entities for, 2/3
Commercial general liability (CGL) insurance policies, 3/23
Commercial leases
insurance costs of, 3/13–14
insurance requirements of, 3/23–24
rent amount of, 3/12
sublease clause of, 3/14
termination of, 3/14
two types of, 3/12
Computers
insurance for, 3/19
security for, 13/10–11
Conception of invention
definition/example of, 11/3
joint inventor's contribution to, 11/6, 11/7–8
notebook's documentation of, 9/3–4
patent implications of, 14/10
sample record of, 9/6
without pre-assignment agreement, 11/9
witnesses to notebook entry on, 9/7–8
Condominium workplace, 3/11
Confidentiality
of auditor-licensee relationship, 17/16
employment agreement on, 10/10, 10/12
independent contractor agreement on, 10/30
nondisclosure agreement on, 13/11–13
trade secrets protected by, 13/4, 13/10–11; 13/12–13
Copyright notices, 16/7–8
Copyrights
advantages/disadvantages of, 16/8
assignment of, by independent contractor, 10/30, 16/8–9

automatic existence of, 12/5, 12/8

of design elements of invention, 16/3–5

earnings from licensing/assignment of, 16/5

infringement of, recourse to, 16/5, 16/7

notice of, on published works, 16/7–8

of patent application drawings, 16/2–3

protections, length of, 12/6, 16/6

protections, limitations on, 16/5–6

qualifications for eligibility, 16/6

registration benefits, 16/6–7

registration fee, 16/7

works protected by, 12/5, 16/2

Corporations

assignment of ownership to, 11/29

attracting investors to, 2/18–19

bankruptcy option for, 2/13

defined, 2/3–4

documentation requirements of, 2/5–6

Employer Identification Number of, 3/16–17, 10/39

fees for forming, 2/6

how to form, 2/6, 2/9–11

income tax treatment of, 2/8–9, 2/19–20, 8/6, 8/11

as independent contractor, 10/39

IRS filing rules for, 5/3, 7/9

legal name of, 3/4

liability rules for, 2/15–17

personal liability protections of, 2/20

signature of, on employment contract, 10/20

trade name of, 3/4–5

unqualified as patent holders, 8/4

Correspondence audits by IRS, 5/11

Costs. *See* Fees and costs

Covenants, Conditions and Restrictions (CC&Rs), 3/11

CPAs (certified public accountants), 5/9–10, 17/15

Credit cards

for business purchases, 4/4, 4/10

for quarterly tax payments, 8/16

Current expenses

building/testing prototypes as, 7/15

capital expenses versus, 7/25

expenses excluded from, 7/16

"first year expensing" assets as, 7/18–19

long-term assets as, 7/10, 7/14–15

requirements for, under Section 162, 7/23–27

research and experimentation as, 7/10, 7/11–13, 7/25–26

Section 162 types of, 7/22

Section 179 deduction limit on, 7/20

tangible personal assets as, 7/19–20

when/how to claim, 7/17–18

See also Research and experimentation expenses

D

DDP (Disclosure Document Program), 9/8–9

Deductions from net sales, 17/13–15

Delegation of duties clause, 10/37

Depreciated assets

assets defined as, 7/10, 7/29–30

calculation methods for, 7/31–32

versus IRC Section 179 deduction, 7/19

listed property as, 4/12, 7/32

periods of depreciation for, 7/30–31

purchased computer software as, 7/15

as R&E expense, under Section 174, 7/30–31

retention of records on, 4/12

See also Amortized assets

Depreciation

defined, 7/29

methods of, 7/31–32

time periods for, 7/30–31

Design patents

application for, 12/9, 14/15

copyrighted drawings of, 16/2–3

copyrights versus, 16/8

fees for application, 14/15, 16/8

protections of, 12/4, 12/6, 14/14

qualifications for, 14/15

Direct expenses

home office deduction of, 7/38

research and experimentation as, 7/13

Directors of corporations, defined, 2/3

Disclosure clauses, 10/12, 10/30, 11/14, 11/24–25
Disclosure Document Deposit Request Form
   (PTO/SB/95), 9/9
Disclosure Document Program (DDP), 9/8–9

E

Earthquake insurance, 3/18
EAs (enrolled agents), defined, 5/9
EIN (Employer Identification Number)
   of corporation, acting as independent contractor,
      10/39
   how to obtain, 3/17
   required business types, 3/16–17
Email security, 13/10–11
Employees
   with conflicting obligations, 10/12
   corporate owners as, 2/8–9
   employment agreement with, 10/7, 10/9–10
   family members as, 10/24
   federal tax withholding from, 10/22, 10/23
   IRS qualifying factors for, 10/6
   new versus current, 10/10
   non-inventive type, 11/20–21
   nontechnical type, 10/9
   pros/cons of hiring, 10/5, 10/7, 10/8
   state tax withholding from, 10/25
   state unemployment compensation for, 10/24–25
   workers' compensation insurance for, 3/21–22,
      10/25–26
   See also Employment agreements; Employment
      taxes; Inventors as employees
Employer Identification Number. See EIN
Employment agreements
   assignment clauses, 10/12, 10/14, 11/13, 16/9
   confidentiality clauses, 10/10, 10/12
   conflicting obligations clause, 10/12
   "consideration" for signing, 10/9
   with current employee, 10/10
   disclosure of developments clause, 10/12
   general provisions clauses, 10/18, 10/20
   mediation/arbitration clause, 10/16, 10/18, 11/26

   with new employee, 10/10
   nondisclosure clause, 10/10, 10/12, 13/12
   with nontechnical employee, 10/9
   prior developments clause, 10/16
   purpose of, 10/9
   sample form, 10/11, 10/13, 10/15, 10/17, 10/19,
      10/21
   signatures on, 10/20
   See also Pre-invention assignment agreements
Employment taxes (payroll taxes)
   of family members as employees, 10/24
   federal income tax, 10/23
   federal unemployment tax, 2/6, 10/22–23
   FICA taxes, 10/22
   methods/frequency of payment, 10/23–24
   research resources on, 18/9–10
   state disability insurance, 10/25
   state income tax, 10/25
   state unemployment compensation, 10/24–25
   withholding of, for employees, 5/7, 5/9
   See also Medicare taxes; Social Security taxes
Enrolled agents (EAs), defined, 5/9
Entertainment/meal/travel expenses, 4/10–11, 7/43
Environmental permits, 3/14–15, 3/16
Environmental pollution insurance, 3/21
Estimated taxes
   and address change notification, 8/17
   based on estimated taxable income, 8/14
   based on last year's tax, 8/12–14
   based on quarterly income, 8/14–15
   due dates for, 5/3–4, 8/15–16
   of independent inventor with job, 8/10, 8/12
   IRS bookkeeping errors on, 8/16
   over/underpayment of, 8/13–14
   payment methods, 8/16
   payment vouchers for, 8/16
   penalties on, 8/17
   penalties on, how to avoid, 8/12
   who must pay, 5/8, 8/10, 8/11
Expenses
   accounting methods for, 4/13

capital types of, 7/25–26

categories of, 4/6

currently deductible types of, 7/10

depreciable types of, 7/10

direct versus indirect, 7/13, 7/38

for entertainment/meals/travel, 4/10–11, 7/43

how to record, 4/4–6

how to record, sample form, 4/7

inventory excluded as, 7/28

on IRS Schedule C, 7/3–4

non-R&E types of, 7/22–23

retention of records on, 4/12

supporting documents for, 4/10–11

as tax deductions, legal requirements, 7/3, 7/44–45

See also Amortized assets; Current expenses;
   Depreciated assets

F

Fax security, 13/11

Federal government employees, 11/21–22

Fees and costs

   copyright registration, 16/7

   corporate formation, 2/6

   design patent application, 14/15, 16/8

   Disclosure Document Deposit Request Form, 9/9

   endorsements to homeowner's insurance, 3/22–23

   fictitious business name, 3/6

   general liability insurance, 3/19

   in-home insurance policies, 3/23

   local business license, 3/16

   patent infringement insurance, 3/20–21

   patents, over life of patent, 14/6

   provisional patent application, 9/10, 14/12

   recorded patent assignment, 11/29

   tax professionals, 5/10

   trademark registration, 15/5

   trademark reservation, 15/5

   See also Attorney fees

FICA (Federal Income Contributions Act) taxes. See
   Medicare taxes; Social Security taxes

Fictitious business name

   fee for registration, 3/6

   how to register, 3/6

   for opening checking account, 4/3

   for partnerships, 2/5

   for sole proprietorship, 2/4

   trademark versus, 3/6

   who needs to register, 3/5–6

Field audits by IRS, 5/11

FITW (federal income tax withholding), 10/23, 10/24

Flood insurance, 3/18

Foreign countries

   licensing of patents in, 17/6–7

   patent applications in, 14/13

   royalty payments in, 17/11

   website resources, 18/4–5

Forms on CD-ROM, Appendix A

Freelancers. See Independent contractor(s)

FUTA (federal unemployment taxes), 10/22–23,
   10/24

G

General business license, 3/15

General liability insurance

   categories of coverage, 3/19–20

   cost of, 3/19

   of landlord's policy, 3/23

GMAR (guaranteed minimum annual royalty), 17/9,
   17/12–13

Gross leases

   defined, 3/12

   insurance costs of, 3/14, 3/23

   insurance requirements of, 3/24

Group insurance plans, 3/24

H

Hazardous waste permits, 3/14–15, 3/16

Hobby loss rule, 6/4, 6/5

Holdover clause of pre-invention assignment
   agreements, 11/5, 11/15, 11/16

Home office deduction
  calculation of, 7/38
  capital gains consequences of, 7/40–41
  for inventory storage, 7/37
  IRS reporting requirements, 7/41–42
  IRS rules for, 7/34–36
  profit limit on, 7/34, 7/39–40
  renters with, 7/39, 7/41–42
  of separate business structure, 7/37
  ways to solidify, 7/36
Homeowner's insurance, 3/22–23
Home workplace
  condominium restrictions on, 3/11
  home office deduction of, 7/35–37
  insurance requirements for, 3/22–23
  lease restrictions on, 3/11–12
  neighbor relations with, 3/9–10
  property deed restrictions on, 3/11
  pros and cons of, 3/7
  zoning restrictions on, 3/7–9
  See also Business workplace

I

ICs. *See* Independent contractor(s)
Income
  accounting methods for, 4/13
  adjusted gross, of high-income taxpayers, 8/13
  audit rate/type based on, 5/11
  capital gains versus ordinary, 8/2
  of hired independent contractors, 10/39–40
  how to record, 4/4–5, 4/6
  how to record, sample form, 4/7
  on IRS Schedule C, 7/3–4
  losses in excess of, 7/9
  net self-employment income, 8/6–8
  retention of records on, 4/12
  supporting documents for, 4/9–10
  See also Capital gains; Profits
Income-producing activities (IRS category), 6/12
Income splitting, 2/19–20

Income tax brackets (2005), 7/7–8
Income taxes
  calendar of filing dates, 5/5–6
  in calendar versus fiscal year, 4/13–14
  on capital gains versus ordinary income, 8/2–3
  of C corporations, 2/9
  of C corporations, with income splitting, 2/19–20
  cities with, 5/5
  computer calculations of, 5/8
  EIN for filing of, 3/16–17
  filing of federal, 5/2–3
  filing of state, 5/4
  insurance premium deductions from, 3/26
  of limited liability companies, 2/11–12
  of partnerships, 2/7–8
  quarterly payment deadlines, 5/3–4, 8/15–16
  research resources on, 5/9, 18/9–10
  of S corporations, 2/10
  of sole proprietorships, 2/7
  withholding of, for employees, 5/7, 10/23
  withholding of, for independent contractors, 10/39–40
  See also Estimated taxes; Tax deductions
Independent contractor(s)
  copyrightable works of, 16/8–9
  with federal government contracts, 11/22
  inventor hired as, 11/13
  IRS qualifying factors, 10/3–5, 10/6
  long-term property purchased/built by, 7/14–15
  new hire reporting requirements for, 10/41
  payments to, methods of, 10/27, 10/30
  pros/cons of hiring, 10/5, 10/7, 10/8
  reporting the income of, 10/39
  tips for dealing with, 10/5
  withholding taxes from, 10/39–40
Independent contractor agreements
  applicable state's law on, 10/35
  assignment/delegation clause, 10/37
  attorney fees provision, 10/32, 10/35
  confidentiality/nondisclosure clause, 10/30, 13/12

disclosure of developments clause, 10/30

excluded from assignment restrictions, 11/18

indemnification clause, 10/32

invoice submission clause, 10/30

materials clauses, 10/27, 10/32

no partnership clause, 10/35, 10/37

notice options of, 10/35

payments clause, 10/27

purpose of, 10/26

record keeping provision, 10/30

references to contractor in, 10/26–27

sample form, 10/28–29, 10/31, 10/33–34, 10/36, 10/38

services performed clause, 10/27

signatures on, 10/37

termination clause, 10/30, 10/32

warranties clause, 10/32

See also Pre-invention assignment agreements

Independent discovery of trade secrets, 13/5–6

Indirect expenses

home office deduction of, 7/38

research and experimentation as, 7/13

Infringement

of copyrights, 16/5, 16/7

liability for, 3/4–5

of patents, 3/20–21, 14/13

of pending patents, 14/4–5

of trademark rights, 15/6–7

In-home insurance policies, 3/23

Insurance

on business property, 3/18–19

on car used for business, 3/21

for computer replacement, 3/19

cost of, as tax deduction, 3/26

for environmental pollution, 3/21

general liability, 2/17–18, 3/19–20

for home workplace, 3/22–23

how to find policies, 3/24–25

net lease costs of, 3/13–14

net lease requirements for, 3/23–24

for patent infringement, 3/20–21

ratings on companies, website, 3/25

for worker's compensation, 3/21–22

Insurance agents, 3/24–25

Intangible assets

as amortized expense, 7/10, 7/29, 7/33

types of, 7/33

without fixable useful life, 7/33

Intellectual property (IP) rights

copyrights, 12/5

defined, 12/2

difficulty of obtaining, 12/8–9

for functional features, 12/5, 12/7

Nolo publications on, 18/13

for nonfunctional features, 12/7–8

patents, 12/3–4

trademarks, 12/5

trade secrets, 12/4

types/examples of, 12/6

websites on laws governing, 18/3

See also Copyrights; Patents; Trademarks; Trade secrets

Inventing business

attorneys specializing in, 18/5–6

hobbies versus, 4/14–15, 6/2

home office deduction rules, 7/34

as income-producing activity, 6/12

IRS behavior test for, 6/6–9

IRS profit test for, 6/2–4

as operating business, under Section 162, 7/23–24

small business resources for, 18/8–9, 18/11–12

start-up costs of, 7/33–34

tax deduction requirements for, 7/2–3

See also Business workplace; Home workplace

Inventions

copyrightable features of, 12/5, 16/3–5

created after employment, 11/15

created before employment, 11/16

created during employment, 11/14

employee/inventor's disclosure of, 11/14, 11/24–25

employee's independent invention of, 11/20

with expired patents, 14/12
of federal employees, 11/21–22
functional features of, 12/5, 12/7
injuries caused by, 2/20, 3/20
joint inventors/owners of, 11/5–6
versus licensed products, 17/6
marketing/licensing records of, 4/14–15, 6/8
nonfunctional features of, 12/7–8, 14/14–15
of non-inventive employees, 11/20–21
notebook's documentation of, 9/3–4
of operating business, under Section 162, 7/23–24
original ownership of, 11/3–4
patentable requirements for, 14/7–9
patent infringement of, 3/20–21, 14/4–5, 14/13
patent protection of, 12/3–4
separable design features of, 16/4–5
with short commercial lives, 13/8, 14/5
solo inventor/owner of, 11/4–5
time spent working on, 6/9
trademark protection of, 12/5
trade secrecy of, 12/4
of university employees, 11/22–24
useful life of, 7/33
Inventories, 7/28, 7/37
Inventors
    conception of invention by, 11/3
    as employee versus independent contractor, 11/13
    as joint inventor, 11/5–6
    original owner status of, 11/4
    patent enforcement responsibility of, 14/13
    recommended business entities for, 2/18, 2/20
    reduction to practice by, 11/3–4
    as separately employed, taxes of, 8/9, 8/10, 8/12
    as solo inventor, 11/4–5
    website resources for, 18/2–3
    See also Inventors as employees; Joint
        inventorship
Inventors as employees
    confirmation of ownership by, 11/26, 11/27
    disclosure tips for, 11/24–25
    employed to invent, 11/19–20

of federal government, 11/21–22
with non-inventive status, 11/20–21
pre-invention assignment by, 11/13, 11/14–16
record keeping strategies of, 11/24
restrictions on assignment by, 11/17–18
in unenforceable assignment agreements,
    11/18–19
of universities, 11/22–24
Inventor's notebook
    alternatives to, 9/8–10
    to avoid joint ownership claims, 11/9
    conception of invention in, sample, 9/6
    contents/purpose of, 9/2–3
    to document business operation, 9/3
    to document patent rights, 9/3–4, 14/10
    how to record entries in, 9/5, 9/7
    of research and development expenses, 7/18
    witnesses to, 9/7–8
Investors in corporations, 2/18–19
IP rights. *See* Intellectual property rights
IRC Section 41, 7/28
IRC Section 162
    on car expenses, 7/42
    common inventor's deductions, 7/27
    on entertainment/meal expenses, 7/43
    expense requirements of, 7/22–25
    on start-up expenses, 7/34
    on travel expenses, 7/43
IRC Section 174
    on amortization claims, 7/17
    on building prototypes, 7/15
    on car expenses, 7/42
    depreciation claims under, 7/30–31
    on entertainment/meal expenses, 7/43
    filing of claims under, 7/17–18
    on long-term property costs, 7/13–15
    on long-term property leases, 7/15
    on non-R&E expenses, 7/16
    preferred use of, 7/22
    "realistic prospect" requirement of, 7/16
    "reasonable expense" requirement of, 7/17

on research and experimentation expenses, 7/11–13

on software development, 7/15

on travel expenses, 7/43

IRC Section 179

depreciating expenses versus, 7/19

filing of claims under, 7/22

"first year expensing" rules of, 7/18–19

home office expenses under, 7/39

minimum use rule of, 7/21

property types, 7/19–20

property value limits, 2003-2008, 7/20

tax deduction limits, 2003-2008, 7/20

IRC Section 195, 7/33

IRC Section 1221, 8/3

IRC Section 1231, 8/3

IRC Section 1235

on patent holder qualifications, 2/11, 8/4

on sale of patent as capital gain, 8/3–6

IRC Section 1245, 8/3

IRS (Internal Revenue Service)

behavior test of, 6/6–9

behavior test of, examples, 6/10–11, 14/14

change of address notification to, 8/17

Employer Identification Number from, 3/17

employment tax regulations of, 10/22–24

home office deduction requirements, 7/35–37

information resources of, 18/9–10

S corporation requirements, 2/10–11

telephone information, 18/10

website, 5/9

worker categories of, 10/3, 10/6

IRS audits

behavior test of, 6/6–9

behavior test of, examples, 6/10–11

correspondence audits, 5/11

declining rate of, 5/10–11

field audits, 5/11

of home office deduction, 7/35

office audits, 5/11

profit test of, 6/2–4

profit test of, postponement of, 6/5

records required at, 5/11–12

supporting documents for, 4/9–11

of tax deductions, 5/6

tax professionals at, 5/12

time limit for, 5/11

IRS Form 940 (Employer's Annual Federal Unemployment Tax Return), 10/24

IRS Form 940-EZ, 10/24

IRS Form 941 (Employer's Quarterly Federal Tax Return), 10/24

IRS Form 1040, 2/7, 5/3, 8/9

IRS Form 1040-ES, 8/16

IRS Form 1045, 7/9

IRS Form 1045X, 7/9

IRS Form 1065 (U.S. Return of Partnership Income), 2/8, 2/11–12, 5/3

IRS Form 1096, 10/40, 10/41

IRS Form 1099-MISC, 7/41–42, 10/39, 10/40–41

IRS Form 1120, 2/9, 2/10

IRS Form 1120-A, 2/9

IRS Form 1120S, 5/3

IRS Form 2210, 8/15

IRS Form 2553, 2/11

IRS Form 4562, 7/22

IRS Form 5213 (Election to Postpone Determination as to Whether the Presumption Applies that an Activity is Engaged in for Profit), 6/5, 6/6

IRS Form 8109-B (Federal Tax Deposit coupon), 10/24

IRS Form 8716 (Election to Have a Tax Year Other Than a Required Tax Year), 4/14

IRS Form 8822 (Change of Address), 8/17

IRS Form 8829 (Expenses for Business Use of Your Home), 7/41

IRS Form 8832 (Entity Classification Election), 2/20

IRS Form SE (Self-Employment Tax), 8/9

IRS Form SS-4 (Application for Employer Identification Number), 3/17

IRS Form W-2 (Wage and Tax Statement), 10/23

IRS Form W-4 (Employee's Withholding Allowance Certificate), 10/23

IRS Form W-9 (Request for Taxpayer Identification Number), 10/39, 10/40

IRS Schedule C (Profit or Loss From Business), 2/7, 5/3, 7/9

completing the form, 7/3–4

sample form, 7/5–6

IRS Schedule D (Capital Gains and Losses), 7/9, 8/7

IRS Schedule E, 2/8, 7/9

IRS Schedule K-1, 2/8, 2/12, 5/3

J

Joint inventorship

decision making by, 11/11

how to avoid, 11/9

improvements/revisions by, 11/12

involuntary form of, 11/7

legal requirements for, 11/7–9

ownership consequences of, 11/5

percentage interests of, 11/11

voluntary form of, 11/6

without partnership, 11/10

Joint ownership agreement

completing the form, 11/11–12

in lieu of partnership agreement, 11/10

L

Lawsuits. *See* Liability

Lawyers. *See* Attorneys

Leases. *See* Commercial leases

Legal names

of corporations, 3/4

defined, 3/3

of LLCs, 3/4

of partnerships, 3/4

of sole proprietorships, 3/3–4

Liability

bankruptcy protections against, 2/13

for CC&R violations, 3/11

of corporations and LLCs, 2/15–17

for defective products, 2/20, 3/20

insurance coverage against, 2/17–18, 3/19–20

of partnerships, 2/14–15

for patent infringement, 3/20–21

"piercing the corporate veil" rule of, 2/17

of sole proprietors, 2/12, 2/14

for trademark infringement, 3/4–5

for zoning violations, 3/8–10

License agreements

alternatives to, 17/3

assignments provision of, 17/6

audit provision of, 17/15–16

business terms of, 17/3

with carryforward provision, 17/12–13

Contract Worksheet for, 17/17–19

deductions provisions in, 17/13–15

dispute resolution clause, 17/16

finalization of, before signing, 17/4

hybrid type of, 17/11–12

length of term of, 17/7–8

negotiation stage of, 17/3

nonrecoupable clause, 17/10

nonrefundable clause, 17/10

oral versus written, 17/7

renewal of, 17/8

sublicense provision of, 17/5–6

territorial scope of, 17/6–7

transfer of rights clauses, 17/5

See also Licensees; Licensing; Royalties

Licensed products, defined, 17/6

Licensees

assignment of rights by, 17/6

auditing the records of, 17/15–16

deductions from net sales by, 17/13–15

finding prospective licensees, 17/4

length of term considerations for, 17/7–8

patent exchange websites for, 17/16

settling disputes with, 17/16

sublicensing by, 17/5–6

territorial rights of, 17/6–7

transfer of rights to, 17/4–5

Licenses and permits. *See* Business licenses and permits

Licensing
   by accused patent infringers, 14/13
   of copyrights, 16/5
   defined, 11/28, 17/4–5
   by federal government, 11/22
   finding prospects for, 17/4, 17/16
   lump sum payment for, 17/10–11
   of patent rights, as preferable, 14/3
   royalties for, 17/8–10
   and sublicensing, 17/5–6
   of trade secrets, 13/3, 13/12
   by universities, 11/23, 11/24
   with/without trademark, 15/3–4
   See also License agreements; Licensees; Royalties
Limited liability companies. *See* LLCs
Limited partnerships, 2/15
Listed assets
   at business location only, 7/21–22
   definition/types of, 4/11
   depreciation of, 7/32
   IRS rules on, 4/12, 7/21
   record-keeping requirement, 4/12
LLCs (limited liability companies)
   assignment of ownership to, 11/29
   bankruptcy option for, 2/13
   deduction of losses in, 2/10, 2/12
   defined, 2/4
   Employer Identification Number of, 3/16–17
   how to form, 2/6
   income splitting benefits of, 2/20
   income tax treatment of, 2/11–12, 8/11
   IRS filing rules for, 5/3, 7/9
   legal name of, 3/4
   liability of, 2/15–17
   personal liability protections of, 2/20
   signature of, on employment contract, 10/20
   trade name of, 3/4–5
Long-term assets
   cost of constructing, 7/14–15
   current deduction of, under IRC Section 179, 7/18–19
   deduction limits on, 7/20
   leasing of, for current deductibility, 7/15
   minimum use rule on, 7/21
   tangible and intangible, 7/10
   "useful" life of, 7/13–14
Losses
   by C corporations, 2/9
   in excess of income, 7/9
   on IRS Schedule C, 7/4
   by limited liability companies, 2/10, 2/12
   by partnerships, 2/8, 2/10
   by S corporations, 2/10
   tax benefits of, 5/6

M

Mediation, 10/16, 11/26, 13/15
   See also Arbitration
Medicare taxes
   computation of, 8/8
   of corporations, 2/8–9
   earnings threshold for, 5/3
   of family members as employees, 10/24
   income splitting's reduction of, 2/19
   of independent inventor with job, 8/9
   quarterly payment of, 5/3–4
   of sole proprietorships, 2/7
   tax rate of, for employers/employees, 10/22
   tax rate of, for self-employed, 8/6–7
   withholding of, for employees, 5/7
Mileage expense deductions, 7/42–43
Municipalities
   licenses and permits of, 3/16
   taxes imposed by, 5/5, 5/8

N

NDAs. *See* Nondisclosure agreements
Net leases, 3/12, 3/13–14, 3/23–24
Net sales licenses, 17/8, 17/10, 17/13–15
Net self-employment income, 8/6–8
NOL (net operating loss). *See* Losses

Nondisclosure agreements (NDAs)
  attorney fees clause, 13/18
  confidentiality clauses, 13/13
  dispute resolution clause, 13/15, 13/18
  with employees, 10/12, 13/12
  injunctive relief clause, 13/18
  sample form, 13/14, 13/16–17, 13/19
  signatures on, 13/20
  successors clause, 13/20
  term options, 13/15
  trade secret licensing without, 13/12
  trade secret protection with, 13/4, 13/11–13
Nonobviousness requirement of patents, 13/9,
  14/8–9
Notebook. See Inventor's notebook
Novelty requirement of patents, 13/9, 14/8

O

Officers of corporations, defined, 2/3
Ordinary income, 8/2

P

Partnerships
  assignment of ownership to, 11/29
  bankruptcy option for, 2/13
  deduction of losses in, 2/10
  defined, 2/3
  Employer Identification Number of, 3/16–17
  exclusion of, in independent contractor agree-
    ment, 10/35, 10/37
  fictitious business name of, 3/5–6
  with home office deduction, 7/41
  income splitting benefits of, 2/20
  income tax treatment of, 2/7–8, 8/11
  informal operation of, 2/4–5
  IRS filing rules for, 5/3, 7/9
  joint ownership's creation of, 11/10
  legal name of, 3/4
  limited form of, 2/15
  LLC's tax treatment as, 2/11–12
  personal liability of, 2/14

  signature of, on employment contract, 10/20
  trade name of, 3/4–5
Patent(s)
  on bookkeeping systems, 4/3
  capital gains treatment of, 2/11, 8/3–6
  claims of, 14/6
  as currently deductible expense, 7/13
  design type of, 12/4, 12/9, 14/14–15
  expiration of, 14/12
  fees for, 14/6
  holder of, qualifications for, 8/4
  hybrid licensing of, 17/11–12
  on impractical inventions, 14/2
  infringement of, 3/20–21, 14/4–5, 14/13
  on invention with short commercial life, 14/5
  as investment attraction, 14/3, 14/4
  license exchanges for, websites, 17/16
  nonobviousness test for, 13/9, 14/8–9
  novelty test for, 13/9, 14/8
  pending patents, 14/4–5, 17/11–12
  profits from, 12/2–3
  profits without, 14/3
  purpose of, 12/3
  searches for, 14/9–10, 18/3–4
  statutory subject matter categories, 14/7–8
  usefulness test for, 12/4, 14/8
  websites on laws governing, 18/3
  See also Patent ownership rights
Patent applications
  after filing disclosure document, 9/9
  approval process for, 14/5–6
  components of, 14/5–6
  copyrighted drawings of, 16/2–3
  for design patents, 12/9, 14/15
  filing deadline rule, 14/10–11
  in foreign countries, 14/13, 18/4–5
  joint owners' filing of, 11/5
  ownership issues of, 11/2–3
  pendency period of, 14/4–5
  professional assistance with, 14/7
  to prove business behavior, 14/14

provisional, 9/9–10

trade secrets disclosed in, 13/6–8

for utility patents, 12/9

where to file, 12/4

without foreign patent rights, 13/8

See also Provisional patent applications

Patent infringement, 3/20–21, 14/4–5, 14/13

Patent ownership rights

actual versus potential, 11/2

assignment's transfer of, 11/26, 11/28

attorneys specializing in, 14/7, 18/5–6

dealing with disputes over, 11/26

of employer, by default, 11/19–21

enforcement of, responsibility for, 14/13

in federal government sector, 11/21–22

"first to invent" rule of, 14/10

in foreign countries, 14/13, 17/6–7, 18/4–5

of independent inventor with job, 9/4

against infringement during pendency, 14/4–5

of joint inventors, 11/5–7

length of protection, 14/12

licensing of, 11/28, 14/3

notebook's documentation of, 9/3–4, 14/10

of original owner, 11/3–4

pre-invention assignment of, 11/13, 11/14–16

of solo inventor, 11/4–5

trade secrecy versus, 13/6, 13/7

transfer of, for capital gains treatment, 8/3–6

transfer of, to related person, 8/6

in university sector, 11/22–24

Patent searches, 14/9–10, 18/3–4

Payroll taxes. *See* Employment taxes

Pending patents

hybrid licensing of, 17/11–12

infringement of, 14/4–5

Peril insurance policies, 3/18–19

Permits. *See* Business licenses and permits

Personal guarantees, 2/15–16

Personal injury coverage, 3/20

Personal liability. *See* Liability

Phone line deductions, 7/36

Piercing the corporate veil (legal doctrine), 2/17

Power of attorney clause, 11/14–15

PPAs. *See* Provisional patent applications

Pre-invention assignment agreements

assignment provision of, 11/14

to avoid joint ownership, 11/9

disclosure provision of, 11/14, 11/24–25

with employee, 10/12, 10/14, 11/13

employer's default ownership without, 11/19–21

holdover clause, 11/5, 11/15

with independent contractor, 10/30, 16/8–9

by joint owners, 11/5, 11/11

power of attorney provision, 11/14–15

state restrictions on, 10/14, 10/16, 10/22, 11/17–18

as unenforceable, 11/18–19

with universities, 11/23–24

waiver provision, 11/16

See also Assignment of rights

Prior art

examples of, 14/9

patent search on, 14/9–10

Product liability protection, 2/20, 3/20

Profit and loss statements, 4/14

Profits

of C corporations, 2/9

and home office deduction rules, 7/34, 7/39–40

income splitting of, 2/19–20

as IRS business test, 6/2–4, 6/7

on IRS Schedule C, 7/4

of limited liability companies, 2/11–12

of partnerships, 2/8

from patents, 12/2–3

of S corporations, 2/10

time needed to make, 6/6

without patents, 14/3

Property. *See* Assets

Property damage coverage, 3/20

Property deeds, 3/11

Property leases. *See* Commercial leases

Prototypes, as current expense, 7/15

Provisional patent applications (PPAs)
    advantages to filing, 14/11–12
    to document reduction to practice, 9/9–10
    filing deadline rule, 14/11
    filing fee, 9/10, 14/12

R

Recordation Form Cover Sheet (USPTO), 11/29
Reduction to practice
    by co-inventor, 11/4
    definition/example of, 11/3–4
    as joint inventorship, 11/8
    notebook's documentation of, 9/3–4
    patent implications of, 14/10
    provisional patent's documentation of, 9/9–10
R&E expenses. *See* Research and experimentation
  expenses
Renters, with home office deduction, 7/39, 7/41–42
Replacement cost policies, 3/18
Research and experimentation (R&E) expenses
    amortization of, 7/17
    as capital versus current expenses, 7/25–26
    car expenses as, 7/42
    current deductibility requirements, 7/11–13, 7/16
    defined, 7/10
    as depreciation deduction, 7/30–31
    entertainment/meal expenses as, 7/43
    IRC Section 174 on, 7/11
    long-term property as, 7/14–15
    record keeping of, 7/18
    software development as, 7/15
    tax credit on, 7/28
    travel expenses as, 7/43
    when/how to claim, 7/17–18
Research resources
    on federal tax law, 18/9–10
    industry and trade associations, 18/8
    at law libraries, 18/9
    Service Corps of Retired Executives, 18/9
    Small Business Association, 18/8–9
    for small businesses, online, 18/11–12

    on state law, 18/10–11
    state offices, 18/13–19
Residential leases, 3/11–12
Reverse engineering of trade secrets, 13/5
Royalties
    advances against, 17/9
    deductions against, 17/13–15
    defined, 17/8
    earned, in excess of GMAR, 17/12
    earned, less than GMAR, 17/12–13
    fluctuating rates of, 17/11
    of hybrid licenses, 17/11–12
    lump sum payment versus, 17/9, 17/10–11
    minimum annual payment of, 17/9
    net sales type, 17/8, 17/10, 17/13
    per unit type, 17/8, 17/10
    per use type, 17/9, 17/10
    from sale of patent, 8/5

S

Sale of invention
    by joint owners, 11/5, 11/11–12
    patent filing deadline after, 14/11
Sales tax permits, 3/15–16
SBA (Small Business Administration), 3/15, 18/8–9
SCORE (Service Corps of Retired Executives), 18/9
S corporations (small business corporations)
    with home office deduction, 7/41
    income tax treatment of, 2/10, 8/11
    IRS filing rules for, 5/3, 7/9
    IRS requirements for forming, 2/10–11
SE (self-employment) taxes. *See* Self-employment
  taxes
Section 41, 7/28
Section 162. *See* IRC Section 162
Section 174. *See* IRC Section 174
Section 179. *See* IRC Section 179
Section 1235. *See* IRC Section 1235
Security deposits on commercial workspace, 3/13
Self-employment (SE) taxes
    annual payment of, 8/9

business expense deductions from, 7/7–8

computation of, 8/8

earnings threshold for, 5/3, 8/6

home office deduction from, 7/39

income splitting's reduction of, 2/19–20

of independent inventor with job, 8/9

on net self-employment income, 8/7–8

quarterly estimated payment of, 5/3–4, 8/15–16

research resources on, 18/9–10

of sole proprietorships, 2/7

tax rates of, 7/8, 8/6–7

who must pay, 8/6, 8/10, 8/12

See also Estimated taxes

Service Corps of Retired Executives (SCORE), 18/9

Service marks, 15/3

Shareholders of corporations

defined, 2/3

as investment resource, 2/18–19

liability protections for, 2/15–17

of S corporations, 2/10

Shop right rule, 11/21

Signatures

on employment contract, 10/20

on independent contractor agreement, 10/37

on joint ownership agreement, 11/10, 11/12

on nondisclosure agreement, 13/20

Small Business Administration (SBA), 3/15, 18/8–9

Social Security taxes

computation of, 8/8

of corporations, 2/8–9

earnings threshold for, 5/3

of family members as employees, 10/24

income splitting's reduction of, 2/19–20

of independent inventor with job, 8/9

quarterly payment of, 5/3–4

of sole proprietorships, 2/7

tax ceiling for, 8/7

tax rate of, for employer/employees, 10/22

tax rate of, for self-employed, 8/6–7

withholding of, for employees, 5/7

Software development, as expense item, 7/15

Sole proprietorships

advantages of, 2/4, 2/9

bankruptcy option for, 2/13

bookkeeping items for, 4/2

business checking account of, 4/3–4

defined, 2/2

Employer Identification Number of, 3/17

fictitiousness business name of, 3/5–6

with home office deduction, 7/41

IRS filing rules for, 5/2–3

legal name of, 3/3–4

liability of, 2/12, 2/14

LLC's tax treatment as, 2/11, 2/12

self-employment taxes of, 2/7, 8/6–10

trade name of, 3/4

Solo inventors, 11/4–5

Special form insurance policies, 3/19

Start-up expenses, 7/10, 7/23, 7/33–34

State income taxes

filing deadlines for, 5/4, 5/6

states without, 5/4

withholding of, for employees, 5/7, 10/25

States

applicable law of, on contracts, 10/35

business license requirements, 3/15

business taxes, 5/5

disability insurance, 10/25

laws of, resources on, 18/10–11

patent ownership policies, 11/22

reporting rules, on hired independent

contractors, 10/41

with restrictions on assignment, 10/14, 10/16,

10/22, 11/17–18

sales tax requirements, 3/15–16, 5/4–5, 5/8

self-employment taxes, 8/10

small business resources of, 18/13–19

trademark law protections, 15/2

unemployment compensation taxes, 10/24–25

workers' compensation requirements, 3/21–22

Straight line depreciation, 7/31–32

Strict liability, defined, 2/20

Sublease of business space, 3/14

Sublicensing, 17/5–6

T

Tangible assets

calculating depreciation of, 7/31–32

as current expense, 7/10, 7/19–20

as depreciated expense, 7/10, 7/29

recovery period for, 7/31

Tax credits, 7/28

Tax deductions

amount of savings from, 7/7–8

for business expenses, 4/10

for business losses, 5/6, 7/9

for car expenses, 4/8–9

for current expenses, 7/10

for depreciated expenses, 7/10

for entertainment/meal expenses, 4/10–11, 7/43

hobby loss rule on, 6/4

for income-producing activities, 6/12

on IRS Schedule C, 7/3–4

against net sales, 17/14

for R&E expenses, under IRC Section 174, 7/11–13, 7/14–15, 7/16

requirements for, 7/2–3

Section 179 limit on, 2003-2008, 7/20

for travel expenses, 4/10–11, 7/43

See also Amortized assets; Current expenses; Depreciated assets; Home office deduction

Taxpayer identification number. *See* EIN (employee identification number)

Tax professionals

fees of, 5/10

how to find, 5/10

at IRS audit, 5/12

types of, 5/9–10, 18/8

See also Research resources

Tax refund forms, 7/9

Tax returns

calendar of filing deadlines, 5/5–6

federal, 5/2–4

with IRC Section 179 claim, 7/22

preparation of, 5/7–8

state, 5/4

Tax year

calendar versus fiscal, 4/13–14

payment filing deadlines of, 5/6

Termination

of commercial leases, 3/14

of independent contractor agreement, 10/30, 10/32

of patent transfer, under IRC Section 1235, 8/5

Trademarks

amortization period of, 7/33

dilution of, 15/7

examples of, 12/5, 15/2

federal registration symbol of, 15/5, 15/7

fictitious business name versus, 3/6

financial value of, 15/2

"first use" rights of, 15/3, 15/4, 15/5

infringement of, recourse to, 3/4–5, 15/6

licensing your invention with, 15/3–4

for nonfunctional features, 15/3

registration fee, 15/5

registration of, with USPTO, 12/8–9, 15/5

reservation of, before using, 15/5

search for, before selecting, 15/5–6

service mark type of, 15/3

strong versus weak, 15/4

"TM" or "SM" symbols of, 15/7

trade name versus, 15/3

Trade names

checking account under, 4/3

defined, 3/3

fictitious business name versus, 3/6

protections for, 3/4–5

of sole proprietorships, 3/4

trademarks versus, 15/3

Trade secrets

as amortized asset, 7/33

automatic existence of, 12/4, 13/3

defined, 12/4

disclosure of, in patent application, 13/6–8

examples of, 13/2–3, 13/9

how to preserve secrecy of, 12/8, 13/9–11

independent discovery of, 13/5–6

legal requirements for, 13/8–9

licensing of, for profit, 13/3

nondisclosure agreement on, 10/10, 10/12, 13/11–20

original owner of, 11/30

protections of, 11/30, 13/4, 13/7

reverse engineering of, 13/5

short commercial life strategy of, 13/8

term of protection, 13/6

Travel expenses, 4/10–11, 7/43

U

Unemployment taxes

for employee of corporation, 2/6

of family members as employees, 10/24

federal, 10/22–23

state, 10/24–25

Universities

federally funded inventions of, 11/23

inventor employees of, 11/22–24

U.S. Patent and Trademark Office (USPTO)

application process with, 11/2, 12/4, 14/5–6

attorneys licensed to practice before, 18/5–6

Disclosure Document Program of, 9/8–9

patent search at, 14/10

recording of assignment with, 11/29

trademark database of, 15/6

trademark registration with, 12/8–9, 15/5

trademark reservation with, 15/5

website, 15/6

Usefulness test for patents, 12/4, 14/8

USPTO. *See* U.S. Patent and Trademark Office

Utility patents. *See* Patent(s)

W

Websites

business licensing requirements, 3/15

computer insurance companies, 3/19

copyright registration, 16/7

depreciation periods of assets, 7/31

Disclosure Document Deposit Request Form, 9/9

encryption programs, 13/10

environmental permits, 3/15

foreign patent rights, 18/4–5

income tax brackets, 7/7

insurance company ratings, 3/25

intellectual property law, 18/3

inventor resources, 18/2

IRS forms/publications, 5/9

newsgroups, 18/12

Nolo, 18/5

patent and license exchanges, 17/16

patent attorneys, 18/6

patent law, 18/3

patent searches, 18/3–4

quarterly tax payments, 8/16

Service Corps of Retired Executives, 18/9

Small Business Association, 18/9

small business issues, 18/11–12

spreadsheet templates, 4/6

state sales tax, 3/16, 5/5

trademark registration, 15/5

trademark search, 3/5, 15/6

trade name search, 3/5

USPTO, 15/6

workers' compensation requirements, 3/22

Witnesses to inventor's notebook, 9/7–8

Workers' compensation insurance, 3/21–22, 10/25–26

Z

Zoning laws

how to change, 3/9, 3/10

purposes of, 3/7–8

types of restrictions, 3/8

where to obtain, 3/8

■

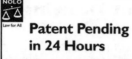

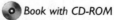

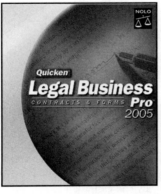

Remember:

Little publishers have big ears.
We really listen to you.

Take 2 Minutes & Give Us Your 2 cents

Your comments make a big difference in the development and revision of Nolo books and software. Please take a few minutes and register your Nolo product—and your comments—with us. Not only will your input make a difference, you'll receive special offers available only to registered owners of Nolo products on our newest books and software. Register now by:

PHONE
1-800-728-3555

FAX
1-800-645-0895

EMAIL
cs@nolo.com

or **MAIL** us
this registration card

- - - - - - - - - - - - - fold here - - - - - - - - - - - - - -

Registration Card

NAME _____ DATE _____

ADDRESS _____

_____

CITY _____ STATE _____ ZIP _____

PHONE _____ EMAIL _____

WHERE DID YOU HEAR ABOUT THIS PRODUCT? _____

WHERE DID YOU PURCHASE THIS PRODUCT? _____

DID YOU CONSULT A LAWYER? (PLEASE CIRCLE ONE)   YES   NO   NOT APPLICABLE

DID YOU FIND THIS BOOK HELPFUL?   (VERY)   5   4   3   2   1   (NOT AT ALL)

COMMENTS _____

_____

_____

WAS IT EASY TO USE?   (VERY EASY)   5   4   3   2   1   (VERY DIFFICULT)

We occasionally make our mailing list available to carefully selected companies whose products may be of interest to you.
❏ If you do not wish to receive mailings from these companies, please check this box.
❏ You can quote me in future Nolo promotional materials.
  Daytime phone number _____.

ILAX 2.0

"Nolo helps lay people perform legal tasks without the aid—or fees—of lawyers."
—USA TODAY

Nolo books are ..."written in plain language, free of legal mumbo jumbo, and spiced with witty personal observations."*
—ASSOCIATED PRESS

"...Nolo publications...guide people simply through the how, when, where and why of law."
—WASHINGTON POST

"Increasingly, people who are not lawyers are performing tasks usually regarded as legal work... And consumers, using books like Nolo's, do routine legal work themselves."
—NEW YORK TIMES

"...All of [Nolo's] books are easy-to-understand, are updated regularly, provide pull-out forms...and are often quite moving in their sense of compassion for the struggles of the lay reader."
—SAN FRANCISCO CHRONICLE

fold here

- -

Nolo
950 Parker Street
Berkeley, CA 94710-9867

Attn: ILAX 2.0